london

a  pocket guide

First published in 2001
Virgin Publishing Ltd, London W6 9HA

contents

Written by 20 contributors in-the-know, this guide gives the inside take on London. The focus is on having fun; where to hang out, shop, eat, relax, enjoy and spoil yourself. And there's a selection of the top cultural hot spots...

area lowdown 4–9

index 10–23

shops 24–80
- accessories 24–25
- antiques 25–27
- auctions 27
- art 27–28
- body decoration 28
- books 28–30
- british designers 30
- cds, records & tapes 30–32
- children's clothing 33
- cigars & cigarettes 33
- clubwear 33–34
- crafts 34
- department stores 34–36
- designer clothes 36–42
- discount stores 43
- drink 43
- electronics 44
- eyewear 44
- fabrics 44
- fetish 45
- food 45–47
- gifts 47–49
- hats 49
- health & beauty 49–51
- high street shops 51–53
- interiors 53–59
- international designers 59–60
- jewellery 60–63
- kites 63
- lingerie 63
- magazines & newspapers 63–64
- markets 64–67
- menswear 67–69
- new age 69
- secondhand clothing 69–72
- sex shops 72
- shoes 72–75
- shoe chains 75–76
- sportswear & equipment 76–77
- stationery & art materials 77
- streetwear 77–79
- tea & coffee 79
- toys & games 79–80
- watches 80

restaurants & cafés 81–119
- afghan 81
- african 81
- belgian 82
- brasseries 82
- breakfast/brunch 83
- british 83–85
- cafés 85–87
- caribbean 87–88
- chinese 88–89
- coffee houses 89
- creperies 90
- fish & chips 90
- french 90–93
- gastropubs 93–94
- global & fusion 94–95
- greek 95
- haute cuisine 95–96
- ice cream 97
- indian & bengali 97–98
- internet cafés 98–99
- italian 99–102
- japanese 102–103
- juice bars 103

kids' restaurants 103
late-night opening 104
latin american 105
mediterranean 105–106
middle eastern 106
modern european 107–113
north american 113–114
patisseries 114
russian & eastern european 114–115
seafood 115–116
southeast asian 116
spanish 117
teas 117–118
turkish 118
vegetarian 118–119
vietnamese 119

bars 120–137
bars & art 120
bar/restaurants 120–121
cigar bars 121
club bars 121–124
cocktail joints 124–125
happy hours 125
hip hangouts 126–129
hotel bars 129
irish pubs 130
late night bars 130–131
live music 131
pool bars 131
the pub experience 132–136
sports bars 136
theme bars 136–137
wine bars 137

clubs 138–142

gay scene 143–145

entertainment 146–149
the papers 146
radio 146
television 146
listings mags 146–147
websites 147
cinema 147
theatre 147–148
poetry 148
dance 148
opera & classical music 148–149
comedy 149

events 150–155

sights, museums & galleries 156–189
landmarks 156–158
viewpoints 158–159
the royals 160–162
the changing of the guard 162
great churches 162–163
famous five 164–167
townhouses 167–170
blue plaques 170
stately homes 170–171
one offs 171–176
galleries 176–179
major exhibition spaces 179–181
galleries – alternative spaces 181–182
photography & design galleries 183
commercial galleries 183–184
kids' attractions 184–187
parks & gardens 187–189

body & soul 190–194

games & activities 195–199

hotels 200–209

practical information 210–219

transport 220–233

maps 234–253

acknowledgements 255

symbols 256

area lowdown

Take a look at London's key zones: from Highgate to Holborn and Holland Park to Hoxton, each area has its own character and allure.

bankside

map 15

Home of the Globe Theatre, Design Museum, smart restaurants, and a stretch of the Thames path with great views of St Paul's. Bankside Power Station is the site of the new Tate Modern.

barbican

map 9

Originally controversial 70s arts centre-cum-residential enclave. A labyrinth of walkways; follow the yellow line to lead you in.

battersea

off map

Dominated by the once intact power station, abandoned in mid-redevelopment. There's a great park and rows of Victorian cottages – a very local neighbourhood.

bayswater

maps 5 & 11

Full of restaurants and shops, with Whiteley's shopping complex at its centre.

belgravia

maps 12 & 18

Embassies and private residences: five-storey grandeur at six-digit prices.

bloomsbury

map 8

Full of literary connections; home to the British Museum and University of Central London. Georgian elegance and squares.

camden

map 2

The spiritual home of Britpop, rough-and-ready Camden Town is still big on the capital's music circuit. The area has, and no doubt always will have, a few bohemians living in its garrets, but its central location and cheap rents have drawn slick media types too; restaurants and bars are opening *en masse* to milk their expense accounts. Despite this gentrification, it remains an amazing social hotchpotch, with club-goers and diners rubbing shoulders with down-and-outs and drifters outside the landmark underground station.

Camden's beating heart is its world-famous market where the style-obsessed and the young at heart hang out on sunny weekends. Things have really changed over the last 20 years and Camden is definitely on the up and up.

chelsea

map 18

More than 30 years ago the King's Road was the epicentre of the swinging 60s, with a battalion of models and designers hanging out in trendy boutiques. It had the *frisson* of a renaissance during punk rock's apogee in the 1970s and, although now no longer the parade ground of preference for fashion's avant-garde, it hasn't lost its zip. Essentially the area is all about walking the King's Road, a haven for shoppers, diners, and those simply out on the pose patrol. It remains a great place to spot London's many tribes: from stripey shirt-clad boys, and girls in pearls (the original Sloane Ranger), to models oozing street cred and sex appeal, and minor celebs hiding behind their shades. The combination suggests affluence and sophistication, but the area does have room for the hoi polloi... it's a melange worth savouring

clerkenwell

map 9

Up-and-coming Clerkenwell is in steep flux, with an ever-growing list of places to eat, drink, and shop. Once a grimy, hidden urban stew – a centre of clockmaking, and home to Mediterranean immigrants – it has undergone a recent leap in popularity. This is partly due to its central location, but also because of the warehouse properties, many of which have been converted into NY-style loft dwellings. Business still predominates, and local barflies divide between office workers and more recent arrivals involved in the local creative and media industries: designers, photographers, architects, and art directors who like the location and this urban pearl's relatively secret but central buzz.

covent garden

maps 8 & 14

Covent Garden exudes cosmopolitan glamour and street chic in equal measure, with a healthy dose of its recent 'alternative' past thrown in. There is always action on the piazza where the tourists gather. Street performers cajole the crowd, the craft market trades in the quirky and quixotic, and the Italianate colonnades of the former fruit and veg market are interspersed with Italian coffee, ice cream, and pasta outlets. North of Long Acre, the area's main drag, the roads are narrower and people eye each other surreptitiously on the cobbled catwalk of Neal Street. Celebs hop from cab to restaurant and back again, watched nonchalantly by those propping up the many bars. The tiny triangle of Neal's Yard is a hippy haven of potted trees, California juice, and enough wholefood to sink an armada. And among the plethora of shops, bars, and restaurants, young DJs in basement record stores try out the tracks they'll later lay down in clubs all across town.

docklands

off map

80s boom city; Canary Wharf is just one of the modern developments. Check it out on the DLR.

earl's court
off map

Aka Kangaroo Valley, favourite antipodean haunt and centre of cheap backpackers' hotels and hostels.

greenwich
off map

A way downriver, Greenwich stands apart from the buzz of central London. Its relaxed, out-of-town air has attracted an unusually large complement of artists, craftspeople and musicians. But it is best known for its maritime past and the impressive architectural ensemble of the Royal Naval College, Maritime Museum and Queen's House. And, of course, there's the burgeoning weekend market and the wide open expanse of the park. On a sunny weekend it seems as though half of South London has come here to unwind.

Sitting astride the meridian, the point from which the world sets its clocks, Greenwich was the allotted hub for Cool Britannia's fervent millennium activity. The controversial Dome dominates the skyline at neighbouring Blackwall, and restaurants and bars are opening with increasing regularity – the millennium borough is booming.

hampstead
off map

From its lofty position on a hill above London, Hampstead radiates an air of comfortable affluence. The spirit of its former glory days as a fashionable spa still pervades the area's tree-lined avenues and Georgian villas; its height, and the vast expanse of Hampstead Heath, bless it with cleaner air than its surrounds. Such rare urban luxuries and its villagey feel have, over the years, attracted artistic and literary types, who've created a quirky, bohemian feel. These days, a mixed crowd of the upwardly mobile has joined the high life of Hampstead and the rich and famous have fostered it as a celebrity haven.

highgate
off map

London's highest 'village', with great views and a famous cemetery.

holland park
off map

A beautiful park (with free-range peacocks) and grand ambassadorial residences. Very expensive.

hoxton & shoreditch
map 4

Take one dilapidated chunk of the East End, toss in an impressive mix of contemporary artists and writers, open some fantastic bars and restaurants, *et voilà*: you have the painfully fashionable Hoxton and Shoreditch. Because rents were cheap, a community of artists flourished here in the 1990s, but the pressure of fashion is irresistable and now the rents are inevitably rising. If you wander the streets before sunset, you might wonder what all the fuss is about, but come nightfall you'll soon get the picture. Some of the coolest new bars and restaurants in London have opened in these once run-down warehouses. But it may not last forever; the arrival of Pizza Express is viewed as the start of a high street invasion destined to ruin their style.

islington

map 3

One of London's glossiest urban villages, Islington is favoured by the upwardly mobile for its elegant architecture, plentiful cafés, bars, restaurants, and shops, and a relaxed vibe. But the area wasn't always so fashionable. Some 30 years ago, it was considered drab; out of touch, and out of bounds. Then middle-class families with a zest for baring the floorboards of their Georgian/Victorian properties arrived, and Islington opened up. Professionals, actors, and writers moved in – and never left. The area became known for its tolerance and liberal-mindedness, and as a left-wing stronghold; 'the People's Borough of Islington', appropriately enough, was home to Tony Blair. As the quality of life crept up, the area became the home of the rich-with-a-conscience, who were soon lampooned by comedians for being 'champagne socialists'. The cost of accommodation has soared: few young people can afford to move here today (though they still come to hang out); most of those who can would live nowhere else.

kensington

off map

Posh houses (including Kensington Palace), and squares; and the swathe of greenery that is Kensington Gardens and Hyde Park.

king's cross

off map

Major transport hub (railway station). Red light district with lots of dodgy characters, but mostly just at night.

knightsbridge & south kensington

maps 17 & 18

Knightsbridge is a gracious playground for the wealthy and well connected. Brompton Road and Sloane Street are lined with exclusive boutiques and designer flagship stores, but the area's real hubs are the high temples of style, Harrods and Harvey Nichols. People seemingly out of fashion mags (and others craving their recognition) converge here *en masse* in search of the latest designer outfit. This is, after all, London's classiest shopping zone.

Despite having similarly lavish Victorian crescents and squares, South Kensington doesn't have the same cachet as its neighbour. Low-key shops exist side by side with top designer outlets and internationally-renowned museums: grand and small scale sit together more easily. A tranche of France, courtesy of the French Institute, as well as a little café society, enhance the chic and cheerful ambience.

little venice
off map

Houseboat heaven. Moorings for residential barges with access to a pleasant path along the Regent's Canal.

marble arch
map 6

The beginning of Edgware Road, aka Little Lebanon, is full of restaurants and shops beloved by London's Middle Eastern expat community.

marylebone
map 6

Upmarket mansion flats, the private doctors of Harley Street, and a fashionable high street. One of the capital's most central yet secret 'villages'.

north soho
map 7

North of Oxford Street, this area, sometimes known as Noho, is packed with restaurants – especially on Charlotte Street.

notting hill
map 1

The cool glamour of Notting Hill has been featured in fashion and style magazines from the US to Japan. According to these, it would seem impossible not to trip over Madonna dashing into her favourite jewellers, or to bump into Björk queuing for flowers in Wild at Heart. Celebs might not be quite this thick on the ground, but rare indeed is the shop or restaurant that has never served an actress, writer, supermodel, or rock star.

Lurking beneath the area's glossy veneer, however, is a rather less salubrious side. A history of slumland barons, race riots and, in more recent years, a thriving drug scene, have left their marks and given the area its distinct edge. The slums have long disappeared, cultures have slowly integrated, and the drug dealers have mostly moved north, but to some extent parallel lives do still exist. Portobello Market cuts through the whole Notting Hill spectrum; from the bijou opulence of Notting Hill Gate's candy-coloured stucco houses, to the grittier area around Golborne Road. Chic shops and louche hang-outs add to the area's identity and charm, making it a magnet for London trendies and visitors, especially since the film *Notting Hill* was released. But its main buzz is generated by the genuinely cosmopolitan feel and the many up-and-coming artists, designers, and musicians for whom this area has been a haunt since the swinging 60s.

piccadilly & mayfair
maps 12 & 13

This is clubland, but not the kind that might first spring to mind. There are no strobe lights and there's no throbbing music. St James's is the domain of gentlemen's clubs (the buildings with doormen, brass nameplates, and 200-year-old rules). Shops service gents' whims and needs, and parade, discreetly, their links with the royal family. With tradition so ingrained, the populist tack and glittering neon whirlwind of Piccadilly Circus nearby makes even more of an impact.

Neighbouring Mayfair is prime real estate – it's the home of pricey hotels, opulent apartments, and top fashion houses. There are designer stores as far as the eye can see along Bond Street. Shepherd Market, meanwhile, is the 'village' centre of Mayfair with its tiny cobbled streets and flurry of bars, cafés, and restaurants.

soho

maps 7 & 13

Soho has, for many years, been the epicentre of cool London, from the rock 'n' roll clubs of the 50s and swinging Carnaby Street in the 60s, right through to the 24-hour party zone it is today. A warren of streets, this area is one of the oldest surviving parts of the capital, but it's definitely not a dry heritage zone. Soho lives for the moment, and is constantly changing...

Turn off the main roads that bound Soho and the mood immediately changes: the streets are narrower, the shops quirkier, and the people buzzier. Despite being a magnet for visitors, Soho has held on to its atmosphere and authenticity. The area is a hive of creative industry: film and advertising businesses thrive alongside one-off shops, coffee bars, and all manner of drinking, dancing, and eating establishments. Throughout the day, actors sip lattes, film-makers have boozy 'meetings', office workers get hammered, and the smart set glide into private members' clubs, while down-and-outs beg for money. All life is here. Notoriously, Soho is also the centre of London's sex industry, with a bevy of porn stores, brothels, clip and strip joints. Indeed, some corners are positively sleazy, but in some ways this has helped contribute to the area's raffish charm.

For three centuries Soho has attracted immigrants and non-conformists. Italians, Maltese, French Huguenots, and Chinese have all become part of the local fabric. In recent years, it has also become a gay mecca, but it never has been, and never will be, a ghetto. However crowded, Soho always manages to absorb more people into its vibrant mix.

south bank

map 14a

Big arts complex and riverside area; focus of free festivals and events in summer.

victoria

off map

Major transport hub (railway and coach stations).

westminster

maps 13 & 14

London's political heart: seat of British government and location of Downing Street and Westminster Abbey.

area index

bankside, bermondsey & london bridge

RESTAURANTS & CAFÉS
Café Rouge (brasserie) 82

SIGHTS, MUSEUMS & GALLERIES
Bermondsey Market (market) 64
Delfina (gallery - alternative space) 182
Globe Theatre (one-off) 172–3
Millennium Bridge (viewpoint) 159
Tate Modern (gallery) 178–9
Vinopolis: City of Wine (one-off) 176

bayswater

BARS
Elbow Room (pool bar) 131

RESTAURANTS & CAFÉS
Assaggi (Italian) 99
Magic Wok (Chinese) 88
Veronica's (British) 85
Westbourne (gastropub) 94
Zucca (Mediterranean) 106

SHOPPING
The Cross (designer clothes) 38

bethnal green & mile end

BARS
Royal Oak (pub experience) 135

SIGHTS, MUSEUMS & GALLERIES
Bethnal Green Museum of Childhood (kids attraction) 185
Chisenhale (gallery - alternative space) 182
Interim Art (commercial gallery) 184
Matt's (gallery - alternative space) 182
The Showroom (gallery - alternative space) 182

clapham, battersea & brixton

BARS
Brixtonian Havana Bar (cocktail joint) 124
Bug Bar (club bar) 122
Dogstar (club bar) 122
Fridge Bar (club bar) 122
The Junction (club bar) 123
Neon (hip hangout) 128
Sand (late night) 131
South Circular (happy hour) 125
Tea Rooms des Artistes (club bar) 123

CLUBS
Mass 141

SHOPPING
Brixton Market (market) 64

SIGHTS, MUSEUMS & GALLERIES
Battersea Pk (parks & gardens) 187
Battersea Power Station (landmark) 156

bromley

SHOPPING
French Connection/Nicole Farhi (discount store) 43

camden & chalk farm

BARS
Bar Solo (late night) 130
Bar Vinyl (club bar) 121
Bartok (live music) 131
Black Cap (gay scene) 143
The Camden Head (pub experience) 132
Cotton's (cocktail joint) 124
Dublin Castle (live music) 131
Falcon (live music) 131
Good Mixer (hip hangout) 127
Jazz Café (live music) 131
The Liberties Bar (Irish pub) 130
Monarch (hip hangout) 128
WKD (club bar) 124

CLUBS
Camden Palace 138
Electric Ballroom 139

RESTAURANTS & CAFÉS
Bar Gansa (Spanish) 117
Belgo Noord (Belgian) 82
Blakes (gastropub) 93
Café Delancey (brasserie) 82
Camden Cantina (Latin American) 105
Crown & Goose (gastropub) 93

Daphne (Greek) 95
The Engineer (gastropub) 94
Mango Room (Caribbean) 87–8
Marine Ices (ice cream) 97
New Culture Revolution (Chinese) 88
Silks & Spice (Southeast Asian) 116
Taste of Siam (Southeast Asian) 116

SHOPPING

Ashvale International (interiors) 54
Bar Vinyl (CDs, records & tapes) 30
Camden Jean Co (streetwear) 77
Camden Lock Designs (interiors) 54
Camden Market 64–5
Compendium (books) 28
Gohil's (accessories) 24
Holt (shoes) 73
LA1 (sportswear & equipment) 76
Modern Age Vintage Clothing (secondhand clothing) 71
Offstage (books) 29
Out on the Floor (CDs, records & tapes) 32
Regent Bookshop (books) 29
Rhythm Records (CDs, records & tapes) 32
Rokit (streetwear) 78
Stables Antique Market (market) 67
Stitch Up (secondhand clothing) 72
Tann-Rokka (interiors) 58
This & That (interiors) 58
Thyme (interiors) 58
Tumi (interiors) 59
Village Games (toys) 80

chelsea & fulham

BARS

Chelsea Potter (pub experience) 132
Cooper's Arms (pub experience) 132
Phene Arms (pub experience) 135
Po Na Na (late night) 131
Surprise (pub experience) 135

RESTAURANTS & CAFÉS

Bersagliera (Italian) 99
Bluebird (modern European) 108
Busabong Tree (Southeast Asian) 116
Café Milan (Italian) 99
Chelsea Kitchen (café) 86
The Dome (brasserie) 82
Gordon Ramsay (haute cuisine) 96
Habitat (café) 86
La Delizia (Italian) 100
Picasso (Italian) 100
Pizza Express (Italian) 101
Soviet Canteen (Russian & Eastern European) 115
Starbucks (coffee houses) 89

SHOPPING

After Noah (interiors) 54
Amazon (discount store) 43
American Classics (streetwear) 77
Antiquarius (antiques) 25
Antony Price (designer clothes) 36
Bluebird (food) 45
Brats (gifts) 47
Brora (designer clothes) 37
The Common Market (clubwear) 33
Daisy & Tom's (toys) 79
Designers Guild (interiors) 56
Emporio Armani (international designer) 60
Erickson Beamon (jewellery) 61
Free Lance (shoes) 73
Gina (shoes) 73
Guinevere (antiques) 26
Hackett (menswear) 68
Hobbs (high street shop) 52
The Holding Company (interiors) 56
Jane Asher (food) 46
Jo Malone (health & beauty) 50
Joanne Booth (antiques) 26, (fabrics) 44,
Joanna Tent (designer clothes) 39
Johnny Moke (shoes) 74
Joseph (designer clothes) 39
Joseph Sale Shop (discount store) 43
L'Artisan Parfumeur (health & beauty) 50
Les Senteurs (health & beauty) 50
LK Bennett (shoes) 74
M.A.C. (health & beauty) 50
Magpie (antiques) 26
Manolo Blahnik (shoes) 74
Mimi (designer clothes) 40
Office (shoe chain) 75
Oliver Bonas (gifts) 48
Patrick Cox (shoes) 74
Peter Jones (department store) 35
Pimpernel & Partners (antiques) 26
Rococo (food) 47
Steinberg & Tolkien (secondhand clothing) 72
Voyage (designer clothes) 42
VV Rouleaux (fabrics) 44
West Village (designer clothes) 42
Whistles Sale Store (discount store) 43

SIGHTS, MUSEUMS & GALLERIES

Chelsea Physic Garden (parks & gardens) 187

chiswick & isleworth

SIGHTS, MUSEUMS & GALLERIES
Chiswick House (stately home) 171
Osterley Park House (stately home) 171

clerkenwell & the city

BARS
Café Kick (theme bar) 137
Dust (club bar) 122
Fluid (hip hangout) 127
Hope & Sir Loin (pub experience) 134
Jerusalem Tavern (pub experience) 134
La Grande Marque (wine bar) 137
LED (hip hangout) 127
Match Bar (cocktail joint) 125
O'Hanlon (Irish pub) 130
Three Kings (pub experience) 136

CLUBS
Fabric 140
Trade @ Turnmills (gay scene) 145
Turnmills 142

RESTAURANTS & CAFÉS
Al's Diner (late-night opening) 104
Cicada (global & fusion) 94
Club Gascon (French) 90—1
The Eagle (gastropub) 93
Gaudi Restaurante (Spanish) 117
The Kolossi Grill (Greek) 95
Maison Novelli (modern European) 111
Moro (Spanish) 117
Quality Chop House (British) 83
Rudland & Stubbs (seafood) 116
St John (British) 84
Sir Loin (breakfast/brunch) 83
Smiths of Smithfield (British) 84
Tinseltown (late-night opening) 104

SHOPPING
Antique Watch Company (watches) 80
Antoni & Alison (designer clothes) 36
Clerkenwell Green Association (crafts) 34
EC One (jewellery) 61
Immaculate House (interiors) 57
Into You (body decoration) 28
Leather Lane (market) 66
Lesley Craze (jewellery) 62
Malapa (designer clothes) 40
North 2 (menswear) 68
Papier Marché (crafts) 34
SCP (interiors) 58
Smithfield Market 67
Viaduct (interiors) 59
Wedding Ring Shop (jewellery) 63

SIGHTS, MUSEUMS & GALLERIES
Andrew Mummery (commercial gallery) 184
Bank of England (landmark) 156
Barbican (major exhibition space) 179
Barbican Cinema (kids attraction) 186
Blue Print Café (viewpoint) 159
Eagle Gallery (commercial gallery) 184
Guildhall Art Gallery (gallery) 177
Lloyd's Building (landmark) 157
Monument (viewpoint) 159
Museum of London (one-off) 174
St Paul's Cathedral (great church) 162, (landmark) 158, (viewpoint) 159
Tower 42 (landmark) 157
Tower Bridge (landmark) 158, (viewpoint) 159
Tower of London (landmark) 158, (the royals) 161–2
Twentyfour Restaurant (viewpoint) 159

covent garden, leicester square & the strand

BARS
The Box (gay scene) 143
Cork & Bottle (wine bar) 137
Denim (hip hangout) 126
Detroit (cocktail joint) 124
Freedom Brewing Company (hip hangout) 127
Freud (bars & art) 120
Gordon's (wine bar) 137
Kudos (gay scene) 144
La Perla (theme bar) 137
Lamb & Flag (pub experience) 134
The Lobby Bar (hotel bars) 129
Sound (club bar) 123
The Spot (late night) 131
Voodoo Lounge (hip hangout) 129

CLUBS
Africa Centre 138
The End 139
Heaven (gay scene) 145
Home 140

RESTAURANTS & CAFÉS

Amphitheatre Restaurant (modern European) 107
Any Amount of Books (books) 28
Asia de Cuba (global & fusion) 94
Bank (modern European) 107
Belgo Centraal (Belgian) 82
Bradley's (café) 85
Café Santé (vegetarian) 118
Chez Gérard Opera Terrace (brasserie) 82
Christopher's American Grill (North American) 113
Food For Thought (vegetarian) 118
Frank's (café) 86
Gaby's (Middle Eastern) 106
The Ivy (modern European) 110
J Sheekey (seafood) 115
Joe Allen (North American) 113
Jus (juice bar) 103
Le Palais du Jardin (French) 91
Livebait (seafood) 116
Monmouth Coffee House 89
Murder One (books) 29
Navajo Joe (Latin American) 105
Neal's Yard Café Society (café) 86
Photographer's Gallery (café) 87
Poetry Café (café) 87
Rainforest Café (kids' restaurants) 103
Rock & Sole Plaice (fish & chips) 90
Rules (British) 84
Silver Moon Women's Bookshop (books) 29
Simpson's-in-the-Strand (breakfast/brunch) 83
Smollensky's Balloon (kids' restaurants) 103
Sofra (Turkish) 118
Thai Pot (Southeast Asian) 116
Zwemmer Media Arts (books) 30

SHOPPING

Accessorize (accessories) 24
Bead Shop (jewellery) 61
Bell, Book & Radmell (books) 28
Bertie (shoe chain) 75
Birkenstock (shoes) 72
Bizarre (fetish) 45
Blackout II (secondhand clothing) 70
Blazer (high street shop) 52
Buffalo (shoes) 72
Burro (menswear) 67
Camper (shoes) 73
Carhartt (streetwear) 77
Carluccio's (food) 45
Cenci (secondhand clothing) 70
Covent Garden Market 65
Cyberdog (clubwear) 33
Dexter Wong (streetwear) 77
Diesel (streetwear) 78
Diesel Stylelab (streetwear) 78
Dockers (streetwear) 78
Dr Martens Department Store (shoes) 73
Duffer of St George (streetwear) 78
Equinox - The Astrology Shop (new age) 69
Foyle's (books) 28
Gap (high street shop) 52
Gap Kids (high street shop) 52
Inner Space (new age) 69
Janet Fitch (jewellery) 62
Jones (menswear) 68
Jones the Bootmaker (shoe chain) 75
Kirk Originals (eyewear) 44
Kite Store (kites) 63
Koh Samui (designer clothes) 40
Kookai (high street shop) 52
The Loft (secondhand clothing) 71
Lush (health & beauty) 50
Mango (high street shop) 53
Miss Sixty (secondhand clothing) 71
Monmouth Coffee House (tea & coffee) 79
Morgan (high street shop) 53
Natural Shoe Store (shoes) 74
Neal Street East (gifts) 48
Neal's Yard Dairy (food) 47
Neal's Yard Remedies (health & beauty) 51
Next (high street shop) 53
Octopus (gifts) 48
Offspring (shoes) 74
Ordning & Reda (stationery & art materials) 77
Paul Smith (designer clothes) 41
Press & Bastyan (designer clothes) 41
Reiss (high street shop) 53
Screen Face (health & beauty) 51
Shu Uemura (health & beauty) 51
Slam City Skates (sportswear & equipment) 76
Sole Trader (shoes) 75
Space NK (health & beauty) 51
Stanfords (books) 30
Stephen Jones (hats) 49
Storm (watches) 80
Stüssy (streetwear) 79
Supersports (sportswear & equipment) 76
Swear (shoes) 75
Tesco Metro (food) 47

Virgin Megastore (CDs, records & tapes) 32
Warehouse (high street shop) 53
Yesterday's Bread (secondhand clothing) 72

SIGHTS, MUSEUMS & GALLERIES
London Transport Museum (kids attraction) 185
National Gallery (gallery) 177
National Portrait Gallery (gallery) 177
Photographer's Gallery (photography and design gallery) 183
Somerset House (gallery) 178
Special Photographer's Gallery (photography & design gallery) 183
Tottenham Court Road
Trafalgar Square (landmark) 158

dulwich & forest hill

SIGHTS, MUSEUMS & GALLERIES
Dulwich Picture Gallery (gallery) 176
Horniman Museum (one-off) 173

docklands

SIGHTS, MUSEUMS & GALLERIES
Canary Wharf (landmark)

edgware road & little venice

RESTAURANTS & CAFÉS
Maroush (late-night opening) 104
Ranoush Juice Bar (late-night opening) 104

SIGHTS, MUSEUMS & GALLERIES
Puppet Theatre Barge (kids attraction) 187

eltham

SIGHTS, MUSEUMS & GALLERIES
Eltham Palace (stately home) 171

embankment

BARS
Shoeless Joe's (sports bar) 136

SIGHTS, MUSEUMS & GALLERIES
Hungerford Foot Bridge (viewpoint) 159

greenwich

BARS
Bar du Musée (wine bar) 137
Cutty Sark Tavern (pub experience) 133
Richard I (pub experience) 135
Trafalgar Tavern (pub experience) 136

RESTAURANTS & CAFÉS
North Pole (gastropub) 94
Royal Teas (vegetarian) 119
Saigon (Vietnamese) 119
Spread Eagle (French) 92
Tai Won Mein (Chinese) 89
Ye Olde Pie House (British) 85

SHOPPING
Autumn & May (jewellery) 61
Bullfrogs (streetwear) 77
Bullfrogs Shoes (shoes) 72
Cheese Board (food) 46
Creek Antiques (antiques) 25
The Dab Hand (food) 46
Different Music (CDs, records & tapes) 30
Emporium (secondhand clothing) 70
Essential Music (CDs, records & tapes) 31
Flying Duck Enterprises (gifts) 48
Greenwich Market 65–6
Halcyon Books (books) 29
Hide All (accessories) 24
Marcet Books (books) 29
Museum Store (gifts) 48
The Observatory (secondhand clothing) 71
Spread Eagle Antiques (antiques) 27
sights, museums & galleries
Cutty Sark & Gypsy Moth (one-off) 171
The Dome (one-off) 172
Greenwich Park (parks & gardens) 187–8
National Maritime Museum & Queen's House (one-off) 174–5
Old Royal Observatory (one-off) 175

hackney & dalston

BARS
291 (bars & art) 120

SIGHTS, MUSEUMS & GALLERIES
Geffrye Museum (one-off) 172

SHOPPING
Ridley Road (market) 66

hammersmith & west brompton

RESTAURANTS & CAFÉS
The Gate (vegetarian) 118–19
River Café (Italian) 101

SHOPPING
Baroque & Roll (antiques) 25

hampstead, belsize park & highgate

BARS
Bar Room Bar (hip hangout) 126
Flask (pub experience) 133
Freemason's Arms (pub experience) 133
The Hollybush (pub experience) 134
King William IV (gay scene) 144
Ye Olde White Bar (pub experience) 136

RESTAURANTS & CAFÉS
Al Casbah (African) 81
The Brewhouse (breakfast/brunch) 83
Caffè Bianco (Southeast Asian) 116
Coffee Cup (coffee houses) 89
Gaucho Grill (Latin American) 105
Giraffe (breakfast/brunch) 83
Gresslin's (modern European) 109
House on Rosslyn Hill (global & fusion) 94
La Cage Imaginaire (French) 91
La Creperie (creperie) 90
Lemonia (Greek) 95
Maison Blanc (patisserie) 114
The New End (British) 83
Odette's (modern European) 111
Toast (modern European) 113
Villa Bianca (Italian) 102
Zen W3 (Chinese) 89

SHOPPING
Catto Gallery (art) 27
Channels (interiors) 55
Designs (secondhand clothing) 70
Exclusivo (secondhand clothing) 70
Hampstead Antique Emporium (antiques) 26
Hampstead Bazaar (streetwear) 78
Hampstead Indoor Market 66
Hobbs (shoe chain) 75
Joy (food) 46
Keith Fawke's (books) 29
Livingstone Studio (designer clothes) 40
Nine West (shoe chain) 75
Ronit Zilkha (designer clothes) 41
YD, UK (sportswear & equipment) 77
Zana Boutique (designer clothes) 42
Zebra/Zebra Two (art) 28

SIGHTS, MUSEUMS & GALLERIES
Camden Arts Centre (major exhibition space) 179
Freud Museum (townhouse) 168
Hampstead Heath & Parliament Hill (parks & gardens) 188
Highgate Cemetery (parks & gardens) 188
Keats' House (townhouse) 168
Kenwood House (townhouse) 168–9
Saatchi Gallery (major exhibition space) 180–1
Two Willow Road (townhouse) 170

holborn

BARS
Terry Neill's Sports Bar & Brasserie (sports bar) 136

RESTAURANTS & CAFÉS
Axis (modern European) 107
Indigo (modern European) 110
Maggiore's Italian Kitchen (Italian) 100

SHOPPING
Black's (sportswear & equipment) 76
Galerie Singleton (gifts) 48
Skoob (books) 29
Ulysses (books) 30

SIGHTS, MUSEUMS & GALLERIES
Sir John Soane's Museum (townhouse) 169–70

holland park

RESTAURANTS & CAFÉS
The Room at the Halcyon (haute cuisine) 96
Wiz (global & fusion) 95

SHOPPING
Cath Kidston (interiors) 55
Virginia (secondhand clothing) 72

SIGHTS, MUSEUMS & GALLERIES
Leighton House (townhouse) 169

hoxton, shoreditch & liverpool street

BARS
The Aquarium (club bar) 121
Bluu Bar (club bar) 122
Bricklayer's Arms (pub experience) 132
Cantaloupe (hip hangout) 126
Charlie Wright's International Bar (late night) 130
Dragon Bar (club bar) 122
The George (hotel bar) 129
Home (hip hangout) 127
Hoxton Square Bar & Kitchen (hip hangout) 127
The Light (club bar) 123
Plastic People (club bar) 123
The Pool (pool bar) 131
Reliance (pub experience) 135
Shoreditch Electricity Showroom (hip hangout) 128
Vibe Bar (club bar) 124

CLUBS
333 142

RESTAURANTS & CAFÉS
The Blue Orange (café) 85
Brick Lane Beigel Bake (café) 85
Brick Lane Market 64
Cantaloupe (Mediterranean) 106
Columbia Road (market) 65
Frockbrokers (secondhand clothing) 70
Gilt by Association (art) 27
Global Gypsy (designer clothes) 39
Great Eastern Dining Room (modern European) 109
Lee's Seafoods (seafood) 115
The Real Greek (Greek) 95
Spitalfields (market) 67
Terminus Bar & Grill (North American) 114
Timothy Everest (menswear) 69
Viet-Hoa (Vietnamese) 119

SHOPPING
@Work (jewellery) 61
Atlantis (stationery & art materials) 77
Eat My Handbag Bitch (interiors) 56
Sh! (sex shop) 72
White Cube² (art) 28

SIGHTS, MUSEUMS & GALLERIES
18 Folgate Street (townhouse) 167–8
The Lux Gallery (photography & design gallery) 183
One in the Other (gallery – alternative space) 182
30 Underwood Street (gallery – alternative space) 182
White Cube² (commercial gallery) 184

islington & king's cross

BARS
Albion (pub experience) 132
Blue Bar (club bar) 122
Bierodrome (theme bar) 136
Central Station (gay scene) 143
The Crown (pub experience) 132
Embassy Bar (club bar) 122
Filthy McNasty's (Irish pub) 130
The Island Queen (pub experience) 134
The King's Head (pub experience) 134
The Medicine Bar (hip hangout) 128
Narrow Boat (pub experience) 135
Nubar (happy hour) 125
The Old Red Lion (pub experience) 135
Rosemary Branch (bars & art) 120
Salmon & Compass (club bar) 123

CLUBS
The Cross 139
Scala 141

RESTAURANTS & CAFÉS
Afghan Kitchen (Afghan) 81
Bliss (patisserie) 114
Casale Franco (Italian) 99
Crafts Council (café) 86
Duke of Cambridge (gastropub) 93
Euphorium (modern European) 109
Frederick's (French) 91
Gallipoli (Turkish) 118
Granita (modern European) 109
Lola's (modern European) 110
Maremma (Italian) 100
Ravi Shankar (Indian & Bengali) 97
Santa Fe (North American) 114
Upper Street Fish Shop (fish & chips) 90

SHOPPING
Acadia (interiors) 53

Annie's (secondhand clothing) 69
Aria (interiors) 54
Camden Passage (market) 65
Camel (interiors) 54
Canal (interiors) 54
Chapel Market 65
Cloud Cuckoo Land (secondhand clothing) 70
Coexistence (interiors) 55
Comfort & Joy (designer clothes) 37, (streetwear) 77
Cover Girl (shoes) 73
Crafts Council (crafts) 34
Cross Street Gallery (art) 27
Cubitt (gallery -alternative space) 182
Diverse (designer clothes) 38, (menswear) 67
Donay (antiques) 25
Emma Hope (shoes) 73
Flashback (secondhand clothing) 70
Gill Wing Gifts (gifts) 48
Hart Gallery (crafts) 34
High Society (secondhand clothing) 71
Home to Be (interiors) 57
North 1 (menswear) 68
Out of Time (interiors) 57
Past Caring (secondhand clothing) 71
Plasterworks (crafts) 34
Sara Lemkow & Rookery Farm (antiques) 26
Sefton (designer clothes) 41
Stephen Einhorn (crafts) 34
20th Century Design (interiors) 59

SIGHTS, MUSEUMS & GALLERIES
Estorick Collection (gallery) 176
Little Angel Theatre (kids attractions) 187
Unicorn Theatre for Children (kids attraction) 187
Victoria Miro (commercial gallery) 184

kensington

RESTAURANTS & CAFÉS
Clarke's (modern European) 108
Easyeverything (internet cafés) 98

SHOPPING
Crabtree & Evelyn (health & beauty) 49
The Homeplace (interiors) 57
Pied à Terre (shoe chain) 76
River Island (high street shop) 53
Urban Outfitters (streetwear) 79

SIGHTS, MUSEUMS & GALLERIES
Albert Hall & Memorial (landmark) 156
Holland Park Adventure Playpark (kids attraction) 186
Kensington Gardens (parks & gardens) 188
Kensington Palace (the royals) 161
Natural History Museum (famous five) 165–6
Royal College of Art (major exhibition space) 180
Science Museum (famous five) 166
Serpentine Gallery (major exhibition space) 181
Victoria & Albert Museum (famous five) 166–7

knightsbridge & belgravia

BARS
Boisdale (cigar bar) 121
Fox & Hounds (pub experience) 133
Grenadier (pub experience) 134

RESTAURANTS & CAFÉS
Café Internet (internet cafés) 98
The Capital (haute cuisine) 95
Fifth Floor Harvey Nichols (modern European) 109
Floriana (Italian) 100
Garden Restaurant (Mediterranean) 106
Isola (Italian) 100
Oriel (brasserie) 82
Pizza Organic (Italian) 101
Stefano Cavallini at the Halkin (Italian) 101
Stockpot (café) 87
Veg (vegetarian) 119
Zafferano (Italian) 102

SHOPPING
À la Mode (designer clothes) 36
Alberta Ferretti (designer clothes) 36
Anya Hindmarch (accessories) 24
Bentleys (accessories) 24
Bertie Golightly (secondhand clothing) 70
Betsey Johnson (designer clothes) 37
Bonhams (auctions) 27
Catherine Prevost (jewellery) 61
Christian Dior (designer clothes) 37

Christian Louboutin (shoes) 73
Cutler & Gross (eyewear) 44
Egg (designer clothes) 38
Elspeth Gibson (designer clothes) 38
Giorgio Armani (international designer) 60
Gucci (international designer) 60
Harrod's (department store) 35
Harvey Nichols (department store) 35
Janet Reger (lingerie) 63
Jimmy Choo (shoes) 74
Margaret Howell (designer clothes) 40
Prada (international designer) 60
Rigby & Peller (lingerie) 63
The Room (art) 27
Tommy Hilfiger's (designer clothes) 41

SIGHTS, MUSEUMS & GALLERIES
Serpentine Lido (kids attraction) 185
Hyde Park (parks & gardens) 188

marylebone & regent's park

BARS
Atlantis (hip hangout) 126

RESTAURANTS & CAFÉS
The Chapel (gastropub) 93
Ozer (Turkish) 118
Patogh (Middle Eastern) 106
Purple Sage (Italian) 101
Seashell (fish & chips) 90
T-Bar (tea) 118

SHOPPING
Alfies (market) 64
Aveda (health & beauty) 49
Sue Ryder (secondhand clothing) 72

SIGHTS, MUSEUMS & GALLERIES
BBC Experience (kids attraction) 185
Lisson Gallery (commercial gallery) 184
London Zoo (kids attraction) 184
Madame Tussaud's & London Planetarium (one-off) 174
Regent's Park (parks & gardens) 189

mayfair & bond street

BARS
Claridge's Bar (cigar bar) 121
Dorchester Bar (cocktail joint) 124
Hush (bar/restaurant) 120
Met Bar (hotel bar) 129
Red Lion (pub experience) 135
Trader Vic's (hotel bar) 129

RESTAURANTS & CAFÉS
Brown's (tea) 117
Cave (Russian & Eastern European) 114–15
Caviar Kaspia (Russian & Eastern European) 115
Chez Nico (haute cuisine) 95
Coast (modern European) 108
The Connaught (haute cuisine) 96
Firebird (Russian & Eastern European) 115
Mirabelle (French) 92
Noble Rot (modern European) 111
Nobu (Japanese) 102
The Oriental (Chinese) 88–9
Pétrus (haute cuisine) 96
Rasa W1 (Indian & Bengali) 97
Sartoria (Italian) 101
Sotheby's (tea) 117
The Square (French) 92
Tamarind (Indian & Bengali) 98

SHOPPING
Angela Hale (jewellery) 60
Asprey & Garrard (jewellery) 61
Berry Bros & Rudd (drink) 43
Browns (designer clothes) 37
Browns Labels for Less (discount store) 43
Calvin Klein (international designer) 59
Chanel (international designer) 59
Christie's (auctions) 27
Comme des Garçons (designer clothes) 38
Davidoff (cigars and cigarettes) 33
Designworks (designer clothes) 38
DKNY (designer clothes) 38, 59
Dolce & Gabbana (international designer) 60
Donna Karan (international designer) 60
Fenwicks (designer clothes) 39
Geo F Trumper (health & beauty) 50
George Cleverley (shoes) 73
Gianni Versace (international designer) 60
Grays (market) 65
Harvie & Hudson (menswear) 68
Hermès (accessories) 24
HMV (CDs, records & tapes) 31
Issey Miyake (designer clothes) 39, 60

Jigsaw (high street shop) 52
John Lobb (shoes) 74
Krizia (designer clothes) 40
Louis Vuitton (international designer) 60
Maggs Brothers (books) 29
Miu Miu (international designer) 60
Moschino (designer clothes) 40
Mulberry (designer clothes), (accessories) 25
Nicole Farhi (designer clothes) 40–1
Paul Smith (discount store) 43
Phillips (auctions) 27
Polo Ralph Lauren (international designer) 60
Richard James (menswear) 69
Russell & Bromley (shoe chain) 76
Selfridges (department store) 36
Sotheby's (auctions) 27
Tiffany (jewellery) 63
Turnbull & Asser (menswear) 69
Vivienne Westwood (designer clothes) 41, 60
Whistles (designer clothes) 42
YMC (designer clothes) 42, 60
Yohji Yamamoto (designer clothes) 42, 60
Yves St Laurent Rive Gauche (designer clothes) 42

SIGHTS, MUSEUMS & GALLERIES

Antony D'Offay Galleries (commercial gallery) 184
Apsley House (townhouse) 167
Entwhistle (commercial gallery) 184
Hyde Park Corner (landmark) 157
Windows (viewpoint) 159
Zelda Cheatle (photography and design gallery) 183

north soho (noho) & bloomsbury

BARS

AKA (club bar) 121
Long Bar (hotel bar) 129
Myhotel (hotel bar) 129
The Social (club bar) 123

RESTAURANTS & CAFÉS

AKA (late-night opening) 104
Costa Dorada (late-night opening) 104
Eyre Bros (café) 86
Intercafé (internet cafés) 99
Mash (modern European) 111
Pied-à-Terre (French) 92
RK Stanley (British) 84
Spoon (modern European) 112
Villandry (French) 92–3

SHOPPING

Habitat (interiors) 56
Heal's (interiors) 56
Laurence Corner (secondhand clothing) 71
Paperchase (stationery & art materials) 77
Planet Organic (food) 47
Purves & Purves (interiors) 58
Villandry (food) 47

SIGHTS, MUSEUMS & GALLERIES

British Museum (famous five) 164, (kids attraction) 186
British Telecom Tower (landmark) 156
Coram's Fields (kids attraction) 184
The Heights (viewpoint) 158
Pollock's Toy Museum (kids attraction) 185
Wallace Collection (gallery) 179

notting hill, portobello & westbourne grove

BARS

Babushka (hip hangout) 126
Beat Bar (club bar) 121
Duke of Wellington (pub experience) 133
Ion (hip hangout) 127
Liquid Lounge (cocktail joint) 125
Market Bar (hip hangout) 128
Pharmacy (hip hangout) 128

CLUBS

Notting Hill Arts Club 141
Subterania 142

RESTAURANTS & CAFÉS

Alastair Little (modern European) 107
Al Duca (Italian) 99
Bali Sugar (global & fusion) 94
Books for Cooks (café) 85
Café Grove (café) 85
Coins Bar & Grill (café) 86
Costas (fish & chips) 90
The Cow (gastropub) 93
Dakota (North American) 113
Geale's (fish & chips) 90
Japanese Canteen (Japanese) 102
Leith's (modern European) 110

Lisboa (patisserie) 114
Mandola (African) 81
Mas Café (Mediterranean) 106
Moroccan Tagine (African) 81
192 (modern European) 112
Ruby in the Dust (North American) 114
Sausage & Mash Café (British) 84
Tom's (café) 87
206 (café) 87

SHOPPING

& Clarke's (food) 45
Aero (interiors) 53
Agnès b (designer clothes) 36
Aime (designer clothes) 36
APC (designer clothes) 37
Bill Amberg (accessories) 24
Books for Cooks (books) 28
Bowles & Linares (interiors) 54
Carden & Cunietti (interiors) 54
Ceramica Blue (interiors) 55
Christa Davies (designer clothes) 37
Coach House (antiques) 25
David Champion (interiors) 55
David Wainwright (interiors) 55
Dinny Hall (jewellery) 61
Dub Vendor (CDs, records & tapes) 31
Emma Bernhardt (gifts) 48
Frontiers (jewellery) 62
Garden Books (books) 29
Ghost (designer clothes) 39
Gong (interiors) 56
Graham & Green (designer clothes) 39, (interiors) 56
Honest Jon's (CDs, records & tapes) 31
Intoxica! (CDs, records & tapes) 31
Jacksons (accessories) 25
John Jesse (antiques) 26
Jonathan Horne (antiques) 26
Lulu Guinness (accessories) 25
Music & Video Exchange (CDs, records & tapes) 31
Natural Selection (streetwear) 78
Nick Ashley (menswear) 68
Nothing (streetwear) 78
Ormonde Gallery (antiques) 26
Oxfam (secondhand clothing) 71
Portobello (market) 66
Retro Man/Retro Woman (secondhand clothing) 71
Richard Dennis (antiques) 26
Roger Doyle (jewellery) 62
Rough Trade (CDs, records & tapes) 32
Scorah Pattullo (shoes) 74
Sigerson Morrison (shoes) 75
Solange Azagury-Partridge (jewellery) 62
Space (interiors) 58
Travel Bookshop (books) 30
Wall (streetwear) 79
Wild at Heart (gifts) 49

oxford circus & marble arch

SHOPPING

All Saints (menswear) 67
The Body Shop (health & beauty) 49
Borders (books) 28
Burton (high street shop) 52
Cinch (designer clothes) 37
Debenhams (department store) 34–5
Dorothy Perkins (high street shop) 52
French Connection (high street shop) 52
Hamleys (toys) 80
Harold Moores (CDs, records & tapes) 31
Hennes (high street shop) 52
JJB Sports (sportswear & equipment) 76
John Lewis (department store) 35
Karen Millen (high street shop) 52
Levi's (streetwear) 78
Marks & Spencer (department store) 35
Miss Selfridge (high street shop) 53
Muji (interiors) 57
Niketown (sportswear & equipment) 76
Oasis (high street shop) 53
Ravel (shoe chain) 76
Shelly's (shoe chain) 76
SU214 (menswear) 69
Top Shop (high street shop) 53
Underground Shoes (shoes) 75
Woodhouse (high street shop) 53

peckham

SIGHTS, MUSEUMS & GALLERIES

South London Gallery (major exhibition space) 181

piccadilly & st james's

BARS
Che (cigar bar) 121
ICA (bars & art) 120
Lounge-jing (late night) 130
Sports Café (sports bar) 136
10 Tokyo Joe's (cocktail joint) 125

RESTAURANTS & CAFÉS
China House (Chinese) 88
Criterion (French) 91
L'Odéon (French) 91
Momo (African) 81
The Oak Room (haute cuisine) 96
Quaglino (modern European) 112
The Ritz (tea) 117
Veeraswamy (Indian & Bengali) 98

SHOPPING
Burberry (international designer) 59
Caviar House (food) 45
Charbonnel et Walker (food) 45
Disney Store (toys) 79—80
DR Harris & Co (health & beauty) 49
Favourbrook (menswear) 68
Floris (health & beauty) 50
Fortnum & Mason (food) 46
Georgina von Etzdorf (accessories) 24
Hatchards (books) 29
Lillywhite's (sportswear & equipment) 76
Lina Stores (food) 46
Ozwald Boateng (menswear) 69
Paxton & Whitfield (food) 47
Penhaligons (health & beauty) 51
Tower Records (CDs, records & tapes) 32
Waterstones (books) 30
White Cube (art) 27
Wright & Teague (jewellery) 63
Zara (high street shop) 53

SIGHTS, MUSEUMS & GALLERIES
Green Park (parks & gardens) 187
ICA (major exhibition space) 180
Piccadilly Circus (landmark) 157
Royal Academy of Arts (major exhibition space) 180
St James's Palace (landmark) 158
St James's Park (parks & gardens) 189
White Cube (commercial gallery) 184

richmond, barnes, twickenham, kew & hampton court

SIGHTS, MUSEUMS & GALLERIES
Ham House (stately home) 171
Hampton Court Palace (the royals) 161
Kew Gardens (parks & gardens) 189
Marble Hill House (stately home) 171
Richmond Park (parks & gardens) 189
Wetland Centre (parks & gardens) 189

soho

BARS
Alphabet (hip hangout) 126
Balans (gay scene) 143
Bar Code (gay scene) 143
Bar Sol Ona (happy hour) 125
Café Bohème (late night) 130
Candy Bar (gay scene) 143
The Clinic (hip hangout) 126
Coach & Horses (pub experience) 132
De Hems (pub experience) 133
Dog & Duck (pub experience) 133
The Edge (gay scene) 144
Ego (club bar) 122
Est (bar/restaurant) 120
Freedom (gay scene) 144
French House Dining Room (pub experience) 133
GAY @ LA2 & the Astoria (gay scene) 145
The George (pub experience) 133
Intrepid Fox (pub experience) 134
K Bar (hip hangout) 127
Ku Bar (gay scene) 144
Lab (cocktail joint) 124
Lupo (hip hangout) 127
Manto's Soho (gay scene) 144
Mezzo (bar/restaurant) 121
'O' Bar (happy hour) 125
The Player (theme bar) 137
Pop (club bar) 123
Rupert St (gay scene) 144
Saint (hip hangout) 128
10 Room (cocktail joint) 125
Toucan (Irish pub) 130
Two Floors (hip hangout) 128
The White Horse (pub experience) 136
The Yard (gay scene) 145

CLUBS
The Annexe 138
Bar Rumba 138
China White 139
Hanover Grand 140
Le Scandale 140
Madame Jo Jo's 140
Ronnie Scott's 141

RESTAURANTS & CAFÉS
Amato (breakfast/brunch) 83, (patisserie) 114
Andrew Edmunds (modern European) 107
Bar & Grill (North American) 113
Aurora Café (Mediterranean) 105
Bar Italia (late-night opening) 104
Blue Room (café) 85
Blues Bistro & Bar (North American) 113
Bonbonnière (café) 85
Busaba Eathai (Southeast Asian) 116
Café Bohème (late-night opening) 104
Café Royal Grill Room (French) 90
Caffè Nero (café) 86
Circus (modern European) 108
Cranks (vegetarian) 118
French House Dining Room (modern European) 109
Frith Street (French) 91
Global Café (internet cafés) 99
Harbour City (Chinese) 88
Jimmy's (Greek) 95
Jus Café (juice bar) 103
Kettners (Italian) 100
Leith's Soho (modern European) 110
L'Escargot (French) 91
Maison Bertaux (patisserie) 114
Melati (Southeast Asian) 116
Mezzo (modern European) 111
Mildred's (vegetarian) 119
New Diamond (late-night opening) 104
New Mayflower (Chinese) 88
New Piccadilly (café) 86
Pâtisserie Valérie (patisserie) 114
Quo Vadis (French) 92
Ryo (late-night opening) 104
Schnecke (French) 92
Soho Spice (Indian & Bengali) 97
Sugar Club (global & fusion) 94
Tactical Café (café) 87
Teatro (modern European) 112
Titanic (modern European) 113
Wagamama (Japanese) 102
Webshack (internet cafés) 99
Wong Kei (Chinese) 89
Yo! Sushi (Japanese) 103

SHOPPING
A Moroni & Son (magazines & newspapers) 63
Ad Hoc (clubwear) 33
Agent Provocateur (lingerie) 63
Alexander McQueen (designer clothes) 36, 59
Algerian Coffee Stores (tea & coffee) 79
Anything Left-handed (interiors) 54
Beau Monde (designer clothes) 37
Berwick Street Market (food) 45
Clone Zone (fetish) 45
Errol Peak (designer clothes) 38
G-Factory (watches) 80
Gerry's (drink) 43
The Great Frog (jewellery) 62
I Camisa & Sons (food) 46
Jess James (jewellery) 62
Kokon Tozai (gifts) 48
Liberty (department store) 35
Mr Bongo (CDs, records & tapes) 31
Mr CD (CDs, records & tapes) 31
Oxfam Original (secondhand clothing) 71
Pineal Eye (clubwear) 33
Plum (clubwear) 33
Ray's Jazz Shop (CDs, records & tapes) 32
Selectadisc (CDs, records & tapes) 32
Shop (clubwear) 33
Sohi Soho (clubwear) 34
Tag (CDs, records & tapes) 32
Vexed Generation (streetwear) 79
Vintage Magazine Shop (magazines & newspapers) 64
Yasmin Cho (designer clothes) 42

south bank & southwark

RESTAURANTS & CAFÉS
Fina Estampa (Latin American) 105
Oxo Tower Restaurant, Bar & Brasserie (modern European) 112
Le Pont de la Tour (modern European) 110
People's Palace (modern European) 112

SIGHTS, MUSEUMS & GALLERIES
BFI IMAX (kids attraction) 186
Design Museum (one-off) 171–2
Golden Hinde (kids attraction) 186
Hayward Gallery (major exhibition space) 179–80

HMS Belfast (one-off) 173
London Aquarium (kids attraction) 185
London Eye (landmark) 157, (viewpoint) 159
National Film Theatre (kids attraction) 187
Oxo Tower (viewpoint) 159

SHOPPING
Farringdon Records (CDs, records & tapes) 31
Jenny Atkinson (accessories) 25

southall

SHOPPING
Southall Market (market) 67

south kensington

BARS
Blenheim (pub experience) 132
The Collection (hip hangout) 126
The Crescent (wine bar) 137

RESTAURANTS & CAFÉS
Bibendum (modern European) 107–8
Cactus Blue (Latin American) 105
Cambio de Tercio (Spanish) 117
Daquise (Russian & Eastern European) 115
Fluid (juice bar) 103
Itsu (Japanese) 102
Paparazzi Café (Italian) 100
Raison d'Être (café) 87
Troubadour (coffee houses) 89
Zaika (Indian & Bengali) 98

SHOPPING
Butler & Wilson (jewellery) 61
Campbellini (children's clothing) 33
Conran Shop (interiors) 55
Divertimenti (interiors) 56
Galerie Gaultier (designer clothes) 39
Jerry's Home Store (interiors) 57
Kara Kara (interiors) 57
The Library (menswear) 68
Officina di Santa Maria Novella (health & beauty) 51
Tocca (designer clothes) 41
Theo Fennell (jewellery) 62

SIGHTS, MUSEUMS & GALLERIES
Science Museum (kids attraction) 186
V&A Canon Photography Gallery (photography & design gallery) 183

vauxhall, lambeth & elephant & castle

CLUBS
The Colosseum 139
Crash (gay scene) 145
Ministry of Sound 141

SIGHTS, MUSEUMS & GALLERIES
Imperial War Museum (famous five) 164–5
Milch (gallery - alternative space) 182

victoria & pimlico

SHOPPING
Cornucopia (secondhand clothing) 70

SIGHTS, MUSEUMS & GALLERIES
Tate Britain (gallery) 178—9

westminster

SIGHTS, MUSEUMS & GALLERIES
Buckingham Palace (the royals) 160
Houses of Parliament & Big Ben (landmark) 157
Royal Mews & Queen's Gallery (the royals) 160–1
Westminster Abbey (great church) 163, (landmark) 158
Whitehall 163

whitechapel

RESTAURANTS & CAFÉS
Café Naz (Indian & Bengali) 97
Café Spice Namaste (Indian & Bengali) 97
Le Taj (Indian & Bengali) 98

SHOPPING
Same (interiors) 58

SIGHTS, MUSEUMS & GALLERIES
Whitechapel Art Gallery (major exhibition space) 181

wimbledon

SIGHTS, MUSEUMS & GALLERIES
Polka Children's Theatre (kids attraction) 187

shops

Sexy, sassy, or just plain chic, innovative design has transformed London into a shoppers' paradise. This is where the world now comes to do some serious shopping.

accessories

☆ ACCESSORIZE *A14*
Scarves, hats, and trinkets – the latest look at a fraction of designer prices.
22 The Market, Covent Garden ☎ 7240 2107 ⊖ Covent Garden

Anya Hindmarch *F11*
No-nonsense contemporary handbags that are hard to beat.
15–17 Pont Street, Knightsbridge ☎ 7838 9177 ⊖ Knightsbridge

Bentleys *F11*
Specialist in elegant antique luggage, selling eccentric accessories.
204 Walton Street, Knightsbridge ☎ 7584 7770 ⊖ Knightsbridge

☆ BILL AMBERG *F1*
Known as the leather man, Amberg does everything with hides, from wallets and laptop bags to handbags and pouches for babies.
10 Chepstow Road, Notting Hill ☎ 7727 3560 ⊖ Notting Hill Gate

Georgina von Etzdorf *C13*
One place really worth a splurge. Von Etzdorf is the undisputed queen of rich velvet scarves.
1–2 Burlington Arcade, St James ☎ 7409 7789 ⊖ Green Park

Gohil's *D2*
This shop is crammed full of handmade leather goods, from belts to briefcases, sandals and handbags – all exceptionally good value.
246 Camden High Street, Camden ☎ 7485 9195 ⊖ Camden Town

Hermès *A13*
Classic, luxury leather goods, silk scarves, and more.
155 New Bond Street, Mayfair ☎ 7499 8856 ⊖ Bond Street

Hide All *off map*
This luggage outfitter has bags galore, with one-offs imported from Italy.
Unit 9, Greenwich Market, Greenwich ☎ 8858 6104 Ⅲ Greenwich

Jacksons ⚲A1
Fun 60s-style accessories like flowery flip-flops and beaded jewellery.
5 All Saints Road, Notting Hill ☎ 7792 8336 ⊖ Westbourne Park

Jenny Atkinson ⚲14a
For hand-knitted separates and bags.
Unit 121, Oxo Tower Wharf, Bargehouse Street, Southwark ☎ 7229 2970 ⊖ Waterloo

Lulu Guinness ⚲B1
Best known for quirky evening bags, like the – now classic – velvet flowerpot.
66 Ledbury Road, Notting Hill ☎ 7221 9686 ⊖ Westbourne Park

☆ MULBERRY ⚲A13
Mulberry is a well-known purveyor of luxury goods. Their leather handbags, belts, and shoes are instantly recognizable as totems of British style the world over.
41–42 New Bond Street, Bond Street ☎ 7493 2546 ⊖ Bond Street

antiques

Antiquarius ⚲D17
Over 120 antique stalls selling everything from art nouveau silver to luggage.
131–141 King's Road, Chelsea ☎ 7351 5353 ⊖ Sloane Square

☆ BAROQUE & ROLL ⚲*off map*
A theatrical antique shop crammed with objects and furniture of all styles, ranging from shabby chic to gleaming gilt.
291 Lillie Road, West Brompton ☎ 7381 5008 ⊖ West Brompton, then 🚌 74, 190

Coach House ⚲D1
Only if you have serious money to blow. Peter Petrou's shop is packed with glorious antique eccentricities.
189 Westbourne Grove, Notting Hill ☎ 7229 8306 ⊖ Notting Hill Gate

Creek Antiques ⚲*off map*
A marvellous mixture of bizarre signs and weird and wonderful objects – a good place to browse.
23 Greenwich South Street, Greenwich ☎ 8293 5721 DLR Greenwich

Donay ⚲C3
This store (open Wed & Sat) in Islington's quaint antique quarter is a good choice for the home and boasts fabulous antique games.
3 Pierrepoint Row, Camden Passage, Islington ☎ 7359 1880 ⊖ Angel

☆ GUINEVERE *off map*
Lovely French country pieces, and old textiles.
574–580 King's Road, Chelsea ☎ 7736 2917 ⊖ Fulham Broadway

Hampstead Antique Emporium *off map*
An eclectic mix of stalls and shops selling everything from Victorian silverware to classic teddy bears.
12 Heath Street, Hampstead ☎ 7794 3297 ⊖ Hampstead

Joanna Booth *C18*
Antique tapestries and decorative textiles.
247 King's Road, Chelsea ☎ 7352 8998 ⊖ Sloane Square

☆ JOHN JESSE *off map*
Focuses on early to mid-20th century design.
160 Kensington Church St, Notting Hill ☎ 7229 0312 ⊖ Notting Hill Gate

☆ JONATHAN HORNE *off map*
Wonderful ceramics and particularly good for Delftware.
66c Kensington Church St, Notting Hill ☎ 7221 5658 ⊖ Notting Hill Gate

☆ MAGPIE *off map*
With a vast selection of antique decorative items for the home, Magpie is particularly strong on kitchen-related collectables.
152 Wandsworth Bridge Rd, Chelsea ☎ 7736 3738
⊖ Fulham Broadway then 28, 295

Ormonde Gallery *C1*
Alongside serious antiques is a never-predictable selection of Far Eastern ephemera.
156 Portobello Road, Notting Hill ☎ 7229 9800 ⊖ Ladbroke Grove

☆ PIMPERNEL & PARTNERS *off map*
Specialists in old textiles.
596 King's Road, Chelsea ☎ 7731 2448 ⊖ Fulham Broadway

☆ RICHARD DENNIS *off map*
Contemporary and antique studio pottery.
144 Kensington Church St, Notting Hill ☎ 7727 2061 ⊖ Notting Hill Gate

Sara Lemkow & Rookery Farm *C3*
For desirable antique enamelware.
12 Camden Passage, Islington ☎ 7359 0190 ⊖ Angel

Spread Eagle Antiques *off map*
Worth investigating for *objets d'art* from a bygone era. It has period costumes, secondhand books, and curios including Oriental vases, brass and rugs.
9 Nevada Street, Greenwich ☎ 8305 1666 Greenwich

auctions

Auctions are a fun way to buy antiques. **Sotheby's**, **Christie's**, and **Phillips** are the largest and most famous, and hold regular headline-hitting sales. Just as reputable is the less well-known **Bonhams**.

Bonhams *F11*
Montpelier Street, Knightbridge ☎ 7393 3900 ⊖ Knightsbridge

Christie's *A13*
8 King Street, Mayfair ☎ 7839 9060 ⊖ Green Park; Piccadilly Circus

Phillips *A13*
101 New Bond Street, Mayfair ☎ 7629 6602 ⊖ Bond Street

Sotheby's *A13*
34 New Bond Street, Mayfair ☎ 7293 5000 ⊖ Bond Street; Oxford Circus

art

Catto Gallery *off map*
Mainly contemporary figurative and representational work.
100 Heath Street, Hampstead ☎ 7435 6660 ⊖ Hampstead

Cross Street Gallery *B3*
Focuses on pleasingly affordable paintings and prints by artists such as Bridget Riley and Walter Sickert.
40 Cross Street, Islington ☎ 7226 8600 ⊖ Angel

Gilt by Association *D10*
Sells iconography and huge gilt mirrors.
8 Dray Walk, Shoreditch ☎ 7426 0001 ⊖ Liverpool Street

The Room *B17*
A small showcase for 'functional art' by contemporary British designers.
158 Walton Street, Knightsbridge ☎ 7225 3225 ⊖ Knightsbridge

White Cube *A13*
Where it's at for contemporary art. Jay Jopling deals in work by his super-artists: Damien Hirst, Tracey Emin and Antony Gormley.
44 Duke Street, St James's ☎ 7930 5373 ⊖ Green Park

White Cube² ₰F4
A small space owned by Jay Jopling. One of the top gallerists of his generation.
48 Hoxton Square, Hoxton ☎ 7930 5373 ⊖ Old Street

Zebra/Zebra Two ₰*off map*
As testimony to its creative past, Hampstead has a thriving art scene. Zebra and Zebra Two house Ecole de Paris and modern British prints by artists such as Henry Moore and David Hockney.
Zebra, Perrin's Court, Hampstead ☎ 7794 1281 ⊖ Hampstead
Zebra Two, 87 Heath Street, Hampstead ☎ 7435 3340 ⊖ Hampstead

body decoration

Into You ₰D9
This reputable tattooist and body piercer takes body art to a new level and sells pieces to adorn your various possible piercings.
144 St John Street, Clerkenwell ☎ 7253 5085 ⊖ Farringdon

books

☆ ANY AMOUNT OF BOOKS ₰B13
Look for bargains in the basement.
67 Charing Cross Rd, Leicester Square ☎ 7240 8140 ⊖ Leicester Square

☆ BELL, BOOK & RADMELL ₰A14
Twentieth-century first editions with some rare gems.
4 Cecil Court, Covent Garden ☎ 7240 2161 ⊖ Leicester Square

☆ BOOKS FOR COOKS ₰C1
A real heaven for foodies, this small shop is well stocked with books about all aspects of cooking, from recipes to diets.
4 Blenheim Crescent, Notting Hill ☎ 7221 1992 ⊖ Ladbroke Grove

☆ BORDERS ₰E7
150,000 books, 3000 magazines, music, and a café to read in.
203 Oxford Street, Oxford Circus ☎ 7292 1600 ⊖ Oxford Circus

Compendium ₰D2
Caters for all off-beat literary needs.
234 Camden High Street, Camden ☎ 7485 8944 ⊖ Camden Town

☆ FOYLE'S ₰B13
Trying to find a book in this vast store is an experience in itself.
113–119 Charing Cross Rd, Tottenham Court Rd ☎ 7437 5660 ⊖ Tottenham Court Road

Garden Books *C1*
An exquisitely-presented store for gardening enthusiasts and pros.
11 Blenheim Crescent, Notting Hill ☎ 7792 0777 ⊖ Ladbroke Grove

Halcyon Books *off map*
Has a vast collection of secondhand titles at knock-down prices.
1 Greenwich South St, Greenwich ☎ 8305 2675 Greenwich

Hatchards *A13*
Books to cater for every taste with over 100,000 titles.
187 Piccadilly, Piccadilly Circus ☎ 7439 9921 ⊖ Piccadilly Circus

Keith Fawkes *off map*
Hampstead's oldest antiquarian bookshop.
1–3 Flask Walk, Hampstead ☎ 7435 0614 ⊖ Hampstead

☆ MAGGS BROTHERS *B12*
Helpful staff and a huge collection of rare books make this a haunt for serious antique book lovers.
50 Berkeley Square, Mayfair ☎ 7493 7160 ⊖ Green Park

Marcet Books *off map*
A tiny shop chock full of interesting secondhand books.
4a Nelson Road, Greenwich ☎ 8853 5408 ⊖ North Greenwich

☆ MURDER ONE *B13*
An arresting selection for readers with a criminal bent.
71–73 Charing Cross Road, Leicester Square ☎ 7734 3485 ⊖ Leicester Square

Offstage *A2*
Stage and screen aficionados come for books about life under the spotlight.
37 Chalk Farm Road, Camden ☎ 7485 4996 ⊖ Chalk Farm

Regent Bookshop *C2*
This bookshop usually has lots of signed editions courtesy of local authors.
73 Parkway, Camden ☎ 7485 9822 ⊖ Camden Town

☆ SILVER MOON WOMEN'S BOOKSHOP *B13*
Leave your fella at the door for this excellent women's bookshop.
64–68 Charing Cross Road, Leicester Square ☎ 7836 7906 ⊖ Leicester Sq

☆ SKOOB *C8*
Comprehensive stock of secondhand books offering great value.
15 Sicilian Avenue, Holborn ☎ 7404 3063 ⊖ Holborn

☆ **STANFORDS** ⌖A14
For travel, this well-stocked shop is an excellent bet. Maps galore also.
12–14 Long Acre, Covent Garden ☎ 7836 2260 ⊖ Leicester Square

☆ **TRAVEL BOOKSHOP** ⌖C1
A point of departure for all London travellers in the know.
13–15 Blenheim Crescent, Notting Hill ☎ 7229 5260 ⊖ Ladbroke Grove

☆ **ULYSSES** ⌖E8
20th-century first editions.
40 Museum Street, Holborn ☎ 7831 1600 ⊖ Holborn

☆ **WATERSTONES** ⌖B13
Check out the glamorous new HQ on Piccadilly of this ubiquitous chain.
203 Piccadilly, St James's ☎ 7851 2400 ⊖ Piccadilly Circus

☆ **ZWEMMER MEDIA ARTS** ⌖B13
Splash out on coffee table art books. Specialists in photography and film.
80 Charing Cross Road, Leicester Square ☎ 7240 4157 ⊖ Leicester Square

british designers

Since 94, British fashion has undergone a transformation of epic proportions, and its twice-yearly fashion week has captured the world's imagination. The group of designers whose talent and vision caused this renaissance include: **Alexander McQueen** (also a designer at Givenchy) who now has his own store and whose daring antics caused a serious stir in the fashion world; **Clements Ribeiro**, the mix and matchers; **Hussein Chalayan**, the modernist; **Sonja Nuttall**, quiet, boyish elegance; and **Copperwheat Blundell**, the streety trendsetters. A newer breed has also emerged with **Tracey Mulligan**'s strong, feminine clothes, **Andrew Groves**' edgy tailoring, **Elspeth Gibson**'s girlie creations, and **Mark Whitaker**'s kooky, colourful dresses. The beauty of the British scene is that there are so many others to discover – the best places to spot all of the above are the department stores.

cds, records & tapes

Bar Vinyl ⌖A2
The latest club sounds and a bar upstairs to boot.
6 Inverness Street, Camden ☎ 7681 7898 ⊖ Camden Town

Different Music ⌖*off map*
This shop, based in the market building, has a large jazz section.
16 Greenwich Market, Greenwich ☎ 8305 1876 ⅡⅠ Greenwich

Dub Vendor *C1*
The place for reggae sounds.
150 Ladbroke Grove, Notting Hill ☎ 8969 3375 ⊖ Ladbroke Grove

Essential Music *off map*
For chart CDs and lots of bargains.
334 Creek Road, Greenwich ☎ 8293 4982 Ⅲ Greenwich

☆ FARRINGDON RECORDS *D14*
With one of the best selections of classical music, Farringdon Records can be relied upon to have all the significant recordings of any one piece of music.
Royal Festival Hall, South Bank ☎ 7620 0198 ⊖ Waterloo; Embankment

☆ HAROLD MOORES *E7*
The basement is crammed with classical rarities on vinyl. This is also a great source for easy listening and exotica.
2 Great Marlborough Street, Oxford Circus ☎ 7437 1576 ⊖ Oxford Circus

☆ HMV *F6*
Mainstream releases and impressive world music and jazz sections.
360 Oxford Street, Bond Street ☎ 7514 3600 ⊖ Bond Street

☆ HONEST JON'S *C1*
A popular haunt for musos looking for jazz, jazz-funk, dance music, reggae, and soul.
276–278 Portobello Road, Notting Hill ☎ 8969 9822 ⊖ Ladbroke Grove

Intoxica! *C1*
Collectors' discs and encyclopedically-knowledgeable staff.
231 Portobello Road, Notting Hill ☎ 7229 8010 ⊖ Ladbroke Grove

Mr Bongo *E7*
Tops for Latin music.
44 Poland Street, Soho ☎ 7287 1887 ⊖ Oxford Circus

☆ MR CD *E7*
Few places can beat this for bargain basement prices.
80 Berwick Street, Soho ☎ 7439 1097 ⊖ Oxford Circus

☆ MUSIC & VIDEO EXCHANGE *F1*
A useful hunting ground for old vinyl and CDs with helpful staff and regular price reductions.
38–40 Notting Hill Gate, Notting Hill ☎ 7243 8573 ⊖ Notting Hill Gate

Out on the Floor ⚲A2
Good for re-issues and rare gems.
10 Inverness Street, Camden ☎ 7267 5989 ⊖ Camden Town

☆ RAY'S JAZZ SHOP ⚲B13
Still run by the man himself, a drumming contemporary of Charlie Watts. Not only is this one of London's best sources of jazz records (stock covers modern, avant-garde, blues & roots), it is also crammed with memorabilia.
180 Shaftesbury Avenue, Soho ☎ 7240 3969 ⊖ Tottenham Court Road

Rhythm Records ⚲D2
Great for more obscure grooves, like 60s rock, and a range of black music.
281 Camden High Street, Camden ☎ 7267 0123 ⊖ Camden Town

☆ ROUGH TRADE ⚲C1
The city's most eclectic and intelligent range of independent label releases. Stock ranges from rare punk through to drum 'n' bass and a good selection of dance music.
130 Talbot Road, Notting Hill ☎ 7229 8541 ⊖ Ladbroke Grove

☆ SELECTADISC ⚲E7
An excellent choice of secondhand and new CDs, especially for indie, jazz, dance, and soul.
34–35 Berwick Street, Soho ☎ 7734 3297 ⊖ Oxford Circus

Tag ⚲B13
A wide selection of house, techno and drum 'n' bass.
5 Rupert Court, Soho ☎ 7434 0029 ⊖ Piccadilly Circus

☆ TOWER RECORDS ⚲B13
For a wide range of dance, R&B, and hip-hop this store – which is open until midnight – easily rivals some of the city's specialist shops.
1 Piccadilly Circus, Piccadilly Circus ☎ 7439 2500 ⊖ Piccadilly Circus

☆ VIRGIN MEGASTORE ⚲F7
The world's largest entertainment store. Its greatest draw is the vast selection of CDs and music paraphernalia – books, mags, videos, games, and sheet music.
14–16 Oxford Street, Tottenham Court Road ☎ 7631 1614
⊖ Tottenham Court Road

childrens' clothing

Campbellini ⚲A17
Bibs, woollen bootees and nappy bags for the more discerning baby, by famed interior designer Nina Campbell.
9 Walton Street, South Kensington ☎ 7225 1011 ⊖ South Kensington

cigars & cigarettes

Davidoff ⚲C13
London's largest cigar specialist.
35 St James's Street, Mayfair ☎ 7930 3079 ⊖ Green Park

clubwear

Ad Hoc ⚲B13
Clubby, contemporary, psychedelic street fashion from skimpy clubwear to skateboarding kit.
10–11 Moor Street, Soho ☎ 7287 0911 ⊖ Leicester Square

The Common Market ⚲C18
An eclectic collection of club gear which includes a good line in work wear labels such as the hugely popular Diesel and Carhartt.
121 King's Road, Chelsea ☎ 7351 9361 ⊖ Sloane Square

Cyberdog ⚲E8
Mid-priced items for hardcore clubbers include T-shirts with flashing lights.
9 Earlham Street, Covent Garden ☎ 7836 7855 ⊖ Covent Garden

☆ PINEAL EYE ⚲E7
This futuristic über-environment is a must-see store for cutting-edge design talent, avant-garde hand-me-downs, and art magazines. One-off pieces by fashion's young turks rub shoulders with secondhand classics by the likes of Comme des Garçons and Yohji Yamamoto.
49 Broadwick Street, Soho ☎ 7434 2567 ⊖ Oxford Circus

Plum ⚲E7
A popular port of call for grown-up clubbers and those with a yen for designer, rather than ex-army, combat gear.
79 Berwick Street, Soho ☎ 7734 0812 ⊖ Oxford Circus

Shop ⚲E7
Venture inside if labels matter and you fancy a little slip dress by Tocca or a quirky T-shirt from the Hysteric Glamour label.
4 Brewer Street, Soho ☎ 7437 1259 ⊖ Oxford Circus

Sohi Soho *⌕E7*
An excellent source for clubbers, with colourful bindis, racks of hippy clothing, trashy make-up and nail varnish, and space-age bongs for mellow evenings.
5 Berwick Street, Soho ☎ 7287 1295 ⊖ Oxford Circus

crafts

Clerkenwell Green Association *⌕C9*
Real craft addicts should contact this association who can put you in touch with the 70 or so artisans (milliners to musical instrument makers) in the area.
Pennybank Chambers, 33–35 St John's Square, Clerkenwell ☎ 7251 0276 ⊖ Farringdon

☆ CRAFTS COUNCIL *⌕off map*
As well as a programme of exhibitions, the council has a shop displaying a constantly-updated selection of imaginative work by contemporary British artisans. There's also a good range of specialist crafts books.
44a Pentonville Road, Islington ☎ 7806 2500 ⊖ Angel

Hart Gallery *⌕C3*
A showcase for some of the best names in contemporary ceramics.
113 Upper Street, Islington ☎ 7704 1131 ⊖ Highbury & Islington

Papier Marché *⌕C9*
Collectors of kitsch love this bright, fun emporium which sells inexpensive pieces, like mirror frames and bizarre decorative objects, all made from – papier-mâché!
53 Clerkenwell Close, Clerkenwell ☎ 7251 6311 ⊖ Farringdon

Plasterworks *⌕B3*
Traditional items made out of plaster of Paris; everything from cornicing to perfectly-formed body parts of Greek gods.
38 Cross Street, Islington ☎ 7226 5355 Ш Essex Road

Stephen Einhorn *⌕C3*
This designer works mostly in metal, producing an eyebrow-raising range of 'gothic' home accessories and jewellery.
210 Upper Street, Islington ☎ 7359 4977 ⊖ Angel

department stores

☆ DEBENHAMS *⌕F6*
Clever deals with top designers such as Ben de Lisi and Lulu Guinness have resulted in covetable clothes, hats, and evening bags at affordable prices. This collaborative approach has now moved into the interiors

department where there are new lines by interior designer of the moment, Kelly Hoppen, as well as a homeware collection by Jasper Conran.
334–348 Oxford St, Oxford Circus ☎ 7580 3000 ⊖ Bond St; Oxford Circus

☆ HARRODS *F11*

Al Fayed's fascinating and fabulously ostentatious tourist trap has everything from perfumery to pets – all at a huge premium. The world's most famous store is well worth a visit for the food halls alone and the spectacular Christmas department which opens in August.
87–135 Brompton Road, Knightsbridge ☎ 7730 1234 ⊖ Knightsbridge

☆ HARVEY NICHOLS *F11*

Excellent fashion with the most desirable designer labels; home furnishing concessions; make-up, perfume, accessories; and a top-floor food hall for all foodies and anyone passionate about packaging. The chic Fifth Floor Restaurant and Café, and an Aveda Concept Salon round things off in true style.
109–123 Knightsbridge, Knightsbridge ☎ 7235 5000 ⊖ Knightsbridge

☆ JOHN LEWIS/PETER JONES *E7*

John Lewis and its reliable Chelsea cousin, Peter Jones, sell everything under the sun from socks to china and electronics. Their fabric and bedlinen departments are particularly popular. The 'never knowingly undersold' policy for both stores ensures excellent value, and if you find any item cheaper they will refund the difference. A safe – if somewhat conservative – bet.
John Lewis, 278–306 Oxford St, Oxford Circus ☎ 7629 7711 ⊖ Oxford Circus
Peter Jones, Sloane Square, Chelsea ☎ 7730 3434 ⊖ Sloane Square

☆ LIBERTY *E7*

A charming store brimming with seductive goods from furniture (Arts & Crafts to Matthew Hilton), rugs (contemporary to antique kilims), and lighting; through to fashion, make-up, and jewellery. Most famous for its printed fabrics, Liberty also has a strong own-label clothes collection, which hangs alongside gorgeous Ghost, wacky Westwood, and many other designer labels. British designers are well represented.
32 Kingly Street, Soho ☎ 7734 1234 ⊖ Oxford Circus

☆ MARKS & SPENCER *E6*

Every Londoner shops in one of the city's 40-odd M&S branches. M&S excels in the basics: undies, T-shirts, and knitwear, and every season it will pull off one great coup: a brilliant take on a classic look from the catwalk. Over the years they have used Paul Smith, Ally Capellino, and more recently Timothy Everest, as fashion consultants. M&S's other great strength is its food – it has managed to transform the TV dinner into an art form.
458 Oxford Street, Marble Arch ☎ 7935 7954 ⊖ Marble Arch

☆ **SELFRIDGES** *F6*
Particularly impressive are the spacious and decidedly glam floors devoted to fashion; all the big labels are there, among them Joseph, Calvin Klein, MaxMara, and Ralph Lauren. Downstairs, customers are greeted by the largest perfumery in Europe and a great international food hall.
400 Oxford Street, Bond Street ☎ 7629 1234 ⊖ Bond Street

designer clothes

Aime *B1*
The lifestyle emporium which mixes exclusive French fashion with chic but quirky gifts for the home.
32 Ledbury Road, Notting Hill ☎ 7221 7070 ⊖ Westbourne Park

☆ **À LA MODE** *E12*
A well-stocked shop, with sophisticated, glamorous clothing from directional, international designers of the moment: Fendi, Chloe, and Matthew Williamson's beaded fancies are worth a look.
36 Hans Crescent, Knightsbridge ☎ 7584 2133 ⊖ Knightsbridge

Agnès b *B1*
Chic mens and womens clothing interpreted through classic and comfortable fabrics.
235 Westbourne Grove, Notting Hill ☎ 0792 1947 ⊖ Westbourne Park

Alberta Ferretti *E12*
Ferreti pleases the jet set with his timeless designs.
205–206 Sloane Street, Knightsbridge ☎ 7235 2349 ⊖ Knightsbridge

Alexander McQueen *B13*
The super-cool king of fashion's first London HQ showcases collections straight off the catwalk. Transparent changing rooms frost over with your body heat.
47 Conduit Street, Soho ☎ 7734 2340 ⊖ Piccadilly Circus

Antoni & Alison *C9*
The Brit design duo are especially known for their wickedly witty slogan T-shirts, vacuum-packed in clear plastic. Their designs extend to chic simple clothing, undies, and some very neat accessories.
43 Rosebery Avenue, Clerkenwell ☎ 7833 2002 ⊖ Farringdon

☆ **ANTONY PRICE** *off map*
The designer's first shop in 10 years allows impatient fans access to his prêt-à-porter range. Price's designs are unashamedly glamorous: sexy tailoring for suits, floaty shifts in intricately cut chiffon, and lots of hot pants.
17 Langton Street, Chelsea ☎ 7376 7250 ⊖ Fulham Broadway

APC *B1*
Highly hip, almost anti-fashion purveyor of fabulously-cut boyish clothes which last a lifetime.
40 Ledbury Road, Notting Hill ☎ 7229 4933 ⊖ Westbourne Park

Beau Monde *B13*
Dressy, quietly elegant women's attire.
43 Lexington Street, Soho ☎ 7734 6563 ⊖ Piccadilly Circus

Betsey Johnson *D17*
Flirty, girly creations in a brilliant yellow, rose-encrusted boutique.
106 Draycott Avenue, Knightsbridge ☎ 7591 0005 ⊖ South Kensington

Brora *C18*
Sloane Rangers make tracks here for its cute cashmere jumpers. They also snap up accessories like picnic rugs and bags.
344 King's Road, Chelsea ☎ 7352 3697 ⊖ Sloane Square

☆ BROWNS *F6*
Famous for championing John Galliano, London's best-known designer boutique is mostly for the rich, famous, and seriously stylish. Their six stores in total make it an excellent all-rounder, and an ideal place to spot up-and-coming designers.
23–27 South Molton Street, Mayfair ☎ 7491 7833 ⊖ Bond Street

Christa Davies *C1*
Feminine chiffon and crepe numbers in rich colours and with wonderful detailing.
35 All Saints Road, Notting Hill ☎ 7727 1998 ⊖ Ladbroke Grove

Christian Dior *E12*
One of fashion's biggest names makes its mark on this haughty stretch of Knightsbridge.
22 Sloane Street, Knightsbridge ☎ 7235 1357 ⊖ Knightsbridge

Cinch *E7*
'Curated' by Luke Oxly, the store is filled with a capsule collection called Levi's Red, secondhand books, handmade jewellery, and even changing art exhibitions. Not the corporate image at all.
5 Newburgh Street, Oxford Circus ☎ 7287 4941 ⊖ Oxford Circus

Comfort & Joy *C3*
An own-label shop selling designs with a street feel.
109 Essex Road, Islington ☎ 7359 3898 ⊖ Angel

☆ COMME DES GARÇONS *F6*

Rei Kawakubo's store requires a degree of chutzpah to enter and then a bit more to try on the clothes. This is conceptual fashion by one of the world's most respected designers. Her complex constructions are an acquired taste.
59 Brook Street, Mayfair ☎ 7493 1258 ⊖ Bond Street

☆ THE CROSS *E1*

Rarely does an edition of *Vogue* appear without featuring something from The Cross. Clothes, shoes, and accessories are either exquisite, fabulous, ingenious, indulgent, or just plain funky. The collection includes Oriental dresses and bags, beautiful knits, and floaty frocks.
141 Portland Road, Bayswater ☎ 7727 6760 ⊖ Holland Park

Designworks *F6*

A reliable source of snappy suits and separates.
19 Avery Row, Mayfair ☎ 7495 5846 ⊖ Bond Street

Diverse *A3*

Choose from funky labels such as Amaya Arzuaga, Ghost, and Ally Capellino.
294 Upper Street, Islington ☎ 7359 8877 ⊖ Highbury & Islington

DKNY *F6*

Worth a visit for the cappuccino bar alone: if you can't afford the logoed sports gear, buy a coffee instead and watch others flex their plastic.
27 Old Bond Street, Mayfair ☎ 7499 8089 ⊖ Green Park

☆ EGG *F12*

Serenity emanates from this shop, which has established a cult following. The exquisite handmade robes, best described as designer ethnic, include *djellabas*, throw-on dresses, and loose shirts, sourced mainly from the Far East.
36 Kinnerton Street, Knightsbridge ☎ 7235 9315 ⊖ Hyde Park Corner

Elspeth Gibson *F11*

Cute camisoles and pretty skirts trimmed with beads.
7 Pont Street, Knightsbridge ☎ 7235 0607 ⊖ Knightsbridge

Errol Peak *E7*

Hi-tech fabrics are the inspiration for the one-time architect's stylish jean jackets, dresses, and coats.
13 Newburgh Street, Soho ☎ 7434 4456 ⊖ Oxford Circus

Fenwicks ♀A13
If one-stop shopping appeals, try this store with its excellent selection of designer labels and some cheaper lines.
63 New Bond Street, Mayfair ☎ 7629 9161 ⊖ Bond Street

☆ GALERIE GAULTIER ♀D17
Jean-Paul's London boutique is home to his mainline collection of flamboyant clubwear, beautiful tailoring, funky denim, and body-conscious evening clothes, as seen on the catwalks of Paris. Strictly for extroverts and statement dressers with a sense of fun.
171 Draycott Avenue, South Kensington ☎ 7584 4648 ⊖ South Kensington

☆ GHOST ♀D1
Tania Sarne's simple, flattering, unashamedly feminine clothes (in viscose) are ever popular. Beautiful knitwear too.
36 Ledbury Road, Notting Hill ☎ 7229 1057 ⊖ Notting Hill Gate

Global Gypsy ♀D10
Stocks urban designerwear and sassy accessories to match.
2 Dray Walk, Shoreditch ☎ 7247 3434 ⊖ Liverpool Street

Graham & Green ♀C1
The eclectic selection of stylish women's clothes and accessories features regularly in the glossies.
4, 7, & 10 Elgin Crescent, Notting Hill ☎ 7727 4594 ⊖ Ladbroke Grove

☆ ISSEY MIYAKE ♀B12
The Japanese designer who brought tiny engineered pleats to the fashion world has a legion of fans who adore his Pleats Please range. So much so he opened a shop for it.
20 Brook Street, Mayfair ☎ 7581 3760 ⊖ Bond Street

Joanna's Tent ♀C18
A reliable source of elegant womenswear and childrenswear with Ghost, Issaye Miayake, and Betsey Johnson making appearances.
289B King's Road, Chelsea ☎ 7352 1151 ⊖ Sloane Square

☆ JOSEPH ♀C17
Joseph's own label provides chic, well-made must-haves for the girl- or man-about-town, throwing in a distinctive dose of glamour from the catwalks too. It also stocks pieces by many international designers.
77 Fulham Road, Chelsea ☎ 7823 9500 ⊖ South Kensington

☆ KOH SAMUI *A14*

This original boutique is a fashion-lover's heaven. Each rail is like a dream wardrobe: snappy suits by Copperwheat Blundell mixed with Clements Ribeiro cashmere knits, and captivating silk dresses by Christa Davies.

65 Monmouth Street, Covent Garden ☎ 7240 4280 ⊖ Leicester Square

Krizia *E7*

The ultra-stylish classic Italian label.

24–25 Conduit Street, Mayfair ☎ 7491 4987 ⊖ Oxford Circus

Livingstone Studio *off map*

An experience in itself. A veritable sanctuary of silk, cotton, and linen garments by Jurgen Lehl; the rest of the studio exhibits one-offs by graduate designers from the Royal College of Art.

36 New End Square, Hampstead ☎ 7435 9586 ⊖ Hampstead

Malapa *off map*

Stocks a wide selection of young British labels, such as Boudicca, Flip Jackson, and Eugene Rocha, as well as clothes by recent fashion graduates.

41 Clerkenwell Road, Clerkenwell ☎ 7490 5229 ⊖ Farringdon

☆ MARGARET HOWELL *F11*

Howell's timeless, minimal clothes draw on traditional British style and add a dash of contemporary fashion. She is most famous for her classic suits, white shirts, and stylish slouch trousers.

29 Beauchamp Place, Knightsbridge ☎ 7584 2462 ⊖ Knightsbridge

☆ MIMI *C18*

A spacious shop for feminine modernists seeking dresses in sumptuous colours by Elspeth Gibson, Gharani Strok, and others, plus great knitwear.

309 King's Road, Chelsea ☎ 7349 9699 ⊖ Sloane Square

☆ MOSCHINO *B13*

All the witty irreverence and kitsch high drama of its namesake (the late Franco Moschino) has been distilled into its clothes and decor. Cheap and Chic! and Moschino Jeans are available here too.

28–29 Conduit Street, Mayfair ☎ 7318 0555 ⊖ Piccadilly Circus

☆ MULBERRY *A13*

The luggage, leather, fashion, and homeware emporium.

41–42 New Bond Street, Mayfair ☎ 7491 3900 ⊖ Bond Street

☆ NICOLE FARHI *A13*

Farhi, with seven London branches, is one of Britain's best-loved fashion

designers. Classic clothes are understated, softly structured, and elegant, with muted colours and an emphasis on textures.
158 New Bond Street, Mayfair ☎ 7499 8368 ⊖ Green Park

☆ PAUL SMITH *E8*
Paul 'classically English with a humorous twist' Smith is the UK's most successful fashion export thanks to the quality and attention to detail in all his clothes for men, women, and children.
40–44 Floral Street, Covent Garden ☎ 7379 7133 ⊖ Covent Garden

Press & Bastyan *E8*
Simple, feminine designs are the hallmark here. The long-established style may look a little jaded, but would-be Lolitas will doubtless find their flat sandals and little seersucker dresses hard to resist.
17–19 Neal Street, Covent Garden ☎ 7240 4401 ⊖ Covent Garden

Ronit Zilkha *off map*
Classy clothes in soft neutral colours for career women are a key feature of Ronit Zilkha's lines.
17 Hampstead High Street, Hampstead ☎ 7431 0253 ⊖ Hampstead

Sefton *A3*
Chic mens- and womenswear is available at these two stores, run by Gill Wing's son, by both less well-known and more established designers.
196 & 271 Upper Street, Islington ☎ 7226 7076 & 7226 9822
⊖ Highbury & Islington

Tocca *D17*
Mimi Lowe's colourful lifestyle emporium sells enticing clothes, trinkets for the home, and beauty products.
169 Draycott Avenue, Fulham ☎ 7225 1002 ⊖ South Kensington

Tommy Hilfiger's *E12*
For a more sporty image. Hilfiger's 'Collection' range is found only here and in Beverly Hills.
6 Sloane Street, Knightsbridge ☎ 7235 2500 ⊖ Knightsbridge

☆ VIVIENNE WESTWOOD *E7*
The influential Queen of Punk is now the mistress of the refined. She still runs the original King's Road store (selling Anglomania, Red, and Gold), and now has two upmarket boutiques flaunting her feisty catwalk collections: Gold (elegant haute couture) on Davies Street; Red (more sassy) and Man (classic) on Conduit Street.
44 Conduit Street, Mayfair ☎ 7439 1109 ⊖ Oxford Circus

☆ **VOYAGE** *B17*

If you're not rich, beautiful, or powerful enough, you are unlikely to get into this store, renowned for its strict door policy – a business card can help. The clothes, dubbed 'hippy bohemia' are hand-dyed, and hand-finished. They are beautiful, but breathtakingly expensive. One shop for women (115) and one for men (175).

115 & 175 Fulham Road, Chelsea ☎ 7823 9581 ⊖ South Kensington

☆ **WEST VILLAGE** *off map*

A tiny slice of the Big Apple in west London. All the designers, bar a couple of shoe makers, hail from New York. Designers include Patch NYC, Alice & Trixie, Sofka bags, and owner Lucy Benzecry's own line, Menza.

364 Fulham Road, Chelsea ☎ 7795 2611 ⊖ Fulham Broadway

☆ **WHISTLES** *A13*

An excellent source of established labels and newcomers, Whistles (with six London branches) is well known for its vaguely ethnic, feminine, and dressy designer clothes, as well as its own label.

12–14 St Christopher's Place, Mayfair ☎ 7487 4484 ⊖ Bond Street

Yasmin Cho *E7*

Yasmin Cho's studio-cum-shop is like arriving at your best friend's apartment and being encouraged to try on her entire wardrobe. Funky designers include Madam a Paris, Susan Cianciolo, AS Vandervorst, and Carol Christian Poell.

Level One, 22 Poland Street, Soho ☎ 7287 6922 ⊖ Oxford Circus

YMC *A13*

Standing for You Must Create, this store defies its name, with one definite look on sale – it's pretty much all urban utility wear, but the best natural fabrics and functional form to be found.

6 Conduit Street, Mayfair ☎ 7629 1747 ⊖ Bond Street

☆ **YOHJI YAMAMOTO** *E7*

Mechanical, austere, and modern, Yamamoto's store is pure Zen. His clothes can be challenging, but they are simply divine, and well worth the effort.

14–15 Conduit Street, Mayfair ☎ 7491 4129 ⊖ Oxford Circus

Yves St Laurent Rive Gauche *A13*

Simple, classy French chic is what YSL's ready-to-wear line is about.

137 New Bond Street, Mayfair ☎ 7493 1800 ⊖ Bond Street

Zana Boutique *off map*

A mix of contemporary designs and antique-inspired clothing.

6 Flask Walk, Hampstead ☎ no phone ⊖ Hampstead

discount stores

☆ **AMAZON** *off map*

Clustered at the lower end of Kensington Church Street, these shops all sell discount clothing. No. 1 sells designer wear, but the others stock high street clothes (like InWear and French Connection) at half the usual price.
1, 3, 7, 19–21 22 Kensington Church Street, Chelsea ☎ 7937 4692 ⊖ High Street Kensington

☆ **BROWNS LABELS FOR LESS** *F6*

Last year's clothes (men's and women's) at a fraction of the original price.
50 South Molton Street, Mayfair ☎ 7514 0052 ⊖ Bond Street

☆ **FRENCH CONNECTION/NICOLE FARHI** *off map*

For those who are prepared to go out of their way for a bargain – you'll find all those items you coveted last season at half the price.
3 Handcock Road, Bromley ☎ 7399 7000 ⊖ Bromley-by-Bow

Joseph Sale Shop *C18*

Crammed with end-of-season discounted items. And to satisfy regular bargain hunters, new goods arrive every Friday.
53 King's Road, Chelsea ☎ 7730 7562 ⊖ Sloane Square

☆ **PAUL SMITH** *F6*

A real deal. Mostly last season's stock, and mostly menswear from the king of style at 50–60% off. Indulge.
23 Avery Row, Mayfair ☎ 7493 1287 ⊖ Bond Street

Whistles Sale Store *C18*

Last season's clothes and accessories at up to 75% off retail price.
31 Sloane Square, Chelsea ☎ 7730 9819 ⊖ Sloane Square

drink

Berry Bros & Rudd *C13*

Purveyors of fine wine.
3 St James's Street, Mayfair ☎ 7396 9600 ⊖ Bond Street

Gerry's *B13*

Bottles of virtually every spirit known to man are stacked up as far as the eye can see. A locked cabinet contains liqueurs in miniature and in the window there are tiny jugs of 'Very English' honey mead.
74 Old Compton Street, Soho ☎ 7734 4215 ⊖ Leicester Square

electronics

The UK isn't renowned for its electronic goods, but if you are on the hunt for something of that ilk, **Tottenham Court Road** is the place to head for. There is little to differentiate one shop from another and getting a good deal is a matter of thorough research and determined haggling. Prices are unpredictable and can vary dramatically. The most fundamental rule is to bargain. Work your way systematically along from Tottenham Court Road or Goodge Street underground stations, armed with pen and paper to jot down prices and shop names – as they are easy to confuse. Chatting to a few assistants can usually set you straight on what model and make to opt for, and from then the bargaining antics begin; most shops will drop their prices, especially if you quote cheaper prices given by neighbours. Some will also give a better price for cash deals. After an hour or two, and a fair amount of deliberating, you will usually come away with a good buy. TV and video systems, and voltage levels, vary from country to country, so double-check on these before you purchase.

eyewear

Cutler & Gross *F11*
For budding Jackie O's, this is the only place to get shades. Choose from a wide range of wonderful 50s and 60s inspired designs.
16 Knightsbridge Green, Knightsbridge ☎ 7581 2250 ⊖ Knightsbridge

Kirk Originals *E8*
Original eyewear is the hallmark in this store where glasses and sunglasses are handmade, often using limited-edition material.
36 Earlham Street, Covent Garden ☎ 7240 5055 ⊖ Covent Garden

fabrics

Joanna Booth *off map*
For antique tapestries and decorative textiles.
247 King's Road, Chelsea ☎ 7352 8998 ⊖ Fulham Broadway

VV Rouleaux *C18*
Filled with roll upon roll of beautiful ribbons in silk, organza, velvet and even paper, perfect for breathing new life into tired clothes.
54 Sloane Square, Chelsea ☎ 7730 3125 ⊖ Sloane Square

fetish

Bizarre *A14*

Fashion and fetishwear for all persuasions.

4A Peter Street, Covent Garden ☎ 7287 7666 ⊖ Covent Garden

Clone Zone *B13*

Fetish fans can let their fantasies rip in this Soho store.

64 Old Compton Street, Soho ☎ 7287 3530 ⊖ Leicester Square

food

☆ & CLARKE'S *off map*

Known for its heavenly bread, this fine deli is also full of other delights: freshly baked biscuits, handmade truffles, excellent quiches and pizzas, and cakes made to order. Locals love it and the café is a popular haunt.

122 Kensington Church St, Notting Hill ☎ 7229 2190 ⊖ Notting Hill Gate

Berwick Street Market *F7*

Buy fruit and veg, or giant £1 slabs of brie, and dip into London market life.

Berwick Street, Soho ⊖ Oxford Circus; Tottenham Court Road

☆ BLUEBIRD *C18*

This spectacularly stylish food hall is a foodies' dream. Staff are knowledgeable and food is readily proffered for tasting. Fruit, veg, and flowers are sold outside and there's a farmers' market every Wednesday – when the sun shines it is easy to imagine yourself in a French market.

350 King's Road, Chelsea ☎ 7559 1154 ⊖ Sloane Square, then 🚌 1, 22, 211, 319

☆ CARLUCCIO'S *E8*

Antonio Carluccio's passion for mushrooms is evident the minute you set foot in his chic, and very tiny, shop. In addition to the dried and fresh mushrooms (imported and native), there is a fantastic selection of unusual pastas, and a deli counter serving delicious slices of focaccia and pizzas.

28a Neal Street, Covent Garden ☎ 7240 1487 ⊖ Covent Garden

Caviar House *C13*

A shrine to the good stuff – Iranian and sometimes Russian; it also stocks excellent vodkas.

161 Piccadilly, St James's ☎ 7409 0445 ⊖ Green Park

Charbonnel et Walker *B13*

A tiny heaven for chocolate lovers and a fave with the Queen.

1 Royal Arcade, Piccadilly Circus ☎ 7491 0939 ⊖ Green Park

Cheese Board *off map*

Revive yourself with a picnic in the park, put together here. This place is a real find, specializing in bread and foreign cheeses

26 Royal Hill, Greenwich ☎ 8305 0401 Greenwich

The Dab Hand *off map*

A fishmonger and deli that does a great seafood pizza.

20 Royal Hill, Greenwich ☎ 8858 2268 Greenwich

☆ FORTNUM & MASON *C13*

Plush red carpets and assistants in tailcoats make this one of London's most unusual purveyors of fine food. Potted stilton with port is a real treat.

181 Piccadilly, St James's ☎ 7734 8040 ⊖ Green Park

I Camisa & Sons *B13*

Regulars queue up for the wide selection of cheeses, fresh pastas, Italian wines, and more.

61 Old Compton Street, Soho ☎ 7437 7610 ⊖ Leicester Square

Jane Asher *A17*

A tiny Chelsea cake shop belonging to the actress.

24 Cale Street, Chelsea ☎ 7584 6177 ⊖ South Kensington

☆ JOY *off map*

This beautiful little food hall has acquired something of a cult status, as has its owner, the knowledgeable gourmand Kevin Gould. Nearly all the stock is organic, with an emphasis on quality. Take-away specials cater for veggies.

511 Finchley Road, Hampstead ☎ 7435 7711 ⊖ Finchley Road

☆ LINA STORES *B13*

One of London's best Italian delis, Lina Stores hasn't changed its appearance since before the war. The aroma transports you to Italy. Fresh pasta is made daily, and there are tempting breads, olive oils, salamis, and cheeses.

18 Brewer Street, Piccadilly Circus ☎ 7437 6482 ⊖ Piccadilly Circus

☆ NEAL'S YARD DAIRY *E8*

Staff are cheese evangelists and talk at length about the varieties on offer and how best to serve each cheese. Everything is bought directly from small farm-based British and Irish makers, and the maturing or ripening process is carefully monitored. Tasting is encouraged.

17 Shorts Gardens, Covent Garden ☎ 7645 3550 ⊖ Covent Garden

Paxton & Whitfield *C13*

The cheeses are among the finest in the capital.

93 Jermyn Street, Piccadilly ☎ 7930 0259 ⊖ Green Park

☆ PLANET ORGANIC *D7*

Source of dried goods, health staples, fruit and veg, fresh bread, and excellent meat and fish; London's first organic supermarket offers one-stop shopping for health-conscious foodies. There is also a wheat-grass juice bar.

22 Torrington Place, North Soho ☎ 7702 1116 ⊖ Goodge Street

☆ ROCOCO *C18*

Chocolate-lovers will find a tiny corner of heaven in the form of this elegant shop. Dedicated to raising chocolate to gourmet status, there are no vegetable fats here – strictly cocoa butter only. At Easter this shop is the place to get the best, chicest, and wittiest eggs in town.

321 King's Road, Chelsea ☎ 7352 5857 ⊖ Sloane Square, then 🚌 11, 22, 211, 319

Tesco Metro *E8*

Supermarket fare on which to picnic in nearby St Paul's churchyard.

22–25 Bedford Street, Covent Garden ☎ 7853 7500 ⊖ Covent Garden

☆ VILLANDRY *C7*

An inspirational deli with an excellent restaurant. Regular deliveries from France include cheeses and succulent fruit and veg. There is also a wide range of breads and a variety of tempting treats.

170 Great Portland Street, North Soho ☎ 7631 3131 ⊖ Great Portland Street

gifts

☆ BRATS *C18*

An excellent source for gift ideas – bags, clocks, candles, jewellery, stationery – for the girl- or man-about-town who has everything.

281 King's Road, Chelsea ☎ 7351 7674 ⊖ Sloane Square then 🚌 22

Chain Reaction *off map*

For pure kitsch and gimmicky gifts this shop leads the way.

208 Chalk Farm Road, Camden ☎ 7284 2214 ⊖ Chalk Farm

Emma Bernhardt *⌕C1*
For out-and-out kitsch – this store sells everything from gilt shrines to feather dusters – all from Mexico.
301 Portobello Road, Notting Hill ☎ 8960 2929 ⊖ Ladbroke Grove

Flying Duck Enterprises *⌕off map*
For a psychedelic treat, full of every conceivable kind of 50s, 60s, and 70s gaudy kitsch, from nodding dogs to plastic plants that light up.
320–322 Creek Road, Greenwich ☎ 8858 1964 Ⅲ Greenwich

☆ GALERIE SINGLETON *⌕D8*
This shop is a showcase for young local designers: clocks, mirrors, ceramics, and glassware – from the frivolous to the sublime.
40 Theobalds Road, Holborn ☎ 7831 6928 ⊖ Chancery Lane

Gill Wing Gifts *⌕A3*
Anything and everything from blow-up egg cups to Matisse deckchairs and lava lamps.
194–195 Upper Street, Islington ☎ 7359 7697 ⊖ Highbury & Islington

Kokon Tozai *⌕B13*
For gadgety gifts and weird paraphernalia, this shop is hard to beat; Tokyo's finest oddities sit alongside hyper-trendy clothes, footwear, and records.
57 Greek Street, Soho ☎ 7434 1316 ⊖ Leicester Square

Museum Store *⌕off map*
Does a good line in copies of famous works from museums all over the world.
4 Perrin's Court, Greenwich ☎ 7431 7156 Ⅲ Greenwich

☆ NEAL STREET EAST *⌕E8*
An Aladdin's cave of goods from books, jewellery, and fabrics to homewares and furniture, all from the East.
5 Neal Street, Covent Garden ☎ 7240 0135 ⊖ Covent Garden

Octopus *⌕E8*
The trendy collection is characterized by its kitsch, quirkiness, and brazen colours – among it a flamboyant bustier adorned with plastic flowers, and some funky washing-up gloves.
54 Neal Street, Covent Garden ☎ 7836 2911 ⊖ Covent Garden

☆ OLIVER BONAS *⌕off map*
Well-chosen items – jewellery, glassware, clothing, furniture – some ethnic and some designer. You can't fail to find a suitable pressie.
801 Fulham Road, Chelsea ☎ 7736 8435 ⊖ Parsons Green

Wild at Heart ⌕D1

For a natural high, check out the extraordinary minimalist floral creations in the shop, or their stall – a Westbourne Grove landmark sharing premises with an award-winning public loo.

49a Ledbury Road, Notting Hill ☎ 7727 3095 ⊖ Notting Hill Gate

hats

☆ STEPHEN JONES ⌕E8

London's main man for hats, Stephen Jones's shop is a Pandora's box of hats from couture to off-the-peg (mainly for women).

36 Great Queen Street, Covent Garden ☎ 7242 0770 ⊖ Holborn; Covent Garden

health & beauty

☆ AVEDA ⌕C6

It's only right that a cult brand such as touchy-feely-set-the-world-to-rights Aveda should establish a dedicated place of worship. All the range is here, plus a relaxed organic restaurant and an elegant flower stall. Splurge on scents for your soul and organic treats for your body.

28 Marylebone High Street, Marylebone ☎ 7224 3157 ⊖ Baker Street

☆ THE BODY SHOP ⌕E7

This long-established, feel-good, do-good chain has conquered the world with its eco-friendly lotions and potions. Many products are based on ancient recipes which the shop's tireless founder, Anita Roddick, has sourced from around the world.

268 Oxford Street, Oxford Circus ☎ 7629 9365 ⊖ Oxford Circus

☆ CRABTREE & EVELYN *⌕off map*

Although still trading on its quintessentially English image, Crabtree & Evelyn is sharpening up its act with the launch of a range of aromatherapy oils and scented candles.

6 Kensington Church Street, Kensington ☎ 7937 9335 ⊖ High Street Kensington

DR Harris & Co ⌕C13

From 8.30am, staff at this old-fashioned chemist tend to the needs of hungover Londoners who pop in for a glass of Harris's patented pick-me-up.

29 St James's Street, St James's ☎ 7930 3915 ⊖ Green Park

Floris C13

A real taste of the past – it's wonderfully dingy with vast wooden cabinets groaning under the weight of soaps and perfumes.

89 Jermyn Street, Piccadilly ☎ 7930 2885 ⊖ Green Park

Geo F Trumper F12

The most venerable of gentlemen's groomers, this tiny store sells the signature colognes and shaving soaps upstairs while customers get their whiskers trimmed downstairs.

9 Curzon Street, Mayfair ☎ 7499 1850 ⊖ Hyde Park Corner

☆ JO MALONE E12

Demand for the facials from the queen of the fashion pack, Jo Malone, is such that she has no plans to take on new clients. But the tools of her trade – skin tonics, cleansing milks, and bath oils – are all available in their smart Chanel-esque livery alongside an excellent range of colognes which can be worn alone or combined to create a constantly changing aroma.

150 Sloane Street, Chelsea ☎ 7581 1101 ⊖ Sloane Square

☆ L'ARTISAN PARFUMEUR A17

This smart little shop has some of the most original and delicious scents in the world such as hazelnut, fig, and even crushed pepper. Mûres et Musc (blackberries and musk) for women, and Méchant Loup (spices, honey, and Tonka bean) for men, are two of the most popular.

17 Cale Street, Chelsea ☎ 7352 4196 ⊖ Sloane Square, South Kensington

☆ LES SENTEURS C18

Choosing from the vast range of unique scents can be daunting, but helpful staff assist in a search for your own 'signature' fragrance. Creed, Diptych, and Annick Goutal are probably the most famous.

71 Elizabeth Street, Chelsea ☎ 7730 2322 ⊖ Sloane Square

☆ LUSH E8

Beauty products for you and your fridge include freshly pulped bananas and other fruit-based face packs, body scrubs, and shampoos. Soaps are sliced like cheese off giant blocks and many of the products come with sell-by dates. Best sellers are bath bombs which fizz in the water.

7 & 11 The Market, Covent Garden ☎ 7240 4570 ⊖ Covent Garden

M.A.C. C18

The cult make-up company may look terrifyingly cool but staff are friendly and will give advice on the extensive range of colours and application.

109 King's Road, Chelsea ☎ 7349 0022 ⊖ Sloane Square

☆ **NEAL'S YARD REMEDIES** *E8*

Aromatherapy is the order of the day here with row upon row of blue glass bottles containing deliciously scented essential massage and burning oils. They also stock homeopathic remedies and wonderful bathtime treats.
15 Neal's Yard, Covent Garden ☎ 7379 7222 ⊖ Covent Garden

Officina di Santa Maria Novella *A17*

Sensuous scents, oils, soaps, and even honey.
117 Walton Street, South Kensington ☎ no phone ⊖ South Kensington

Penahaligons

This perfumer expanded in the 70s and has ranges for men and women.
16 Burlington Arcade, Piccadilly ☎ 7629 1416 ⊖ Green Park

☆ **SCREEN FACE** *E8*

In among the vast range of nail varnish, eyeshadows, lipsticks, brushes, and false eyelashes, there are clues to the store's professional status, with pots of goo labelled 'fresh bruise', 'congealed blood', and 'scab'.
48 Monmouth Street, Covent Garden ☎ 7836 3955 ⊖ Covent Garden

Shu Uemura *E8*

Founded by a Japanese make-up artist who worked with the likes of Marilyn Monroe, Shu Uemura offers an impressive array of lipsticks, eyeshadows, and more in myriad shimmering shades.
16 Thomas Neals, 29–41 Earlham Street, Covent Garden ☎ 7379 6627 ⊖ Covent Garden

☆ **SPACE NK** *E8*

It's easy to lose track of time in this bright box of glass and chrome filled with every beauty treatment and achingly fashionable make-up brand imaginable (like Nars and Stila). It takes a strong will to leave empty-handed.
4 Thomas Neals, 37 Earlham Street, Covent Garden ☎ 7379 7030 ⊖ Covent Garden

high street shops

British highstreet stores are keeping up with catwalk trends and collaborating with top-name designers. London is possibly the best place in the world to find style, quality, and originality at affordable prices. There are plenty of stores to choose from, so competition is fierce. Most of the chains can be found on Oxford Street, High Street Kensington, or in Covent Garden. One of the most inspirational happenings on the high street is **Top Shop**'s mega-relaunch of their flagship store (Top Man for men). The four-floor fashion theme park includes a catwalk with live shows and a café; not to mention affordable capsule collections by hip designers such as modernist Hussein Chalayan. Also at the cheaper end of the market are: **Dorothy Perkins,** with new capsule collections by top catwalk creators; eclectic, fashionable **Hennes**; and **Warehouse** (women only), which always seems ahead of the pack for new trends. **Miss Selfridge**, **River Island**, **Oasis**, **Morgan**, and **Kookai**, all of which are for women only, have skimpy, flirtatious numbers for twentysomethings. Spanish chains **Zara** (more upmarket women's clothes) and **Mango** (cheap and cheerful) are also taking a slice of the action. For a slightly more conservative, mostly unisex range there are: **Next**, **Gap** and **Gap Kid**; and **Hobbs** (women only) and **Jigsaw** (men's outlet is called Uth), both purveyors of timeless, understated clothing. **French Connection** and **Karen Millen** are in the same league – the former is slightly more trend-conscious, the latter (women only) is marginally more adventurous. A good variety of cutting-edge menswear for all ages is the hallmark of **Reiss**, **Burton**, and **Woodhouse**; **Blazer** is similar but offers a little more street cred.

Blazer *E8*
29 King Street, Covent Garden ☎ 7632 9733 ⊖ Covent Garden

Burton *E7*
West One Shopping Centre, 379 Oxford Street, Oxford Circus ☎ 7495 6282 ⊖ Oxford Circus

Dorothy Perkins *E7*
West One Shopping Centre, 379 Oxford Street, Oxford Circus ☎ 7495 6181 ⊖ Oxford Circus

French Connection *E7*
429 Regent Street, Oxford Circus ☎ 7493 3124 ⊖ Oxford Circus

Gap *A14*
30–31 Long Acre, Covent Garden ☎ 7379 0779 ⊖ Covent Garden

Gap Kids *A14*
121–123 Long Acre, Covent Garden ☎ 7836 0646 ⊖ Covent Garden

Hennes *E7*
261–271 Regent Street, Oxford Circus ☎ 7493 4004 ⊖ Oxford Circus

Hobbs *C18*
84–88 King's Road, Chelsea ☎ 7581 2914 ⊖ Sloane Square

Jigsaw *A13*
126–127 New Bond Street, Mayfair ☎ 7491 4484 ⊖ Bond Street

Karen Millen *E7*
262–264 Regent Street, Oxford Circus ☎ 7287 6158 ⊖ Oxford Circus

Kookai *E8*
Unit 13, The Piazza, Covent Garden ☎ 7379 1318 ⊖ Covent Garden

Mango ⇧E8
8 Neal Street, Covent Garden ☎ 7240 6099 ⊖ Covent Garden

Miss Selfridge ⇧E7
221–223 Oxford Street, Oxford Circus ☎ 7434 0405 ⊖ Oxford Circus

Morgan ⇧F7
7 Oxford Street, Tottenham Court Road ☎ 7437 2768
⊖ Tottenham Court Road

Next ⇧A14
19–20 Long Acre, Covent Garden ☎ 7836 1516 ⊖ Covent Garden

Oasis ⇧E7
Unit G12 The Plaza, Oxford Street, Oxford Circus
☎ 7580 4763 ⊖ Oxford Circus

Reiss ⇧A14
116 Long Acre, Covent Garden ☎ 7240 7495 ⊖ Covent Garden

River Island ⇧*off map*
124–126 Kensington High Street, Kensington ☎ 7937 0224
⊖ High St Kensington

☆ TOP SHOP ⇧E7
214 Oxford Street, Oxford Circus ☎ 7636 7700 ⊖ Oxford Circus

Warehouse ⇧A14
24 Long Acre, Covent Garden ☎ 7240 8242 ⊖ Covent Garden

Woodhouse;. ⇧E7
99 Oxford Street, Oxford Circus ☎ 7437 2809 ⊖ Oxford Circus

Zara ⇧B13
118 Regent Street, Piccadilly Circus ☎ 7534 9500 ⊖ Piccadilly Circus

interiors

Acadia ⇧C3
Designer lighting as well as stylish furniture and furnishings.
11–13 Essex Road, Islington ☎ 7354 4464 ⊖ Angel

☆ AERO ⇧D1
A classy outlet producing its own designs: clever flat-pack mirrors, lamps, and dual-purpose items like napkin rings which double as egg cups. The own-label stock is bolstered with a selection of the best in contemporary design with emphasis on the minimal and functional.
96 Westbourne Grove, Notting Hill ☎ 7221 1950 ⊖ Notting Hill Gate

After Noah *C18*
An inspirational shop specializing in a constantly changing mix of retro furniture, period collectibles, revamped junk, and commissioned pieces.
261 King's Road, Chelsea ☎ 7351 2610 ⊖ Sloane Square

Anything Left-handed *B13*
For those whose lives have been blighted by right-handed scissors, potato peelers, and even notebooks.
57 Brewer Street, Soho ☎ 7437 3910 ⊖ Piccadilly Circus

Aria *A3*
This discerning shop features classics by Alessi and Philippe Starck in its home accessories shop.
133 Upper Street, Islington ☎ 7226 1021 ⊖ Highbury & Islington

Ashvale International *B2*
Ethnic treats, like Indian rugs and throws, are good value here.
47 West Yard, Camden ☎ 7482 5049 ⊖ Camden Town

Bowles & Linares *F1*
A truly textural modernist experience, where much of the furniture, accessories, and lighting is handcrafted.
32 Hereford Road, Notting Hill ☎ 7229 9886 ⊖ Notting Hill Gate

Camden Lock Designs *B2*
Well-priced ethnic knick-knacks are the deal here.
6a Camden Lock Place, Camden ☎ 7284 2219 ⊖ Camden Town

Camel *E3*
Covetable deco ceramics.
34 Islington Green, Islington ☎ 7359 5242 ⊖ Angel

Canal *E3*
Old and contemporary jewellery, antiques, textiles, pashminas, and more ethnic goodies.
642 Cross Street, Islington ☎ 7704 0222 ⊖ Angel

☆ CARDEN & CUNIETTI *off map*
This interior design duo presents an eclectic combination of style and period: 60s chairs are displayed alongside hand-stitched cushions, throws made from antique fabrics, and Orient-influenced items such as bamboo-handled cutlery.
83 Westbourne Park Road, Notting Hill ☎ 7229 8559 ⊖ Royal Oak

☆ CATH KIDSTON *C1*
Cath Kidston is the doyenne of 50s floral chic. The shop is a charming melange of eiderdowns and items made from her own range of nostalgic fabrics featuring slightly kitsch chintzy roses. Current best-sellers include lampshades, pyjamas, bath hats, and bedlinen.
8 Clarendon Cross, Holland Park ☎ 7221 4000 ⊖ Holland Park; Ladbroke Gr

Ceramica Blue *C1*
Vibrant ceramics including one-offs from the De Simone family, who taught Picasso to glaze.
10 Blenheim Crescent, Notting Hill ☎ 7727 0288 ⊖ Ladbroke Grove

Channels *off map*
Commissions, and sells, avant-garde glassware and modern furniture.
84 Heath Street, Hampstead ☎ 7431 8844 ⊖ Hampstead

Coexistence *A3*
Specializing in 1950s classic furniture.
288 Upper Street, Islington ☎ 7354 8817 ⊖ Highbury& Islington

☆ CONRAN SHOP *C17*
The Conran Shop may be something of a byword for expense, but it also caters to more limited budgets. If it's stylish and well-designed it's here – regardless of price. This means that there are plenty of affordable treats: vases, kids' toys, kitchen accessories, and stationery; as well as loads of must-have furniture that will break the bank.
Michelin House, 81 Fulham Road, South Kensington ☎ 7589 7401
⊖ South Kensington

David Champion *off map*
This eclectic store encompasses David's own designs, commissions from craftsmen, and antiques, textiles, and *objets trouvés* from around the world: prices range from two to five figures.
199 Westbourne Grove, Notting Hill ☎ 7727 6016 ⊖ Notting Hill Gate

David Wainwright *C1*
Concentrates on the solely decorative end of the market, with furniture and accessories mainly from India, Indonesia, and China.
251 Portobello Road, Notting Hill ☎ 7792 1988 ⊖ Ladbroke Grove

☆ DESIGNERS GUILD ⌕C18

Tricia Guild has long reigned over the vibrant interior, and her shop is very much a reflection of her modern Mediterranean style: lots of terracotta, acid green, and hot pink fabrics, paints, and accessories. Downstairs there's a chic little espresso bar and plenty of lovely kitchen gear.
267–271 King's Road, Chelsea ☎ 7351 5775 ⊖ Sloane Square, then 🚌 11, 22, 211, 319

Divertimenti ⌕C17

The smart set flock to Divertimenti where the shelves groan under the weight of wonderful Italian and French crockery and loads of stainless steel utensils.
139–141 Fulham Road, South Kensington ☎ 7581 8065 ⊖ South Kensington

Eat My Handbag Bitch ⌕D10

In vogue 20th-century vintage furniture, lighting, and home accessories.
4 Dray Walk, 91–95 Brick Lane, Shoreditch ☎ 7375 3100 ⊖ Liverpool Street

Gong ⌕C1

The owner, Jo Plismy, has collected chic pieces from China and Japan.
182 Portobello Road, Notting Hill ☎ 7565 4162 ⊖ Ladbroke Grove

Graham & Green ⌕C1

Contemporary, ethnic, and antique furniture, accessories, and textiles. The owner scours degree shows in search of talented young designers.
4, 7, & 10 Elgin Crescent, Notting Hill ☎ 7727 4594 ⊖ Ladbroke Grove

☆ HABITAT ⌕D7

The great leveller of the interiors world, Habitat produces affordable and fashionable lookalikes of whatever the top end of the market is doing. Lots of modular furniture, bargain lighting, and soft furnishings, as well as kitchen equipment, china, and glass to be snapped up.
196 Tottenham Court Road, Bloomsbury ☎ 7631 3880 ⊖ Goodge Street

☆ HEAL'S ⌕D7

Heal's has a gleaming and covetable selection of everything you've dreamed of for the home: exceptional contemporary furniture and lighting; delicious treats for foodies; great cookware and china; and tempting things for the bathroom and bedroom.
196 Tottenham Court Road, Bloomsbury ☎ 7636 1666 ⊖ Goodge Street

The Holding Company ⌕F17

The obsessively tidy can indulge in endless imaginative storage devices.
241–245 King's Road, Chelsea ☎ 7352 1600 ⊖ South Kensington

Home to Be
♯E3
Period items blended with appropriately chosen contemporary work.
70 Amwell Street, Islington ☎ 7833 3611 ⊖ Angel

The Homeplace
♯off map
This vast store offers style-on-a-shoestring. Select carefully and elegant china, classic stainless-steel cookware, classy lighting, and innovative accessories can be yours without creating a dent in your bank balance.
26–40 Kensington High Street, Kensington ☎ 7937 2626
⊖ High St Kensington

Immaculate House
♯D10
A haven for worshippers of luxury, with its home accessories, sumptuous bathrobes and handmade soaps.
57–59 Brushfield Street, City ☎ 7375 1844 ⊖ Liverpool Street

Jerry's Home Store
♯C17
Customers get a healthy dose of kitsch kitchenalia, plus a range of exclusive leather chairs and sofas.
163–167 Fulham Road, South Kensington ☎ 7581 0909
⊖ South Kensington

☆ KARA KARA
♯F17
Everything in this tiny shrine-like outlet is handmade: exquisite tea cups, intricately-carved chopsticks, delicately painted silk cushions from Japan, Indonesia, and India. This is the place for understated yet luxurious treats, like embroidered place mats and green tea from Mount Fuji.
2a Pond Place, South Kensington ☎ 7591 0891 ⊖ South Kensington

☆ MUJI
♯E7
A minimalist's dream come true, this understated Japanese chain has everything for the home, ranging from futon sofabeds to cardboard storage crates, all in plain colours. No frills, no fuss or extravagance, just well-designed, functional pieces. There is also a limited range of clothing and a good selection of Japanese snacks.
187 Oxford Street, Oxford Circus ☎ 7437 7503 ⊖ Oxford Circus

Out of Time
♯off map
Specialists in Americana: art deco and 1950s pieces at reasonable prices.
21 Canonbury Lane, Islington ☎ 7354 5755 ⊖ Highbury & Islington

☆ PURVES & PURVES *D7*

This husband and wife team has travelled the world in search of exciting new design. The main store has an impressive lighting section and wide range of furniture that's more funky than classic.
80–81 & 83 Tottenham Court Road, Bloomsbury ☎ 7580 8223 ⊖ Goodge Street

☆ SAME *off map*

This vast, white minimal East London space, punctuated by innovative furniture and lighting, is a destination for modern design enthusiasts. Same is a launch pad for designers from all over the world – British names of note include Michael Young and Tom Dixon. Regular exhibitions relating to the work are held in a separate exhibition gallery.
The Bridge, 146 Brick Lane, Whitechapel ☎ 7480 5967 ⊖ Aldgate East

☆ SCP *off map*

One of London's best design showcases, SCP is a patron of young designers. Two showrooms display furniture by the likes of Jasper Morrison and Matthew Hilton, as well as smaller, classic items such as Duralex glassware and Michael Marriot's croquet shelving.
135–139 Curtain Road, City ☎ 7739 1869 ⊖ Old Street

☆ SPACE *off map*

Contrary to its name, this is a tiny shop, into which three levels have been cunningly squeezed. The stock ranges from space-age furniture which wouldn't look out of place on the set of a 60s sci-fi movie, to elegant ceramics and glassware with a strong contemporary edge.
214 Westbourne Grove, Notting Hill ☎ 7229 6533 ⊖ Notting Hill Gate

☆ TANN-ROKKA *off map*

Tann-Rokka offers an eclectic mix of treats for the home. Founded by two Romany gypsies, the shop has established itself as an excellent source of pieces from the Orient, such as 17th-century altar pieces and kitsch knick-knacks.
123 Regent's Park Road, Camden ☎ 7722 3999 ⊖ Chalk Farm

This & That *off map*

A delightful collection of beds, chests, and Mexican wooden furniture.
50 Chalk Farm Road, Camden ☎ 7267 5433 ⊖ Chalk Farm

Thyme *off map*

Elegant, contemporary designs with mirrors, glasses and other art deco accessories priced lower than you might expect.
4a Murray Street, Camden ☎ 7482 3529 Ⅲ Camden Road

Tumi *off map*
The place for Latin American goodies, from jewellery to family-sized hammocks.
23 Chalk Farm Road, Camden ☎ 7485 4152 ⊖ Chalk Farm

20th Century Design *A3*
Deals with the best of modern furniture design, especially 1960s classics.
274 Upper Street, Islington ☎ 7288 1996 ⊖ Highbury & Islington

Viaduct *C9*
A major London showcase for modern European design; much of the stock includes larger items, but they also have smaller accessories and lights by design luminaries such as Philippe Starck and Sebastian Bergne.
1–10 Summer's Street, Clerkenwell ☎ 7278 8456 ⊖ Farringdon

international designers

Calvin Klein, Donna Karan, Ralph Lauren, Prada, Gucci, Armani, Dolce & Gabbana: these names are mantras to dedicated followers of fashion. All these world-famous designers have concessions in the department stores, as well as flagship stores which cluster around the moneyed areas of Bond Street and Sloane Street. **Prada**, **Dolce & Gabbana**, **Armani**, **Chanel** and **Gucci** are all dotted along Sloane Street, while Bond Street is home to **Calvin Klein**, **Polo Ralph Lauren**, **Louis Vuitton**, **Donna Karan**, and **Gianni Versace**. Fortunately most of these designers have more affordable diffusion line stores: **Miu Miu** (Prada); **DKNY** (Donna Karan) and a chain of **Emporio Armani** boutiques courtesy of Armani. Conduit Street is also back on the map with a mix of home-grown and international names: **Vivienne Westwood**, **Yohji Yamamoto**, **Burberry**, **Issey Miyake**, **YMC**, and none other than **Alexander McQueen**.

Alexander McQueen *B13*
47 Conduit Street, Soho ☎ 7734 2340 ⊖ Piccadilly Circus

Burberry *B13*
165 Regent Street, Piccadilly Circus ☎ 7734 4060 ⊖ Piccadilly Circus

Calvin Klein *A13*
53–55 New Bond Street, Mayfair ☎ 7491 9696 ⊖ Bond Street

Chanel *A13*
26 Old Bond Street, Mayfair ☎ 7493 5040 ⊖ Green Park

DKNY *F6*
27 Old Bond Street, Mayfair ☎ 7499 8089 ⊖ Green Park

Dolce & Gabbana ₽A13
6–8 Bond Street, Mayfair ☎ 7659 9000 ⊖ Green Park

Donna Karan ₽A13
19 New Bond Street, Mayfair ☎ 7495 3100 ⊖ Bond Street

Emporio Armani ₽B17
191 Brompton Road, Chelsea ☎ 7823 8818 ⊖ South Kensington

Gianni Versace ₽A13
34–36 Old Bond Street, Mayfair ☎ 7499 1862 ⊖ Green Park

Giorgio Armani ₽E12
37 Sloane Street, Knightsbridge ☎ 7235 6232 ⊖ Knightsbridge

Gucci ₽E12
17–18 Sloane Street, Knightsbridge ☎ 7235 6707 ⊖ Knightsbridge

☆ ISSEY MIYAKE ₽B12
20 Brook Street, Mayfair ☎ 7581 3760 ⊖ Bond Street

Louis Vuitton ₽A13
17–18 New Bond Street, Mayfair ☎ 7399 4050 ⊖ Bond Street

Miu Miu ₽A13
123 New Bond Street, Mayfair ☎ 7409 0900 ⊖ Bond Street

Polo Ralph Lauren ₽A13
1 New Bond Street, Mayfair ☎ 7535 4600 ⊖ Bond Street

Prada ₽E12
43–45 Sloane Street, Knightsbridge ☎ 7235 0008 ⊖ Knightsbridge

☆ VIVIENNE WESTWOOD ₽E7
44 Conduit Street, Mayfair ☎ 7439 1109 ⊖ Oxford Circus

YMC ₽A13
6 Conduit Street, Mayfair ☎ 7629 1747 ⊖ Bond Street

☆ YOHJI YAMAMOTO ₽E7
14–15 Conduit Street, Mayfair ☎ 7491 4129 ⊖ Oxford Circus

jewellery

☆ ANGELA HALE ₽A13
This wonderful boutique bristles with well-priced quirky and exquisite costume jewellery and accessories. The A-list clientele includes Paloma Picasso, and Julie Christie.
5 Royal Arcade, Old Bond Street, Mayfair ☎ 7495 1920 ⊖ Green Park

Asprey & Garrard *A13*
The prestigious royal jewellers. Also sells silverware and leather items.
167 New Bond Street, Mayfair ☎ 7493 6767 ⊖ Bond Street

@Work *B10*
Silverwork from recent jewellery design graduates.
156 Brick Lane, Shoreditch ☎ 7377 0597 ⊖ Shoreditch

Autumn & May *off map*
If it's contemporary jewellery you're after, this is the place for lots of silver and amber – some designed by the mother-daughter team who own the shop.
9a Greenwich Market, Greenwich ☎ 8293 9361 Ⅲ Greenwich

Bead Shop *E8*
Budding jewellery-makers can while away a good hour making their selection in this wonderful bead store.
21a Tower Street, Covent Garden ☎ 7240 0931 ⊖ Covent Garden

☆ BUTLER & WILSON *C17*
Glitzy and extravagant: London's famed costume jeweller specializes in 'antique chic' crystal, faux pearls, jet, and beading in every guise.
189 Fulham Road, South Kensington ☎ 7352 8255 ⊖ South Kensington

Catherine Prevost *A17*
Designs and sells distinctive pieces.
109 Walton Street, Knightsbridge ☎ 7584 8860 ⊖ South Kensington

Dinny Hall *F1*
Delicate, understated, modern jewellery.
200 Westbourne Grove, Notting Hill ☎ 7792 3913 ⊖ Notting Hill Gate

EC One *C9*
A range of work from local craftspeople – young, cool, urban, cutting-edge, and eminently affordable.
28 Exmouth Market, Clerkenwell ☎ 7713 6185 ⊖ Farringdon

☆ ERICKSON BEAMON *C18*
This boutique is for lovers of avant-garde costume jewellery. Designers include Erik Halley and Scott Wilson who have worked for McQueen and Galliano.
38 Elizabeth Street, Chelsea ☎ 7259 0202 ⊖ Sloane Square; Victoria

Frontiers ⌕F1
Beautiful antique jewellery from Asia, Africa, and the Middle East.
37–39 Pembridge Road, Notting Hill ☎ 7727 6132 ⊖ Notting Hill Gate

The Great Frog ⌕E7
Heavy metal enthusiasts are lured by gothic brooches, rings, and studs.
10 Ganton Street, Soho ☎ 7439 9357 ⊖ Oxford Circus

☆ JANET FITCH ⌕E8
Four London shops showcase the work of over 200 innovative designers. The collections include understated silver pieces, camp-and-kitsch love jewels, trinkets, and accessories.
37a Neal Street, Covent Garden ☎ 7240 6332 ⊖ Covent Garden

☆ JESS JAMES ⌕E7
One of the front-runners for contemporary design talent, this boutique specializes in reasonably-priced silver and precious pieces for both sexes.
3 Newburgh Street, Soho ☎ 7437 0199 ⊖ Oxford Street

Lesley Craze ⌕C9
A huge collection of jewellery in both precious and non-precious metals. Her clutch of shops also sells contemporary textiles in every conceivable form, from scarves to cushions.
34 Clerkenwell Green, Clerkenwell ☎ 7608 0393 ⊖ Farringdon

Roger Doyle ⌕D1
Rings of semi-precious stones and black matt anodised aluminium are made to be noticed.
38 Ledbury Road, Notting Hill ☎ 7727 5797 ⊖ Notting Hill Gate

Solange Azagury-Partridge ⌕F1
Their most outrageous creation to date is a £3,000, 24-carat gold ring enamelled to look like a cluster of chocolate Smarties. The 'Material Girl' regularly shops here.
171 Westbourne Grove, Notting Hill ☎ 7792 0197 ⊖ Notting Hill Gate

Theo Fennell ⌕C17
Head here for a taste of the high life – grandeur, glamour, and lots of gold accessories and jewellery.
169 Fulham Road, South Kensington ☎ 7591 5000 ⊖ South Kensington

☆ TIFFANY ⚲A13

Tiffany's is still the ultimate in chic and its allure will never fade. Objects of desire include silver key-fobs, eternity rings and crystal crucifix chains.

25 Old Bond Street, Mayfair ☎ 7409 2790 ⊖ Green Park

Wedding Ring Shop ⚲C9

This shop claims to sell over 4,000 different designs.

97 Hatton Garden, Clerkenwell ☎ 7405 2453 ⊖ Chancery Lane

☆ WRIGHT & TEAGUE ⚲A13

The duo famous for etching words of love into silver pendants and rings now have their own shop selling silver, 18-carat gold, platinum, and antique jewellery.

1a Grafton Street, Piccadilly ☎ 7629 2777 ⊖ Green Park

kites

Kite Store ⚲E8

Kites of all colours and all styles priced from under £20 upwards.

48 Neal Street, Covent Garden ☎ 7836 1666 ⊖ Covent Garden

lingerie

☆ AGENT PROVOCATEUR ⚲F7

Designer Vivienne Westwood's son, Joe Corre, is the brain behind these emporia of pricey, erotic underwear, which have revolutionized the concept of knicker shopping in London. Seeing is believing.

6 Broadwick Street, Soho ☎ 7439 0229 ⊖ Tottenham Court Road

Janet Reger ⚲F11

Indulge in slinky, silk underwear and negligées.

10 Beauchamp Place, Knightsbridge ☎ 7584 9360 ⊖ Knightsbridge

☆ RIGBY & PELLER ⚲F11

The Queen's corsetières certainly know a thing or two about fitting bras and underwear; their specialists can tell sizes at a swift glance. Buy your undies here and you'll never look back. A reassuringly expensive experience.

2 Hans Road, Knightsbridge ☎ 7589 9293 ⊖ Knightsbridge

magazines & newspapers

A Moroni & Son ⚲B13

Supplying Soho's cosmopolitan crowd with a vast range of British and foreign newspapers and magazines.

68 Old Compton Street, Soho ☎ 7437 2847 ⊖ Leicester Square

Vintage Magazine Shop ✆B13
This amazing store offers an impressive range of collectors' mags, film posters, and comics. You can also try www.vinmag.com for online shopping.
39–43 Brewer Street, Soho ☎ 7439 8525 ⊖ Piccadilly Circus

markets

☆ ALFIES ✆D5
The antique shops which make up this market (open 10am–6pm Tue–Sat) at the northern end of Church Street, are all under one roof, making it ideal for a rainy afternoon. A warren of stalls on several levels sell everything from costume jewellery to arts and crafts furniture and art deco ornaments. The rooftop café serves tasty food and there's a terrace.
13–25 Church Street, Marylebone ⊖ Edgware Road; Marylebone

☆ BERMONDSEY ✆D15
Open from 2.30am–midday on Fridays, Bermondsey is best visited before dawn, when dealers can be seen examining silver marks through magnifying glasses by torchlight. Most of the stallholders specialize in silverware. Furniture is sold in the surrounding warehouses.
Bermondsey Square, Bermondsey ⊖ Borough; London Bridge

☆ BRICK LANE ✆*off map*
One of the East End's best-known markets selling anything and everything. Open 6am–1pm Sundays.
Brick Lane, Shoreditch ⊖ Liverpool Street; Aldgate East

☆ BRIXTON ✆*off map*
Wonderful African fabrics, fresh food, and a good reggae beat in the air from 8am 'til 5.30pm every day except Sunday.
Station Rd, Atlantic Rd, Electric Ave, Popes Road, Brixton ⊖ Brixton

☆ CAMDEN ✆D2
The height of trendiness in the 70s, Camden's weekend markets are now somewhat tired and over-touristed, and get busy, busy, busy at weekends. The best time for the discerning shopper is around 10am when the stalls are setting up and before the hordes descend. Some parts are rather shabby, but the atmosphere verges on the carnival at times, with different nationalities (both buyers and sellers) making it London's most cosmopolitan meeting place. And if you skip the stalls selling tourist tat, you'll still find originality and a huge variety of items for sale. Shoes, street- and clubwear, and secondhand clothes are sold in the covered Camden Market on the right as you head up to the Lock from the tube. Over the bridge is a passageway, also on the right, full of great

secondhand gear. Stalls in and around the Lock Building on the left (the original Camden Lock Market) are more craft-orientated, with world music, handmade clothes, and hammocks to lure you in.
Camden High Street, Camden ⊖ Camden Town

Camden Passage *C3*
Islington's cutesy antique quarter is packed with tiny shops, but bustles extra hard on Wednesday and Saturdays when the antiques market sets up. Prices can be nearly as breathtaking as the often weird, and usually wonderful stock.
Camden Passage, off Upper Street, Islington ☎ 7359 9969 ⊖ Angel

Chapel Market *E3*
This is a side of Islington that's much more down to earth. Diamond geezers (market stallholders are often second or third generation) flog good-value household goods; cheap-and-cheerful clothes, accessories, and shoes; and fruit and veg. Open 9am–4pm daily; to 1pm Sundays.
Chapel Street, Islington ⊖ Angel

☆ COLUMBIA ROAD *off map*
In a quaint Victorian terraced street, this colourful flower market (8am–2pm Sunday) is a magnet for London's gardeners. The market is best for house and garden plants and cut flowers.
Columbia Road (east of Ravenscourt Street), Shoreditch 🚌 26, 48, 55

☆ COVENT GARDEN *A14*
An artsy-craftsy enclave selling handmade goodies. Filling the central piazza are numerous small shops specializing in all sorts of things from candles, lace, and doll's house toys, to tobacco, herbs, and aromatherapy. In between, stalls run by enterprising individuals sell jewellery and crafts including wood, ceramics, jazzy plastics, handmade clothes, and all you need to become a first-rate juggler. A larger covered market happens daily in nearby Jubilee Hall: antiques on Mondays; the usual hotch-potch of cheap clothes and accessories on other weekdays; and arts and crafts at the weekend.
Covent Garden Piazza, Covent Garden ⊖ Covent Garden

☆ GRAYS *A13*
A mass of stalls under one roof – with a bias towards antique jewellery. Glassware, textiles, and knick-knacks too. Open 10am–6pm weekdays.
58 Davies Street & Davies Mews, Mayfair ⊖ Bond Street

☆ GREENWICH *off map*
Worth the outing for its quaint villagey atmosphere and arts and crafts stalls. The busy weekend market (Fri–Sun) is actually split into three. The village

market on Stockwell Street is packed with record stalls, rare books, ex-army clothes, strange bric-a-brac, and racks and racks of secondhand clothing. The antique market on Greenwich High Road has car boot sale-style odds and ends, while the craft market in the market building just off Greenwich Church Street offers anything and everything handmade. It's often a bit of a jumble, but it's charming and there are gems to be found here.
Stockwell Street & Greenwich High Road, Greenwich Ⅲ Greenwich

Hampstead Indoor Market *off map*
Every Saturday locals set up shop to market their wares in-between eating homemade cakes and gossiping. The stallholders sell handcrafted works – anything from wood carvings and decorative mosaics, to tiles and jams.
78 Hampstead High Street, Hampstead ☎ 7794 8313 ⊖ Hampstead

Leather Lane *C1 & D1*
Great for the odd bargain be it a fake fur coat or cheap accessories. Open weekdays 10.30am–2pm.
Leather Lane, Clerkenwell ⊖ Chancery Lane

☆ PORTOBELLO *C1 & D1*
Favoured by Notting-Hillbillies, Portobello Market can be divided into several parts. The much-photographed southernmost part, closest to Notting Hill Gate (Sat only), caters predominantly to tourists. This stretch is all about pricey antiques and silver, and gradually gives way to more mundane stalls of flowers, fruit and veg, household goods, and cheapo clothes (Mon–Sat). Further on, under the Westway flyover, stalls become more varied (Fri–Sun); vendors sell jewellery, old kitchenware, lamps, and all sorts of household desirables. Under the canopy, top designers may be seen searching for inspiration among the racks of young design work and secondhand stuff; over the road, great junk finds await discovery. Jumbles of old clothes and retro items lead up to the Golborne Road (Fri–Sat), which has a more local identity. Lined with stalls selling bric-a-brac, secondhand clothes, and exotic and not-so-exotic fruit and veg, this street also has some interesting, though pricier, antique shops. In behind the Gate cinema is the popular Farmers' Market with fresh, fresh, fruit and veg from the home counties (Sat only).
Portobello Road & Golborne Road, Notting Hill ⊖ Ladbroke Grove; Notting Hill Gate; Westbourne Park

☆ RIDLEY ROAD *off map*
Stalls selling food, designer fakes, household goods, and music reflects the Afro-Caribbean, Asian, and Turkish communities which live in the area. Open 9am–5pm Tue–Sat.
Ridley Road, Dalston Ⅲ Dalston Junction

Smithfield Market *C9*
Meat is the bag of this market, but don't let that put you off visiting this architectural wonder. Before the crack of dawn (weekdays only), it's a hive of activity, with local pubs and caffs open all hours.
Charterhouse Street, Clerkenwell ⊖ Farringdon; Barbican

☆ SOUTHALL *off map*
In the heart of London's Asian community, Southall's Saturday market (9am–5pm) sells anything from shalwar kameez to bargain bags of pistachio nuts.
The Cattle Market, High Street, Southall ⊖ Ealing Broadway then 273

☆ SPITALFIELDS *off map*
Vintage clothes, organic food, and handicrafts are housed in this spacious former fruit and veg market building. A collection of eateries, cafés, and bars dish up global food making it an all day affair for a young, trendy crowd. Best on Sundays but also open weekdays (9am–6pm).
Commercial Street, Shoreditch ⊖ Liverpool Street

Stables Antique Market *off map*
The warren of passageways and converted railway arches (where the Clash used to rehearse) is bursting with ethnic bits and bobs, funky 70s clothes, and 20th-century design classics. Open daily but best on weekends.
Camden Market ☎ no phone ⊖ Camden Town

menswear

☆ ALL SAINTS *E7*
Bridging the gap between designer and high street, this label is a success. The clothes always hit the right note, and appeal to men who opt for smart, casual separates, rather than the usual suits.
9 Foubert's Place, Oxford Circus ☎ 7494 3909 ⊖ Oxford Circus

☆ BURRO *A14*
Burro shows on the catwalks of Paris, and has established quite a following. Great shirts, casual trousers, smart jackets with a 70s-turned-millennium twist for the young man-about-town with a disposable income.
29 Floral Street, Covent Garden ☎ 7240 5120 ⊖ Covent Garden

Diverse *off map*
Carhartt, John Rocha, Armand Basi, and the like for the boys.
286 Upper St, Islington ☎ 7359 0081 ⊖ Highbury & Islington

Favourbrook ⚲B13
Racks of sumptuously embroidered waistcoats and dapper coats for men and women.
18 Piccadilly Arcade, Piccadilly Circus ☎ 7493 5060 ⊖ Piccadilly Circus

☆ HACKETT ⚲E12
The vast stock of this flagship branch includes everything from multi-coloured socks to silk top hats. Casual and formal wear can be found as well as Hackett's well-known 'flag' jumpers. The store is also equipped with a barbers and alteration department.
136-138 Sloane Street, Chelsea ☎ 7730 3331 ⊖ Sloane Square

Harvie & Hudson ⚲A13
Highly rated shirtmakers.
77 Jermyn Street, Mayfair ☎ 7930 3949 ⊖ Green Park

☆ JONES ⚲A14
Frequented by the likes of George Michael and David Bowie, Jones has two stores. No. 13 houses casual directional lines such as Helmut Lang Jeans while No. 15 has a broad range of clothes by some of the world's most revered designers.
13 & 15 Floral Street, Covent Garden ☎ 7240 8312 ⊖ Covent Garden

☆ THE LIBRARY ⚲B17
One of the best places in London to find up-and-coming and established international menswear designers, the Library offers the trends of tomorrow and doubles as an arty bookshop. An inspirational collection of clothing by fashion's young guns.
268 Brompton Road, South Kensington ☎ 7589 6569 ⊖ South Kensington

Nick Ashley ⚲D1
The son of Laura Ashley, designs menswear for bikers and other macho outdoor types in 'high performance' fabrics, like Teflon-impregnated Harris tweed.
57 Ledbury Road, Notting Hill ☎ 7221 1221 ⊖ Notting Hill Gate

North 1 ⚲E3
Dapper menswear to kit you out from head to toe.
34 Penton Street, Islington ☎ 7278 3365 ⊖ Angel

North 2 ⚲C9
Purveyor of well-priced menswear, as well as snappy suits and separates for women.
31 Exmouth Market, Clerkenwell ☎ 7837 5822 ⊖ Farringdon

☆ OZWALD BOATENG *B13*
Well-known for his highly desirable, streamlined, and brightly coloured 'bespoke couture' (and ready-to-wear) suits.
9 Vigo Street, Piccadilly ☎ 7734 6868 ⊖ Piccadilly Circus

☆ RICHARD JAMES *A13*
Racy off-the-peg collections every season, which can also be specially made-to-measure. Bespoke shirts start at around £100 per piece.
31 Savile Row, Mayfair ☎ 7434 0605 ⊖ Green Park

☆ SU214 *E7*
The brash, new SU214 majors on designer labels from the likes of Lime Haus and Soviet – all competitively priced.
214 Oxford Street, Oxford Circus ☎ 7927 0214 ⊖ Oxford Circus

☆ TIMOTHY EVEREST *D10*
Everest learnt his trade on Savile Row and has brought the tradition of bespoke (and semi-bespoke) suits bang up-to-date with his sharp eye for colour, proportion, and quality.
32 Elder Street, Shoreditch ☎ 7377 5770 ⊖ Liverpool Street

☆ TURNBULL & ASSER *A13*
First class shirtmakers.
71–72 Jermyn Street, Mayfair ☎ 7808 3000 ⊖ Green Park

new age

Equinox – The Astrology Shop *E8*
Seekers of truth and meaning can get their astrology chart drawn up by computer for around £20.
78 Neal Street, Covent Garden ☎ 7497 1001 ⊖ Covent Garden

Inner Space *E8*
A friendly drop-in meditation centre. Books, tapes, and buddhas are on sale for those unable to kick the spending habit.
36 Shorts Gardens, Covent Garden ☎ 7836 6688 ⊖ Covent Garden

secondhand clothing

Annie's *C3*
Gorgeous vintage clothing (mostly 20th-century but also earlier).
10 Camden Passage, Islington ☎ 7359 0796 ⊖ Angel

☆ **BERTIE GOLIGHTLY** *F11*
The pickings are usually rich at this up-market Knightsbridge dress agency.
48 Beauchamp Place, Knightsbridge ☎ 7584 7270 ⊖ Knightsbridge

☆ **BLACKOUT II** *E8*
An extrovert's paradise choc-a-bloc with tack, trash, and glamour from the 20s to the 80s. Hanging alongside vintage bikinis and flares are stylish cocktail dresses for sale and hire.
51 Endell Street, Covent Garden ☎ 7240 5006 ⊖ Covent Garden

Cenci *E8*
Classic Italian men's and women's retro clothing.
31 Monmouth Street, Covent Garden ☎ 7836 1400 ⊖ Covent Garden

☆ **CLOUD CUCKOO LAND** *E3*
Specialists in clothes from 1910–1950.
6 Charlton Place, Islington ☎ 7354 3141 ⊖ Angel

☆ **CORNUCOPIA** *B18*
The overcrowded rails are a magnet to fashion students and stylists on the lookout for unusual fabrics and detailing.
12 Tachbrook Street, Victoria ☎ 7828 5752 ⊖ Victoria

Designs *off map*
Top-notch labels discarded by Hampstead's wealthy inhabitants.
60 Rosslyn Hill, Hampstead ☎ 7435 0100 ⊖ Hampstead

Emporium *off map*
Racks of good-quality period clothing from the flouncy 50s to the tailored 80s.
330–332 Creek Road, Greenwich ☎ 8305 1670 III Greenwich

☆ **EXCLUSIVO** *off map*
A dress agency selling designer label cast offs.
24 Hampstead High St, Hampstead ☎ 7431 8618 ⊖ Hampstead

Flashback *B3*
Good vintage vault with rock bottom prices.
50 Essex Road, Islington ☎ 7354 9356 III Essex Road

☆ **FROCKBROKERS** *D10*
A relative newcomer where Armani, Westwood, and even Voyage can be found alongside the work of fashion students who sell off their graduation collections. Clothes can be pricey, but one-offs are plentiful.
47 Brushfield Street, Shoreditch ☎ 7247 4222 ⊖ Liverpool Street

High Society ⚲E3
Quality secondhand men's gear as well as new clothes by Ben Sherman and Fred Perry.
46 Cross Street, Islington ☎ 7226 6863 ⊖ Angel

☆ LAURENCE CORNER ⚲A7
Famous for surplus military gear.
62–64 Hampstead Road, Bloomsbury ☎ 7813 1010 ⊖ Warren Street

☆ THE LOFT ⚲A14
Rummage around here for secondhand DKNY, John Rocha, and the like.
35 Monmouth Street, Covent Garden ☎ 7240 3807 ⊖ Leicester Square

Miss Sixty ⚲E8
A fun Italian store with a mish-mash of retro and utility wear.
39 Neal Street, Covent Garden ☎ 7836 3789 ⊖ Covent Garden

Modern Age Vintage Clothing ⚲*off map*
An impressive collection of secondhand gear (the 1940s are a speciality), from swimsuits to flying jackets.
65 Chalk Farm Road, Camden ☎ 7482 3787 ⊖ Chalk Farm

The Observatory ⚲*off map*
Cheap retro gear including crimplene jackets and Adidas tracksuits.
20 Greenwich Church Street, Greenwich ☎ 8305 1998 Ⅲ Greenwich

Oxfam ⚲*off map*
One of London's best hunting grounds for label lovers on a budget
245 Westbourne Grove, Notting Hill ☎ 7229 5000 ⊖ Notting Hill Gate

☆ OXFAM ORIGINAL ⚲E7
This slick little shop breathes new life into its most interesting donations – the best of Oxfam's 60s and 70s donations.
26 Ganton Street, Soho ☎ 7437 7338 ⊖ Oxford Circus

Past Caring ⚲B3
The kind of place where you can pick up an old Roberts Radio along with a 1970s lamé evening frock.
76 Essex Road, Islington Ⅲ Essex Road

Retro Man/Retro Woman ⚲F1
Hard up label victims sort through discarded designer items here.
Man: 34 Pembridge Road, Notting Hill ☎ 7792 1711 ⊖ Notting Hill Gate
Woman: 32 Pembridge Road, Notting Hill ☎ 7727 4805 ⊖ Notting Hill Gate

☆ STEINBERG & TOLKIEN *C18*
For some excellent vintage couture, this is where fashion designers flock for inspiration. Prices can be high, but there are plenty of cheaper finds.
193 King's Road, Chelsea ☎ 7376 3660 ⊖ Sloane Square

Stitch Up *C2*
Exclusive, but affordable, reconditioned cashmere, vintage jeans, and more.
45 Parkway, Camden ☎ 7482 4404 ⊖ Camden Town

☆ SUE RYDER *C6*
A haunt of the shrewd hunter whose favourite pastime is rummaging around in charity shops.
2 Crawford Street, Marylebone ☎ 7935 8758 ⊖ Baker Street

☆ VIRGINIA *E1*
A shop which seems to have stepped back in time. Beautiful high end vintage clothing at sky high prices.
98 Portland Road, Holland Park ☎ 7727 9908 ⊖ Holland Park

Yesterday's Bread *A14*
A psychedelic box of 60s, 70s, and 80s delights. Relive the past and slip into crocheted tank tops, spandex halternecks, and denim flares.
29 Foubert's Place, Covent Garden ☎ 7287 1929 ⊖ Covent Garden

sex shops

Sh! *F4*
Fetish gear and sex toys in a female-friendly boudoir.
39 Coronet Street, Hoxton ☎ 7613 5458 ⊖ Old Street

shoes

☆ BIRKENSTOCK *E8*
The German comfy sandal company whose range gets better by the year.
37 Neal Street, Covent Garden ☎ 7240 2783 ⊖ Covent Garden

☆ BUFFALO *E8*
The birthplace of the Spice Girls' favourite elevated platform.
47–49 Neal Street, Covent Garden ☎ 7379 1051 ⊖ Covent Garden

Bullfrogs Shoes *off map*
Cool lines from Base and Red or Dead.
12 Nelson Road, Greenwich ☎ 8305 1102 Ⅲ Greenwich

☆ **CAMPER** ⚲A14
The 100-year-old Spanish company have captured the market with quirky trainer/shoe hybrids, kooky sandals, and their unique canvas summer shoe.
39 Floral Street, Covent Garden ☎ 7379 8678 ⊖ Covent Garden

☆ **CHRISTIAN LOUBOUTIN** ⚲F11
The Frenchman whose fetish for footwear went from a childhood obsession to a career designing wild, women's shoes, all of which feature fiery red soles.
23 Motcomb Street, Knightsbridge ☎ 7823 2234 ⊖ Knightsbridge

Cover Girl ⚲B3
A specialist fetish shoe shop selling stilettos to teeter in and thigh-high boots (by appointment only).
44 Cross Street, Islington ☎ 7354 2883 ⅢI Essex Road

☆ **DR MARTENS DEPARTMENT STORE** ⚲A14
This five-storey store is the obvious place for good old DMs of every conceivable shape and size.
1–4 King Street, Covent Garden ☎ 7497 1460 ⊖ Covent Garden

☆ **EMMA HOPE** ⚲E3
Emma Hope sells covetable, exquisitely crafted shoes; prices are high, but fair for the quality.
33 Amwell Street, Islington ☎ 7833 2367 ⊖ Angel

Free Lance ⚲F17
Unusual and funky designs that ensure you stand out in the crowd.
253 King's Road, Chelsea ☎ 7351 4038 ⊖ South Kensington

☆ **GEORGE CLEVERLEY** ⚲A13
A good and reliable choice for quality men's shoes.
13 Royal Arcade, Old Bond Street, Mayfair ☎ 7493 0443 ⊖ Green Park

☆ **GINA** ⚲E12
Very feminine shoes which have graced many a catwalk and can jazz up any little black party dress – at a cost.
189 Sloane Street, Chelsea ☎ 7235 2932 ⊖ Knightsbridge

Holt ⚲B2
Frequented by everyone from vicars to skinheads, the Gallagher brothers to ZZ Top, this family-run shop – in business since 1894 – delights in its reputation as a supplier (the first) of competitively priced Dr Martens shoes.
5 Kentish Town Road, Camden ☎ 7485 8505 ⊖ Camden Town

☆ **JIMMY CHOO** *ℱF11*

This store stocks the signature snakeskin shoes for women, as well as a more classic line for men.
20 Motcomb Street, Knightsbridge ☎ 7235 0242 ⊖ Knightsbridge

☆ **JOHN LOBB** *ℱC13*

Classic, quality leather shoes (for men and women) at high prices.
St James's Street, Mayfair ☎ 7930 3664 ⊖ Green Park; Piccadilly Circus

☆ **JOHNNY MOKE** *ℱC18*

Like Jimmy Choo and Gina, Johnny Moke is a British label giving Blahnik a run for his marabou mules. An eclectic and inspirational collection of footwear, clothing, and accessories.
396 King's Road, Chelsea ☎ 7351 2232 ⊖ Sloane Sq, then 🚌 11, 19, 22, 211, 319

☆ **LK BENNETT** *ℱC18*

Elegant, handmade footwear for the sophisticated woman.
83 King's Road, Chelsea ☎ 7352 8066 ⊖ Sloane Square

☆ **MANOLO BLAHNIK** *ℱC18*

The king of the fashion shoe cobbles for supermodels and celebs, and is adored by fashion editors and stylists alike, who coo over the workmanship and sensuality of his delicate creations. His prices, ranging from £230 to over a grand, leave mere mortals in the cold.
49–51 Old Church St, Chelsea ☎ 7352 3863 ⊖ Sloane Sq then 🚌 11, 22, 211, 319

☆ **NATURAL SHOE STORE** *ℱE8*

The place for wholesome and super-comfortable footgear.
21 Neal Street, Covent Garden ☎ 7836 5254 ⊖ Covent Garden

☆ **OFFSPRING** *ℱE8*

Excellent for well-selected fashionable trainers, including Nike, Adidas, New Balance, Reebok, and Converse.
60 Neal Street, Covent Garden ☎ 7497 2463 ⊖ Covent Garden

☆ **PATRICK COX** *ℱC18*

Dedicated to selling the famous Wannabe collection, which also includes clothing. In the early 90s, his Wannabe loafer was the shoe to wear (over a million pairs sold to date).
129 Sloane Street, Chelsea ☎ 7730 8886 ⊖ Sloane Square

Scorah Pattullo *ℱoff map*

Girls about town get their kicks from this impressive array of top designer footwear.
193 Westbourne Grove, Notting Hill ☎ 7792 0100 ⊖ Notting Hill Gate

Sigerson Morrision
⚲off map
Very feminine, Cinderella-ish shoes from the American duo.
184 Westbourne Grove, Notting Hill ☎ 7229 8465 ⊖ Notting Hill Gate

Sole Trader
⚲E8
Stocks most major labels – Converse, Cats, Timberland, and Kickers.
72 Neal Street, Covent Garden ☎ 7836 6777 ⊖ Covent Garden

Swear
⚲E8
This Portuguese outfit is one of the wildest shoeshops, with myriad variations on the platform trainer.
61 Neal Street, Covent Garden ☎ 7240 7673 ⊖ Covent Garden

Underground Shoes
⚲E7
Make a statement with your feet and purchase a pair of towering platforms or Japanese *geta* thongs.
3 Marlborough Court, Oxford Circus ☎ 7494 2338 ⊖ Oxford Circus

shoe chains

London has plenty of good chain shoe stores to choose from. These range from stylish but timeless women's designs at **Bertie** and **Hobbs** through to the myriad unisex creations on the shelves at **Shelly's** which feature old favourites as well as funky, outrageous designs – something for everyone. Sensible, understated, and good value footwear is the hallmark of **Ravel** and **Jones the Bootmaker**, while **Office** is more adventurous, imaginative, and youthful – and their reasonable prices make it feasible to keep up with ever-changing trends. If you can't find what you're looking for in Office, try **Nine West** for well-made, ultra-trendy designer footwear. **Pied à Terre**'s irresistible designs are equally up-to-the-minute, but not as affordable. Top of the price range is **Russell & Bromley**, which stocks some designer names such as DKNY and Joseph Azagury, as well as their own label.

Bertie
⚲A14
25 Long Acre, Covent Garden ☎ 7836 7223 ⊖ Covent Garden; Leicester Sq

Hobbs
⚲off map
9 Hampstead High Street, Hampstead ☎ 7431 2228 ⊖ Hampstead

Jones the Bootmaker
⚲A14
women: 16 New Row, Covent Garden ☎ 7240 6558 ⊖ Covent Garden
men: 7 Langley Court, Covent Garden ☎ 7836 5079 ⊖ Covent Garden

Nine West
⚲off map
31 Hampstead High Street, Hampstead ☎ 7435 0613 ⊖ Hampstead

Office
⚲C18
100 King's Road, Chelsea ☎ 7581 8750 ⊖ Sloane Square

Pied à Terre ⌕off map
102 Kensington High St, Kensington ☎ 7376 0296 ⊖ High St Kensington

Ravel ⌕E7
184–188 Oxford Street, Oxford Circus ☎ 7631 4135 ⊖ Oxford Circus

Russell & Bromley ⌕A13
24–25 New Bond Street, Mayfair ☎ 7629 6903 ⊖ Bond Street

Shelly's ⌕E7
266–270 Regent Street, Oxford Circus ☎ 7287 0939 ⊖ Oxford Circus

sportswear & equipment

☆ BLACK'S ⌕D8
A wide range of outdoor equipment and clothing unrivalled in the city.
10–11 Holborn, Holborn ☎ 7404 5681 ⊖ Chancery Lane

☆ JJB SPORTS ⌕E7
A huge range of clothing and footwear from major sports names.
301–309 Oxford Street, Oxford Circus ☎ 7409 2619 ⊖ Oxford Circus

LA1 ⌕B2
For the very best range of surfwear in north London.
17 Chalk Farm Road, Camden ☎ 7267 2228 ⊖ Chalk Farm; Camden Town

☆ LILLYWHITE'S ⌕B13
A reliable and reasonably priced all-rounder with six floors of sporting gear from trainers to cricket and golfing kits.
24–36 Regent Street, Piccadilly ☎ 7930 3181 ⊖ Piccadilly Circus

☆ NIKETOWN ⌕E7
The mother of all sports shops. It has anything and everything sporty with the ubiquitous giant swoosh.
236 Oxford Street, Oxford Circus ☎ 7612 0800 ⊖ Oxford Circus

Slam City Skates ⌕E8
Purveyor of skateboards, shoes, and skating fashion for over a decade.
16 Neal's Yard, Covent Garden ☎ 7240 0928 ⊖ Covent Garden

☆ SUPERSPORTS ⌕F7
A good solid sports emporium with an extensive range of shoes, clothing, and accessories in their numerous London branches. Prices are competitive.
111 Oxford St, Tottenham Court Rd ☎ 7439 1082 ⊖ Tottenham Court Rd

YD, UK *off map*
Reasonably priced, groovy surfing and skateboarding gear in lairy colours.
82 Heath Street, Hampstead ☎ 7431 9242 ⊖ Hampstead

stationery & art materials

Atlantis *off map*
A huge range of artists' materials and a fab contemporary gallery to boot.
146 Brick Lane, Shoreditch ☎ 7377 8855 ⊖ Shoreditch

☆ ORDNING & REDA *A14*
Stationery to drool over – stylish bits and pieces in bright Smartie colours.
22 New Row, Covent Garden ☎ 7240 8090 ⊖ Leicester Square

☆ PAPERCHASE *F7*
This huge airy shop probably has the biggest choice of stationery in town.
213 Tottenham Court Road, Bloomsbury ☎ 7467 6200 ⊖ Goodge Street

streetwear

American Classics *off map*
Dedicated to Hawaiian shirts, vintage Levis, and tuxedos.
398–400 King's Road, Chelsea ☎ 752 2853 ⊖ Fulham Broadway

Bullfrogs *off map*
Moving into the millennium, with clubby separates and mainstream lines.
22 Greenwich Church Street, Greenwich ☎ 8305 2404 Ⅲ Greenwich

Camden Jean Co *D2*
A good bet for jeans, old and new.
235 Camden High Street, Camden ☎ 7485 6656 ⊖ Camden Town

☆ CARHARTT *E8*
This American workwear brand has emerged as trendy streetwear in the UK – baggy carpenter jeans and cozy hooded tops to last a lifetime.
56 Neal Street, Covent Garden ☎ 7836 5659 ⊖ Covent Garden

Comfort & Joy *C3*
An own-label shop selling designs with a street feel.
109 Essex Road, Islington ☎ 7359 3898 ⊖ Angel

Dexter Wong *E8*
Specialists in tough, space-age fabrics such as plasticized linen. The reasonably priced unisex clothes include carbon pedal pushers.
17 Monmouth Street, Covent Garden ☎ 7240 7692 ⊖ Covent Garden

☆ DIESEL *E8*

The Italian casual and jeanswear brand with a kitsch, humorous approach has a three-floor store for men, women, children, and the androgynous.

43 Earlham Street, Covent Garden ☎ 7497 5543 ⊖ Covent Garden

Diesel Stylelab *A14*

The Diesel offshoot with more exclusive items in a gallery-like space.

12 Floral Street, Covent Garden ☎ 7836 4970 ⊖ Covent Garden

Dockers *A14*

Dockers utility wear has a cult following of urbanites who crave the basics: flat-fronted khakis, mechanics' jeans, and quality white T-shirts.

Unit 6, North Piazza, Covent Garden ☎ 7240 7908 ⊖ Covent Garden

Duffer of St George *E8*

The collection ranges from military-style T-shirts to some of the fruitiest creations in town.

29 Shorts Gardens, Covent Garden ☎ 7379 4660 ⊖ Covent Garden

Hampstead Bazaar *off map*

One of the first clothes shops to open in the village back in 1969. The rails are ablaze with colours inspired by the nomadic peoples of north Africa.

30 Heath Street, Hampstead ☎ 7431 3343 ⊖ Hampstead

Levi's *E7*

The concept store of the famous jeans brand, with a customization area – add embroidery, laser-etching, or artificially age your new purchase; and at night the store becomes a club and multimedia entertainment venue.

174 Regent Street, Oxford Circus ☎ 7287 4559 ⊖ Oxford Circus

Natural Selection *F1*

For a hippyish mood, head to this store for bias-cut dresses, subtly-hued cotton-and-linen items, and stunning hand-dyed silk shifts.

57b Pembridge Road, Notting Hill ☎ 7792 2717 ⊖ Notting Hill Gate

Nothing *C1*

Models like Helena Christiansen are fans of the simple, well-fitting, long-lasting, urban separates that are the hallmark of this reasonably-priced store.

230 Portobello Road, Notting Hill ☎ 7221 2910 ⊖ Ladbroke Grove

Rokit *D2*

Good quality retro-chic can be found here. Best visited at the weekend when the best stuff is for sale on the top floor.

225 Camden High Street, Camden ☎ 7267 3046 ⊖ Camden Town

Stüssy *E8*

Dish of the day for T-shirts with attitude. You'll be as impressed by the state-of-the art store (the door opens when you touch a hand sticker) as you are with the gear and accessories for boys and girls.

19 Earlham Street, Covent Garden ☎ 7836 9418 ⊖ Covent Garden

☆ URBAN OUTFITTERS *off map*

This well-known American chain sells urban casualwear, denims, and secondhand clothes. Aimed at students, it has a bar, a resident DJ, and sells kitsch home accessories too.

36–38 Kensington High St, Kensington ☎ 7761 1001 ⊖ High St Kensington

☆ VEXED GENERATION *E7*

Well-priced clothes for urban warriors (men and women): trousers and jackets with protective padding and hooded anoraks which preserve the wearer's anonimity when it matters.

3 Berwick Street, Soho ☎ 7287 6224 ⊖ Oxford Circus; Leicester Square

Wall *F1*

Made to last, quiet, luxurious and versatile clothes.

1 Denbigh Road, Notting Hill ☎ 7243 4623 ⊖ Notting Hill Gate

tea & coffee

Algerian Coffee Stores *B13*

To satiate even the keenest caffeine addict, with an impressive range of rare and unusual coffees and teas.

52 Old Compton St, Soho ☎ 7437 2480 ⊖ Leicester Square

Monmouth Coffee House *E8*

A wonderful and eclectic range of coffees (try the delicate and complex Ethiopian Yirgacheffe).

27 Monmouth Street, Covent Garden ☎ 7379 3516 ⊖ Covent Garden

toys & games

Daisy & Tom's *C18*

This friendly emporium has one of the biggest kids' book departments in the country (over 7000 titles), plus a clothes store and soda bar. The emphasis is on fun. There's a carousel to ride and free half-hourly puppet shows.

181 King's Road, Chelsea ☎ 7352 5000 ⊖ Sloane Square

Disney Store ‡B13

All the merchandise – including toys, T-shirts, books, costumes, and videos – ties in with Disney. The top sellers tend to be anything and everything to do with the latest movie releases.

140–144 Regent Street, Piccadilly Circus ☎ 7287 6558 ⊖ Piccadilly Circus

Hamleys ‡E7

Since opening in 1760, this shop has got bigger and bigger. Now seven floors hold 40,000 toys. On the ground floor you're bombarded by demonstrations of the latest gizmos. It can be overwhelming, so tackle Hamleys at the start of the day when you've got the energy.

188–196 Regent Street, Oxford Circus ☎ 7494 2000 ⊖ Oxford Circus

Village Games ‡B2

Guaranteed to provide mental stimulation with its puzzles, games, and magic tricks.

65 West Yard Camden Lock, Camden ☎ 7485 0653 ⊖ Camden Town

watches

Antique Watch Company ‡C9

A small shop selling big name classic watches, including Cartier and Rolex: the real thing at secondhand prices.

19 Clerkenwell Road, Clerkenwell ☎ 7250 3734 ⊖ Farringdon

☆ G-FACTORY ‡E7

Chunky, stainless-steel, and digital, with sleek futuristic styling. These watches look good and they're reliable.

32 Carnaby Street, Soho ☎ 7437 1441 ⊖ Oxford Circus

☆ STORM ‡E8

Colourful dials and stainless-steel outers are Storm's trademark. So much choice, it's hard to make up your mind.

30 Neal Street, Covent Garden ☎ 7836 3088 ⊖ Covent Garden

restaurants & cafés

London's restaurant scene has never been so alluring; superchefs and restaurateurs such as Marco Pierre White and Sir Terence Conran are busy redefining the concept of British dining, and for sheer diversity, this cosmopolitan city is hard to beat. Eating out is often a total aesthetic experience, and one that satisfies the most exacting foodie. Pacific-rim cuisine is one to look out for, but whatever you choose, try to book a long way ahead.

afghan

Afghan Kitchen *C3*
Expect to share a table at this popular restaurant, which proffers tasty, filling vegetarian and meaty mains – but no starters or puds.
35 Islington Green, Islington ☎ 7359 8019 ⊖ Angel £

african

Al Casbah *off map*
With its wafting incense and bedouin aura, this is a bit of a misfit on Hampstead High Street, but the chef, from Marrakech, cooks a mean tajine.
42 Hampstead High Street, Hampstead 7435 7632 ⊖ Hampstead £

Mandola *D1*
A mellow Sudanese place popular with a hip, scruffy, vaguely arty-muso crowd. It's BYO, which keeps the price down.
139–141 Westbourne Grove, Notting Hill ☎ 7229 4734 ⊖ Notting Hill Gate £

☆MOMO *A13*
Wow. Exquisite interiors of the palatial kind embody Moroccan life that could grace *Vogue*. An equally splendid bar is open to diners (otherwise it's members only). Authentic dishes include salad *zaalouk* (grilled aubergine, coriander and olive oil), *couscous maison* (lamb, *merguez* and skewered lamb), and *patilla de dattes* (pastry filled with dates).
25 Heddon Street, Piccadilly ☎ 7434 4040 ⊖ Piccadilly Circus ££–£££

Moroccan Tagine *A1*
Authentic and wonderfully cheap eatery, which dishes up sizzling national specialities such as couscous and tagine (last orders at 8pm, no alcohol).
95 Golborne Road, Notting Hill ☎ 8968 8055 ⊖ Ladbroke Grove £

belgian

☆ BELGO CENTRAAL ⚲E7

A myriad of Flemish favourites: Belgo's signature kilo pots of mussels; smoked wild boar sausages and Belgian mash or beef braised in beer are less messy but equally delicious. Wash it all down with your choice from 105 Belgian beers available. Good lunchtime deals. Other branches including Notting Hill (124 Ladbroke Grove).

50 Earlham Street, Covent Garden ☎ 7813 2233 ⊖ Covent Garden ££–£££

Belgo Noord ⚲*off map*

Cuisine from temperate climes is represented by top-notch *moules et frites* (and great lunchtime deals) at the first Belgo of the chain, where the waiters are resplendent in monks' garb: the attached beer shop has over one hundred Belgian beers to take away.

72 Chalk Farm Rd, Camden ☎ 7267 0718 ⊖ Chalk Farm; Camden Town £–££

brasseries

Café Delancey ⚲D2

This calm brasserie-style eatery with a leafy courtyard has attracted a mixed-age bunch for years.

3 Delancey Street, Camden ☎ 7387 1985 ⊖ Camden Town ££

Café Rouge ⚲*off map*

An atmospheric brasserie chain that can be found on most London high streets, offering reliable *croque monsieurs, steak frites*, and the like at reasonable prices.

Hays Galleria, 3 Tooley St, London Bridge ☎ 7378 0097 ⊖ London Bridge ££

Chez Gérard Opera Terrace ⚲A14

Classic brasserie fare. Its first-floor location ensures good vantage points for observing piazza activities, and it has an alfresco terrace.

45 The Market, Covent Garden ☎ 7379 0666 ⊖ Covent Garden ££–£££

The Dome ⚲C18

It's an all-day affair at Chelsea's branch of this highly successful chain. The classic French trimmings and good-value set menus make it a hot spot.

354 King's Road, Chelsea ☎ 7352 2828 ⊖ Sloane Square £

Oriel ⚲C18

The brasserie experience *par excellence*, which thrives on a timeless art deco look and all-time favourite dishes. It also makes the most of having the best pavement frontage on Sloane Square.

50–51 Sloane Square, Belgravia ☎ 7730 2804 ⊖ Sloane Square ££

breakfast/brunch

☆ AMATO *B13*
Full English breakfast served all day, and, as you'd expect from an Italian joint, strong shots of espresso too.
14 Old Compton Street, Soho ☎ 7734 5733 ⊖ Leicester Square £

☆ THE BREWHOUSE *off map*
Wholesome organic breakfasts – followed by a walk on nearby Hampstead Heath to work it all off.
Kenwood House, Hampstead Lane ☎ 8341 5384 ⊖ Highgate; Hampstead £

Giraffe *off map*
Hip Hampstead café with a global menu and great breakfasts.
46 Rosslyn Hill, Hampstead ☎ 7435 0343 ⊖ Hampstead £

☆ SIMPSON'S-IN-THE-STRAND *A14*
If you want an upmarket breakkie, try the trad English fry up here. Booking is essential.
100 The Strand ☎ 7836 9112 ⊖ Covent Garden ££

☆ SIR LOIN *D7*
The Sir Loin (above the Hope pub) comes into its own for boozing in the early hours, and its hearty English breakfasts – so large you can't see the plate.
94 Cowcross Street, Clerkenwell ☎ 7253 8525 ⊖ Farringdon £–££

british

The New End *off map*
Elaborate modern British cuisine (veal cutlets with almond fondue) served in an elegant interior.
102 Heath Street, Hampstead ☎ 7431 4423 ⊖ Hampstead ££–£££

☆ QUALITY CHOP HOUSE *A9*
This former working-class caff has retained its bench seats and wooden tables, introduced a new menu (part old-fashioned Brit grub such as jellied eels and salmon fish cakes, part French brasserie food like Toulouse sausages), added a wine list, and has emerged as one of London's most sought-after restaurants. The window may still read 'Progressive Working Class Caterers', but these days the clientele is more la-di-dah.
92–94 Farringdon Road, Clerkenwell ☎ 7837 5093 ⊖ Farringdon ££–£££

☆ RK STANLEY ⌕E7

Fans of sausages and beer should make a beeline to this slick, modern diner. Take your pick from wines, cocktails, and a huge range of bottled and draught British beers at the bar, then slide into one of the red leather banquettes and choose from the menu's 'Magnificent Seven': the game and the Thai sausages are particular faves. Portions aren't huge – another dollop of mashed potato wouldn't go amiss – but you can fill up on dessert. The creamy rhubarb burnt cream really hits the spot.

6 Little Portland Street, North Soho ☎ 7462 0099 ⊖ Oxford Circus ££

☆ RULES ⌕A14

Rules is London's oldest surviving restaurant (1798): Dickens tucked into the steak and kidney pies, and King Edward VII entertained his mistresses here. The heritage theme might be laid on a little thick, but in this genuinely beautiful building, trad English country house food is served with a discreet modern zing. Wild rabbit casserole comes with sugar-snap peas; roast cod gets a pepper-and-tomato sauce, and potatoes are mashed with herbs or cauliflower. At all costs, leave room for one of Britain's greatest culinary contributions – steamed treacle sponge pudding.

35 Maiden Lane, Covent Garden ☎ 7836 5314 ⊖ Covent Garden £££

Sausage & Mash Café ⌕C1

Good value comfort food in a relaxed atmosphere. Bangers range from Thai to good veggie options like leek and blue cheese.

298 Portobello Road, Notting Hill ☎ 8968 8898 ⊖ Ladbroke Grove £

☆ ST JOHN ⌕D9

This restaurant, part of an old smokehouse, constitutes a reintroduction of frugal British ingredient-led cuisine with the accent on meat. The decor and staff uniforms are suitably simple too; there's no music, frills, or frou-frou tendencies here – even the menu features entries that simply read 'cheese' or 'salad'. As such, the food has to work hard and it manages admirably, with dishes like roast bone marrow and parsley salad; plaice and leeks; and pork chops with chutney; which more than adequately line the stomachs of the architect- and designer-heavy clientele.

26 St John Street, Clerkenwell ☎ 7251 0848 ⊖ Farringdon ££–£££

Smiths of Smithfield ⌕C9

Making use of ingredients from Smithfield's market, this informal second-floor brasserie serves trad Brit food like steak and chips. The roof-top restaurant is posher, focussing on quality dining and fine wine. There are also two bars in the complex – a café-cum-bar on the ground floor and a slick cocktail joint above.

66–67 Charterhouse Street, Clerkenwell ☎ 7236 6666 ⊖ Farringdon ££–£££

☆ VERONICA'S *D1*

In days of old, when knights were bold... they ate devilled whitebait, haddock pie, and treacle pudding. The same can now be found a short walk from Westbourne Grove, at an intimate and slightly eccentric eaterie, where historical British dishes are served with evangelical pride to a mainly local clientele. The recipes are based on old historical documents, but the health-conscious can opt for low-fat, non-cholesterol alternatives.

3 Hereford Road, Bayswater ☎ 7229 5079 ⊖ Westbourne Grove ££–£££

Ye Olde Pie House *off map*

Excellent pies – of course.

45 Greenwich Church Street, Greenwich ⅢⅠ Greenwich £

cafés

The Blue Orange *off map*

A bohemian café serving quality coffee, hot choc, and Portuguese pastries.

65 Columbia Road, Hoxton ☎ 7366 9272 ⊖ Old Street £

Blue Room *F7*

A cool arty café serving fruit smoothies.

3 Bateman Street, Soho ☎ 7437 4827 ⊖ Tottenham Court Road £

Bonbonnière *E7*

Have a cup of tea here if you're investigating the pop history of Carnaby Street – it will lend some authentic 60s atmosphere to your quest.

36 Great Marlborough Street, Soho ☎ 7437 2562 ⊖ Oxford Circus £

Books for Cooks *C1*

Reserve a table for what could be the best lunch in town. Cookery writers and other food pros take turns to make lunch.

4 Blenheim Crescent, Notting Hill ☎ 7221 1992 ⊖ Ladbroke Grove ££

Bradley's *A14*

This minimalist Tuscan café, is one of the classiest sandwich options around, with a good selection of classic Italian creations.

9 King Street, Covent Garden ☎ 7240 5178 ⊖ Covent Garden £

Brick Lane Beigel Bake *off map*

Satisfies 24/7 with over-stuffed beigels, all for less than £1.60.

159 Brick Lane, Shoreditch ☎ 7729 0616 ⊖ Liverpool Street £

Café Grove *C1*

The first-floor terrace is ideal for watching the Portobello goings-on.

253a Portobello Road, Notting Hill ☎ 7243 1094 ⊖ Ladbroke Grove £

Caffè Nero *F7*
A good meeting place which dishes up tasty pizza slices. Numerous branches around London.
43 Frith Street, Soho ☎ 7434 3887 ⊖ Tottenham Court Road £

Chelsea Kitchen *C18*
This ever-crowded eatery is a cheap and cheerful pit stop, where the most expensive dish on the European menu is under a fiver.
98 King's Road, Chelsea ☎ 7589 1330 ⊖ Sloane Square £

Coins Bar & Grill *F1*
A cool café with a 50s look, is relaxed by day and buzzy at night, when locals drop in for the evening's specials.
105–107 Talbot Road, Notting Hill ☎ 7221 8099 ⊖ Notting Hill Gate £

Crafts Council *E3*
Relax in this little-known coffee and snack bar.
44a Pentonville Road, Islington ☎ 7806 2500 ⊖ Angel £

Eyre Bros *D7*
Take away food has been raised to new heights; starting early (at 8am) with gammon sarnies, then moving on to soups, sandwiches, and restaurant-quality hot dishes over the counter.
35–42 Charlotte Road, North Soho ☎ 7739 5345 ⊖ Goodge Street £

Frank's *E7*
A prime example of a 'greasy spoon' and the perfect hangover cure.
52 Neal Street, Covent Garden ☎ 7836 6345 ⊖ Covent Garden £

Habitat *C18*
This light and spacious café has a welcoming Mediterranean feel and a varied menu. The perfect stopping off point for any King's Road spending spree.
208 King's Road, Chelsea ☎ 7351 1211 ⊖ Sloane Square £

Neal's Yard Café Society *E7*
A bright and vibrant fruitopia and gelateria serving freshly squeezed juices, ice creams, and tasty ciabatta sandwiches.
13 Neal's Yard, Covent Garden ☎ 7240 1168 ⊖ Covent Garden £

New Piccadilly *B13*
The favourite haunt for fry-ups for fans of 50s interiors.
8 Denman Street, Soho ☎ 7437 8530 ⊖ Piccadilly Circus £

Photographer's Gallery ⚲B13

For some of the cheapest rolls, salads, and cakes around, try this café where you can survey the photographic exhibitions while tucking in.

5 Great Newport Street, Covent Garden ☎ 7831 1772 ⊖ Leicester Square £

Poetry Café ⚲E7

This attracts publishers, aspiring poets, and anyone in the know who wants to escape the throng. Its pared-down, modern style evokes Japanese haiku rather than Rupert Brooke-lyricism. A limited menu revolves around soups, quiches, and cakes. About four times a week poetry readings and other events are held .

22 Betterton Street, Covent Garden ☎ 7420 9888 ⊖ Covent Garden £

Raison d'Être ⚲C17

Home-baked bread is crammed with imaginative fillings. Outside tables are available, and they serve some of the best coffee around.

18 Bute Street, South Kensington ☎ 7584 5008 ⊖ South Kensington £

Stockpot ⚲F11

Solid nosh at a snip. It's not smart, it's not *haute* cuisine, but it's the cheapest meal for miles.

6 Basil Street, Knightsbridge ☎ 7589 8627 ⊖ Knightsbridge £

Tactical Café ⚲F7

A chilled goatee-and-poetry kind of experience.

26–27 D'Arblay Street, Soho ☎ 7287 2823 ⊖ Oxford Circus £

Tom's ⚲D1

A busy deli-cum-café owned by Tom Conran, which serves delicious snacks and has tables in its tiny garden.

226 Westbourne Grove, Notting Hill ☎ 7221 8818 ⊖ Ladbroke Grove; Westbourne Park £

206 ⚲D1

A popular Italian café drawing local hipsters.

206 Westbourne Grove, Notting Hill ☎ 7221 1535 ⊖ Ladbroke Grove £

caribbean

☆ MANGO ROOM ⚲B4

At last, a modern Caribbean restaurant and, appropriately enough, in the heart of multi-ethnic Camden Town. This place is a little bubble of good times with reggae on the system, colourful art on bare brick walls, and delicious food on the menu. Traditional ingredients are paired with

alternative partners, like spinach and plantain or salt cod fritters with apple chutney. Familiar dishes have a fresh approach, spicy chargrilled jerk chicken certainly kicks the tastebuds awake. Keep the good feeling going and retire to the adjoining bar (open late) for a nightcap or three.....
10 Kentish Town Road, Camden ☎ 7482 5065 ⊖ Camden Town ££

chinese

China House *B13*
A multiplex of the Orient, featuring two restaurants (of innovative modern Chinese cuisine), two bars, and a shop.
160 Piccadilly, Piccadilly ☎ 7499 6996 ⊖ Piccadilly Circus ££–£££

☆ HARBOUR CITY *B13*
Dumpling heaven. A steady stream of Chinese punters confirms this restaurant's pedigree. Harbour City uses only the freshest ingredients and cooks them with skill. Best at lunchtime, when Chinese families linger over plates of dim sum: delicate won ton, spring rolls, fried squid, paper-wrapped prawns and steamed beef-and-tofu balls. There's a full Cantonese and Peking-style menu in the evenings (but no dim sum).
46 Gerrard Street, Soho ☎ 7439 7859 ⊖ Leicester Square £££

☆ MAGIC WOK *off map*
Always packed and lively, this is the best of Queensway's Chinese restaurants. Specialities include the weird and wonderful (steamed eels), as well as more traditional dishes: king prawn curry has a generous number of crustaceans in a rich, coconut-heavy sauce; fillet steak Cantonese style has tender slices of meat in a barbecue sauce; and smoked crispy chicken with chilli comprises slivers of chicken covered in a spicy batter then deep-fried. Free tea and fortune cookies round things off nicely.
100 Queensway, Bayswater ☎ 7792 9767 ⊖ Bayswater, Queensway £–££

New Culture Revolution *C2*
An alternative taste of the Orient with bargain basement noodles and dumplings. They'll fill you up with tasty basics for less than a fiver.
43 Parkway, Camden ☎ 7267 2700 ⊖ Camden Town £

New Mayflower *B13*
A cut above other Chinatown eateries, selling dishes like stewed belly pork.
68–70 Shaftesbury Avenue, Soho ☎ 7734 9207 ⊖ Leicester Square £££

☆ THE ORIENTAL *D12*
A series of rooms, lavishly decorated with Asian textiles and antiques, leads to three ornate private rooms, and a staircase up to a rather less embellished main dining room. Sensational Cantonese food, ranging

from dim sum to roasted Peking duck, is presented in a sophisticated, Oriental manner by a skilled team of devotees
Dorchester Hotel, 53 Park Lane, Mayfair ☎ 7317 6328 ⊖ Hyde Park Corner £££

Tai Won Mein *off map*
Head here for huge bowls of noodles at rock-bottom prices. It's always packed so there's usually a short wait for one of the long, shared benches.
47–49 Greenwich Church Street, Greenwich ☎ 8858 1668 Greenwich £

Wong Kei *F7*
Celebrated for the legendary rudeness of the waiters as much as its cheap food. Be prepared to share your table.
41 Wardour Street, Soho ☎ 7437 8408 ⊖ Oxford Circus; Tottenham Court Road £

ZEN W3 *off map*
Hampstead's smartest Chinese restaurant, featuring a cascading waterfall. The culinary emphasis is on a finely-tuned blend of healthy, spicy dishes.
83 Hampstead High Street, Hampstead ☎ 7794 7863 ⊖ Hampstead £££

coffee houses

Coffee Cup *off map*
Fifty years ago, an Austrian refugee craved the delicacies of his homeland, and the Coffee Cup was born. Always the first port of call for Hampstead veterans, its snug, woody interior offers home comforts.
74 Hampstead High Street, Hampstead ☎ 7435 7565 ⊖ Hampstead £

Monmouth Coffee House *E7*
You name it and they'll brew it. An eclectic range of coffees served in snug, private wooden booths.
27 Monmouth Street, Covent Garden ☎ 7379 3516 ⊖ Covent Garden £

Starbucks *C18*
The now ubiquitous American coffee stop.
123 King's Road, Chelsea ☎ 7376 4678 ⊖ South Kensington; Sloane Square £

☆ TROUBADOUR *off map*
Trad coffee house with loads of character. Special events: poetry readings, comedy, and music.
265 Old Brompton Road, South Kensington ☎ 7370 1434 ⊖ Earl's Court £–££

creperies

La Creperie *off map*
A landmark stall on the High Street, is a seven-day-a-week operation, whipping up delicious sweet and savoury crepes to order.
Perrin's Lane, Hampstead ☎ no phone ⊖ Hampstead £

fish & chips

Costas *F1*
A spartan restaurant dishing up cheap, good fish-and-chips.
18 Hillgate Street, Notting Hill ☎ 7727 4310 ⊖ Notting Hill Gate £

Geale's *F1*
Posh fish-and-chips, with photos of smiley fish-and-chip-loving celebs like Sir Elton on the walls.
2 Farmer Street, Notting Hill ☎ 7727 7969 ⊖ Notting Hill Gate £

☆ ROCK & SOLE PLAICE *E7*
The fish is always fresh, and they serve giant-sized portions.
47 Endell Street, Covent Garden ☎ 7836 3785 ⊖ Covent Garden £–££

☆ SEASHELL *D5*
Constant queues outside this good-value fish shop.
49–51 Lisson Grove, Marylebone ☎ 7224 9000 ⊖ Marylebone £–££

☆ UPPER STREET FISH SHOP *C3*
Trad chippy/homey restaurant, serves lobster and crab as well as good old fish and chips. Ace.
324 Upper Street, Islington ☎ 7359 1401 ⊖ Angel £–££

french

Café Royal Grill Room *B13*
Those searching for the spirit of Oscar Wilde can opt for this old-fashioned restaurant – one of the places where the great wit exercised his epigrams. The Victorian dining room exemplifies rococo extravagance, and superchef Marco Pierre White delivers contemporary French classics.
68 Regent Street, Soho ☎ 7437 9090 ⊖ Piccadilly Circus £££

☆ CLUB GASCON *D9*
Not a club in the sense that membership is required – but it is a case of like-minded diners united by foie gras (and everything else a goose provides). Balancing restraint/excess and tradition/innovation, the deliberately modest portions enable you to order from any part of the

menu, and in any sequence. If the winged-one is not for you, other southwestern French specialities beckon like tuna with andouille and chervil sauce. Always popular: City guys for lunch, foodies at night. Step nextdoor to Cellar Gascon for swanky snacks and an impressive wine list.
57 West Smithfield Street, Clerkenwell ☎ 7253 5853 ⊖ Barbican £–££

Criterion *B13*
If your taste is for the neo-Byzantine, then the 'Arabian nights' theatricality combines perfectly with the modern French menu – another Marco Pierre White creation.
224 Piccadilly, Piccadilly ☎ 7930 0488 ⊖ Piccadilly Circus £££

Frederick's *C3*
A plush, old-fashioned, and fairly expensive French restaurant.
Camden Passage, Islington ☎ 7359 2888 ⊖ Angel £££

Frith Street *F7*
Serves exquisite modern French cuisine to well-healed, fortysomethings in an immaculate, minimalist setting.
63–64 Frith Street, Soho ☎ 7734 4545 ⊖ Tottenham Court Road ££

La Cage Imaginaire *off map*
A pretty house at the end of a row of tiny cottages, this really is like eating French food in a cozy living room.
16 Flask Walk, Hampstead ☎ 7794 6674 ⊖ Hampstead ££

Le Palais du Jardin *A14*
The smart, modern interior exemplifies the merits of a brasserie, but draws a more soigné crowd. An innovative menu is supplemented by a separate seafood bar.
136 Long Acre, Covent Garden ☎ 7739 5353 ⊖ Covent Garden ££

L'Escargot *F7*
It's extravagant, French, and several decades old; try the brasserie, or splash out at the restaurant upstairs.
48 Greek Street, Soho ☎ 7437 2679 ⊖ Tottenham Court Road ££–£££

☆ L'ODÉON *A13*
Although a mega-sized venue, the art deco-esque L'Odéon is cleverly divided into a series of smaller dining areas. A superlative brasserie-style modern French menu is prepared with panache: wild mushroom risotto or lobster risotto flavoured with smoked paprika, chocolate tart with chantilly cream. The bar area offers a separate menu and live music, and is en route to the dining area, so it's ideal for people watching.
65 Regent Street, Piccadilly ☎ 7287 1400 ⊖ Piccadilly Circus £££

☆ **MIRABELLE** *C13*

A perfect balance of restraint and art deco-style flamboyance. Immaculately served French cuisine sees technical finesse heightened by inherent flair. The smoked salmon omelette with salad is a simple yet sensational dish, while the terrine of lamb and parsley *en gelée* tailors a rustic dish to metropolitan palates. Raspberry soufflé looks amazing and tastes the same. An incredible wine list includes 50 vintages of Château d'Yquem.

56 Curzon Street, Mayfair ☎ 7499 4636 ⊖ Green Park £££

☆ **PIED-À-TERRE** *D7*

Bold, passionate, single-minded dedication to quality makes this one of the best French restaurants in town. Gourmets hunker down to a faultless procession of fish and meats, robustly flavoured with morels, truffles, foie gras, beetroot or salsify. The meal is punctuated by delicate *amusegueules* (a frothy espresso-cup of pea soup, or a miniature vanilla cream). Pied-à-Terre's masterstroke is to take the intimidation out of haute cuisine, serving exquisite food in a relaxed, friendly, modern setting.

34 Charlotte Street, North Soho ☎ 7636 1178 ⊖ Goodge Street £££

Quo Vadis *F7*

This has been around for decades, but has been reinvented and refurbished by Marco Pierre White and artist Damien Hirst. The food is quite expensive, but the cocktail bar enables you to drink and enjoy a clubby environment with attitudinal Brit art on the walls.

26–29 Dean Street, Soho ☎ 7437 9585 ⊖ Tottenham Court Road £££

Schnecke *C13*

The Alsatian restaurant, whose *tartes flambées* are absolute heaven.

58–59 Poland Street, Soho ☎ 7287 6666 ⊖ Oxford Circus £–££

Spread Eagle *off map*

For a real blowout, go to the unreservedly romantic Spread Eagle: an old Greenwich coaching inn with a modern British and French menu.

1–2 Stockwell Street, Greenwich ☎ 8853 2333 Ⅲ Greenwich £££

The Square *F6*

Modern French, in a vibrant setting is the *raison d'être*, with connoisseurs drawn by its second Michelin star.

6–10 Bruton Street, Mayfair ☎ 7839 8787 ⊖ Bond Street £££

☆ **VILLANDRY** *C7*

Villandry got too popular for its original location, so it moved – and is still flourishing. The latest venue has the same dedicated feel; all the staff know their onions, foodwise, and the kitchen still churns out wonderful,

gutsy dishes without a blip. A duck breast with crêpe parmentier, turnip, greens, and tarragon jus packs a full-flavoured right hook; and it would be hard to beat the cheese plate: much of the produce comes daily from Paris and it shows.
170 Great Portland St, North Soho ☎ 7631 3131 ⊖ Great Portland St ££–£££

gastropubs

☆ BLAKES A2
The menu is imaginative and complex and it's worth taking the plunge on the unknowns: baked ricotta with mango chutney in a filo parcel or curried penne. Desserts are more familiar.
31 Jamestown Road, Camden ☎ 7482 2959 ⊖ Camden Town ££–£££

☆ THE CHAPEL D5
With a global wine list and a decent range of beers, this is a great place to go for a drink – but the food is hard to resist. Cuisine is modern British with a nod to Europe and the Orient, and the short blackboard menu changes daily.
48 Chapel Street, Marylebone ☎ 7402 9220 ⊖ Edgware Road ££

The Cow C1
Owned by Tom Conran (son of Terence). The downstairs bar specializes in seafood; upstairs modern European food is served in a French bistro environment.
89 Westbourne Pk Road, Notting Hill ☎ 7221 0021 ⊖ Ladbroke Grove ££

Crown & Goose D2
This pub has been pulling in a loud crowd since before it won an award in 1992.
100 Arlington Road, Camden ☎ 7485 2342 ⊖ Camden Town ££

☆ DUKE OF CAMBRIDGE E3
The excellent organic menu, which is changed daily, and extensive beer selection make this laid-back gastropub a real must.
30 St Peter's Street, Islington ☎ 7359 3066 ⊖ Angel ££

☆ THE EAGLE A9
London's orginal gastropub. Serves great food in big portions, often with a grilled and Portuguese bent, such as spicy sausages, grilled mackerel on leaves, and bif ana, its popular steak sandwich. There's a good selection of wine and beer too.
159 Farringdon Road, Clerkenwell ☎ 7837 1353 ⊖ Farringdon £–££

The Engineer ₰A2
An exceptional menu, but at times this Camden hang-out is just too cool and crowded for its own good.
65 Gloucester Avenue, Camden ☎ 7722 0950 ⊖ Chalk Farm ££

North Pole *₰off map*
This recent addition to the Greenwich scene is full of appreciative locals tucking into modern European food.
131 Greenwich High Road, Greenwich ☎ 8853 3020 Ⅲ Greenwich £

Westbourne *₰off map*
A vibrant place that packs in a young, good-looking set who enjoy a daily menu of Mediterranean dishes.
101 Westbourne Grove, Park Villas, Bayswater ☎ 7221 1332 ⊖ Bayswater ££

global & fusion

Asia de Cuba *₰A14*
Rules the roost with its mini TVs, books, and Scandinavian styling, serving what can loosely be termed Cuban cuisine. The hotel also has a sushi and seafood counter, Seabar, and a French brasserie Saint M.
45 St Martin's Lane, Covent Garden ☎ 7300 5588 ⊖ Charing Cross £££

Bali Sugar *₰A1*
Formerly Peter Gordon's Sugar Club, which famously turned Madonna away because it was full. Global food shines in this minimalist setting.
33a All Saints Road, Notting Hill ☎ 7221 4477 ⊖ Ladbroke Grove £££

Cicada *₰B9*
Fashionable Pacific Rim-type food and a bar attracting a clientele seemingly plucked from the pages of a style magazine.
132–136 St John Street, Clerkenwell ☎ 7608 1550 ⊖ Farringdon £–££

House on Rosslyn Hill *₰off map*
Enormous portions from a 'global village' menu.
34a Rosslyn Hill, Hampstead ☎ 7435 8037 ⊖ Hampstead ££

☆ SUGAR CLUB *₰B13*
The chefs of the Sugar Club forage in the world's pantries and emerge with mind-boggling, precision-engineered combinations of ingredients and techniques. Grilled chorizo is teamed with soft-boiled egg; while duck breast is served on a bed of vanilla-scented flageolet beans. The resulting cuisine, melding Mediterranean, British, and Asian influences, is totally delicious and served with the minimum of fuss.
21 Warwick Street, Soho ☎ 7437 7776 ⊖ Piccadilly Circus £££

Wiz ⌕E1

A selection of tapas span the globe. The NY-style Sunday brunch makes Wiz a favourite with post-party poseurs.

123a Clarendon Road, Holland Park ☎ 7229 1500 ⊖ Holland Park ££

greek

Daphne ⌕D2

A cheerful friendly Greek-Cypriot haunt.

83 Bayham Street, Camden ☎ 7267 7322 ⊖ Camden Town ££

Jimmy's ⌕A13

A great Soho favourite with the young and hard-up, where a typical meal comprises moussaka and chips.

23 Frith Street, Soho ☎ 7437 9521 ⊖ Leicester Square £

The Kolossi Grill ⌕A9

A no-frills Greek restaurant representing old Clerkenwell.

56–60 Rosebery Avenue, Clerkenwell ☎ 7278 5758 ⊖ Farringdon ££

☆ LEMONIA ⌕*off map*

Situated in one of north London's most chichi neighbourhoods, this well-established Greek-Cypriot restaurant has a ready-made clientele of well-heeled urbanites. It serves all the family favourites: grilled sardines, calamari, stifado, moussaka, and dolmades, but while this menu can seem tired elsewhere, the dishes here are clean-cut, fresh, and well-presented.

89 Regent's Park Road, Belsize Park ☎ 7586 7454 ⊖ Chalk Farm ££–£££

The Real Greek ⌕A10

Refined cooking using top-notch Greek ingredients.

15 Hoxton Market, Hoxton ☎ 7739 8212 ⊖ Old Street ££–£££

haute cuisine

The Capital ⌕F11

Arguably Knightsbridge's top restaurant. French in style, it costs a packet but the cooking is simply superb.

22 Basil Street, Knightsbridge ☎ 7589 5171 ⊖ Knightsbridge £££

☆ CHEZ NICO ⌕E6

Nico Ladenis's total dedication to the high art of cuisine emanates from every dish on the menu at his marvellously old-school restaurant. Creations include baked turbot hollandaise; and duck with honey, roast vegetables, and cassis sauce. The set lunch is the 'budget' option, or go for broke with the 8-course gastronomic menu. The wine list follows suit.

90 Park Lane, Mayfair ☎ 7409 1290 ⊖ Marble Arch ££–£££

☆ THE CONNAUGHT C13

People who eat here are deadly serious about their food and you need to be with these prices – but the experience is more than worth it. This is a traditional restaurant in the mould of the great Parisian institutions. Nothing informal or modern here. Jackets and ties are the norm, and they're not afraid to use cream. The classics tumble from the menu: homard d'Ecosse grillé 'My Way', filet de boeuf en croûte légère 'Strasbourgeoise' – the list goes on and on. Feast and then roll home at the end of it.

Carlos Place, Mayfair ☎ 7499 7070 ⊖ Green Park £££

☆ GORDON RAMSAY C18

Just in case you didn't catch the chef's name, it's Gordon Ramsay – but the experience is all about you, with expertly trained staff that create an engaging momentum. It's *très Parisien*. So is the setting, with plenty of glass – decorative screens and flamboyant specimens of the glass-blower's art. The food? Also an art form. Technically perfect, and presented with an innovative aestheticism: ravioli of lobster poached in a lobster bisque, served with a fine basil purée; pigeon poached in a bouillon of ceps, sautéed foie gras served in ceps consommé; and tatin of apples with caramel ice cream. Don't just dream it, go eat it.

68 Royal Hospital Road, Chelsea ☎ 7352 4441 ⊖ Sloane Square £££

The Oak Room A13

An indulgent helping of Edwardiana, courtesy of über-chef Marco Pierre White, is the deal here, with a menu combining classicism with innovation.

Le Meridien Hotel, 21 Piccadilly, Piccadilly ☎ 7734 8000 ⊖ Piccadilly Circus £££

Pétrus C13

Kudos has been given to this dining spot by owner Marcus Warehing, former head chef at Gordon Ramsay's. Fine haute cuisine and well-priced set menus are the draw.

33 St James's Street, Mayfair ☎ 7930 4272 ⊖ Green Park £££

☆ THE ROOM AT THE HALCYON E1

The classic/modern look stems from a combination of French and English country-house style: a charming patio garden is a wonderful and entirely traditional extra. Light, full-flavoured contemporary Provençal cooking is elegantly presented and perfected by chef Nigel Davies' culinary skills and creativity: pressed foie gras terrine with poached pear, accompanied by toasted brioche; grilled duck breast with caramelized pear and green peppercorns, and chilled nougatine parfait with apricot coulis. Sit back and enjoy.

129 Holland Park Avenue, Holland Park ☎ 7221 5411 ⊖ Holland Park £££

ice cream

Marine Ices *off map*

Famous throughout North London for its gorgeous gelati.

8 Haverstock Hill, Camden ☎ 7482 9003 ⊖ Chalk Farm £

indian & bengali

Café Naz *off map*

Brick Lane's chic curry house leads the way with contemporary Bangladeshi cooking – authentic food at good prices.

46–48 Brick Lane, Whitechapel ☎ 7247 0234 ⊖ Shoreditch £–££

☆ CAFÉ SPICE NAMASTE *off map*

As familiar as fish and chips, curry is usually as predictable. Café Spice Namaste, however, is on a mission to upgrade the image of food from the Indian sub-continent, by proudly presenting (in a very informative menu) a wide variety of its cuisines: delicious Tamil-style chicken from Sri Lanka, mushroom curry from Goa, and Kashmiri lamb dishes. Situated in Victorian chambers, in an area long-associated with immigration from India and Bangladesh, this restaurant is beloved by City dealers who, quite frankly, can get a little too loud at times.

16 Prescot Street, Whitechapel ☎ 7488 9242 ⊖ Aldgate East; Tower Hill ££

☆ RASA W1 *F6*

The colourful, aromatic vegetarian cooking of Kerala's Nair caste has been faithfully reproduced in London at this bright restaurant, a larger branch of the award-winning original in northeast London. Begin with intricately shaped Keralan crisps, served with pickles which are home-made and unmissable. A mild starter of deep-fried plantain with peanut and ginger sauce is one of the most popular: wonderful curries include the subtle flavours of *moru kachiatu*, made with mangoes and plantain yoghurt, and several dry stir-fries called *thorans*. An exquisite experience. There are two other branches – in Stoke Newington and Charlotte Street, W1.

6 Dering Street, Mayfair ☎ 7629 1346 ⊖ Oxford Circus; Bond Street. ££

Ravi Shankar *E3*

This Indian has good, cheap vegetarian food that makes up for its slightly cramped surroundings.

422 St John Street, Islington ☎ 7833 5849 ⊖ Angel £

Soho Spice *F7*

This funky colourful Indian is a buzzy, cheap and cheerful option.

124–126 Wardour Street, Soho ☎ 7434 0808 ⊖ Tottenham Court Road £££

Le Taj *off map*
Quality Bangladeshi specialities.
134 Brick Lane, Whitechapel ☎ 7247 4210 ⊖ Shoreditch £–££

☆ TAMARIND *C13*
Regional north Indian cuisine that is full of revelations, combining subtlety with charisma: *hara kebab* (pan fried cake of potato, spinach, chick peas, and lentils), *hari machchi* (John Dory with crispy spinach and tamarind), culminating in *malai pista kulfi* (egg-free saffron and pistachio ice cream). Decor follows suit, placing traditional elements, such as framed textiles, in a minimal but nevertheless warm setting.
20 Queen Street, Mayfair ☎ 7629 3561 ⊖ Green Park ££–£££

☆ VEERASWAMY *A13*
Reflecting modern India, Veeraswamy's streamlined decor makes the most of traditional sari colours, while antique Indian artefacts provide focal points. The menu presents regional specialities, with a good choice of rewarding vegetarian dishes, such as *lala puri* (flat wheat biscuits layered with herbs, potatoes, and three chutneys). Among the carnivorous delights are *apple dopiaza* (lamb curry with chillies, caramelized onion, and apples), and *dumka murgh* (chicken baked in yoghurt, poppy seeds, green chillies, and caramelized onions). Sunday is family day.
99 Regent Street, Piccadilly ☎ 7734 1401 ⊖ Piccadilly Circus ££–£££

☆ ZAIKA *C17*
Zaika literally translates as 'sophisticated flavours'. It certainly applies whether its a traditional number like lamb and lentil patties stuffed with egg and onion, *roganjosh* and butter chicken, or chef Vineet Bhatia's own signature dishes such as the inspired smoked salmon kebab. A five course Juhalbandi degustation menu is irresistible at £22, with wines to match each course for another £8. A notable addition to sw3.
257–259 Fulham Road, South Kensington ☎ 7351 7823
⊖ South Kensingtion £££

internet cafés

Café Internet *E13*
Refuel and surf the net for £1.50–£2 per hour.
22–24 Buckingham Palace Road, Belgravia ☎ 7233 5786 ⊖ Victoria

Easyeverything *off map*
Dirt cheap internet access at just £1 hour, available round the clock.
160–166 Kensington High St, Kensington ☎ 7233 8456 ⊖ High St Kensington

Global Café ⌖B13

A tantalizing taste of the future, this cyber-café is a favourite for music machine-heads. By day, enjoy access to the net with a drink. By night, you'll find one of a cycle of DJs broadcasting live on the internet. Art, music, and film events are common.

15 Golden Square, Soho ☎ 7287 2242 ⊖ Piccadilly Circus

Intercafé ⌖B13

Order a beer and access the web for £5 per hour.

Portland Street, North Soho ☎ 7631 0063 ⊖ Oxford Circus

Webshack ⌖F7

A fiver an hour for internet access. Open 'til 11pm except Sundays.

15 Dean Street, Soho ☎ 7439 8000 ⊖ Tottenham Court Road

italian

Al Duca ⌖D1

A chichi modern Italian with classic dishes and friendly service.

4–5 Duke of York Street, Westbourne Grove ☎ 7839 3090 ⊖ Notting Hill Gate ££–£££

Assaggi ⌖*off map*

You'll need to book well in advance for this friendly, relaxed, but pricey Italian, as this is one of the most popular restaurants in the area.

39 Chepstow Place, Bayswater ☎ 7792 5501 ⊖ Bayswater £££

Bersagliera ⌖C18

'Old school' Italian dishes are the draw, served in a no-frills, unstuffy setting.

372 King's Road, Chelsea ☎ 7352 5993 ⊖ Sloane Square ££

Café Milan ⌖C18

The complete Italian experience is stylishly proffered at this restaurant where you take your pick between contemporary restaurant, antipasti bar, espresso bar, gelateria, and juice bar.

312–314 King's Road, Chelsea ☎ 7351 0101 ⊖ Sloane Square ££

Casale Franco ⌖A3

Several years ago this modern Italian restaurant was *the* place to go in Upper Street. Now it's slightly out of the limelight, but the food's still good (great pizzas), and the tiny open-air courtyard makes a nice lunch spot in summer.

134–137 Upper Street, Islington ☎ 7226 8994 ⊖ Highbury & Islington ££

Floriana ⚲F11
Progressive Italian cuisine capitalizing on speciality ingredients.
15 Beauchamp Place, Knightsbridge ☎ 7838 1500 ⊖ Knightsbridge £££

☆ ISOLA ⚲F11
This restaurant has all the hallmarks of retro-metropolitan Italianate power dining. A spectacular glass façade gives you total visibility of passers-by, and vice-versa. Modern Italian dishes that are sophisticated in their simplicity ensure that head chef Bruno Loubet remains ahead of the field: potato gnocchi with osso buco sauce and *gremolata*, artichoke and goats' cheese terrine with tapenade and celery pesto, and, of course, tiramisu.
145 Knightsbridge, Knightsbridge ☎ 7838 1044 ⊖ Knightsbridge £££

Kettners ⚲B13
Fairly unexciting pizzas/pastas, but Kettners offers a great atmosphere in shabby but elegant surroundings with a fun champagne bar.
29 Romilly Street, Soho ☎ 7437 6437 ⊖ Leicester Square ££

La Delizia ⚲C18
A modern, streamlined, but rather cramped pizzeria, with another branch in the Chelsea Farmer's Market.
64 Chelsea Manor Street, Chelsea ☎ 7376 4111 ⊖ Sloane Square ££

Maggiore's Italian Kitchen ⚲A14
If you fancy an Italian lunch for just under a fiver, this place has an excellent-value two-course set menu.
17–21 Tavistock Street, Holborn ☎ 7379 9696 ⊖ Temple £

Maremma ⚲C3
An upmarket Italian for serious restaurant-goers.
11–13 Theberton Street, Islington ☎ 7226 9400 Ⅲ Essex Road ££–£££

Paparazzi Café ⚲C17
A little pricey, but open late. Pasta and pizzas are the order of the day.
58 Fulham Road, South Kensington ☎ 7589 0876 ⊖ South Kensington £

Picasso ⚲C18
Cheap and cheerful Italian staples are served up here – it justifies its name with a few (repro) line drawings by the great maestro. It's popular with a mixed crowd including locals and Harley-Davidson bikers.
127 King's Road, Chelsea ☎ 7352 4921 ⊖ Sloane Square ££

Pizza Express *⚲C18*

One of London's premier pizza chains. Housed in The Pheasantry, an ornate neoclassical building, it includes a private forecourt set with tables.

152–154 King's Road, Chelsea ☎ 7351 5031 ⊖ Sloane Square ££

Pizza Organic *⚲F11*

For the most wholesome pizzas in the west.

20 Old Brompton Road, Knightsbridge ☎ 7589 9613 ⊖ Knightsbridge £

☆ PURPLE SAGE *⚲D5*

More terracotta than purple sage, the walls of this contemporary Italian are bare, but there's an open kitchen, handsome waiters, and a mixed bunch of happy eaters to look at should conversation pall. And of course there's the food: marinated raw tuna with capers and anchovies is a wonderfully toothsome starter; specials include roast monkfish with rocket and red peppers; or you can plump for *crostatina* with wild berries and homemade walnut ice cream to finish.

92 Wigmore Street, Marylebone ☎ 7486 1912 ⊖ Bond Street ££–£££

☆ RIVER CAFÉ *⚲off map*

This very fashionable restaurant started life as the staff canteen for Richard Rogers's architectural practice next door and is still run by his wife Ruth, and her partner Rose Gray. The food is inspired by rural Italian cooking, with lots of vegetables and herbs which are grown in the courtyard outside. Meat, seafood, and game are mostly chargrilled or wood-roasted; there's also wonderful fresh pasta and masterful desserts. At these prices, flying to Italy could be an option, but Hammersmith is closer.

Thames Wharf, Rainville Road, Hammersmith ☎ 7381 8824 ⊖ Hammersmith £££

Sartoria *⚲A13*

A typical Conran-ism, where the design draws on Italian rationalism and the menu features modern Italian classics.

20 Savile Row, Mayfair ☎ 7534 7000 ⊖ Oxford Circus £££

☆ STEFANO CAVALLINI AT THE HALKIN *⚲F12*

Post-modern, north Italian style – plenty of marble and elegant drapes – set within one of London's most innovative deluxe hotels. Stefano Cavallini's menu yields superlative flavours: duck ravioli with savoy cabbage and foie gras, roasted fillet of veal with Parma ham, potatoes, courgettes, and shiitake; chocolate soufflé with orange and cardamom sorbet. All served by staff impeccably dressed in Armani. It's like mamma used to make, only much much better.

5–6 Halkin Street, Belgravia ☎ 7333 1234 ⊖ Hyde Park Corner £££

Villa Bianca *off map*

Sitting beneath a balcony covered with hanging baskets; Villa Blanca is a favourite among locals for its upmarket but authentic repertoire of Italian dishes.

1 Perrin's Court, Hampstead ☎ 7435 3131 ⊖ Hampstead ££–£££

☆ ZAFFERANO *F11*

This is Belgravia but not dauntingly so: a relaxed environment and a faultless display of Italian cooking guarantees Zafferano's popularity. Even the simplest dishes are presented with verve and imagination. The pasta is excellent, from buttery *pappardelle* with broad beans and rocket, to ricotta and aubergine parcels. Influences span the Italian peninsula from Sicilian caponata to Sardinian cheese parcels with honey, and the coffee can't be beat.

15 Lowndes Street, Belgravia ☎ 7235 5800 ⊖ Knightsbridge £££

japanese

Itsu *D17*

Sushi and sashimi glide past on a gleaming conveyor belt. Presentation is all, and that applies to the clientele too. Upstairs, there's a saké bar where diners can wait to be seated.

18 Draycott Avenue, South Kensington ☎ 7584 5522 ⊖ South Kensington £££

Japanese Canteen *A1*

A joyous, funky addition to Portobello, serving fragrant noodle soups and hot dishes as well as beautifully presented sushi and sashimi.

305 Portobello Road, Notting Hill ☎ 8968 9968 ⊖ Ladbroke Grove ££

☆ NOBU *F12*

East meets South, as Japanese specialities, made contemporary with South American influences, create a spectacular alliance. Japanese aesthetics determine the decor and presentation, heightening the appeal of culinary masterpieces: *matsuhisa* shrimp with caviar; black cod with *miso; hamachi sashimi* with jalapeños. An accompaniment of saké is available in fruit flavours, and there are also wonderful views of Hyde Park to salivate over. A separate sushi bar serves the very finest specimens.

19 Old Park Lane, Mayfair ☎ 7447 4747 ⊖ Hyde Park Corner £££

☆ WAGAMAMA *B13*

Specializing in fresh Japanese noodes (plus curries, miso soups, and rice dishes), this is Oriental dining designer-refectory style. The menu also features Japanese beer and saké. plus great juices. Always busy but queues move quickly. Other branches on Wigmore Street, Bloomsbury, High Street Kensington, and Jamestown Road in Camden.

10a Lexington Street, Soho ☎ 7292 0990 ⊖ Piccadilly Circus £–££

☆ YO! SUSHI ⚲E7

Fashionable, fast, and furious – this Japanese sushi bar is a pit stop for film and music wannabes. Diners sit on bar stools around a conveyor belt laden with delicious but affordable sushi, sashimi, and tempura. Not a place for a quiet intimate meal – music and conversation here are loud. And beware of painful collisions at groin height with the mobile robotic trolley. Other branches on Finchley Road, in Selfridges on Oxford Street, and on the Fifth Floor of Harvey Nichols in Knightsbridge.

52 Poland Street, Soho ☎ 7287 0443 ⊖ Oxford Circus ££

juice bars

Fluid ⚲E17

The big squeeze: design your own combinations juices. Other branches at Elgin Crescent W11, Hanover Square W1.

208 Fulham Road, Fulham ☎ 7352 4372
⊖ Fulham Broadway; Earl's Court; South Kensington £

Jus ⚲A14

Delish juices and smoothies plus plenty of healthy-looking salads if you're hungry.

New Row, Covent Garden ☎ 7240 8984 ⊖ Covent Garden; Leicester Square £

Jus Café ⚲D3

For the best vitamin infusion in the area, serving smoothies and freshly squeezed juices.

30–32 Foubert's Place, Soho ☎ 7734 7522 ⊖ Oxford Circus £

kids' restaurants

Rainforest Café ⚲B13

Any day of the week you can walk into a misty rainforest environment with robotic animatronics, such as gorillas and a croc that periodically comes 'to life'. The food is decent and varied, but expect queues. Kids can have Jurassic chicken and a Rainforest Rick's apple crisp to follow.

20 Shaftesbury Avenue, Covent Garden ☎ 7434 3111 ⊖ Piccadilly Circus ££

Smollensky's Balloon ⚲A14

At weekends this modern American brasserie opens its doors to kids. There are cartoons, bright balloons, and Nintendo games. A section is cleared for pedal cars, and a resident clown does a first-rate show. Children's brunches include kids koktails, or you can order a child's portions from the adult's menu.

105 Strand, Covent Garden ☎ 7497 2101 ⊖ Charing Cross ££

☆ AKA ꟻF7

Up-market grub for late-night clubbers.

18 West Central St, Bloomsbury ☎ 7836 0110 ⊖ Tottenham Court Rd ££–£££

Al's Diner ꟻA9

A café-cum-bar that swings through the night thanks to its late licence. It's a great spot for Sunday brunch too.

11–13 Exmouth Market, Clerkenwell ☎ 7837 4821 ⊖ Farringdon ££

☆ BAR ITALIA ꟻF7

A 50s Italian joint, serving the best coffee of all the Soho cafés. There's lots of late-night buzz and it's open 24 hours a day (except 4–7am Mon).

22 Frith Street, Soho ☎ 7437 4520 ⊖ Tottenham Court Road £

☆ CAFÉ BOHÈME ꟻB13

Parisian brasserie for late-night stop outs.

13 Old Compton Street, Soho ☎ 7734 0623 ⊖ Leicester Square £–££

Costa Dorada ꟻF7

Party and feast Spanish style till 3am.

47 Hanway Street, North Soho ☎ 7636 7139 ⊖ Tottenham Court Road ££

☆ MAROUSH ꟻE6

Authentic Lebanese cuisine, live Arabic music, and belly dancing.

21 Edgware Road, Edgware Road ☎ 7262 1090 ⊖ Marble Arch ££

New Diamond ꟻB13

Great Chinese, and it's open late.

23 Lisle Street, Soho ☎ 7437 2517 ⊖ Leicester Square; Piccadilly Circus ££

☆ RANOUSH JUICE BAR ꟻE6

Order the tastiest juices and kebabs in west London or try their best seller: Lebanese starters, such as falafel and houmous, served as tasty sandwiches.

43 Edgware Road, Edgware Road ☎ 723 5929 ⊖ Marble Arch £

Ryo ꟻB13

Busy night-time noodle shop usually full of bedraggled clubbers.

84 Brewer Street, Soho ☎ 7287 1318 ⊖ Piccadilly Circus £–££

Tinseltown ꟻD9

A late night haunt for clubbers as it serves meals (like burgers, pastas, salads etc) round the clock. Licensed for drinks until midnight.

44–46 St John Street, Clerkenwell ☎ 7689 2424 ⊖ Farringdon £

latin american

☆ CACTUS BLUE *E17*

South Ken's well-heeled residents have plenty of restaurants to choose from, but many of its more boho locals gravitate to this groovy bar-cum-restaurant. Native American artefacts and paintings loom over diners who munch on a loose version of Tex-Mex that successfully brings in Creole, Cajun, Caribbean and even Chinese influences. Wash it all down with Mexican beer or some of the best margaritas in town.

86 Fulham Rd, South Kensington ☎ 7823 7858 ⊖ South Kensington ££–£££

Camden Cantina *off map*

Plain old (but excellent) Mexican comida and a steady flow of margaritas.

34 Chalk Farm Road, Chalk Farm ☎ 7267 2780 ⊖ Chalk Farm ££££–££

☆ FINA ESTAMPA *C16*

In the basement kitchen of this classy, yet relaxed, restaurant, Doña Bianca rustles up her Peruvian specialities: *ocopa* (new potatoes draped in a rich, spicy peanut and walnut sauce garnished with king prawns); or *carapulcra* (a filling stew of pork and chicken with dried potatoes and cassava). Salsa music plays, and no-one would stop you from dancing after dinner, though a gentle stroll would probably be more realistic. Come hungry, and kick off your Latin adventure with a spot-on pisco sour.

150 Tooley St, Southwark ☎ 7403 1342 ⊖ London Bridge; Tower Hill ££–£££

Gaucho Grill *off map*

The newest arrival on Hampstead's (rather limited) culinary scene . From its bovine interior, it is obvious that this joint pulls no punches with its cowskin chairs and a grill sizzling with steaks.

64 Heath Street, Hampstead ☎ 7431 8222 ⊖ Hampstead ££

Navajo Joe *A14*

A remarkable 200 or more tequilas to accompany South American/Mexican cuisine. Lunchtimes are quiet, so if you're after some action, prepare to jostle with the evening crowd.

34 King Street, Covent Garden ☎ 7240 4008 ⊖ Covent Garden ££

mediterranean

Aurora Café *A13*

Despite its name, this is a small restaurant in a gorgeous old house with a weekly-changing Mediterranean menu.

49 Lexington Street, Soho ☎ 7494 0514 ⊖ Piccadilly Circus ££

☆ CANTALOUPE *B10*

This industrial-style and size bar-restaurant has done phenomenally well since it opened in 1997, and is packed at weekends. But the quieter back room offers a pleasant dining experience, featuring well-cooked, no-nonsense food: chicken with okra and chickpeas, roast lamb with basil mash, confit of duck, and big salads. There's also a good-value wine list, plus bottled beers, cocktails, single cigars, and a relaxed policy on people who just want to snack.

35–42 Charlotte Road, Hoxton ☎ 7613 4411 ⊖ Old Street ££

Garden Restaurant *F11*

Overlooking (and making use of) an overgrown garden, this café has day-long dining and a Mediterranean menu.

General Trading Co, 141 Sloane Street, Knightsbridge ☎ 7730 2001 ⊖ Knightsbridge £

Mas Café *A1*

Young, street, cheap and clubby in feel with zinging Mediterranean food. Mas Café (currently under refurbishment so phone ahead) was formerly known as the Mangrove – a late night shebeen, which fell under the gaze of the media in the 60s. It was here that call-girl Christine Keeler seduced both the Minister of Defence, John Profumo, and a Russian spy, causing Profumo's resignation and nearly bringing down the government.

6–8 All Saints Road, Notting Hill ☎ 7243 0969 ⊖ Ladbroke Grove ££

Zucca *off map*

The delicious food based on top quality fresh ingredients, is cooked by one of Alastair Little's protégés.

188 Westbourne Grove, Bayswater ☎ 7727 0060 ⊖ Bayswater ££

middle eastern

Gaby's *A14*

A good, budget stop-off with excellent falafels and a vast selection of salads.

30 Charing Cross Road, Covent Garden ☎ 7836 4233 ⊖ Leicester Square £

☆ PATOGH *D5*

Patogh is usually packed with Middle Eastern expats, but it's no surprise as every dish on the short menu is tops. Start with *masto moosir*, a thick, creamy dip of yoghurt and finely chopped spring onions or cucumber (*masto khiar*); or nibble on an assortment of crunchy pickles. Keep going with succulent chicken on a bed of buttery rice, or tender lamb accompanied by cartwheel-sized flat bread hot from the oven. No alcohol is served, but all meat is good quality, helpings are copious, and service friendly.

8 Crawford Place, Marylebone ☎ 7262 4015 ⊖ Edgware Road £–££

☆ **ALASTAIR LITTLE** *C1*

Lancaster Road used to be the wrong end of Notting Hill, but Mr Little's arrival in 1996 proved that this hippest of neighbourhoods knows no boundaries. The food is as good, if not better, than at its Soho sister, with dishes like the *bollito misto* with *salsa verde* leaving you wondering how they did it. Convivial and friendly, this place has wowed the locals – even though it's more like a local bistro than some of the area's slicker eateries. Set course dinners only.

136a Lancaster Road, Notting Hill ☎ 7243 2220 ⊖ Ladbroke Grove ££–£££

Amphitheatre Restaurant *E7*

The spectacular views over the Piazza are open to Royal Opera House ticket holders only at night; everyone else can enjoy them during the day.

Royal Opera House, Bow Street, Covent Garden ☎ 7212 9254 ⊖ Covent Garden £££

☆ **ANDREW EDMUNDS** *F7*

Some of the best food in Soho is served at this intimate bistro. Its bohemian, slightly scruffy decor only adds to its romance. The ever-imaginative menu might include serrano ham, Manchego cheese, figs, and piquillo peppers, followed by a sublime seared rare tuna with boulangère potatoes, tomato and chilli salsa, and deep fried capers. English puds, like the perfect summer pudding with crème fraîche, are at their best.

46 Lexington Street, Soho ☎ 7437 5708 ⊖ Piccadilly Circus ££

Axis *B14*

An adventurous take on Modern European classics in a stylish 1930s setting.

1 Aldwych, Holborn ☎ 7300 0300 ⊖ Temple ££–£££

☆ **BANK** *B14*

A glass act: the glazed walkway leads past an open-plan kitchen to the dining room, where endless rows of glass fins are suspended from the ceiling. This fashionable venue continues to draw crowds of fast-track media and City players. The well-executed menu spans modern Europeanism. Crab linguine with chilli, pea risotto, and other Italian numbers rub shoulders with English classics, such as fish and chips and mushy peas. It's a perfect marriage of nostalgia and innovation.

1 Kingsway, Covent Garden ☎ 7379 9797 ⊖ Holborn ££–£££

☆ **BIBENDUM** *C17*

Occupying part of the beautiful Michelin building, this restaurant has the perfect dining room – light, airy and you could almost drive buses

between the tables. You pay top whack, but the food is truly sublime: grilled scallops with artichoke purée, rocket and truffle oil lead a delicious dance around the tastebuds. And the sautéed sweetbreads with broad bean purée and mint are an offal-lover's dream. After a lunch to remember, why not blow the rest of your credit card limit in the Conran Shop downstairs? Gorge on molluscs and tank up on champagne in the elegant Oyster Bar downstairs.
81 Fulham Road, South Kensington ☎ 7581 5817 ⊖ South Kensington £££

☆ BLUEBIRD *D17*
Conran's huge restaurant/café/supermarket, once a garage, is a welcome address on a street not renowned for great dining opportunities. The first-floor restaurant is elegant, and the friendly and attentive service from blue-jacketed flunkies fits the bill too. The menu covers a wide range, with reliable classics (pasta, steak-frites, fishcakes), and wood-roasted dishes (including lobster and pigeon) a speciality. There's a suitably fashionable wine list too...
350 King's Road, Chelsea ☎ 7559 1000 ⊖ Sloane Square then 🚌 11, 22 ££

Circus *B13*
A softly minimal restaurant with a seasonal menu of mostly modern European dishes, served to a trendy media crowd.
1 Upper James Street, Soho ☎ 7534 4000 ⊖ Piccadilly Circus £££

☆ CLARKE'S *F1*
Serious foodies won't be disappointed by this sedate little restaurant, where the emphasis is on the freshest ingredients cooked with skill, but no pyrotechnics. Owner and chef Sally Clarke's philosophy comes from California: use only the best of locally found ingredients and allow them to speak for themselves. Lunch and dinner menus are set, to make the most of the day's produce, and dishes are composed of superb-quality vegetables around the likes of Cornish turbot or Romney Marsh lamb.
124 Kensington Church Street, Kensington ☎ 7221 9225
⊖ Notting Hill Gate ££–£££

☆ COAST *C13*
Less is more – as long as you like less – and this is a minimal space, emphasized by a vast glazed frontage. The modern European menu scores high on presentation and flavour: pan-fried raviolis of braised beef, roasted pumpkin, braising juices and parmesan; pan-fried chorizo and sweet potato gnocchi with lentil dressing; poached pear with pannacotta and ginger shortbread. Slick service completes the seductive package. Eating is believing...
26b Albemarle Street, Mayfair ☎ 7495 5999 ⊖ Green Park £££

Euphorium ℘A3
Not-so-special Modern European fare in a striking setting. Less exquisite and less expensive than its sister restaurant, Granita.
203 Upper Street, Islington ☎ 7704 6909 ⊖ Highbury & Islington £££

☆ FIFTH FLOOR HARVEY NICHOLS ℘F11
Imagination plus deft technical execution turns this restaurant on the top floor of London's most fashionable department store into more than just an add-on to the Harvey Nichols shopping experience. Cracking views and a continent-hopping menu make it the haunt of the absolutely fabulous shopping set. Classics like steak tartare are joined by innovative combinations; rock oysters with grilled spicy sausages, as well as rustic chic dishes such as pot roast rabbit with ale gravy and herb dumplings. A subtly minimal dining room puts diners (rather than the restaurant design) in the spotlight.
109–123 Knightsbridge ☎ 7235 5250 ⊖ Knightsbridge £££

☆ FRENCH HOUSE DINING ROOM ℘B13
An old-fashioned dining room above a pub, the 'French' is renowned for substantial helpings of quintessential English food with a twist. Pig's trotters appear in an unctuous salad; sweetbreads are served with watercress and bacon; rabbit with chicory and mustard sauce; and skate is accompanied by samphire. Side orders include one of London's best Welsh rarebits, and the cheeses are a selection of the UK's best from Neal's Yard Dairy.
1st floor, 49 Dean Street, Soho ☎ 7437 2477 ⊖ Tottenham Court Road ££–£££

Granita ℘A3
Supposedly where Tony Blair hatched the New Labour plan, this is a minimalist refectory that is less chilly than it appears through its picture window. The menu features cosmopolitan dishes such as squid in a lime, tamarind, and chilli sauce.
127 Upper Street, Islington ☎ 7226 3222 ⊖ Highbury & Islington £££

Great Eastern Dining Room ℘B10
Italianesque food served in a beautifully converted fabric warehouse.
54–56 Great Eastern Street, Hoxton ☎ 7613 4545 ⊖ Old Street ££

Gresslin's ℘off map
Modern European in taste, with a hint of the Orient which can verge on the experimental. It attracts 'ladies who lunch', drawn by a reasonably-priced menu.
13 Heath Street, Hampstead ☎ 7794 8386 ⊖ Hampstead ££

Indigo ⍟A14

A sleek, high-style restaurant, dispensing modern European food.

1 Aldwych, Holborn ☎ 7300 0400 ⊖ Temple £–£££

☆ THE IVY ⍟B13

This is the post-theatre restaurant in London. Statesmen, movie, and pop stars sprinkle the art deco dining room. But there's no second-class status here – the staff treat everyone with the same friendly courtesy. The food is simple, fresh, and delicious. For vegetarians, you can't beat the herb risotto; for carnivores, the steak tartare is the best around... and the vodka martinis definitely hit the spot.

1 West Street, Covent Garden ☎ 7836 4751 ⊖ Leicester Square ££–£££

Leith's ⍟C1

A well-established reputation and an enticing Modern European menu with lots of choice for vegetarians.

92 Kensington Pk Rd, Notting Hill ☎ 7229 4481 ⊖ Ladbroke Grove £££

Leith's Soho ⍟B13

Serves up trad favourites, like cauliflower cheese and bangers and mash, in a divine setting with impeccable service.

41 Beak Street, Soho ☎ 7287 2057 ⊖ Oxford Circus; Piccadilly Circus £££

☆ LE PONT DE LA TOUR ⍟C16

At one of Conran's most expensive restaurants, the Anglo-French cooking is good, though not as exquisite as the prices suggest. You're paying for the wonderful riverside views, so be sure to book one of the terrace tables, which come well-equipped for the vagaries of alfresco dining in London. Shellfish bisque with armagnac cream, roast salad of rabbit with creamed borlotti beans and rosemary, and caramel mousse with Calvados sauce are typical of the gastronomic offerings. The pre-theatre set dinners and Sunday menu offer the best value.

36d Shad Thames, Butler's Wharf, Southwark ☎ 7403 8403
⊖ London Bridge; Tower Hill £££

☆ LOLA'S ⍟C3

A recipient of a lot of culinary back-slapping, Lola's really is worth the hype. Gary Lee's daily changing menu is truly varied: a chilled chickpea soup with *horiatiki* and flat bread, and a fantastic fennel and broad bean risotto could seduce even a confirmed carnivore, but a more red-blooded diner would purr with pleasure over the plump fillet steak with chips and Caesar salad. Variety, freshness, and deftness are the hallmarks..

The Mall Building, 359 Upper Street, Islington ☎ 7359 1932
⊖ Angel ££–£££

☆ **MAISON NOVELLI** *A9*

This is the first and most famous of superchef Jean-Christophe Novelli's restaurants. Aficionados love the intricacy of his creations (much artful drizzling of sauces), and the intensity of the flavours, colours, and textures of the ingredients used. Dishes feature sophisticated re-treads of French classics such as bouillabaisse, as well as global hook-ups like Chinese noodles and baby squid. The French staff are starchily formal, as befits a restaurant of this stature, but service can be unbelievably slow.
29 Clerkenwell Green, Clerkenwell ☎ 7251 6606 ⊖ Farringdon £££

☆ **MASH** *E7*

This trendy bar-deli-restaurant (from the Oliver Peyton stable) is notable for its futuristic interior design as much as for its food and drink. Customers flock to try the excellent home-brewed ales and cocktails in the bar, and to the more sedate restaurant upstairs. Here, the (mostly!) healthy menu has dishes such as roast salmon with pak-choi, and rib-eye of beef with portobello mushrooms. Staff tend to be as fun as the place itself.
19–21 Great Portland St, North Soho ☎ 7637 5555 ⊖ Oxford Circus ££–£££

Mezzo *B13*

Full of whizz-kids spending their firms' money on brasserie-type food.
100 Wardour Street, Soho ☎ 7314 4000 ⊖ Piccadilly Circus £££

☆ **NOBLE ROT** *E7*

The name may suggest aristocratic excess, but this actually refers to a condition that affects grapes. A varied selection of the finest dessert wines can be enjoyed with plenty of sublime puds, though there are plenty of Modern European dishes to savour en route. They are all prepared with finesse and enlightenment, but also with respect for their heritage: foie gras and chicken liver *parfait,* toasted brioche and pickled figs, and wild mushroom lasagne. The setting is attractively low-key with style meister Nicky Haslam adding elements of the 30s and 40s Happy Valley Crowd. With a package like this, punters will always be happy.
3–5 Mill Street, Mayfair ☎ 7629 8877 ⊖ Oxford Circus £££

☆ **ODETTE'S** *off map*

A homely Primrose Hill town house; the walls are covered with gilt-framed mirrors, and there's a variety of rooms from intimate snugs to a bright conservatory. While the Anglo-French food is a little old-fashioned, it can't be faulted for quality. Dishes might include a flavourful breast of Barbary duck with turnip gratin, caramelized endive, and sweet and sour cherries or grilled fillet of salmon with creamed cabbage and red wine sauce. The wine list is long and serious, and a cheaper menu is served in the basement wine bar.
130 Regent's Park Road, Belsize Park ☎ 7586 5486 ⊖ Chalk Farm ££–£££

192 ♯C1
Where the scene is as essential as the food. Ever-popular in Notting Hill circles, this wine bar-cum-restaurant caters to art, fashion, and film luvvies.
192 Kensington Pk Rd, Notting Hill ☎ 7229 0482 ⊖ Ladbroke Grove £££

☆ OXO TOWER RESTAURANT, BAR & BRASSERIE ♯D14
Chef Simon Arkless works his culinary magic at this London landmark. As well as turning out delicious cuts of meat, he has a real talent for roasting fish: sea bass, monkfish, and cod all feature regularly. The views over the city are terrific; meals with a view are more affordable in the brasserie which does a great pre-theatre menu. Nowhere, you may be relieved to hear, is there any trace of Oxo in the cooking...
8th fl, Oxo Tower Wharf, Barge House Street, South Bank ☎ 7803 3888 ⊖ Waterloo £££

☆ PEOPLE'S PALACE ♯D14
Feast your eyes on this restaurant's uninterrupted views of the Thames, or just feast on its confident, unfussy modern European food. Starters set the tone – well-flavoured salads or robust terrine of salt beef and roast beetroot. Fish is seared, pan-fried, or roasted; lamb may come with polenta and baby onions; entrecôte simply with chips. The prompt, attentive service is well-geared to pre-theatre dining.
Royal Festival Hall, South Bank ☎ 7928 9999 ⊖ Waterloo ££–£££

Quaglino ♯C13
Ever since Terence Conran reopened in 1993, this legendary venue has operated on a grand scale: 1,000 people a day order from a modern European menu.
16 Bury Street, St James ☎ 7930 6767 ⊖ Green Park £££

☆ SPOON ♯E7
A stylish and gastronomic indulgence. The all-white Spoon is delightfully whimsical with all its Venetian glass and super-chef Alain Ducasse's exciting menu provides an amazing choice. The menu divides into the usual categories of fish, meat, pasta etc, but each dish within a section divides into a) principal component, b) sauce, and c) garnish; you can choose whichever three elements you like. Sheer genius. Think pasta with black truffle sauce and parmesan, pan-seared tuna with crushed lemon confit and wok-sauteed vegetables, followed by chocolate pizza. A dream.
Sanderson Hotel, 50 Berners St, North Soho ☎ 7300 1444 ⊖ Oxford Circus £££

Teatro ♯B13
This is a bonus to the local gastronomic scene, with good modern British food and a suitably luvvie atmosphere.
93–107 Shaftesbury Avenue, Soho ☎ 7494 3040 ⊖ Leicester Square £££

Titanic ⌖B13
Marco Pierre White's bar/restaurant is amusingly located above the Atlantic. A buzzy, noisy, underwater-themed option.
81 Brewer Street, Soho ☎ 7437 1912 ⊖ Piccadilly Circus ££

Toast ⌖*off map*
Très fashionable Hampsteadites frequent this bar for its modern European cuisine. For those recovering from the weekend's endeavours, a restorative Sunday brunch here includes the all-important 'hair of the dog', along with a full English breakfast.
50 Hampstead High Street, Hampstead ☎ 7431 2244 ⊖ Hampstead ££

north american

Atlantic Bar & Grill ⌖B13
The flagship restaurant/bar of entrepreneur Oliver Peyton. It has the look of an art deco cruise liner, but despite its cavernous size and American-influenced food, it suffers from an over-zealous door policy.
20 Glasshouse Street, Soho ☎ 7734 4888 ⊖ Piccadilly Circus ££–£££

Blues Bistro & Bar ⌖F7
Chowder and crab cakes provide reassurance for homesick Americans.
42 Dean Street, Soho ☎ 7494 1966 ⊖ Tottenham Court Road ££–£££

Christopher's American Grill ⌖E7
For a taste of North America with some panache, this is a reliable option. Food is excellent; the setting grand; service wonderfully discreet and formal.
18 Wellington Street, Covent Garden ☎ 7240 4222 ⊖ Covent Garden £££

☆ DAKOTA ⌖C1
Easy, laid-back and unstudiedly cool, Dakota gained immediate acceptance in the neighbourhood – it's a favourite with design duo Clements Ribeiro, who revealed that Madonna had skipped a booking at the Pharmacy to have dinner here. A high-ceilinged converted pub, it serves startlingly adventurous modern American fare such as prawn, red pepper and sweet potato chowder or chargrilled white tuna with wild rice salad. A heavenly American dream.
127 Ledbury Road, Notting Hill ☎ 7792 9191 ⊖ Notting Hill Gate ££–£££

Joe Allen ⌖A14
A favourite haunt of theatrical-types and theatre-goers, with memorabilia-based decor inspiring luvvie behaviour. The more down-to-earth menu comprises American and international faves.
13 Exeter Street, Covent Garden ☎ 7836 0651 ⊖ Covent Garden ££

Ruby in the Dust *D2*
Laidback, with good snacks to boot, and it's open until midnight.
299 Portobello Road, Notting Hill ☎ 8969 4626 ⊖ Ladbroke Grove £–££

Santa Fe *C3*
A good fix for authentic Southwestern cooking (high on the chilli factor).
75 Upper Street, Islington ☎ 7288 2288 ⊖ Angel ££

Terminus Bar & Grill *D10*
Serving high quality food from early morning until midnight.
Great Eastern Hotel, Liverpool St ☎ 7618 7400 ⊖ Liverpool Street ££–£££

patisseries

Amato *B13*
Mouthwatering pastries.
14 Old Compton Street, Soho ☎ 7734 5733 ⊖ Leicester Square £

Bliss *E3*
Succumb to a perfect pastry (sweet or savoury) at this tiny coffee bar.
428 St John Street, Islington ☎ 7837 3720 ⊖ Angel £

☆ LISBOA *B1*
There's a constant hubbub in this ultra-authentic Portuguese patisserie.
57 Golborne Road, Notting Hill ☎ 8968 5242 ⊖ Westbourne Park £

☆ MAISON BERTAUX *A14*
A Soho old-timer with an arty crowd. Delicious pastries and fine tea.
28 Greek Street, Soho ☎ 7437 6007 ⊖ Leicester Square £

Maison Blanc *off map*
Refined, elegant, and oh-so-French, the tearoom triples up as a boulangerie, pâtisserie, and chocolaterie.
62a Hampstead High Street, Hampstead ☎ 7431 8338 ⊖ Hampstead £

☆ PÂTISSERIE VALÉRIE *B13*
Major Soho hangout and arguably the best gateaux in town.
44 Old Compton Street, Soho ☎ 7437 3466 ⊖ Leicester Square £

russian & eastern european

☆ CAVE *C13*
A delightfully eccentric restaurant: a 'wave' of blue embraces the bar counter, with the theme continued by a maritime mosaic. Various grades of Iranian caviar, served with blinis and soured cream. If you fancy some-

thing else of a deluxe nature, Balik smoked salmon, rock oysters, and lobster salad with black truffle dressing are there for the choosing...
161 Piccadilly, Mayfair ☎ 7409 0445 ⊖ Green Park £££

Caviar Kaspia *F6*
Imperial Russia characterizes this restaurant. Few restaurants are devoted to a single foodstuff, but then caviar does warrant such an honour.
18/18a Bruton Place, Mayfair ☎ 7493 0879 ⊖ Bond Street £££

Daquise *C17*
To enter this family-run Polish eatery is to step back in time: plastic tablecloths and button-back benches accompany great Eastern European food like golabki (stuffed cabbage leaves) and potato pancakes.
20 Thurloe Street, South Kensington ☎ 7589 6117 ⊖ South Kensington £

Firebird *E7*
Three types of caviar are on sale in this opulent, but ostentatious, townhouse; the main menu's pre-Revolutionary Russian cuisine is very authentic, but a bit on the expensive side.
23 Conduit Street, Mayfair ☎ 7493 7000 ⊖ Oxford Circus £££

Soviet Canteen *C18*
For an introduction to East European cooking, bag a chrome table here and choose from. A reasonably priced set menus and 34 types of vodka.
430 King's Road, Chelsea ☎ 7795 1556 ⊖ Sloane Square ££

seafood

☆ J SHEEKEY *A13*
An updated, sleek Sheekey's is back – in style. All that remains of the old restaurant is an emphasis on fish and seafood. The interior is divided into four rooms, which makes for a more intimate club-like atmosphere. Service is charming and the unfussy food is the business: from classics like Lobster Americaine, to simply cooked mixed grilled fish with herb butter, or daily changing specials such as sautéed rabbit with crab. Puds are mostly old-school British, like treacle tart, but there are also savouries for those who like to finish things off on a sharper note.
28–32 St Martin's Court, Covent Garden ☎ 7240 2565 ⊖ Leicester Sq ££–£££

Lee's Seafoods *off map*
Serves fresh cockles and mussels (and jellied eels) from a hole-in-the-wall.
134 Columbia Road, Shoreditch ☎ 7739 3685 ⊖ Shoreditch £

☆ LIVEBAIT *A14*

Livebait's interior is reminiscent of an old-fashioned fishmongers, but there's nothing backward-looking about the menu which changes daily. Imagination is the name of the game: the freshest seafood plays the starring role, while ingredients from around the world (Spanish chorizo, Thai lemongrass etc) act as a supporting cast. The quality cooking and the American-style service ensure a constant stream of satisfied fish fans.
21 Wellington Street, Covent Garden ☎ 7836 7161 ⊖ Covent Garden £££

Rudland & Stubbs *A9*

An old school fish restaurant: all *fruits de mer*, tiles, and white wine.
35–37 Greenhill Rents, Clerkenwell ☎ 7253 0848 ⊖ Farringdon ££

southeast asian

Busaba Eathai *F7*

A no-smoking Thai restaurant in the same canteen vein as Wagamama.
106–110 Wardour Street, Soho ☎ 7255 8650 ⊖ Tottenham Court Road £–££

Busabong Tree *off map*

Set menus (£22 and up) offering the best of Thai cuisine. Its lovely patio garden is another plus.
112 Cheyne Walk, Chelsea ☎ 7352 7534 ⊖ Fulham Broadway ££

Caffè Bianco *off map*

A sandwich place by day and Thai café by night. Great value.
12 Perrins Court, Hampstead ☎ 7431 0363 ⊖ Hampstead £

Melati *B13*

Indonesian food on Soho's most stripper-rich street.
21 Great Windmill Street, Soho ☎ 7437 2745 ⊖ Piccadilly Circus £–££

Silks & Spice *off map*

A relatively new, but well-loved Southeast Asian chain.
28 Chalk Farm Road, Camden ☎ 7267 5751 ⊖ Camden Town ££

Taste of Siam *D2*

Camden has been the home of this homely Thai restaurant for a decade.
45 Camden High Street, Camden ☎ 7380 0665 ⊖ Camden Town ££

Thai Pot *A14*

Fantastic Southeast Asian delights in a chic and intimate setting.
1 Bedfordbury, Covent Garden ☎ 7379 4580 ⊖ Leicester Square £–££

spanish

Bar Gansa ⚲A2
Spanish for goose – a noisy, spirited tapas bar.
2 Inverness Street, Camden ☎ 7267 8909 ⊖ Camden Town £

☆ CAMBIO DE TERCIO ⚲C17
In a quiet backwater between Earl's Court and Gloucester Road, this is a new wave Spanish restaurant where good ingredients are lovingly prepared and cooked. Gourmets will want to start with a plate of exquisite Jabugo ham, from acorn-fed black pigs. Tapas (grilled octopus, *gazpacho*, clams cooked in garlic and paprika) come on big plates; rich, savoury main courses such as cod with a pimento crust, or Segovian suckling pig, show the hand of a chef who really cares about Spain's often-neglected cuisine.
163 Old Brompton Road, South Kensington ☎ 7244 8970
⊖ Gloucester Road ££–£££

Gaudi Restaurante ⚲C9
Elegant and Iberian in flavour. Imaginative concoctions are carried off with flair.
63b Clerkenwell Road, Clerkenwell ☎ 7608 3220 ⊖ Farringdon ££–£££

☆ MORO ⚲A9
Quietly chic rather than screamingly 'designer', this roomy, southern-Mediterranean-style restaurant has proved an instant hit with the local design and media crowd who pile in for treats such as roast cod with caramelized onions and wood roasted pork with quince aioli and rocket. Drinkers at the bar can pick at tapas throughout the day as they quaff the largely Spanish wine list, which includes excellent chilled sherries.
34–36 Exmouth Market, Clerkenwell ☎ 7833 8336
⊖ Angel; Farringdon ££–£££

teas

☆ BROWN'S ⚲C13
Classic English tea served in country-house style – easy to stay all afternoon.
30–34 Albemarle Street, Mayfair ☎ 7518 4108 ⊖ Green Park ££

☆ THE RITZ ⚲C13
Classiest tea in town.
Piccadilly, St James's ☎ 7493 8181 ⊖ Green Park £££

☆ SOTHEBY'S ⚲F6
Trad English tea with scrummy homemade cakes.
34–35 New Bond Street, Mayfair ☎ 7293 5077 ⊖ Bond Street £–££

☆ T-BAR *D5*

Over 50 varieties of tea from Earl Grey to monkey-picked oolong!

72 Baker Street, Marylebone ☎ 7224 1165 ⊖ Baker Street £

turkish

Gallipoli *A3*

A good value, modern Turkish restaurant, which has brought the simple Near-Eastern delights of hummus, aubergine and grilled meats to Islington's culinarily curious. The ambience is amiably ramshackle and pavement chairs and tables are available for fair-weather dining.

102 Upper Street, Islington ☎ 7359 0630 ⊖ Highbury & Islington £

☆ OZER *E7*

Traditional Ottoman cuisine was always a case of adopt and adapt and this Modern Ottaman restaurant is part of the next evolutionary phase. In addition to sensational meze (*borek*, *tabbouleh*, falafel and all the rest), the menu focuses on fish and veggie dishes: vegetables and fragrant herbs in smokey-flavoured aubergine, pan-fried salmon served with stewed courgette, tomato, and okra, with the perfect dessert being a parchment parcel of mixed fruits steamed in Turkish melissa tea. The decor is recognizably Ottoman too with lighting inspired by Istanbul's Blue Mosque and traditional glass lamp holders suspended from a copper raft.

4–5 Langham Place, Marylebone ☎ 7482 5065 ⊖ Oxford Circus ££

Sofra *A14*

Turkish food in a streamlined brasserie setting.

18 Shepherd Street, Covent Garden ☎ 7493 3320 ⊖ Leicester Square £

vegetarian

Café Santé *A14*

Upbeat ethnic, serving cosmopolitan vegetarian fare.

17 Garrick Street, Covent Garden ☎ 7240 7811 ⊖ Leicester Square £

Cranks *E7*

A wholefood approach to the café experience.

8 Marshall Street, Soho ☎ 7437 9431 ⊖ Oxford Circus £

Food For Thought *E7*

A veggie favourite, offering wholesome global dishes.

31 Neal Street, Covent Garden ☎ 7836 0239 ⊖ Covent Garden £

☆ THE GATE *off map*

Probably the best veggie food in west London is served in the Gate's airy,

not-so-mellow-yellow dining room. Seasonal ingredients are imaginatively combined in a monthly-changing menu full of Mediterranean zing as well as other global influences, from wild mushroom risotto to haloumi *kibi*. If the weather's good, dine in the walled courtyard outside. Staff are helpful and accommodating; clientele rather civilized; and wines are regular, organic – and for the seriously committed – even vegan.
51 Queen Caroline Street, Hammersmith ☎ 8748 6932 ⊖ Hammersmith ££

☆ MILDRED'S *F7*
Changing every week, the imaginative and varied veggie menu at this small, friendly and down-to-earth eaterie spans the world. Vegans are well catered for and non-vegetarians should not be hit too hard, with dishes like stir-fry with tiger prawns, and meatless burgers featuring regularly. The close proximity of tables encourages chatter among strangers – the usual interesting Soho mix.
58 Greek Street, Soho ☎ 7494 1634 ⊖ Tottenham Court Road £–££

Royal Teas *off map*
A tiny, simple veggie café with outside seating.
76 Royal Hill, Greenwich ☎ 8691 7270 Greenwich £

Veg *F11*
This Chinese restaurant boasts an entirely meat- and fish-free menu, offering veggie versions of the classics.
8 Egerton Gardens Mews, Knightsbridge ☎ 7584 7007 ⊖ South Kensington £

vietnamese

Saigon *off map*
Traditional decor, silk-clad waitresses, and simply the best crispy aromatic duck.
16 Nelson Road, Greenwich ☎ 8853 0414 Greenwich ££

☆ VIET-HOA *A10*
The best and most authentic Vietnamese restaurant in town still looks and feels like the Vietnamese community centre it once was, despite the move to larger premises. Decor is simple, and the school-hall tables are full of exiles wolfing down bowls of *pho* (noodle soup with prawns or chicken) and spring rolls far more flavoursome than anything on a Saigon food stall. There are also delicious salads: try *goi* – a tangy mixture of shredded vegetables with chicken and prawns; and a huge selection of stir-fry dishes.
70–72 Kingsland Road, Hoxton ☎ 7729 8293 ⊖ Old Street £–££

bars

Good-time London revolves around a dizzying array of pubs and bars. Whether it's Soho's drinking dens, Notting Hill's chic watering holes, an historic inn, or a shiny temple to modernism, London's drinking culture is delightfully disparate.

bars & art

Freud *E7*

Accommodating an unusual melange of the stylishly attired and the bodily pierced, this is a smokey basement bar doubling as exhibition space.

198 Shaftesbury Ave, Covent Garden ☎ 7240 9933 ⊖ Covent Garden

ICA *D3*

Often described as London's best kept secret (although it's not anymore), the bar at the ICA is as cutting edge as the gallery itself. Clean, slick and attracting a trendy, arty (if somewhat pretentious) crowd; Sex Pistol mogul Malcom McLaren was spotted here.

The Mall, St James's ☎ 7930 2402 ⊖ Charing Cross; Piccadilly Circus

291 *B10*

Situated in up-and-coming Hackney, 291 is an arts space in a converted church, with the bar tucked round the side. Drawing a diverse crowd of East End trendies and locals, it gets busy at the weekends.

291 Hackney Road, Hackney ☎ 7613 5686 ⊖ Old Street

☆ ROSEMARY BRANCH *off map*

An idiosyncratic gem, tucked away in the heart of bohemian artist-land. Regular exhibitions, smart-art decor, and a truly eccentric, creative clientele make this an exceptional pub.

2 Shepperton Rd, Islington ☎ 7704 2730 ⊖ Highbury & Islington

bar/restaurants

☆ EST *D3*

A clean, vaguely transatlantic bar/restaurant benefiting from a good location.

54 Frith Street, Soho ☎ 7437 0666 ⊖ Leicester Square

Hush *D3*

A gorgeous bar/restaurant. The food's nothing special, so head upstairs to sip cocktails at the bar.

8 Lancashire Court, New Bond Street ☎ 7659 1500 ⊖ Bond Street

Mezzo ⌖F7
For those wishing to take part in Conran's ever-stylish vision of global domination, step this way.
100 Wardour Street, Soho ☎ 7314 4000 ⊖ Tottenham Court Road

cigar bars

☆ BOISDALE ⌖D18
Over 50 different sorts of well-kept, quality cigars – some old, some new – are the perfect accompaniment to the fine malts in this wood-panelled cocoon.
15 Eccleston Street, Belgravia ☎ 7730 6922 ⊖ Victoria

☆ CHE ⌖C13
This smoker's paradise has the largest cigar collection of any bar in the world. A wall-length humidor contains the 70-plus varieties.
23 St James's Street, St James's ☎ 7747 9380 ⊖ Green Park

☆ CLARIDGE'S BAR ⌖A13
The New York trend for cigar bars has hit Mayfair.
Brook Street, Mayfair ☎ 7429 8860 ⊖ Bond Street

club bars

☆ AKA ⌖F7
The latest addition to DJ Mr C's club, The End, AKA is a bar-restaurant that takes pre-club drinking to a new level. Artfully designed, it attracts a smart older crowd and can be hard to get into.
18 West Central Street, Bloomsbury ☎ 7836 0110 ⊖ Tottenham Court Road

The Aquarium ⌖B10
A Hoxton haunt, playing old-skool breaks.
256 Old Street, Hoxton ☎ 7251 6136 ⊖ Old Street

☆ BAR VINYL ⌖A2
Is it a bar? Is it a club? Is it a record shop? Camden's Bar Vinyl takes the overlap to its logical extreme, selling records, playing them, and serving drinks and tasty snacks to an energetic, music-mad crowd.
6 Inverness Street, Camden ☎ 7681 7898 ⊖ Camden Town

Beat Bar ⌖A1
A funky hang-out, with nights ranging from drum'n' bass to R&B.
265 Portobello Road, Notting Hill ☎ 7792 2043 ⊖ Ladbroke Grove

Blue Bar *D3*

A high-ceilinged, dark place, spun round an imposing central bar. Big with the urban rucksack crew, it has a solid reputation for good music and no-nonsense drinking.

257–259 Pentonville Road, King's Cross ☎ 7837 3218 ⊖ King's Cross

Bluu Bar *B10*

Upstairs it's pretty sleek; while in the basement are intimate cubby holes of soft seats, and DJs playing chilled tunes at conversation-friendly levels.

1 Hoxton Square, Hoxton ☎ 7613 2793 ⊖ Old Street

Bug Bar *off map*

Part of Brixton's invigorated nightlife, the Bug Bar is an intimate and easy-going place to drink late, deep in the crypt of an old church.

St Matthew's Church, Brixton Hill, Brixton ☎ 7738 3184 ⊖ Brixton

☆ DOGSTAR *off map*

Once just a pub, now a rejuvenated centre of cool. Half pub, half club, this is a shabby yet elegant monument to party monsters.

389 Coldharbour Lane, Brixton ☎ 7733 7515 ⊖ Brixton

Dragon Bar *B10*

With fantastic DJ sets (Thu–Sat) providing a friendly crowd with everything from East Coast hip-hop to James Brown.

5 Leonard Street, Hoxton ☎ 7490 7110 ⊖ Old Street

Dust *C9*

Hums at the weekend with a trendy crowd when DJs up the beat.

27 Clerkenwell Road, Clerkenwell ☎ 7490 5120 ⊖ Farringdon

Ego *F7*

DJs provide the soundtrack to an often-international crowd.

23–24 Bateman Street, Soho ☎ 7437 1977 ⊖ Tottenham Court Road

☆ EMBASSY BAR *B3*

DJs from a handful of London's best labels and record shops (Nuphonic, Atlas, Disque) make this a fail-safe place to kick-start a long night off the rails.

119 Essex Road, Islington ☎ 7359 7882 ⊖ Angel

☆ FRIDGE BAR *off map*

Open virtually round-the-clock at weekends, late night really does mean late here. The Fridge Bar is an exceptionally busy haunt for locals and can't-go-home-yet clubbers who get down on the basement dance floor.

Town Hill Parade, Brixton Hill, Brixton ☎ 7326 5100 ⊖ Brixton

☆ **THE JUNCTION** *off map*

This dark, horseshoe-shaped bar has created an intimate, exciting spot at the centre of bar/club fusion. From the chill-out area to the dance floor, it's adored by club kids and drinkers alike.

242 Coldharbour Lane, Brixton ☎ 7274 6696 ⊖ Brixton

The Light *D3*

Airy and industrial; the restaurant serves affordable, if uninspiring, food; and there are DJs three nights a week (Thu–Sat).

233 Shoreditch High St, Shoreditch ☎ 7247 8989 ⊖ Shoreditch

Plastic People *D3*

A previously-roving night that's now planted its roots here to play Latino, house, soul, and hip-hop to a clued-up crowd into the wee hours.

147–149 Curtain Road, Hoxton ☎ 7739 6471 ⊖ Old Street

Pop *F7*

A kitsch red and wood 60s decor creates a warm atmosphere in this clubby bar which draws a lively, up-for-it crowd.

14 Soho Street, Soho ☎ 7734 4004 ⊖ Tottenham Court Road

☆ **SALMON & COMPASS** *E3*

A pub by virtue of its architecture, but a club/bar in all other respects. DJs and a dance floor make for a hectic night out.

58 Penton Street, Islington ☎ 7837 3891 ⊖ Angel

The Social *B13*

Small, stark, and super-cool, The Social leads the way in the revitalisation of Noho. Packed at weekends, with excellent DJs and bands pulling the crowds, it epitomises downbeat London chic.

5 Little Portland Street, Noho ☎ 7636 4992 ⊖ Oxford Circus

Sound *D3*

A teen-dream with mock leopardskin chairs, and MTV Live playing. Frequented by pop kids, tourists, and music industry types. The odd album launch closes off parts to the masses, but enhances the star-spotting opportunities.

Swiss Centre, Leicester Square ☎ 7287 1010 ⊖ Leicester Square

☆ **TEA ROOMS DES ARTISTES** *off map*

Charming, historical, with a faded grandeur going back to the 16th century, this is the place for ambient jazz in a relaxed setting. Weekends hot up with DJs, live music, and a livelier crowd.

697 Wandsworth Road, Clapham ☎ 7652 6526 ⊖ Clapham Common

☆ **VIBE BAR** *off map*
Hyper-cool, with regular arts-led events, attracting young creative sparks. Discreetly lit, with heavy wooden tables and deep sofas, this is perfect for an intimate, if image-conscious, evening.
91–95 Brick Lane, Shoreditch ☎ 7377 2899 ⊖ Aldgate East; Liverpool St

WKD *B2*
With a music policy that changes almost nightly, rounded off with sometime live acts, WKD provides groovier Camdenites with a late-night haunt. Plus, a long happy hour (4–8pm daily) gets them going early.
18 Kentish Town Road, Camden ☎ 7267 1869 ⊖ Camden Town

cocktail joints

Brixtonian Havana Bar *off map*
Run by the extrovert Vincent Osborne (a rum-obsessive), the Brixtonian is a wonderfully eclectic taste of the downbeat Brixton lifestyle. Now in new, larger premises, the Brixtonian remains an SW9 institution.
11 Beehive Place, Brixton ☎ 7924 9262 ⊖ Brixton

☆ **COTTON'S** *off map*
A lively bar-restaurant offering a boisterous experience of West Indian culture. More than 30 different rums accompany sweet Caribbean dishes, and the friendly staff mix a mean Piña Colada. A rum celebration.
55 Chalk Farm Road, Camden ☎ 7482 1096 ⊖ Chalk Farm

Detroit *E7*
A groovy bat cave with a cocktail bar at its core and satellite booths to dine on modern British dishes.
35 Earlham Street, Covent Garden ☎ 7240 2662 ⊖ Covent Garden

☆ **DORCHESTER BAR** *D3*
Oh la la! If you want grown-up elegance, regardless of expense, then this is ideal. Relax in luxurious leather chairs, enjoying ultra-slick service (your cigarette is lit for you) and mouthwatering nibbles, while the pianist plays jazz in the background. A classic experience.
53 Park Lane, Mayfair ☎ 7629 8888 ⊖ Green Park

Lab *D3*
With a retro 70s look, this bar's massive cocktail list is supplemented by a fresh juice bar.
12 Old Compton Street, Soho ☎ 7437 7820 ⊖ Leicester Square

☆ LIQUID LOUNGE *A1*
It's blue, cube-shaped, and the sounds are provided by the resident DJ. The most popular tipple here? None other than the chic, but slightly ironic, vodka martini of course.
209 Westbourne Park Rd, Notting Hill ☎ 7243 0914 ⊖ Westbourne Park

Match Bar *D3*
Suited city boys gather for cocktails and good food.
45–47 Clerkenwell Road, Clerkenwell ☎ 7250 4002 ⊖ Farringdon

10 Tokyo Joe's *D3*
Run by the guys behind 10 Room and dishes out the same class of cocktails, albeit in a more lounge-core setting.
85 Piccadilly ☎ 7495 2595 ⊖ Piccadilly Circus

10 Room *A13*
The ultimate Soho bar experience: tough to gain entry, streetwise decor, and cocktails once you're in, it's always packed to bursting with über-trendy media types. Specially designed drinks menus provide weird and wonderful concoctions in a lush purple, pink, and red setting.
10 Air Street, Soho ☎ 7734 9990 ⊖ Piccadilly Circus

happy hours

Bar Sol Ona *D3*
A surprising basement hideaway in Soho, with loud Latin music and a *muy caliente* ambience.
17 Old Compton Street, Soho ☎ 7287 9932 ⊖ Leicester Square

Nubar *C3*
Epitomy of pub-cum-trendy bar; almost all-day happy hour at weekends.
196 Essex Road, Islington ☎ 7354 8886 ⊖ Angel

'O' Bar *D3*
One of the earlier newcomers to realize that customers wanted more than a pub, and it has become a club-cum-cattle market with youngsters guzzling pitchers of potent cocktails during happy hour.
83–85 Wardour Street, Soho ☎ 7437 3490 ⊖ Piccadilly Circus

South Circular *off map*
Bright Young Things of Battersea meet for a warm-up of happy hour cocktails in this intimate, stylish hang-out. DJs on Saturdays.
89 Battersea Rise, Battersea ☎ 7207 0170 ⊖ Clapham Junction

☆ **ALPHABET** *A13*
Situated within stumbling distance of central London's clubs, the very smart Alphabet also has a handy A–Z printed on the basement floor in case you get really lost. It's nicely clad in beige sofas and school-style tables.
61–63 Beak Street, Soho ☎ 7439 2190 ⊖ Oxford Circus

☆ **ATLANTIS** *C6*
Smart, marine-themed basement bar with kids' corner for self-styled Peter Pans, so expect Jenga and Connect 4 with your imported beer. DJs spin the latest tunes at weekends.
114–117 Crawford Street, Marylebone ☎ 7224 2878 ⊖ Baker Street

☆ **BABUSHKA** *A1*
Guest DJs entertain every night, or you can have a go yourself in the open-DJ slot (Mon–Tue). It has weekend BBQ's in the garden, a mixed and relaxed crowd, and a deserved reputation for understated cool.
41 Tavistock Crescent, Notting Hill ☎ 7727 9250 ⊖ Westbourne Park

☆ **BAR ROOM BAR** *off map*
A design-led drinking spot with an appealing patio attracting a hip following.
48 Rosslyn Hill, Hampstead ☎ 7435 0808 ⊖ Hampstead

☆ **CANTALOUPE** *B10*
Affords prime opportunities for lounging inside and doing some serious drinking, or sitting out at wide wooden tables and soaking up the fashionably relaxed vibe. Great food served out back.
35–42 Charlotte Road, Hoxton ☎ 7613 4411 ⊖ Old Street

The Clinic *D3*
The anti-fashion, anti-designer style makes it a trendy place to hang out and sup vodka-based drinks.
13 Gerrard Street, Soho ☎ 7734 9836 ⊖ Leicester Square

The Collection *D3*
Sashay along the uplit glass catwalk into a converted warehouse, where handsome bar staff serve cool cocktails to the beautiful people.
264 Brompton Road, South Kensington ☎ 7225 1212 ⊖ South Kensington

☆ **DENIM** *E7*
Image-conscious, but never alarmingly so, Denim's sci-fi interior has futuristic touches, such as a wall of pink monitor-style screens. Service is quick and friendly, but drinks are pricey and dining space limited.
4a Upper St Martin's Lane, Covent Garden ☎ 7497 0376 ⊖ Leicester Square

Fluid ⚲C9
Trendy Japanese beers and homemade sushi.
40 Charterhouse Street, Clerkenwell ☎ 7253 3444 ⊖ Farringdon

Freedom Brewing Company ⚲E7
The centrepiece of this new-school micro-brewery must be the huge copper vats in which unique beers are created. Food is modern British, the space minimalist and industrial.
41 Earlham Street, Covent Garden ☎ 7240 0606 ⊖ Covent Garden

Good Mixer ⚲A2
Bands like Blur and Echobelly allegedly once hung out here. That buzz might have moved on, but it's still popular with Camden's 'yoof'.
30 Inverness Street, Camden ☎ 7916 7929 ⊖ Camden Town

☆ HOME ⚲B10
When staying in became the new going out, Home styled itself around a down-at-heel living room and found itself at a premium. Popular with the artsy posse, it has shabby furniture and a refreshingly unassuming ambience.
100–106 Leonard Street, Hoxton ☎ 7684 8618 ⊖ Old Street

Hoxton Square Bar & Kitchen ⚲B10
A must on the circuit, where hip young things slouch on 70s sofas. Resident DJs play whatever happens to be flavour of the month.
2 Hoxton Square, Hoxton ☎ 7613 0709 ⊖ Old Street

☆ ION ⚲A1
A local chill-out zone with good jazz, funk and soul nights.
165 Ladbroke Grove, Notting Hill ☎ 8960 1702 ⊖ Ladbroke Grove

K Bar ⚲D3
For west London dahhlings on the West End razz.
84–86 Wardour Street, Soho ☎ 7439 4393 ⊖ Piccadilly Circus

☆ LED ⚲A9
Street level is a pale red diner, but the basement bar is a fiery nether world of deepest red. Drinks range from smoothies to draft lager, and every Wednesday there's a playstation league.
171 Farringdon Road, Clerkenwell ☎ 7278 4400 ⊖ Farringdon

☆ LUPO ⚲F7
Twentysomething media-darlings drink under dramatic plaster reliefs of cherubs and a lion's head. A labyrinthine concoction of rooms, Lupo is the Soho expert's choice.
50 Dean Street, Soho ☎ 7434 3399 ⊖ Tottenham Court Road

☆ **MARKET BAR** *⌕A1*

High ceilings, wood carvings, heavy tapestry drapes and huge candles give this space a gothic feel. Funky live music pulls in a mixed-age, bohemian crowd. Loud, but not lairy, the Market Bar is a vibrant experience.

240a Portobello Road, Notting Hill ☎ 7229 6472 ⊖ Ladbroke Grove

The Medicine Bar *⌕A3*

A fashionable Islington bar. There are DJs on Friday and Saturday nights when it's supposedly members only.

181 Upper Street, Islington ☎ 7704 8056 ⊖ Highbury & Islington

Monarch *⌕A2*

There's a good chance of spotting a star here

49 Chalk Farm Road, Camden ☎ 7916 1049 ⊖ Camden Town

Neon *⌕off map*

London is plagued with cold, minimal bars, but Neon is one that pulls it off. In bohemian Brixton, this luscious bar attracts a clued-up crowd who indulge in good-time drinking and great Italian rustic food.

71 Atlantic Road, Brixton ☎ 7738 6576 ⊖ Brixton

☆ **PHARMACY** *⌕F1*

Designed by enfant-terrible, Damien Hirst, this is celeb central. Clinical white design, medicinal artwork, and the sort of chic that comes only fleetingly.

150 Notting Hill Gate, Notting Hill ☎ 7221 2442 ⊖ Notting Hill Gate

Saint *⌕D3*

The choosy door staff select the privileged (and most beautiful). Late-night drinking may be enough of an incentive to risk humiliation.

8 Great Newport Street, Soho ☎ 7240 1551 ⊖ Leicester Square

☆ **SHOREDITCH ELECTRICITY SHOWROOM** *⌕B10*

Unconventionally housed in this former showroom, the SES is inspired by functional utility, and frequented by lo-fi trendies. Formica tables foster a low-budget 1960s look and all the juices used for mixers are freshly squeezed.

39a Hoxton Square, Hoxton ☎ 7739 6934 ⊖ Old Street

Two Floors *⌕A13*

Offers, naturally, two floors of an easy drinking nature.

3 Kingly Street, Soho ☎ 7439 1007 ⊖ Piccadilly Circus

☆ VOODOO LOUNGE *D3*

Avoid the members-only bar on the ground floor and head upstairs where lesser mortals are allowed. The Voodoo Lounge lures the cream of Soho into their Leicester Square rooms with themed flame and mirror bars.

7–9 Leicester Square, Leicester Square ☎ 7434 0606 ⊖ Leicester Square

hotel bars

The George *D3*

The George is Conran's idea of a typical English pub, serving classic Brit food and a disappointingly limited array of beers.

Great Eastern Hotel, 40 Liverpool Street ☎ 7618 7400 ⊖ Liverpool Street

The Lobby Bar *E7*

In the (yep, you guessed it) lobby of One Aldwych, this immaculately turned-out bar attracts a mixed and friendly crowd.

One Aldwych Hotel, 1 Aldwych, The Strand ☎ 7300 1000 ⊖ Covent Garden

Long Bar *B13*

Great food and amazing cocktails are served in this very slick, Dali-esque bar designed by Philippe Starck.

Sanderson Hotel, 50 Berners Street, North Soho ☎ 7300 1444 ⊖ Oxford Circus

Met Bar *F12*

Access to London's allegedly coolest cocktail zone, is unrestricted during the day, but reserved for its posey celebrity/media members after 6pm.

Metropolitan Hotel, 19 Old Park Lane, Mayfair ☎ 7447 1000 ⊖ Hyde Park Corner

Mybar *F7*

An ever-so-happening hang-out for cocktails and sushi.

Myhotel, 11–13 Bayley Street, Bloomsbury ☎ 7667 6000 ⊖ Tottenham Court Road

☆ TRADER VIC'S *F12*

This Polynesian fantasy is pure kitsch: whether you consider it a fabulous or odious example of the genre depends on your taste – or how many rum cocktails you've had. Sip a Mai Tai cocktail to Latin music.

Hilton Hotel, 22 Park Lane, Mayfair ☎ 7208 4113 ⊖ Hyde Park Corner

irish pubs

☆ FILTHY MCNASTY'S *⌕A9*
Favoured Irish drinking spot with strong modern literary connections. Aural treats too, with regular readings (Tue & Thu) from the likes of Will Self.
68 Amwell Street, Islington ☎ 7837 6067 ⊖ Angel

The Liberties Bar *⌕D2*
A long-established Irish pub, which still pulls in the exiles to watch traditional sports on weekend afternoons, with a spot of Gaelic partying later on.
100 Camden High Street, Camden ☎ 7485 4019 ⊖ Camden Town

☆ O'HANLON *⌕A9*
Home-brewed beers, hearty food, and Irish without resorting to clichés, this watering hole warms the cockles of your heart. Once bitten, always smitten.
8 Tysoe Street, Clerkenwell ☎ 7837 4112 ⊖ Angel

☆ TOUCAN *⌕F7*
A dark-fronted Soho pub on two levels, serving good Guinness and tasty Irish food. There's a good selection of Irish whiskey in the basement.
19 Carlisle Street, Soho ☎ 7437 4123 ⊖ Tottenham Court Road

late night bars

Bar Solo *⌕D3*
Drink late without paying to get in. As one of few late-openers in the area it's usually packed late on.
20 Inverness Street, Camden ☎ 7482 4611 ⊖ Camden Town

Café Bohème *⌕D3*
A pleasant Parisian-style Soho brasserie open 23 hours Fridays and Saturdays and 'til 3am other nights.
13 Old Compton Street, Soho ☎ 7734 0623 ⊖ Leicester Square

Charlie Wright's International Bar *⌕B10*
The place to be; and it's open later than most.
45 Pitfield Street, Hoxton ☎ 7490 8345 ⊖ Old Street

Lounge-jing *⌕D3*
More kitsch than classy, this is a bar/restaurant with a late license (to 3am), mixing up ambience and trance to a mixed group of punters.
29 Old Burlington Street, Piccadilly ☎ 7437 9933 ⊖ Piccadilly Circus

Po Na Na ₰C18
This late-night bar has an upbeat scene.
316 King's Road, Chelsea ☎ 7352 4552 ⊖ Sloane Square

Sand *₰off map*
Straight out of the Sahara and dropped in Clapham, the lovely Sand oozes North African charm. Sup cocktails with a party crowd 'til 2am every night.
156 Clapham Park Road, Clapham ☎ 7622 3022 ⊖ Clapham Common

The Spot ₰E7
An after-hours hang-out attracting a mixed twentysomething party crowd.
29 Maiden Lane, Covent Garden ☎ 7379 5900 ⊖ Covent Garden

live music

Bartok ₰A2
What was once the Engine Room, is now this stylishly converted bar which dispenses drinks from a pink neon back-lit bar to the sound of live classical music.
78–79 Chalk Farm Road, Camden ☎ 7916 0595 ⊖ Camden Town

Dublin Castle ₰B2
The gig for indie bands starting the climb to the top.
94 Parkway, Camden ☎ 7485 1773 ⊖ Camden Town

Falcon *₰off map*
Probably the oldest indie venue in the area.
234 Royal College Street, Camden ☎ 7485 3834 ≡ Camden Road

Jazz Café ₰D2
Still one of the major stops on the jazz/soul circuit, where you can hang out, drink, eat, and see some excellent bands.
5 Parkway, Camden ☎ 7916 6060 ⊖ Camden Town

pool bars

Elbow Room ₰D3
One of the best spots to sink a cold pint and play some serious pool. With nine tables and a reasonable rate, it can't be beaten.
103 Westbourne Grove, Bayswater ☎ 7221 5211 ⊖ Bayswater

The Pool ₰B10
Doesn't quite live up to its name (there are only three pool tables), but it's a great place to hang out, with big beats, and even bigger beanbags.
104–108 Curtain Road, Hoxton ☎ 7739 9608 ⊖ Old Street

☆ ALBION *A3*

A resolutely old-style pub, with cozy corners, down-to-earth beers, brilliant Sunday roasts, and patios. Full of content locals – a real public haven.

10 Thornhill Road, Islington ☎ 7607 7450 ⊖ Angel

Blenheim *D3*

Despite a make-over, this still retains a local pub feel. Relaxed, comfortable, and serving good beer... in fact everything a pub should be.

27 Cale Street, South Kensington ☎ 7349 0056 ⊖ South Kensington

☆ BRICKLAYER'S ARMS *B10*

The prime example of down-at-heel Hoxton chic; bohemians and art students are joined by media bods to play table football and sup the most affordable drinks in the area. Doorstep sandwiches a speciality.

63 Charlotte Road, Hoxton ☎ 7739 5245 ⊖ Old Street

The Camden Head *C3*

Quite happily stuck in a time warp with an interior full of splendid mirrored Victoriana.

2 Camden Walk, Camden ☎ 7359 0851 ⊖ Camden Town

Chelsea Potter *C18*

One of the liveliest and most characterful pubs on the King's Road.

119 King's Road, Chelsea ☎ 7352 9479 ⊖ Sloane Square

Coach & Horses *F7*

Crowded, louche, and presided over by London's self-styled 'rudest landlord', the Coach & Horses fields a fascinating mix of winners, losers, drunks, and hipsters that makes it easy to understand how its been incorporated into Soho's rich mythology.

29 Greek Street, Soho ☎ 7437 5920 ⊖ Tottenham Court Road

Cooper's Arms *C18*

A more contemporary version of the trad pub, where the old-fashioned character has been lifted by a few minimalist touches.

87 Flood Street, Chelsea ☎ 7376 3120 ⊖ Sloane Square

The Crown *E3*

A spruced up pub with a reasonable menu accompanied by good Fullers beer.

116 Cloudesley Road, Islington ☎ 7837 7107 ⊖ Angel

Cutty Sark Tavern *off map*
A well-kept secret dating from 1804. It has a roaring fire in winter, and is a tranquil spot to sit out in summer.
4–6 Ballast Quay, Greenwich ☎ 8858 3146 Greenwich

De Hems *D3*
London's only Dutch pub – very friendly.
11 Macclesfield Street, Soho ☎ 7437 2494 ⊖ Leicester Square

Dog & Duck *F7*
Famed for its tiled interior and excellent ales.
18 Bateman Street, Soho ☎ 7437 4447 ⊖ Tottenham Court Road

Duke of Wellington *C1*
The Portobello Road pub, known locally as Finch's since the 50s when it was part of a chain of beatnik pubs. It's a plain old boozer which gets packed with alternative types, groovy twenty-somethings, and old soaks.
179 Portobello Road, Notting Hill ☎ 7727 6727 ⊖ Notting Hill Gate

☆ FLASK *off map*
The joy of a proper pub! This Hampstead hideaway is tucked down a pedestrianized alley. Delicious home-cooked food, no-nonsense drinking, and a standard that others rarely reach.
14 Flask Walk, Hampstead ☎ 7435 4580 ⊖ Hampstead

☆ FOX & HOUNDS *C18*
The Fox & Hounds offers a gentle reminder of pub times past. No music, just the hum of conversation and the chinking of glasses...
29 Passmore Street, Belgravia ☎ 7730 6367 ⊖ Sloane Square

Freemason's Arms *off map*
Next to the Hampstead Heath, and with the largest beer garden around, this has been transformed into an upmarket pub.
32 Downshire Hill, Hampstead ☎ 7433 6811 ⊖ Hampstead

French House Dining Room *D3*
Perennially cool – small, busy, and atmospheric; during WWII it was the centre of the French Resistance in exile.
49 Dean Street, Soho ☎ 7437 2477 ⊖ Leicester Square

The George *F7*
A good old-fashioned pub in the heart of Soho.
1 D'Arblay Street, Soho ☎ 7439 1911 ⊖ Oxford Circus

☆ GRENADIER *F12*
If it's rush-free calm you prize in a pub, this one is an ideal respite. Stacked military and drinking-related antiques line the walls, the ale is real, and the atmosphere has a confidence that comes only with age.
18 Wilton Row, Knightsbridge ☎ 7235 3074 ⊖ Hyde Park Corner

The Hollybush *D3*
An authentic English pub, dating back to 1797. It has regular poetry nights on Tuesdays in the Spinning Room.
23 Holly Mount, Hampstead ☎ 7435 2892 ⊖ Hampstead

Hope & Sir Loin *D3*
100% genuine; a market trader's pub, where you can drink from 6.30am. Their breakfasts are an institution.
94 Cowcross Street, Clerkenwell ☎ 7253 8525 ⊖ Farringdon

Intrepid Fox *D3*
Goths will find their Valhalla here. Black-painted fingernails are *de rigueur*.
99 Wardour Street, Soho ☎ 7287 8359 ⊖ Tottenham Court

The Island Queen *D3*
A popular, big established pub with a maritime feel, located on Noel Road, where 30-odd years ago the playwright Joe Orton was killed by his lover Ken Halliwell.
87 Noel Road, Islington ☎ 7226 0307 ⊖ Angel

Jerusalem Tavern *D3*
With its snug cubby holes, is great. The interior's only a few years old but summons up an enjoyable London-via-Disney vibe.
55 Britton Street, Clerkenwell ☎ 7490 4281 ⊖ Farringdon

The King's Head *A3*
The most celebrated pub in Islington, which has a confusing policy of charging in pre-decimal money, and is home to one of London's oldest pub-theatres.
115 Upper Street, Islington ☎ 7226 0364 Ⅲ Essex Road

Lamb & Flag *D3*
The perfect example of the trad British pub: quaint, nostalgic, and bustling.
33 Rose Street, Covent Garden ☎ 7497 9504 ⊖ Leicester Square

☆ **NARROW BOAT** *E3*
Perfect for outdoor summer drinking. Stand on the balcony of this boat-decked pub, and just watch the world go by along the canal towpath. Sunday's acoustic open mic session is a crowd-puller.
119 St Peter's Street, Islington ☎ 7288 9821 ⊖ Angel

The Old Red Lion *E3*
A prime example of a friendly London boozer with a theatre upstairs.
418 St John Street, Islington ☎ 7837 7816 ⊖ Angel

☆ **PHENE ARMS** *C18*
As English as pubs come, the Phene (rhymes with genie) is a well-placed supping spot, with an even better placed terrace. Positively dripping with shabby elegance and charm, it's a Chelsea jewel.
9 Phene Street, Chelsea ☎ 7352 3294 ⊖ Sloane Square then 🚌 11, 19, 22

Red Lion *D3*
A neighbourhood pub that delivers the style of 19th-century London without resorting to faux Victoriana. Home-style cooking is a plus.
1 Waverton Street, Mayfair ☎ 7499 1307 ⊖ Green Park; Hyde Park Corner

Reliance *B10*
Tries its best to get on the pre-clubbing circuit, with DJs at weekends, but sits better in the few-beers-with-your-mates genre.
336 Old Street, Hoxton ☎ 7729 6888 ⊖ Old Street

Richard I *D3*
A friendly boozer tucked away on Royal Hill. Its big garden is a fine place to sample good, simple, home-cooked pub grub.
52–54 Royal Hill, Greenwich ☎ 8692 2996 🚆 Greenwich

Royal Oak *D3*
Do Columbia Road's Sunday Flower Market in style and grab a champagne breakfast here.
73 Columbia Road, Bethnal Green ☎ 7739 8204 ⊖ Bethnal Green

Surprise *C18*
A perfect specimen of the English pub. Sketches of Chelsea life line the walls and classic pub pastimes, like darts and dominoes, are on offer.
6 Christchurch Terrace, Chelsea ☎ 7349 1821 ⊖ Sloane Square

Three Kings *D3*
A welcoming and eccentric watering hole: in summer, drinkers take their ales into the churchyard opposite.
7 Clerkenwell Close, Clerkenwell ☎ 7253 0483 ⊖ Farringdon

Trafalgar Tavern *off map*
This place has hardly changed since it opened in 1837. Whitebait used to be caught in the river nearby, and remains a speciality on the menu. Live bands pack the house on Friday and Saturday nights.
Park Row, Greenwich ☎ 7858 2437 Greenwich

The White Horse *B13*
An old school pub colonized by the young crowd employed in Soho's creative industries.
16 Newburgh Street, Soho ☎ 7479 7971 ⊖ Oxford Circus

☆ YE OLDE WHITE BEAR *off map*
The best way to enjoy this pub (just a short amble from Hampstead Heath), is lingering over a pint and partaking of a plate of cod and chips. Very amiable and highly recommended. Thursday is quiz night.
New End, Hampstead ☎ 7435 3758 ⊖ Hampstead

sports bars

☆ SHOELESS JOE'S *D3*
Popular with the rugby crowd – a great place to watch a big match.
Temple Place, Embankment ☎ 7240 7865 ⊖ Embankment

☆ SPORTS CAFÉ *D13*
Cavernous central London theme bar; lots of post-office Friday-night fever.
80 Haymarket, St James's ☎ 7839 8300 ⊖ Piccadilly Circus

☆ TERRY NEILL'S SPORTS BAR & BRASSERIE *E7*
Functional drinks and ubiquitous televised sport.
53 Holborn Viaduct ☎ 7329 6653 ⊖ Farringdon

theme bars

Bierodrome *D3*
In true Belgian style it has over 200 varieties of beer and tubes of chips and mayo can be bought from the bar.
173–174 Upper Street, Islington ☎ 7226 5835 Essex Road

Café Kick *⚲A9*
Brimming with 60s Italian style, it gets its name from the old-style 'babyfoot' tables; photos of footballers; and the rules of the game ('no spinning') adorn the walls.
43 Exmouth Market, Clerkenwell ☎ 7837 8077 ⊖ Farringdon

La Perla *⚲E7*
Acts as a pedestal for a vast range of tequila and mezcal.
28 Maiden Lane, Covent Garden ☎ 7240 7400 ⊖ Covent Garden

The Player *⚲B13*
Like an 80s hotel bar; but it's meant to be like that, so sit back with a champagne cocktail and a healthy sense of irony. But turn up early 'cos it turns members-only in peak hours.
8–12 Broadwick Street, Soho ☎ 7494 9125 ⊖ Oxford Circus

wine bars

Bar du Musée *⚲off map*
A trendy bar which has an extensive wine list. There's a little garden but this place is best on chilly winter evenings when it's cozy.
17 Nelson Road, Greenwich ☎ 8858 4710 Ⅲ Greenwich

☆ CORK & BOTTLE *⚲D3*
Opened in the earliest days of night fever, and still vintage 70s. Pavement tables for people-watching and a splendid array of global wines make for a good time.
44–46 Cranbourn Street, Leicester Square ☎ 7734 7807 ⊖ Leicester Square

The Crescent *⚲D3*
This stylish yet cozy bolt hole has over 200 wines on its list, many available by the glass. The tiny bar soon fills up, but remains relaxing, and good food is available all day in the larger basement dining room.
99 Fulham Road, South Kensington ☎ 7225 2244 ⊖ South Kensington

☆ GORDON'S *⚲D3*
A lugubrious cellar bar with an ancient pedigree. Charmingly bereft of modern trappings, Gordon's boasts a solid selection of fortified wines.
47 Villiers Street, Strand ☎ 7930 1408 ⊖ Charing Cross; Embankment

☆ LA GRANDE MARQUE *⚲D3*
Previously incarnated as a bank, this site is still firmly tuned to the City crowd. Not even open on Saturday and Sunday, but well worth a weekday trip for the house champagne alone.
47 Ludgate Hill, City ☎ 7329 6709 ⊖ St Paul's

clubs

Since the house music explosion of the late 80s, London clubs have been the global epicentre of dance culture. Whilst pre-acid house pop-centred pick-up joints still exist, they have been superseded by a startling variety of musically innovative clubs playing house, soul, disco, hip-hop, drum & bass, techno, jungle, and speed garage. Whilst the ecstasy revolution is still apparent, the traditional stimulants of drink and enthusiasm are equally prevalent. Wherever you end up – a purpose-built superclub or low-key one-off – you'll discover a unique London vibe.

Africa Centre *E7*
Hots up on weekend club nights. Not as exotic as it sounds, but genuinely friendly. Club nights often feature live performances.
Africa Centre, 38 King Street, Covent Garden ☎ 7836 1973 ⊖ Covent Garden

The Annexe *F7*
A good, intimate place for the fun and funky.
1 Dean Street, Soho ☎ 7287 9608 ⊖ Tottemham Court Road

Bar Rumba *B13*
It may be located in touristy central London, but this is a glittering jewel of musical surprises. Long and lean, it provides sounds from the entire musical spectrum, although not usually all in one night. There's a quality continuum running through Rumba's club nights, so whether it's deep house, nu-skool breaks, drum & bass, or salsa, you can be assured of a top night. Monday's That's How It Is! is Peterson and Wilcox's long-running night, renowned for its open-minded approach to jazz and beats. Ace. Space features deep house from Luke Solomon and Kenny Hawkes, with top notch guests too – not bad for a Wednesday night. Movement, on Thursdays, is the city's finest drum & bass night. Reinforced beats from Bryan Gee, Ray Keith, and Tonic, and regular guests like Roni Size.
36 Shaftesbury Avenue, Soho ☎ 7287 2715 ⊖ Piccadilly Circus

Camden Palace *A2*
Head off to this famous Camden joint. Very studenty and young with huge queues who come for good garage nights.
1a Camden High Street, Camden ☎ 7387 04280 ⊖ Camden Town

Electric Ballroom *D2*
The drinks are expensive, but the extravagant setting – an old Music Hall theatre – can't be beaten.
184 Camden High Street, Camden ☎ 7247 8582 ⊖ Camden Town

The Colosseum *off map*
This is south London's premier garage and house venue, and home to garage spot, Underground Explosion.
1 Nine Elms Lane, Vauxhall ☎ 7720 3609 ⊖ Vauxhall

China White *B13*
You want glamour? Then China White's the spot for you. Notoriously tough to get into (being with a member or a beautiful female helps), China White is the place for champagne guzzling and très chic lounging. Comes into its own at the weekend.
6 Air Street, Soho ☎ 7343 0040 ⊖ Piccadilly Circus

The Cross *off map*
One of a brace of venues in the King's Cross area, The Cross encompasses a labyrinth of brick tunnels and, for when the weather's nice, a courtyard with a canal close by. Specialities are big, glittery house nights; it's the place to find London's Ibiza-ites off-season. Sunday's Vertigo features Italian house-style night full of friendly, dressy Italians. Really good.
Refurbishment has created three rooms with differing styles of music.
King's Cross Goods Yard, off York Way, King's Cross ☎ 7837 0828
⊖ King's Cross

The End *F7*
Owned by ex-Shamen Mr C, The End is designed with a futurist clubber in mind. All metallic edges and techno styling, it has a serious sound system. The music is equally steel-lined. Catch Thursday night's UK underground garage heaven, Atelier – the mixed crowd fuels this laid-back alternative to full-on clubbing, with emphasis on sophisticated mellow sounds. A slick, stylish kick-start to the weekend. Check out the club's smorgasboard of monthly one-offs. Sharp sound system.
Moody body searches.
18 West Central St, Tottenham Court Road, Covent Garden ☎ 7419 9199
⊖ Tottenham Court Road

Fabric C9

Is this the most important thing to have happened to London's club life? Could well be, what with the incredible roster of cutting edge dance nights that draw a clued-up party crowd to the converted meat storehouse that is Fabric. Fabric Live (every Friday of the month) is perhaps your strongest bet, fusing live music and DJs together into a blend of uptempo beats. 👍 Best sound system in Britain. 👎 The queues to get in can verge on the ridiculous.

❶ Try and get into the VIP room; the balcony is great.

77a Charterhouse Street, Clerkenwell ☎ 7490 0444 ⊖ Farringdon

Hanover Grand E7

A spacious Piccadilly venue where glamorous, glitzy club kids come to dress up, dazzle each other, and dance to sugarcoated swing, funky drum & bass, and big-tune house and garage. 👍 Check out Saturday's flagship Future Perfect for a very London, high-profile house night. Wednesday's Fresh 'n' Funky is the club's popular R&B night, where hip-hop, underground garage, and swing meet with dressed-up girls and soul. Busy, so arrive early.

6 Hanover Street, Soho ☎ 7499 7977 ⊖ Oxford Circus

Home B13

The last word in purpose-built clubs, Home is a megaclub with seven storeys, three dancefloors, a restaurant, a street-level café, and a glass elevator. Based in Leicester Square, so you'll have to fight your way through the crowds, but once inside, big name DJs like Danny Rampling and Paul Oakenfold take control. Check out Highrise – an eclectic mix of party beats each and every Thursday, from residents Jon Carter and Tayo.

1 Leicester Square, Leicester Square ☎ 7909 1111 ⊖ Leicester Square

Le Scandale F7

Boasts a different theme every night, ranging from rock to indie.

54 Berwick Street, Soho ☎ 7437 6830 ⊖ Oxford Circus

Madame Jo Jo's E7

Disco divas head here for glitzy glamour, with its fabulous drag cabarets (Thu–Sat).

8–10 Brewer Street, Soho ☎ 7734 3040 ⊖ Oxford Circus

Mass *off map*

Currently jumping with exciting nights, Brixton is home to a plethora of innovative clubs and cool scuzzy venues. Mass is one of the newest and largest, operating in the revamped Brix. The music centres around deep house, drum & bass, techno, funk & trance – and the club prides itself on its facilities for live bands. Popular, youthful, and friendly.

St Matthew's Church, Brixton Hill, Brixton ☎ 7274 6470 ⊖ Brixton

Ministry of Sound *off map*

Opened in the early 90s as London's answer to New York über-clubbing, Ministry of Sound started the UK superclub boom. A spacious venue with impeccable sound system attracting dressed-up club kids, and uplifting house nights hosted by the finest jocks the US can fly over. It's no surprise that Ministry's hard to get into. The club's original 'no alcohol' rule has long been overturned. Move on Fridays is a popular choice.

103 Gaunt Street, Elephant & Castle ☎ 7378 6528 ⊖ Elephant & Castle

Notting Hill Arts Club *F1*

Tucked away in West London, the NHAC is part of the new breed of nightclub that caters to a crowd that wants more than banging house tunes and E-monsters. Consequently, this minimalist paean to concrete hosts a selection of rotating monthly nights including Eastern breakbeat outfits like Outcaste. Saturday's Brazilian Love Affair sees authentic Brazilian funk and bossa novas at this fortnightly affair.

An eclectic mix of music and art; the one-off exhibitions.

21 Notting Hill Gate, Notting Hill ☎ 7460 4459 ⊖ Notting Hill Gate

Ronnie Scott's *F7*

For the older, more mellow crowd – the legendary, Ronnie Scott's is still jazz-central offering a well-established favourite with an impressive line-up of artists.

47 Frith Street, Soho ☎ 7439 0747 ⊖ Oxford Circus

Scala *off map*

Slap bang in the heart of King's Cross, London's sleaze central, is the Scala. This former porn cinema and notorious pool hall is now one of London's foremost club and live music venues, hosting hedonistic Saturday night sessions of breaks and beats, Sonic Mook Experiment. Check if London's premier hip-hop night Scratch is on (monthly Thursdays). One of the liveliest, messiest crowds in London. The walk back through shifty King's Cross; it's a maze inside, so don't get lost.

275 Pentonville Road, King's Cross ☎ 7833 2022 ⊖ King's Cross; St Pancras

Subterania ⌕A1

Compact west London venue, with a handy balcony overlooking the oval dance floor. Subterania hosts Rotation on Friday, a block-rocking R&B party, with hefty chunks of hip-hop, soul, and jazz that keep the dance floor jumping – and new house event, Soulsonic. A generally relaxed venue with R&B leanings, given to engendering a bumping party feel.
12 Acklam Road, Notting Hill ☎ 8960 4590 ⊖ Ladbroke Grove

333 ⌕A10

Now the Blue Note has departed, the 333 is in the enviable position of being the only major nightclub in very hip Hoxton. Subject to much discussion over its state of (dis)repair, the venue has undergone a major facelift. The London home of down-tempo hip-hop and leftfield breakbeats, 333 goes from strength to strength. ♨ Saturday's Off Centre sees left of field hip-hop, jazz, breakbeat drum, and house.
333 Old Street, Shoreditch ☎ 7739 1800 ⊖ Old Street

Turnmills ⌕C9

Clerkenwell's number one spot for late, late hedonism, Turnmills was one of London's first venues with all-night licensing. Home to the hugely popular Gallery – full-on handbag house on a Friday, with an up-for-it, unpretentious crowd, and a chill-out room – and Europe's most famous gay night, Trade. Headstart is proof that you *can* get cutting edge house and electro on a Saturday night, what with the Kahuna Brothers and Carl Clarke as residents. Nice, very nice. The club is much loved by its followers, and has a top-notch sound system to boot.
63b Clerkenwell Road, Clerkenwell ☎ 7250 3409 ⊖ Farringdon

practical information

Magazines like *Sleaze Nation* and *Time Out* carry informative listings [Y132]. Ring and check details before venturing out – clubland changes very swiftly. Flyers, often offering cheap entry, are found at many independent record shops – they're also handed out after gigs, and on Fri/Sat evenings around Leicester Square.

⏱ Clubs open every night, but there's much more choice on Friday and Saturday and, increasingly, Sunday. Clubs usually open around 10pm and fill up about midnight. Most go on until anytime between 3am and 6am.

£ Admission varies from £5 to £15, although you can pay more for special events. Some clubs have specific dress codes, others are more opaque and operate at the door-person's whim. Check press for details.

gay scene

Soho's Old Compton Street is cruise central with a parade of hotties flitting, flirting and flexing their well-toned muscles as they hop from café to bar to restaurant to club. It doesn't get much livelier than this hotbed of nightime activity...

bars

Balans *B13*

A relaxed but image-conscious vibe, slick decor with comfy red banquettes, good global food – and more importantly some seriously good-looking waiters – ensure a constant buzz.

60 Old Compton Street, Soho ☎ 7437 5212 ⊖ Leicester Square

☆ BAR CODE *B13*

DJs, spinning club visuals, and fruit machines – a split-level gay bar designed with the fun-loving and friendly in mind.

3–4 Archer Street, Soho ☎ 7734 3342 ⊖ Piccadilly Circus

☆ BLACK CAP *D2*

Camden never looked as good as it does inside Black Cap's gay disco and cabaret bar, or overlooking the throng on the terrace. A late licence adds to the appeal.

171 Camden High Street, Camden ☎ 7428 2721 ⊖ Camden Town

The Box *E8*

On the fringes of the Soho gay scene, the Box is laid back during the day, but transforms into a cruising ground at night.

30 Monmouth Street, Covent Garden ☎ 7240 5828 ⊖ Covent Garden

Candy Bar *F7*

The best lesbian bar in the area, with a downstairs disco.

4 Carlisle Street, Soho ☎ 7494 4041 ⊖ Tottenham Court Road

Central Station *off map*

Gay sports bar Central Station is home to Stonewall FC, London's champion gay footie team. Live music, drag acts, quiz nights, and strip acts draw in an up-for-it crew into the early hours. Open 'til 5am Fridays and Saturdays.

37 Wharfdale Road, King's Cross ☎ 7278 3294 ⊖ King's Cross; St Pancras

☆THE EDGE *F7*

Mingle in the midst of an all-year-round sparkling Soho crowd. The four floors (not to mention the four bars) and a carefree atmosphere draw café society bohos, post-pubbers and pre-clubbers who can all find a corner to suit their mood. Energy levels rise the higher you go with a dance floor right at the top.

11 Soho Square, Soho ☎ 7439 1313 ⊖ Tottenham Court Road

☆FREEDOM *B13*

Increasingly mixed gay bar where fashionable young things get together under neon lights and contemporary art. Once past the door staff, two bars with an extensive cocktail selection and a café area beckon. A place to see and be seen – plenty of action on the raised platform in front of the huge windows.

60–66 Wardour Street, Soho ☎ 7734 0071 ⊖ Piccadilly Circus

King William IV *off map*

Also known locally as the 'Wicked Willy', this place attracts a lively, gay crowd.

77 Hampstead High Street, Hampstead ☎ 7435 5747 ⊖ Hampstead

Ku Bar *B13*

An unpretentious gay bar with disco on the jukebox that gets the crowd moving and grooving.

75 Charing Cross Road, Soho ☎ 7437 4303 ⊖ Leicester Square

Kudos *E8*

A bit rough around the edges, this is a gay bar of the first order where a cosmo crowd bump and grind. Late-night revelry doesn't feature heavily around here.

10 Adelaide Street, Covent Garden ☎ 7379 4573 ⊖ Leicester Square

Manto's Soho *F7*

The sister bar of the infamous Mancunian watering hole, Manto's has taken to Soho like a duck to water. With a cool, liberal, and fun atmosphere, this is the perfect Old Compton Street stopover, although as a result it can become overcrowded.

30 Old Compton Street, Soho ☎ 7494 2756 ⊖ Tottenham Court Road

☆RUPERT ST *B13*

Named after (and located on) the famous street in the middle of gay Soho, Rupert St is ultra-trendy, busy-busy, and filled with male beauties. Design is simple and smart with comfy sofas and armchairs.

50 Rupert Street, Soho ☎ 7292 7141 ⊖ Piccadilly Circus

☆**THE YARD** ⚲B13
Welcoming, spacious, and alive with the buzz of Soho, The Yard is for the young at heart. The summer courtyard rounds it all off nicely.
57 Rupert Street, Soho ☎ 7437 2652 ⊖ Piccadilly Circus

clubs

Heaven ⚲A14
London's first superclub, and irrefutably the capital's foremost gay venue, Heaven has two decades of pedigree club nights under its belt. Following a big-money facelift, it introduced a super-strong roster of nights, and remains as cavernous, exciting, and inviting as ever. Thumping house and tribal dance are the order of the day at There – the reliable weekly Friday sesh. Great guest DJs are on weekly, but with residents like Nicky Holloway and Leigh Morgan, who needs them? Party nights include Bedrock (first Thursday of month) – one of London's hottest nights. John Digweed's road-blocked monthly draws a young and devastatingly up-for-it crowd to worship at the altar of dark, deep, progressive house.
VIP lifts.
Under the arches, off Villiers Street, The Strand ☎ 7930 2020
⊖ Charing Cross; Embankment

Trade @ Turnmills ⚲C9
Arguably London's most popular gay club night. Sunday early morning see hordes of body beautiful Muscle Mary's descending on Turnmill's dance floor for some hardcore clubbing. It's loud, it's pumping, and it's hard-house and techno all the way from 4am 'til noon.
63b Clerkenwell Road, Clerkenwell ☎ 7250 3409 ⊖ Farringdon

GAY @ LA2 & Astoria ⚲C7
A disco vibe attracts the party crowds to GAY four nights a week. Mondays and Thursdays are at LA2, Fridays and Saturdays at the larger Astoria.
Astoria, 157 Charing Cross Road, Soho ☎ 7743 9592
LA2, 165 Charing Cross Road, Soho ☎ 7434 0403 ⊖ Tottenham Court

Crash ⚲*off map*
This Saturday night sex spot lures a friendly crew south of the river for four bars, two dance floors, and two chill-out zones under Vauxhall's railway arches. House and tribal keep the place hopping 'til late and a shuttle bus takes the serious clubsters on to Trade to continue the heady hedonism.
Arch 66, Goding Street, Vauxhall ☎ 7820 1500 ⊖ Vauxhall

entertainment

London's a go-go; get out on the town.....

the papers

Newspaper production may have moved and modernized, but the traditional tabloid/broadsheet split remains. Vulgar and vibrant, tabloids such as the right-wing *Sun*, the more up-market *Daily Mail*, and the left-wing *Mirror* are colourful rags. Written in punchy, pre-school English, and larded with puns, taste is no object when it comes to selling their salacious scandal.

Serious news coverage can be found in the broadsheets, with the right-wing *Daily Telegraph*, *The Times*, and *The Financial Times* lining up against the left-wing *Guardian*, while *The Independent* occupies the centre ground. Or join commuters devouring cover photos of the latest glitzy charity galas in London's only surviving evening paper, the *Evening Standard*. You'll find these dailies at any newsagent. But for sheer cosmopolitan choice, try the new-stands outside central underground stations – these sell a plethora of international titles. For a quick fix on London's news and events, pick up a copy of *Metro*, a free newspaper distributed at underground stations.

All the dailies have Saturday and Sunday 'doorstoppers' which are loaded with supplements, and tend to be a little pricier. Alternatively, tuck into a Sunday tabloid such as The *News of the World* (affectionately known as 'The News of the Screws') – the journalistic equivalent of a greasy breakfast.

radio

Tune in to BBC Radio One (97.6–99.8 MHz) for pop, Two (88–91 MHz) for easy listening, Three (90.2–92.4 MHz) for classical music, Four (92.4–94.6 MHz, 198 KHz) for news and drama, or Five Live (693, 909 KHz) for sports coverage. Also check out one of the capital's myriad independents – these offer a maverick alternative to the traditional 'Voice of the BBC'.

television

When it comes to television, five terrestrial channels offer no challenge to the US, but British broadcasting makes up in quality what it lacks in quantity. The advert-free BBC1 and BBC2 are run by the British Broadcasting Corporation (established in 1922) and paid for by the licence fee. In the commercial sector, meanwhile, channel-hop between light entertainment on ITV/Carlton, bold 'minority' programming on Channel 4, and trashy made-for-TV movies on the newest arrival, Channel 5.

The news (national and international) is on early evening (6pm BBC1, 6.30pm ITV, 7pm C4 and C5); and at 9pm on BBC1 and 11pm on ITV. With satellite TV in many hotels and pubs, and a blossoming cable network – including the BBC's rolling 24-hour news – there's no doubt that London is the big top of Britain's media circus – so tune in, turn on, and enjoy!

listings mags

London's ultimate living guide is *Time Out* – with exhaustive info about everything from clubbing to sport. Their 'pick of the week' (film, music, etc) is usually sound and the features spotlight latest trends. *What's On* has similar, but tamer, events coverage. But if you don't want to fork out any extra cash, then there's *The Guardian*'s *The Guide*, *The Independent*'s *The Information* and *The Times' Metro* (all on Sat), while (on Thu) there's *Hot Tickets* in the *Evening Standard* – all four list entertainment and preview what's really worth seeing. For a more basic round-up, try *Footloose*, *LAM* (Living Abroad Magazine), and *TNT*, freebies found outside most tube stations. *Heat* has more nationwide coverage and good, long features on what's up and coming.

websites

w www.timeout.com/london and **w** www.londontown.com cover everything from accommodation to clubs with hot tips for the month, last minute deals, and tickets. The Evening Standard is also on line (www.thisislondon.com), And **w** www.book2eat.com is an online restaurant reservation service.

cinema

To see a new release, it's best to book in advance. Book with the cinema direct – most cinemas have a credit card booking line, which incurs a small booking fee.

Weekly programmes run from Friday to Thursday. At most cinemas the first screening is usually at lunchtime, followed by one mid-afternoon, then early evening and the last viewing tends to be around 8.30/9pm. Late shows – after 11pm – only run on Friday and Saturday nights at selected cinemas. The screening begins with ads (often worth a look) and trailers for future films; the film proper starts about 10–15 minutes after the programme time.

Some of the chains have automated booking lines which means your seats are selected for you – early birds will get the best seats.

Expect to pay £6–9 for tickets in the West End. Mondays, matinées, and cinemas further out of town tend to be cheaper. Some of the independents don't take credit cards.

1| Film reviews and information about shows can be found in listings mags. *Time Out* has the most comprehensive reviews and a critics' shortlist, which is usually spot-on. *Scoot* is a useful information line: call to find out what's on near you, or where a particular film is showing.

☎ 0800 192192. National daily newspapers review films on Thursday or Friday.

2| There are five main certificates: U (universal) is suitable for all; PG (parental guidance) means that some scenes may be unsuitable for young children and 12, 15 & 18 are for persons of 12, 15 and 18 years and over.

theatre

By far the best way to get a ticket for any London show is to contact the venue direct. This avoids agency commissions. But the hit musicals are notoriously difficult to get into without paying agencies through the nose. Ticket agencies are found throughout the West End.

Two reliable ones are: Globaltickets ☎ 7734 4555 and First Call ☎ 7420 0000.

Restricted views and tickets for matinees are generally easier to come by. If you're flexible, the Half-Price Ticket Booth in Leicester Square (on the south side) offers great bargains for performances on the day (cash only). It operates on a first-come-first-served basis, so get there early and keep an open mind on what you would like to see. Tickets are limited to two pairs per person, and expect to queue.

12–6.30pm daily (to 3pm Sun).

Shows are mostly Mon–Sat, and usually

start at 7.30/8pm. Matinees are generally on Wednesday or Thursday, and Saturday.

Stalls are in front of the stage and expensive. Dress, grand, or royal circles are above the stalls and sometimes cheaper. The upper circle, the balcony, or seats with restricted view are the cheapest. Boxes are the most expensive option. If necessary, theatres can fax a seating plan to you.

Expect to pay £30 or more for a good seat at one of the West End musicals, £20 or more for a West End play, £12–£15 at off-West End venues, and about £10 on the fringe. Tickets for previews can be a cheaper option.

Theatre reviews and information about shows can be found in listings magazines. *Time Out* has a comprehensive listing and publishes their critic's choice, which is usually reliable. Look out for Michael Billington's reviews in *The Guardian*, and read *The Independent* for daily reviews, or its Wednesday page devoted to theatre features and reviews.

poetry

Tickets are usually available on the door but you'll need to book ahead for major performance poets.

Times of shows vary (check with venue).

Prices vary from free entry to around £3; special events are a bit more but rarely more than £5.

Check the TLS (*Times Literary Supplement*, which lists events and reviews of published poetry each week) or the national papers for up-and-coming big events. *Time Out* has good listings each week.

dance

It is best to book tickets with the venue direct – and, since most shows have a very short run, it is worth booking in advance. If a show is sold out it may be worth queueing for returns, and some big theatres like Sadler's Wells and the Royal Opera House hold back some tickets to sell on the day of performance.

Performances usually start at 7.30/7.45/8pm. Many last for as little as one hour without an interval.

In smaller venues the seats are frequently unreserved – so get there early to ensure a good view.

Smaller venues charge between £7 and £10 for tickets; at larger places expect to pay £10 to £50.

The best all-round coverage week by week is in *Time Out*. The weekly guides in the Saturday editions of *The Independent* and *The Guardian* are useful For reviews try any of the dailies, although only pretty established work will get a mention.

opera & classical music

It's easiest and cheapest to book with the venue direct. Discounts are available for many concerts at the larger venues if you book early or make a block-booking. Opening nights and big-name artists sell out quickly.

Although you still see a few black ties and long evening dresses at the Royal Opera House, the dress code nowadays is much less formal. You'll know from the looks you get if you've gone too far. Sportswear is best avoided.

City churches often have lunchtime concerts. Most evening concerts start between 6.30/7.30pm. Usual start time for performances at the ENO or the Royal Opera House is 7.30pm.

As a guide, centrally placed seats in the stalls or on the lower tiers command the highest prices, but those at the very front will be cheaper. Hiring your own box is, of course, more expensive.

Ticket prices for classical concerts vary between £5 and £65, but are always related to the prestige of the artist(s). Lunchtime concerts in churches are often free. Opera tickets usually start at £5 for standby tickets (available from the venue 3 hours before the performance) but can cost £100+ for the best seats in the house at the Royal Opera or the ENO.

❶ All broadsheet papers print ads giving concert details, and there are limited previews in *Time Out* and other listings mags. Concert reviews generally appear in papers on the following day.

music

Tickets for all London gigs can be bought in advance from the venues. This avoids agency commission. For the majority of small club and pub gigs you can simply turn up on the night. If a show is sold out, you can approach the ticket touts milling outside the venue, but be careful – they are sharks, and will bite. If tickets aren't available from venues try the following agencies:

Albemarle ☎ 7580 3141
City Box Office ☎ 7976 2002
First Call ☎ 7420 1000
Stargreen ☎ 7734 8932
Ticketmaster ☎ 7344 4444

🕐 There are gigs every night of the week but many more on Friday and Saturday nights. Most start between 8/9pm. Big names will often have a support band which will start earlier.

Wembley Arena is all seated, but many venues have standing room and seats. Smaller pub venues are usually standing room only.

£ Tickets for big names are around the £20–£25 mark, but otherwise reckon on paying between £10–£15.

❶ *Time Out* has exhaustive listings of every gig in London each week, but other mags list the best of what's on in the capital. You should also check out the UK's two weekly music magazines *New Musical Express* and *Melody Maker*. They're national, but highly London-focused and packed with gig guides and reviews that are scurrilous, opinionated, insightful, ridiculous, pretentious, and hilarious, often within the same sentence. Monthly magazines *Q* and *Select* are more sober and *Mojo* and *Uncut* approach music with a dusty, museum-like air of veneration.

comedy

It's generally best to phone the venue and book ahead, but tickets are often available on the door. The bigger venues like the Comedy Store sell tickets through Ticketmaster ☎ 7344 4444.

🕐 There are shows every night of the week but many more on Fridays and Saturdays. Most shows start at 8.30/9pm, but doors usually open half an hour before. August is a lean month, as most of the talent heads north to the Edinburgh Festival.

If you don't enjoy ritual humiliation or audience participation, don't book the front row.

£ Smaller venues charge from £4 to £7 for tickets, and larger places £10 to £12. Smaller clubs rarely take credit cards.

❶ Check listings mags for information on shows. For the latest highlights see *Time Out*, *The Guardian's The Guide* (Sat), *The Independent's The Information* (Sat) and the *Evening Standard's Hot Tickets* (Thu).

events

An eventful guide to what's going on in the capital...

summer

Trooping the Colour *C14*
Tickets are sold by ballot months in advance, but you can see the Queen and her troops parade in full regalia along The Mall for free.
Horse Guards Parade, Whitehall ☎ 7414 2479
⊖ Westminster; Charing Cross ◑ *Jun*

Start of the Summer Sales *throughout town*
A cue to start shopping again.
◑ *Jun*

Royal Academy Summer Exhibition *A13*
Open exhibition of over 1200 works, most of which are for sale. Famous names show alongside new British talent.
Burlington House, Piccadilly ☎ 7300 8000
⊖ Green Park; Piccadilly Circus ◑ *end May–mid-Aug*

Royal Ascot *off map*
Ever-so-English event with royalty, racing, and hats galore. Four enclosures with different priced tickets, some available on the day.
Ascot Racecourse, Ascot, Berks ☎ 01344 622211 Ascot ◑ *mid Jun*

Fleadh *off map*
Originally Irish, this happening weekend festival now brings together artists and music with folk or Celtic roots.
Finsbury Park ☎ 8961 5490 ⊖ Finsbury Park ◑ *Jun*

London International Festival of Theatre – LIFT *throughout town*
Every two years, LIFT brings contemporary theatre and performance from around the world to the capital.
Various venues around London ☎ 7490 3964 ◑ *mid Jun–beg Jul*

Wimbledon Tennis *off map*
The strawberries and cream of international tennis. Limited number of tickets available on the day. Queue early.
All England Lawn Tennis Club, Church Road, Wimbledon
☎ 8946 2244 ⊖ Wimbledon; Southfields ◑ *mid Jun–beg Jul*

City of London Festival *⚲throughout town*
Classical concerts and arts performances in some of the City's most splendid buildings.
St Paul's Cathedral, Livery Companies & other City venues
☎ 7377 0540 ◑ *mid-Jun–mid-Jul*

BP Portrait Award *⚲A14*
An annual portrait competition, showing the shortlisted entries from young European artists.
National Portrait Gallery, St Martin's Place, Trafalgar Square
☎ 7306 0055 ⊖ Charing Cross; Leicester Square ◑ *end Jun–beg Oct*

Hampton Court Palace Flower Show *⚲off map*
A gardener's delight, this annual flower event includes the British Rose Festival.
Hampton Court Palace, East Molesey, Surrey ☎ 7649 1885
Hampton Court ◑ *beg Jul*

Lesbian & Gay Pride *⚲throughout town*
One of the biggest all-day parties in the UK follows this annual march through the city.
☎ 07071 781904 ◑ *Jul*

Party in the Park *⚲A11–C12*
An all-day summer concert with bands on three stages that raises money for the Prince's Trust.
Hyde Park ☎ 7766 6000
⊖ Hyde Park Corner; Marble Arch ◑ *Jul*

Test Match Cricket
It doesn't get more quintessentially English than watching the summer test matches at Lord's or the Oval.
Lord's Cricket Ground *⚲off map*
St John's Wood ☎ 7289 1611 ⊖ St John's Wood ◑ *Apr–Sep*
The Oval *⚲off map*
Kennington ☎ 7582 6660 ⊖ Oval ◑ *Apr–Sep*

Kenwood Lakeside Concerts *⚲off map*
Open-air classical and light jazz concerts on summer evenings by the lake.
Kenwood House, Hampstead Lane, Hampstead ☎ 7973 3434
⊖ Golders Green, then 120 ◑ *beg Jul–end Aug*

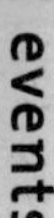

The Proms ⚐E11
Queue to 'promenade' or pay more to sit and experience these world-famous classical concerts in sumptuous surroundings.
Royal Albert Hall, Kensington Gore ☎ 7589 8212
⊖ South Kensington ◑ *mid Jul–mid Sep*

Start of British Football season ⚐*off map*
Discover whether you share the British love of this game one Saturday afternoon.
☎ Call individual clubs for details ◑ *Aug*

Notting Hill Carnival ⚐*map 1*
Second only to Rio, London's biggest street party brings the city alive with floats, music of all kinds, and Caribbean food.
☎ 8964 0544 ⊖ Notting Hill Gate; Westbourne Park (Ladbroke Grove closes during the carnival) ◑ *Aug Bank Holiday*

autumn

Chelsea Antiques Fair ⚐*off map*
A plethora of antiques (mainly pre-Victorian) sold and guaranteed by premier British dealers.
Chelsea Old Town Hall, King's Road, Chelsea ☎ 01444 482514
⊖ Sloane Square ◑ *Sep (also Mar)*

Rugby Union season ⚐*throughout town*
London has only one rugby league team, but many rugby union tournaments are played at London clubs.
☎ Call individual clubs for details
◑ *Aug–May Rugby Union (Mar–Oct Rugby League)*

London Open House ⚐*throughout town*
Over 200 private houses, offices, and corporate headquarters open to the public in celebration of their architectural merits.
Various venues around London ☎ 09001 600061 ◑ *mid Sep*

Soho Jazz Festival ⚐*throughout Soho*
Soho venues buzz with the sound of national and international bands.
Various venues around Soho ☎ 7734 6112 ◑ *end Sep–early Oct*

Dance Umbrella ⚐*throughout town*
International festival of contemporary dance, with opportunities to see many cross-cultural performances.
Various venues around London ☎ 8741 5881 ◑ *Sep–Nov*

Guy Fawkes/Bonfire Night *throughout town*

Guy Fawkes tried to blow up Parliament in the 17th century. Commemorate with traditional festivities such as bonfires, fireworks, and burning a Guy.

Parks all over London ☎ 7971 0026 ◑ ***5 Nov***

London Film Festival *throughout town*

Two weeks of cutting-edge international and British films.

National Film Theatre, South Bank & various venues

☎ 7928 3232 ⊖ Waterloo ◑ ***Nov***

The London Jazz Festival *D9*

Jazz is a broad definition for the sounds that abound at this vibrant celebration.

Barbican Centre, South Bank & various venues

☎ 7405 5974 ◑ ***Nov***

Lord Mayor's Show *F9*

Pageantry and historic costumes as the new Lord Mayor of London parades through the City. Stand in any of the major streets around St Paul's Cathedral and the Barbican to get good views of the show

☎ 7606 3030 ⊖ St Paul's ◑ ***Nov***

Remembrance Sunday *E14*

The Queen, heads of government, and veterans pay tribute to those who lost their lives in two world wars. Two minutes national silence at 11am.

Cenotaph, Whitehall

⊖ Westminster; Charing Cross ◑ ***Sunday nearest to 11 Nov***

State Opening of Parliament *E14*

Good views of the Queen and Household Cavalry arriving and leaving for the welcoming ceremony. Exact date is confirmed about one month in advance.

Houses of Parliament, Whitehall ☎ 7219 3107

⊖ Westminster ◑ ***Nov***

The Turner Prize *off map*

Exhibition of contemporary British artists who have reached the finals of this hugely prestigious award.

Tate Britain, Millbank ☎ 7887 8000

⊖ Pimlico ◑ ***Nov–Jan***

Christmas Lights & Tree *⚲A14 & E7*
The Norwegians donate a Christmas tree which is put up in Trafalgar Square. The Christmas lights on Oxford and Regent Streets are switched on by a celeb. See press for details.
Trafalgar Square; Regent & Oxford Streets ◑ *Nov/Dec*

Carol services *⚲throughout town*
Traditional Christmas songs to welcome the festivities.
Various churches and cathedrals ◑ *Dec*

New Year's Eve Festivities *⚲A14*
Revellers hit Trafalgar Square to jump in the fountains and hear Big Ben's midnight chimes.
Trafalgar Square ⊖ Leicester Square; Charing Cross ◑ *31 Dec*

Art 2000 *⚲C3*
Works from the 100 best contemporary galleries in London on sale from £100 to £100,000.
Business Design Centre, 52 Upper Street, Islington
☎ 7359 3535 ⊖ Angel ◑ *Jan*

Start of the Winter Sales *⚲throughout town*
This is the time to spend all that Christmas money.
◑ *Jan*

London International Mime Festival *⚲throughout town*
Artists from all over the world perform in London.
Various venues ☎ 7637 5661 ◑ *Jan*

Chinese New Year Celebrations *⚲B13 & A14*
The Chinese New Year begins in February. Join in the traditional celebrations around Chinatown.
Leicester Square, Newport Place, Gerrard Street & Lisle Street
⊖ Leicester Square ◑ *Feb*

Spring Loaded Dance Festival *⚲throughout town*
The very best of contemporary British dance.
The Place, 17 Dukes Road and various London venues
☎ 7387 0031 ⊖ Euston; King's Cross ◑ *Mar–Jun*

Chelsea Spring Antiques Fair *off map*

Over 40 stalls of authenticated pre-Victorian antiques, to view and to buy, from British dealers.

Chelsea Old Town Hall, King's Road, Chelsea ☎ 01444 482514
⊖ Sloane Square ◑ *Mar (also Sep)*

Good Friday Procession & Hymns *E14*

Ecumenical procession along Victoria Street, with prayers, meditations, and hymns.

Westminster Central Hall to Westminster Abbey, Westminster
☎ 7222 8010 ⊖ St James's ◑ *Easter weekend*

Oxford & Cambridge Boat Race *off map*

Beer in hand at a pub on the Thames is the best way to see the rowing teams speed past.

River Thames, Putney to Mortlake ☎ 7379 3234 ◑ *Mar*

London Marathon *off map*

Professional athletes and sponsored participants in fancy dress are among the 40,000 who run in this 26-mile race.

Greenwich Park, Tower Bridge, Isle of Dogs, Embankment to The Mall
◑ *Apr*

FA Cup Final *off map*

The culmination of the British football year. Impossible to get tickets but catch the action on TV and in pubs across the city.

Wembley Arena, Empire Way, Wembley ☎ 8902 0902
⊖ Wembley Park; Wembley Central ◑ *May*

Chelsea Flower Show *E18*

The world's most famous floral feast; innovative colours, scents, designer gardens, and exotica.

Royal Hospital, Chelsea ☎ 7649 1885
⊖ Sloane Square ◑ *May*

BOC Covent Garden Festival *throughout town*

Showcasing innovative opera, music, and theatre, some of which is played outside in the Piazza at Covent Garden.

Various venues around London ☎ 7379 0870
⊖ Covent Garden ◑ *May–Jun*

sights, museums & galleries

The choice of London sights and museums is vast, from modest former homes of painters and writers, to celebrated palaces devoted to art, history, nature, and science.

landmarks

Albert Hall & Memorial *E11*

Queen Victoria's consort, Prince Albert, has two impressive eponymous monuments situated in the area of London he did much to develop: the circular, domed concert hall, with its annual season of promenade concerts, and the gleamingly restored memorial opposite.

Kensington Gore, Kensington ⊖ Gloucester Road

Bank of England *E10*

From the windowless building that is the Bank of England emerges every bona fide banknote in England and Wales; while next door at the Royal Exchange, brightly jacketed wheelers and dealers trade on the value of this currency.

Threadneedle Street, City ⊖ Bank

Battersea Power Station *off map*

White smoke once billowed from the four chimneys of Battersea Power Station but since 1974 it has held its breath while endless plans for renewal have been developed and discarded. Its most productive use in the last 25 years has been as a film set for Terry Gilliam's *Brazil*.

Battersea ⊖ Pimlico

British Telecom Tower *C7*

Once famous for its revolving restaurant, which spun gently throughout the 1970s, Telecom Tower's spinning top is now sadly static most of the time, though the building's original function as a transmitting and receiving station remains intact.

Maple Street, North Soho ⊖ Goodge Street

Canary Wharf *off map*

Big business has been lured to the Wharf in Docklands by tax breaks and cheaper rents, and it may yet prove a rival to the City. Canada Tower, the development's Everest, is topped by a pyramid, which for three short months made it the tallest building in Europe.

Canary Wharf, Docklands ⊖ Canary Wharf

Houses of Parliament & Big Ben *E14*

Scene of the battles and banter of Britain's daily political life, the chambers of debate are cocooned within Barry and Pugin's Gothic revival masterwork. The clocktower on the north end is known as Big Ben after the giant bell which tolls on the hour.

Westminster ⊖ Westminster

Hyde Park Corner *F12*

Right in the middle of one of London's biggest roundabouts is Wellington Arch, with its statue of Winged Victory (the world-famous goddess Nike). The arch celebrates Britain's victory over France. Wellington himself lived in Apsley House opposite.

Mayfair ⊖ Hyde Park Corner

Lloyd's Building *F10*

Glass elevators, metal pipes, and spiralling stairs slide and twist their way around this power-plant style building, which dominates the heart of London's financial district. Richard Rogers' homage to high-tech architecture was completed in 1986.

Lime Street, City ⊖ Bank

London Eye *D14*

At 135 metres in stature, not only is the London Eye the world's highest observation wheel with fantastic views for miles around, but it creates an amazing new addition to London's skyline. The wheel, the fourth tallest structure in the city, symbolises regeneration and time, the turning of the new century.

South Bank ⊖ Waterloo

Tower 42 *F10*

Dwarfed by Canada Tower since 1991, bombed by the IRA in 1993, Tower42, formerly known as the NatWest Tower, is nevertheless a sleek piece of 1970s' styling by Richard Seifert, completed just as a new decade of ruthless financial aggression dawned.

12 Throgmorton Avenue, City ⊖ Bank

Piccadilly Circus *F13*

In the middle of the incessant flow of London traffic, and beneath the bright neon lights of ads for Japanese electronics, Coca-Cola, and Australian lager, dances Eros, the tip-toeing messenger of love.

Piccadilly Circus ⊖ Piccadilly Circus

St James's Palace C13

Standing out against the white stuccoed façades along Pall Mall is the red brick of St James's Palace. The oldest remaining part of the Tudor palace is the clocktower, built for Henry VIII in 1540. It is now Prince Charles' London pad.
Pall Mall, St James' ⊖ Green Park

St Paul's Cathedral F9

Designed by Sir Christopher Wren in 1675, the great dome of St Paul's on its colonnaded drum looks most impressive from the South Bank as it hovers protectively over the City. A popular choice for weddings of the privileged, St Paul's is where Charles and Diana exchanged their vows.
Ludgate Hill, City ⊖ St Paul's

Tower Bridge B16

A magnificent piece of late Victorian engineering, the bridge is a river gateway to the City. Two massive mock-medieval towers bear the weight of the bascules which raise the central section to allow ships to pass.
City ⊖ Tower Hill

Tower of London B16

This perfectly preserved medieval fortress is chiefly famous as a prison and place of execution. But its present-day role as the safe deposit of the Crown jewels is what really pulls the crowds to London's top tourist attraction.
Tower Hill, City ⊖ Tower Hill

Trafalgar Square A14

In the centre of this monumental square, Nelson stands atop his 51 m column, ignored by the tourists below, who feed the pigeons and have their photos taken on Landseer's bronze lions. The square is the place of choice for political rallies and New Year's Eve celebrations.
Covent Garden ⊖ Charing Cross

Westminster Abbey E14

This Gothic masterpiece enshrines the history of the British nation: every sovereign (apart from two) has been crowned here. The abbey is also a giant mausoleum – it was the royal burial site for 500 years, and many of Britain's greats are honoured here too.
Broad Sanctuary, Westminster ⊖ Westminster

viewpoints

The Heights E7

St George's Hotel, Langham Place, North Soho ☎ 7580 0111
⊖ Oxford Circus

Twentyfour Restaurant *⌖F10*
24th Floor, Tower 42, Old Broad St, City ☎ 7877 2424 ⊖ Bank

Windows *⌖F12*
28th Floor, London Hilton, Park Lane, Mayfair ☎ 7493 8000
⊖ Hyde Park Corner

Blue Print Café *⌖B16*
Design Museum, Shad Thames, Butler's Wharf, City ☎ 7378 7031
⊖ Tower Hill

Hungerford Foot Bridge *⌖C14*
This recently renovated footbridge overlooks the City and St Paul's.
Victoria Embankment ⊖ Embankment

Millennium Bridge *⌖A15*
London's first new bridge since 1894 is unfortunately closed until further notice. It remains a striking architectural piece linking the new Tate Modern and St Paul's Cathedral.
off Queen Victoria Street ⊖ Blackfriars

Oxo Tower *⌖14a*
Barge House Street, South Bank ☎ 7803 3888 ⊖ Blackfriars

London Eye *⌖D14*
At 135 m, the uppermost point offers unrivalled views day and night.
South Bank ☎ 0870 5000600 ⊖ Waterloo
◑ 10am–9.30pm (to 5.30pm Oct–Mar)

Monument *⌖A16*
311 steps get you to the top of this memorial to the Great Fire of London.
Monument Street ☎ 7626 2717 ⊖ Monument
◑ 10am–5pm Mon–Sat, 11am–5pm Sun.

St Paul's Cathedral *⌖F9*
Climb to the Golden Gallery for a dramatic panoramic vista.
St Paul's Churchyard, The City ⊖ St Paul's

Tower Bridge *⌖D16*
The walkways (on the tour) are great observation points.
Tower Bridge Road ☎ 7403 3761 ⊖ Tower Hill
◑ 10am–6.30pm daily (Nov–Mar: 9.30–5.15pm).

Buckingham Palace *E13*

Home to the Queen and Prince Philip, Buckingham Palace is the HQ of the British monarchy. The Royal Standard flag flies when the Queen is in residence. There are over 400 rooms in Buckingham Palace but visitors only get to see ten of them. The state rooms take up a sizeable chunk of the west wing, and their decorative excess is probably as much as the eye can take. The tour route proceeds through several shades of opulence, from the green, blue, and white drawing rooms to the blood-red dining room, and cavernous gilt-edged throne room. Such fanciful extravagance – a mutual desire of George IV and John Nash to reach new heights of indulgence – was further embellished during Edward VII's reign. The sum total is rather overwhelming, as walls and ceilings hang heavy with relief carving and a panoply of decorative motifs.

Walking into the diffused light of the picture gallery is like coming up for air. For many, this is the highlight of a visit to the palace. The long gallery is home to some magnificent works by such Old Masters as Rembrandt, Rubens, Vermeer, Van Dyck, Frans Hals, and Canaletto: by contrast, the east gallery is full of family portraits, including eccentric George III, playboy prince George IV, and a brighter painting of the coronation of a very youthful Queen Victoria. The visit winds up with a brief sortie into the Palace gardens, but only as far as an improvised gift shop in a temporary pavilion – a reminder that come the Queen's return, all traces of the riff-raff will have been removed. ❶ Pre-booking a ticket saves queueing. All tickets have a specific time allocation. ❶ It's worth paying £4 for the official guide.

Buckingham Palace Road, Westminster ☎ 7321 2233
⊖ Green Park; Victoria ◑ *Aug–Sep: 9.30am–4pm daily.*

Royal Mews & Queen's Gallery *E13*

Once you've wandered along the line of small black carriages, you can then move on to the best of the lot – the Gold State Coach – which the Queen last took for a spin back in 1977 to celebrate her Silver Jubilee. The carriage rests in a room of its own, complete with model horses, just to ensure you grasp the purpose of the contraption. It is, however, a magnificent piece of baroque foppery, built in 1761 for George III, and the preferred mode of transport for coronations since George IV's.

Far more impressive is the Royal Trust Collection, reckoned to be one of the world's largest, with around 7000 pictures. Only a fraction used to be on show at any one time in the Queen's Gallery, but the building is currently under refurbishment to extend the space. Due to open early in 2002, the new space will be a series of interconnecting rooms, allowing themed exhibitions and special events to be held. The new collection will also include the decorative arts and furniture.

Buckingham Palace Road, Westminster ☎ 7839 1377 ⊖ Green Park; Victoria ◑ *Royal Mews (Jul–Oct): 10.30am–4.30pm Mon–Thu.*

Hampton Court Palace *off map*

The massive riverside palace of Hampton Court is one of Britain's most complete Tudor palaces. Cardinal Wolsey built it for himself, but gave it to Henry VIII when he thought it would put him back in the royal good books. Henry added the Real (royal) tennis court and the state apartments, but every royal occupant has left some mark. A fire in 1986 destroyed a wing built by Wren; subsequent restoration has revealed much about the building.

Outside, the extensive gardens feature a baffling maze; the restored Privy Gardens; and the Great Vine, planted by Lancelot 'Capability' Brown over 200 years ago. The romantically inclined might like to approach Hampton Court by riverboat. 1| Great Hall; tour of the Tudor kitchens. 2| The exhibition on the 1986 fire. 3| The river approach to Hampton Court. ❶ Free access to gardens from Bushy Park entrance.

East Molesey, Hampton Court, Surrey ☎ 8781 9500 Hampton Court (from Waterloo) ◑ *10.15am–6pm Mon; 9.30am–6pm Tue–Sun (Nov–Mar: closes at 4.30pm).*

Kensington Palace *off map*

Lording it over Kensington Gardens, Kensington Palace positively drips with history and sumptuous interiors. Part private apartments – once home to mad King George III, and Princess Di, currently Princess Margaret's London pad – and part museum, the newest residents are the waxworks which can be seen 'Dressing for Royalty' in the Royal Dress Collection exhibition. Debutantes get glammed up to prowl for husbands at court, a uniformed ambassador prepares to impress, and sponsors inspect their protegées. There's also an assortment of the Queen's glad rags worn at various state occasions over the last 50 years. Upstairs, in the state apartments, there's a collection of Old Masters, and two rooms display exquisite examples of 18th-century court dress including a 2 m-wide Mantua skirt. 1| King's staircase. 2| Wind-dial.

Kensington Palace Gardens, Kensington ☎ 7937 9561 ⊖ High Street Kensington ◑ *10am–6pm daily (Nov–Feb: 10am–3pm Wed–Sun).*

Tower of London *B16*

Every half hour at the Tower, a stockinged, scarlet-frocked Beefeater delights the hordes with cheery banter and tales of scandal, torture, and loss of heads. The grim attractions of death and misery – such as the chopping block that served as final pillow for Anne Boleyn, cold dungeons, and tower-top prisons used to lock away princes – make strange bedfellows with the Tower's other big attraction, the Crown Jewels. In the anteroom before the royal crown and sceptre, the Queen's coronation

plays continuously on a remarkable piece of film footage. The perpetual crowning moment is a suitable introduction to the next surreal experience: on a slow-moving walkway, you drift in a semi-dreamlike state past the shimmering rocks embedded in gold and cushioned with velvet. Once outside, you may well wonder whether the experience was for real.
👁 1| The cell of condemned man Sir Thomas More, where he spent the last 14 months before execution. 2| Crown Jewels. 3| Royal Armouries.
Tower Hill, City ☎ 7709 0765 ⊖ Tower Hill ◑ *9am–6pm daily (from 10am Sun); Nov–Feb: 9am–5pm daily (from 10am Sun–Mon).*

the changing of the guard

On alternate mornings at 11.30, amid a flourish of red coats and to the sound of trumpets and drums, the guard is changed outside Buckingham Palace. Old and new guard face each other and, in a remarkable piece of mime theatre, the two opposing officers pretend to exchange the keys to the palace. Hey presto, the guard is changed!
Scheduling varies: see the notice on the palace gates for details.

great churches

St Paul's Cathedral *F9*

St Paul's is the ultimate one-stop shop – culture, Christianity, and even counselling are available should the stresses of life or London be too great. This magnificent 17th-century cathedral is Christopher Wren's definitive baroque masterpiece: a house of worship that has become a place of touristic pilgrimage along the way, and visitors are asked to respect its original purpose. The interior is inspirational: a massive space, emphasized by the black and white marble flagstones, the plain glass windows (chosen by Wren to let in as much light as possible), and the muffled underwater-like noise of people in an enclosed, lofty, and sacred space. Much of the decor has evolved through time; originally empty of statuary, today there are countless sculptures, as well as mausoleums and gravestones of famous and not-so-famous VIPs in the crypt. Above the beautifully carved wooden 'quire' is a stunning, sparkling Victorian glass mosaic ceiling.

Uplift yourself even further by climbing the 530 steps up to the exterior Golden Gallery, two levels above the world-famous Whispering Gallery: it affords fantastic views over London and the best way of understanding Wren's use of a double-skinned dome. The second largest in the world (after St Peter's in Rome), it was designed to maximize aesthetics from the inside, and scale from the outside. Ingenious. A memorial to the 32,000 Londoners who died in the devastation of World War II has been erected in the churchyard outside the north transept.
St Paul's Churchyard, The City ☎ 7236 4128 ⊖ St Paul's
◑ *8.30am–4pm Mon–Sat (Sun for services only).*

Westminster Abbey ⁂E14

The sturdy walls of Westminster Abbey hold 1000 years of history. The present entrance, through the north transept, takes you into Henry III's 13th-century section, where you can wait for one of the regular guided tours, muddle your way round with a guidebook, or throw yourself upon the mercy of Patience and Brian, the whimsical double act who voice the audio guide. Whichever way, the route is pretty much prescribed: following a brief foray west to Purcell's tomb, it is east towards Henry VII's flamboyant chapel of bright flags and a magnificent fan-vaulted ceiling; then to the south transept for Poets' Corner; into the central choir area; once round the cloister; and finally through the nave to exit via the west door. Along the way you will encounter traces of Britain's volatile history, from grand memorials to battling monarchs, to the tomb of an unknown soldier killed in WWI. The rather robust Coronation chair has supported many a royal derrière through seven centuries of service. Fascinating details pop out of every chapel and tomb, such as the monk-like figures carved into the feet of Baron Daubeny (in the Chapel of St Paul). The elite of the English language are remembered in Poets' Corner, though sometimes memorials were erected long after a poet's death: even Shakespeare had to wait until 1740. 👁 1| Henry VII Chapel; Poets' Corner; Coronation Chair. 2| Organ recitals in summer. ❶ Get there early to avoid the crush. Chaplains (in red cloaks) know everything about the Abbey – do ask them questions.

Parliament Square, Westminster ☎ 7222 5152 ⊖ Westminster
◑ 9.30am–4.30pm Mon–Sat (Sun services only).

Whitehall ⁂E14

This broad, ceremonial street which runs between Trafalgar Square and the Houses of Parliament is resonant with political and military history. Midway along Whitehall is Inigo Jones's Banqueting House, where Charles I danced, dined, and died. Almost opposite is Horseguards Parade, where, beneath the rusticated arches, sentrymen must maintain a silent, Zen-like concentration, while tourists tease them in the attempt to provoke a response, and jostle for photographs. Fenced off from Whitehall for security, Downing Street has been home to the nation's prime ministers since 1735. Nearby is the Cenotaph, a Lutyens-designed simple stone obelisk (1920), with inscriptions commemorating the dead of two world wars. Statues run the length of Whitehall, and include a dandyish Walter Raleigh, hat cocked at a jaunty angle, undaunted by the other more strapping frames of Haig, Montgomery, and a general called Slim.

British Museum *C8*

The name is misleading; it's not crammed with everything British, but is a storehouse of world treasures. The collection was started almost 250 years ago when Britain was expanding her empire, and the wealthy were 'discovering' the classical world on the Grand Tour. The Napoleonic Wars provided the museum with loads of spoils (pilfered by the French in Egypt), and British ambassadors played a significant part in adding to the collection of antiquities: Lord Elgin 'acquired' the marbles from the Parthenon in Athens in 1816 when he was ambassador at Constantinople.

The museum's two-and-a-half miles of galleries contain over six million exhibits including one of the finest collections of Assyrian reliefs outside the Middle East; Egyptian mummies; Anglo-Saxon treasures; the Lindisfarne Gospels; Chinese porcelain; 3000 clocks and watches; 2.5 million prints, and hoards of Greek finds. No wonder it is the most visited museum in the country. The room numbering is complicated and many collections are spread over more than one floor. The best advice is to concentrate on the highlights (see below) or on one or two of the collections.

The museum is presently undergoing large-scale reorganization – the British Library Reading Room is being transformed into London's first covered public square, designed by Sir Norman Foster, and the ethnographic collection (from the Museum of Mankind) is being reintegrated into the museum. Its first section – the North American gallery – is now open. 1| Nereid monument from southwest Turkey (room 7). 2| Sculptures from the Parthenon, Athens (room 8). 3| Fragments from the mausoleum at Halicarnassus (room 12). 4| Giant man-headed bulls from an 8th-century Assyrian palace (room 16). 5| Egyptian mummies (rooms 60–66). 6| Collection from ancient Mexico (room 33c). 7| Amarvati sculptures from India (33a). The map is a good investment for £1 and has colour plans and suggested tours. For inside information on the exhibits, the highlights tour is worth the £5. The excellent shop has good copies of exhibits, including numerous statues and some Egyptian jewellery.

Great Russell Street, Bloomsbury 7636 1555 Tottenham Court Road
10am–5pm Mon–Sat; 12pm–6pm Sun.

Imperial War Museum *off map*

This museum, with its imaginative portrayal of 20th-century warfare, entices many visitors south of the river. Within the striking neo-classical building, which was once a mental hospital, is a hoard of exhibits and interactive displays which inform, stimulate, fascinate, and shock.

The chaotic scene, with planes dangling from the ceiling of the vast atrium, and wartime machinery – missiles, tanks, and guns – littering the central exhibition hall, seems a fittingly dramatic introduction. The bulk of the exhibition is in the basement where thematic displays trace the two world wars and other conflicts this century. The museum is a bombardment on all the senses – interactive video stations, sound and lighting effects, telephones, and other special effects ensure that you see, feel, hear, and even smell the experience of war. The trench and Blitz experiences both heighten the sense of involvement with walk-through reconstructions. War is consistently brought out of its historic context into a personal realm: poetry, letters, and drawings poignantly convey the heroism, suffering and despair distilled in individual experiences.

Upstairs, there is a cinema; Secret War, an exhibition about the world of espionage and the special forces; and an impressive collection of war art with works by Paul Nash, John Singer Sargent, and others. The top floor houses a challenging but remarkable permanent exhibition, which explores the harrowing story of the Holocaust, through survivors' own emotional testimonies and archive footage. ❶ Admission is free after 4.30pm. ✧ The stylish café is a good place for the war-weary to readjust. **Lambeth Road, Lambeth ☎ 7416 5320 ⊖ Lambeth Road ◑ *10am–6pm daily.***

Natural History Museum ‡A17

The beauty of this building is as awesome as its content: carved Gothic creatures crawl inside and out, and lofty arches dwarf the dinosaur skeleton that greets you. The old British habit of exploration and plunder has resulted in this huge and amazing collection, which ranges from blue whales to butterflies, armadillos, and anthracite. A glittering must-see section is the Earth Gallery. In a £12 million revamp, this three-floor wing tells the history of the Earth in an absorbing and stylish way. It starts with an escalator ride up through a rotating globe and ends with an alarming simulated earthquake in a Japanese supermarket. In between are over 4 billion years' worth of the Earth's history – that's 25 million years per metre of exhibition. And, there are 6000 specimens – globs of gold, fossils, ytterbium, and zircon – to admire.

Before the Earth Gallery arrived on the scene, the ground floor Life Galleries were the most visited, particularly the dinosaur section. The Mammal Galleries are worth a detour with enough stuffed exotics to last a lifetime. Another of the museum's upbeat sections is Ecology. Step inside a giant leaf which shows how photosynthesis works, or find out how humans affect the lifestyles of plant and beast. A great sprawling hive of interest, there is enough space to avoid the crowds and enjoy a mind-blowing collection of nature's goodies. ❶ A useful map is given out free at the museum's entrance and there are touch screen information points in six languages in the Earth and Life galleries. If there are huge queues, nip round to the Earth Gallery entrance on Exhibition Road, or go after 4pm when it's quieter and free. ✧ 1| Earth Galleries; dinosaurs. 2| Three shops include a good gift and book shop. 3| The ground floor café is

the best. 4| The Clore Education Centre that opened early in 2000 houses Investigate, an interactive education initiative for 7–14 year olds.
Cromwell Road, Kensington ☎ 7938 9123 ⊖ South Kensington
◑ 10am–5.50pm daily (from 11am Sun).

Science Museum *A17*
For wannabe Einsteins and polar explorers a little hors d'oeuvre for the brain starts with whatever is being served up in the temporary exhibitions on the ground floor.

The more cerebral should go to the 3rd floor, using the sleek glassy lift, through to Aviation. There's a rollercoaster in space which hurtles past planets and stars. Probably best to have a more sedate ride in the Cessna aeroplane first, and check out how to fly in the earth's atmosphere. Or you could launch a rocket. For a quieter time, nip up to the 4th floor, to the history of medicine, where you can ponder a Tibetan doctor's bag or gaze at some of Lister's original growths of penicillin. There are some gruesome exhibits, so medically sensitive souls should avoid this floor altogether.

For some more action the 1st floor Launch Pad is hands-on science. Guided by 'explainers' who help the truly lost, you can attempt to build bridges, design a train wheel, or create electricity. More hands-on, but only for 2–6 year olds and their parents, the place to be is in the Garden (basement), which has everything except a way of getting kids out peacefully.

The Wellcome Wing (opened in 2000) is a four-floor suite of new and continually updated exhibitions that presents the latest developments in science, medicine, and technology. It includes a 450-seat 3D IMAX cinema (showing some of the most enthralling science films in the world), a space travel simulator, galleries on digital technology, biomedical science, the future of science, and a rapid news section. The second floor houses Digitopolis which uses the most powerful commercial technology to show what digital developments are possible in the future. It also has the computer on which the World Wide Web was invented. Other areas include Who Am I? (exploring human physiology) and Antenna (presenting the most recent discoveries in science). 👁 1| Stevenson's Rocket (ground floor) and Babbage's computer (2nd floor). 2| The shop is full of great gizmos like kits for making your very own hot air balloon or super-sleek Tomboy pens. ❶ Admission is free after 4pm. 👎 There is a sneaky £2 extra for the 'rides'.
Exhibition Road, Kensington SW7 ☎ 7942 4000 ⊖ South Kensington
◑ 10am–6pm daily.

Victoria & Albert Museum *A17*
What isn't in the V&A? Hailed as the world's greatest museum of decorative arts, it also holds paintings by Constable, sculptures by Rodin, portrait miniatures, prints, and architectural installations. Visit this awe-

inspiring and maze-like Victorian 'palace' and navigate your way through rooms full of porcelain, silverware, musical instruments, stained glass, and tapestries. There is little explanation as to why the medieval treasury is next to Ming vases, or why costume jewellery twinkles alongside war and peace frescoes by Leighton, but the eclecticism of the V&A is precisely its charm. No matter how often you visit, you can, and will, always be surprised, delighted, and intrigued by discovering an additional room (or floor) that you never knew existed. 👁 1| The legendary Great Bed of Ware (room 53). 2| The high-security jewellery gallery (room 93). 3| St Thomas Becket casket (room 43). 4| Salt cellar in the shape of a ship (room 25). 5| With over 150 rooms on six floors you will never be so pleased to see a café in your life. The best are the Morris, Gamble & Poynter rooms at the back, which were designed in the 1860s – arguably the first museum café in the world. ❗ There's a free map and guide showing what's where. Admission is free after 4.30pm. 🛍 The shop has excellent reproductions of exhibits, and concessions for those from the Crafts Council.
Cromwell Road, Kensington ☎ 7938 8500 ⊖ South Kensington
◑ *10am–5.45pm daily (from 12pm Mon; to 9.30pm Wed).*

townhouses

Apsley House *F12*

Apsley House has the prestigious address of No. 1 London. In the 18th century, it was the first house encountered after the toll gate into the capital. Victorious from the Battle of Waterloo, the Duke of Wellington converted Apsley House into his des res in 1817. He ripped out the exquisite Robert Adam interiors and added a 27 metre-long picture gallery. His redesign is now a showcase for his memorabilia. The ground floor is packed with impressive gifts he received from the royal houses of Europe – including a 400-piece dinner service decorated with scenes of the 'Iron Duke's' life. Napoleon would have turned in his grave to know that the nude he commissioned of himself, and hated, now stands at the bottom of the staircase. The silk taboret hangings of the first floor are a fitting backdrop for paintings looted from the Spanish royal collection. Although the house was given to the nation in 1947, the present duke still lives here.
Hyde Park Corner, Mayfair ☎ 7499 5676 ⊖ Hyde Park Corner
◑ *11am–5pm Tue–Sun.*

18 Folgate Street *off map*

Tucked away behind Spitalfields Market, 18 Folgate Street is one of London's most remarkable residences. From 1724 to 1919 the Jervis family lived here; today it is the home of the Californian Dennis Severs, who restored and decorated the ten rooms in Georgian and Victorian styles. Less

a museum and more a 'still-life drama', the house is packed full of sights, sounds, and smells, which lead you into another world. A clutter of paintings, porcelain, wigs, peeled fruit, buckled shoes, chamber pots (used!), clothing, and cards abandoned in mid-game, help to erase the 21st century. Smells such as leaf tobacco, oranges, and roasting meats draw you further into the past. The atmosphere is extraordinary and is truly an experience not to be missed. House motto: 'You either see it or you don't'.
18 Folgate Street, Shoreditch ☎ 7247 4013 ⊖ Liverpool Street
◑ ***2–5pm 1st Sun of month; evening of 1st Mon of month; occasional other evenings (booking is essential).***

Freud Museum *off map*
A blue plaque identifies this as Freud's former home. Freud lived here with his daughter Anna for the last year of his life, after fleeing from Austria following its annexation to Germany in 1938. Following Anna's death in 1986, and according to her wishes, the house became a museum. It is an oasis of calm, and the setting is a therapy in itself. Freud's study, a close re-creation of the one he left behind in Vienna, is enormous. Its contents reflect two sides of Freud – the personal and psychoanalytical. Shelves are lined with photos, and many antiquities, including statuettes – which he called his friends, as well as books on every aspect of the mind, archaeology and ancient history. His desk is littered with ephemera, and opposite is the famous couch where patients would spend their 'analytical hour'.
20 Maresfield Gardens, Hampstead ☎ 7435 2002 ⊖ Finchley Road
◑ ***12–5pm Wed–Sun.***

Keats' House *off map*
A lavender-lined path leads you to the door of Keats' House where much of the pleasure comes from the quiet seclusion of its setting. In the garden a small plum tree now replaces the one under which he penned Ode to a Nightingale. The poet's life may have been short, but living here must have been sweet. Inside is a trove of personal effects, as well as evidence of an obsession with the hair of his lover, Fanny Brawne. Two locks are kept in a display case, along with a testimony to her hair's vitality. On a sunny day, incorporate a walk on Hampstead Heath.
Wentworth Place, Keats Grove, Hampstead ☎ 7435 2062
⊖ Hampstead ◑ ***10am–1pm & 2–6pm Mon–Sat (to 5pm Sat); 2–5pm Sun (Nov–Mar: 1–5pm Mon–Fri; 10am–1pm & 2–5pm Sat; 2–5pm Sun).***

Kenwood House *off map*
This beautiful neo-classical house was remodelled in 1764–79 by Robert Adam for the Earl of Mansfield, and remained in the family until the 1920's. It was acquired by the 1st Earl of Iveagh and bequeathed to the

nation after his death in 1928, together with his impressive collection of paintings. Around one million people enjoy its glorious grounds each year, but relatively few visit the building itself.

In the dining room, some of Lord Iveagh's finest Old Masters are to be found: most notably The Guitar Player (1605) by Vermeer, and Rembrandt's Self Portrait. Parts of the house are just as impressive. The library is gorgeous – its shape is based on ancient Roman public baths, and the ceiling, apses, and walls are beautifully decorated. Much of the original contents of the house was sold in the 20s, but similar pieces have since been acquired. Upstairs, rooms are used for temporary exhibitions, while the Collectors' Room contains a stunning array of jewellery and portrait miniatures. ❶ The Brewhouse next door is great for organic breakfasts, snacks, and meals.

Hampstead Lane, Hampstead ☎ 8348 1286
⊖ Highgate, Hampstead ◑ ***10am–6pm daily (Oct–Mar: 10am–4pm).***

Leighton House *off map*

Home to the painter Lord Leighton for more than 30 years, this house was part of an artists' colony which grew up around Holland Park in the late 19th century. The house, designed by Leighton and the architect George Aitchison in 1864, was created not only as a place in which Leighton could live and work, but as 'a palace of art'. It remains a showcase of art, displaying Leighton's own work and that of other Pre-Raphaelite artists such as Burne Jones, alongside contemporary exhibitions and stunning interiors.

The most striking feature of the house itself is the exotic Arab Hall. Based on a Moorish palace, the domed space is adorned with a central fountain and myriad beautiful Islamic tiles and mosaics. Upstairs, Leighton's spacious studio was the focal point of the house – an opulent setting for the musical evenings which were, and still are, held here.

12 Holland Park Road, Holland Park W14 ☎ 7602 3316 ⊖ High Street Kensington, then 🚌 9, 10, 27, 28, 49 ◑ ***11am–5.30pm Wed–Mon.***

Sir John Soane's Museum *F8*

The personal, homely feel of this unusual museum makes an impact the moment you set foot inside. A ring at the doorbell summons someone to welcome you, and from here you step into the unaltered world of the leading 19th-century architect, Sir John Soane. The house and museum which Soane ingeniously designed to create tricks of light and space is brimming with curious and beautiful objects which he collected during his lifetime. Lightwells are adorned with architectural fragments, and a seemingly tiny picture gallery has panels that open out to reveal more than 100 works by artists such as Turner, Hogarth, and Piranesi. Most atmospheric of all are the eerie crypt with the sarcophagus of Pharaoh

Seti I (13th century BC) and the Gothic-style Monk's Parlour, which both feel remarkably remote from city life outside.
13 Lincoln's Inn Fields, Holborn ☎ 7405 2107 ⊖ Holborn
◑ *10am–5pm Tue–Sat.*

Two Willow Road *off map*
This modernist reinvention of a Regency terrace, overlooking Hampstead Heath, was designed by the architect Erno Goldfinger in 1939. He lived here with his wife, the artist Ursula Blackwell, and his family, who remained in the house until 1994.

Despite the controversy of the project – many objected to his brand of concrete classicism – planning permission was granted, and London acquired this modernist gem. Inside, the elegant building displays a stunning sense of light and space as well as Goldfinger's furniture and most of his original art collection. Pieces include those by his wife and other Hampstead residents such as Henry Moore and Sir Roland Penrose. Today, tours around the house, decorated in the original colour schemes, are led by guides who point out the architect's design signatures with enthusiasm and relish. It was said that Goldfinger was a fraction short of a genius. Go to Willow Road and judge for yourself.
2 Willow Road, Hampstead ☎ 7435 6166 ⊖ Hampstead
◑ *Apr–Oct: 12–5pm Thu–Sat.*

blue plaques

But for 226 years, Handel and Hendrix would have been neighbours, a fact recorded by two small ceramic tiles of blue sitting side by side on Brook Street, Mayfair. Over 600 plaques commemorate addresses of the famous in London, giving dates for their period of residence in the capital.

stately homes

Once in the country, now in the outer reaches of the capital's grasp, stately homes huddle in splendour in London's leafy suburbs. Many are gathered to the south and west. **Marble Hill House** (1729), a Palladian residence built for George II's mistress, is right on the banks of the Thames and almost opposite the 17th-century **Ham House**. Both are set in glorious grounds and there's a little ferry between the two. **Chiswick House** (begun 1725) was built by Lord Burlington as a 'temple to the arts' and again is surrounded by landscaped gardens. The slender columns of **Osterley House** (1576) are the result of Adams' remodelling (mid-18th century) of the Jacobean brick building. The gardens are planted with giant cedars and the extensive grounds attract picnickers in summer. For an art deco residence that oozes style, taste, and panache, **Eltham Palace** (1936) hits the spot. See the muralled cage built for the owners' lemur, the stunning black and silver dining room, and the onyx and gold fitted bathroom.

Chiswick House *off map*
Burlington Lane, Chiswick ☎ 8995 0508 Chiswick
10am–6pm daily (Oct–Mar: 10am–4pm Wed–Sun).

Eltham Palace *off map*
off Court Road, Eltham ☎ 8294 2548 Eltham
10am–5pm daily (to 4pm Sun).

Ham House *off map*
Ham Street, Richmond upon Thames ☎ 8940 1950 ⊖ Richmond, then 65 *Apr–Oct: 1–5pm Sat–Wed (grounds 10.30am–6pm).*

Marble Hill House *off map*
Richmond Road, Twickenham, Middlesex ☎ 8892 5115 ⊖ Richmond, then H22, R68, R70, 281, 290, 490 *10am–6pm daily (winter: Wed–Sun 10am–4pm).*

Osterley Park House *off map*
Osterley, Isleworth, Middlesex ☎ 8560 3918 ⊖ Osterley
Apr–Oct: 1–4.30pm Wed–Sun.

one-offs

Cutty Sark & Gypsy Moth *off map*
The Cutty Sark's masts soar above the rooftops of Greenwich. She was built in 1869 by John 'White Hat' Wills, a man with a mission: he wanted her to be the fastest clipper plying the tea trade with China. She was restored to her former glory and given a permanent home in Greenwich in 1954. Below deck, displays chart the history of the clipper – cartoons, posters, old photos, and prints. And there's a surprising collection of original figureheads from shipwrecks, donated to the Cutty Sark by 'Long John Silver'!

Gipsy Moth IV, in the dry dock a few yards away, is a tiny, beautiful vessel in comparison; only 16m long, this is the yacht in which Sir Francis Chichester became the first person to sail single-handedly around the world. Her glorious past is rather sadly now contained behind restrictive security fencing. Still worth a look.
King William Walk, Greenwich ☎ 8858 3445
Greenwich (from Charing Cross) *10am–5pm daily.*

Design Museum *B16*
The museum's pristine white interior is a stylish showcase for the well-presented and innovative collections displayed here which create a fascinating overview of design for mass production.

Exhibitions change regularly, but the main display is on the wonderfully spacious top floor. It is remarkable to see how the things which furnish our everyday lives have developed over the years. Telephones range from the crude cumbersome designs of the 1870s through to sophisticated cordless variations, while TVs start in the 1930s as pieces of art deco furniture and run through to the very latest technical wizardry. Clear, concise information makes the museum accessible to all. ☞ Excellent shop; Blue Print Café has a good vibe and great river views. **Butler's Wharf, Shad Thames, Southwark ☎ 7403 6933 ⊖ Tower Hill; London Bridge ◑ *11.30am–6pm daily (from 10.30am Sat–Sun).***

The Dome *off map*

After stirring up plenty of controversy, The Dome opened its doors to the public on January 1st 2000, after spending a stupendous £780 million. But is it worth it? That's the question on the lips of Britain's taxpayers. Base the answer on ticket sales and it seems the jury's still out, with initial poor take-ups being improved upon. ❶ Initially envisaged as a one-off, year-long public attraction for the millennium, The Dome, is up for sale and will undergo major redevelopments during 2001.
Greenwich ☎ 0870 6062000 ⊖ North Greenwich ◑ *10am–11pm daily.*

Geffrye Museum *off map*

This area of Shoreditch used to be the centre of London's furniture trade, hence the Geffrye Museum's mission to preserve a series of English domestic interiors from 1600 to the present. The early 18th-century almshouses, which enclose a spacious front lawn, make an attractive setting. The furniture and fittings include many fine (and quirky) details – from 17th-century linenfold panelling to a stuffed armadillo.

A large modern extension has doubled the size of the museum and houses the 20th-century rooms, a design centre for contemporary work, and often fantastic temporary exhibitions. Take a break in the peaceful herb garden at the rear of the museum.
Kingsland Road, Hackney ☎ 7739 9893 ⊖ Old Street then 🚌 243 ◑ *10am–5pm Tue–Sun (from 12pm Sun).*

Globe Theatre *A15*

After more than five years of work and an expenditure of some £32 million, this impressive project, inspired by the late Sam Wanamaker, has yet to be fully realized. The reconstruction of Shakespeare's Globe Theatre is complete – the first productions took place in summer 1997 – but the Inigo Jones Winter Theatre is still being built.

This open-air theatre is a rebuilding of the Elizabethan playhouse where Shakespeare himself acted and for which he wrote his plays. A tour gives a fascinating insight into the Bard's life and work, the history of the original theatre and the Elizabethan building methods which have been re-employed. To see a performance here is magical. Some things have inevitably changed – admission no longer costs a penny and casts aren't all-male – but Elizabethan theatre has undoubtedly been captured down to the finest detail.

If following Shakespeare's trail is hot on your agenda, pop round the corner to the Rose Theatre (on Park Street), where the Bard held his first plays. The temporary exhibition is going on indefinitely until enough money has been raised to completely excavate this oldest Bankside theatre. ❶ Visits to the theatre are by guided tour only – every half hour; performances May–Sep. Café and restaurant have great river views.
New Globe Walk, Bankside ☎ 7902 1400 ⊖ Mansion House
10am–5pm daily (May–Sep: 9am–12pm).

HMS Belfast *C16*
This vast battle-cruiser, first launched in 1938, remained in service with the Royal Navy until 1965. It's easy to get lost in the labyrinth of steep stairs, narrow corridors, gangways, and level upon level of decks (seven in total). The more lost you get, the easier it is to immerse yourself in the ship's past and imagine what it must have been like to live aboard this monstrosity during World War II. It can be quite unnerving to find yourself in the explosives room with hundreds of shells facing your direction, and the niggling fear that one could still be active.
Morgans Lane, Southwark ☎ 7940 6328 ⊖ London Bridge
10am–6pm daily (Nov–Feb: 10am–5pm daily).

Horniman Museum *off map*
An extraordinary collection of objects – very much reflecting the tastes and travels of one man, the tea magnate Frederick Horniman – which appropriately brings the world's natural and cultural diversity to multicultural South London.

The static natural history displays are very trad, but the aquarium adds movement and colour. The ecological centre allows you to explore the natural world, and the lovely gardens ensure that living nature is drawn in to the museum. This striking Arts and Crafts building is being revamped (parts will be closed). More prominence will soon be given to the ethnographic treasures – among them world masks, Tibetan buddhas, and an Egyptian mummy. The music room is also to be enlarged in order to accommodate more of the museum's 6,000 instruments, which are accompanied by excellent videos and recordings.
100 London Road, Forest Hill ☎ 8699 1872 ⊖ Forest Hill
10.30am–5.30pm daily (from 2pm Sun).

Madame Tussaud's & London Planetarium *C6*

Let's face it, the closest most of us nobodies will get to rubbing shoulders with a somebody like Bill Clinton, Elizabeth Taylor, or Michael Jackson will be at Madame Tussaud's waxwork exhibition. Here, more than 400 figures, including pop, film, and sports stars, politicians, royalty, and murderers, are shuffled past, peered at, and photographed by over 2.5 million visitors each year – it's a total tourist trap.

Amongst the collection are some very convincing models, such as Martin Luther King and the Dalai Lama (wearing a suitably wry expression); others, like a 1956 Elvis, are less lifelike. The Chamber of Horrors, whose roots date back to Madame Tussaud's original touring exhibition, is a succession of mostly gory tableaux, and is as such one of the most popular sections. The Spirit of London ride, which you visit in a 'time-taxi', is a short blast of an acid trip through 400 years of life in the capital, ending up in modern London.

If you haven't had enough star-gazing, continue on to the Planetarium for a close encounter of the celestial kind. A few interactive demonstrations and displays are on show, but the real draw is the state-of-the-art Digistar II projector in the domed auditorium. The show takes you on a 30-minute 3D voyage of discovery through inner and outer space, accompanied by an informative narrative. ❶ Book by credit card 24 hrs in advance and come early, or late, to avoid the crowds.

Marylebone Road, Marylebone ☎ 0870 400 3000 ⊖ Baker Street
◑ *10am–5.30pm daily.*

Museum of London *D9*

Built virtually on top of London's Roman wall, the Museum of London is jam-packed with anything and everything to do with the capital's history. There are two floors of galleries with objects, artefacts, models, reconstructions, maps, information panels, and even holograms. The content is almost overwhelming, and the layout quite confusing, so it's not a bad idea to adopt the amble-through approach, as treasures abound.

The garden contains a chronological selection of plants introduced by nurserymen from medieval times to the present, and is a great place to escape the crowds. ❶ Admission is free after 4.30pm. Tickets are valid for three months for unlimited return visits.

London Wall, The City ☎ 7600 3699 ⊖ St Paul's; Barbican
◑ *10am–5.50pm daily (from 12pm Sun).*

National Maritime Museum & Queen's House *off map*

Revamped and expanded, the National Maritime Museum is the world's largest nautical museum. There are exhibitions covering all aspects of the maritime world and history, from costume to trade, and the future of the sea. Try your skills at steering a Viking ship into harbour, guiding a paddle along the Thames, or take control of a Seacat ferry. Somewhat calmer is the Ship of War, which is full of models, and rather more intellectual is the 20th-century Sea Power with its interactive operations room. And, perhaps most interesting of all, is the Nelson Gallery which, as you'd expect, is devoted to the great British naval hero.

Adjoining the museum is the Palladian Queen's House (1616), a rare example of the work of Inigo Jones which set the neo-classical style in England. A plain exterior conceals vivid interiors, restored to their 17th-century royal splendour when Charles I's wife, Henrietta Maria, lived here.

Royal connections were broken when the house was transformed into an orphanage for the children of seamen in the 19th century – the long colonnades and wings were added to accommodate them. The most memorable features of the house, the dreamy vistas apart, are the perfect cubical entrance hall and the lovely spiral 'tulip' staircase. Upstairs are the matching royal apartments for king and queen, while the cavernous basement exhibits objects from the treasury.

Greenwich ☎ 8312 6565 Ⅲ Maze Hill (from Charing Cross)
◑ *10am–5pm daily.*

Old Royal Observatory *off map*

The official starting point of the 21st century, and the theoretical centre of world time and space, the observatory (designed by Sir Christopher Wren) is home to the Meridian Line (dividing the eastern and western hemispheres) and Greenwich Mean Time (GMT). This is the point from which the world has set its clocks and measured space since 1884.

The observatory was founded in 1675 by Charles II to find a way to determine longitude at sea. The first Astronomer Royal, John Flamsteed, devoted 45 years to observing the stars from here and for the next 250 years, Greenwich led the world in star mapping and time-keeping.

At the top of the house, above the astronomer's apartments, is the stunning, light-filled octagonal room which is used for observation. Two loud clocks tick hypnotically, setting the rhythm for the basement galleries which are all about the science and history of time.

Amid the hands-on science stations, and many weird and wonderful scientific instruments, is John Harrison's H4 precision clock, which won the £20,000 longitude prize in 1763 and changed the history of navigation forever. A mere fraction of the museum's 7000 scientific instruments is on display at any one time.

Romney Road, Greenwich ☎ 8858 4422
Ⅲ Maze Hill (from Charing Cross) ◑ *10am–5pm daily.*

Vinopolis: City of Wine *D15*

Scared that punters might get bored by a lengthy walk-about before sinking a glass of the good stuff, the people at Vinopolis have thrown it all at this one, from 'old school' mock-ups of Spanish courtyards to 'new school' interactive displays. The latter include scooters for video trips through the Italian countryside, while an audio guide (in six languages) charts the development of wines. It can be unnerving to have Jancis Robinson or Oz Clarke suddenly breathing words in your ear about Bordeaux's 'aristocratic character', but there is some good and interesting information. A tasting session is included in the tour; you get to choose five wines from the 200 available. For an extra £2.50 you can sample another five, or head for the extensive stock on sale in the Majestic Wine Warehouse. Good restaurants open outside museum hours.

1 Bank End, Bankside ☎ 7241 4040 ⊖ London Bridge

10am–5.30pm Tue–Fri (last admission 3.30pm); 10am–late Sat–Mon (last admission 6pm).

galleries

Dulwich Picture Gallery *off map*

Britain's oldest public gallery re-opened in 2000 following a major refurbishment to restore it to Sir John Soane's original 1811 design and add a new wing. This is one case where size most certainly doesn't matter: despite its small collection, the Picture Gallery houses Rubens, Rembrandts, and Van Dycks to die for.

College Road, Dulwich ☎ 8693 5254 Dulwich; West Dulwich

10am–5pm Tue–Sun (from 11am Sat–Sun).

Estorick Collection *off map*

Situated in a converted Georgian house in ultra-chic Islington, this gallery opened in 1997, revealing Eric Estorick's amazing collection of Italian Futurism. He started collecting 40 years after the short-lived movement launched itself in 1909, and his acquisitions include Balla's *Hand of the Violinist* and Boccioni's *Modern Idol*, as well as pieces by Carra, Marinetti, Russolo, and Severini. The finest Futurist collection outside Italy, it is well worth a visit, not least because it has the clout to bring in supplementary exhibitions from Italian national museums. Café with seats in the garden.

39a Canonbury Square, Islington ☎ 7704 9522 ⊖ Highbury & Islington

11am–6pm Wed–Sat; 12–5pm Sun.

Guildhall Art Gallery *E10*

The re-opening of the Guildhall Art Gallery comes after more than 50 years of the collection being housed in a temporary building; the original 1885 building burnt down in 1941. Although quite small in comparison to other national collections, there are some gems to be found. John Singleton Copley's enormous *The Defeat of the Floating Batteries* takes pride of place alongside work by the Pre-Raphaelites, Constable, and Reynolds. There's an assemblage of pictures charting the development of London, and a selection of portraits from the 16th century onwards.

Guildhall Yard, The City (off Gresham St) ☎ 7332 1632
⊖ Bank; St Paul's ◑ *10am–5pm Mon–Sat; 12–4pm Sun.*

National Gallery *A14*

The National Gallery occupies a commanding position on the north side of Trafalgar Square. Its vast collection is highly impressive, especially when you consider that it was initially founded from private collections in the 1820s and 1830s, rather than from a royal foundation. The 1984 Sainsbury Wing houses the gallery's breathtaking early Renaissance paintings and icons, as well as temporary shows. Although there are oodles of Rubens goddesses falling out of their bodices, tranquil 17th-century Dutch landscapes, Velazquez's *Rokeby Venus*, and works by Michelangelo and Titian, it is invariably the Impressionist rooms that are jam-packed. You can see work by all the usual suspects: Monet, Renoir, Degas, Seurat, and Manet, as well as Cézanne and Van Gogh. Constable's *The Hay Wain*; Hogarth's *Marriage à la Mode*; Gainsborough's *Mr and Mrs Andrews*; Velazquez's *Rokeby Venus*. 1| For more info on specific works, or to plan a tour, use the screens in the Micro Gallery. 2| Crivelli's Garden, the top-floor restaurant, offers a great view over Trafalgar Square.

Trafalgar Square ☎ 7839 3321 ⊖ Charing Cross; Leicester Square
◑ *10am–6pm daily (to 9pm Wed).*

National Portrait Gallery *A14*

The National Portrait Gallery was founded in 1856 to form a British 'rogues' gallery of the rich, famous, and dead, a collection which includes the only known portrait of Shakespeare. It is the world's largest portrait collection, one that since 1969 has included works of people alive and well. Now contemporary icons in a variety of media effervesce in the 20th-century galleries: the Queen by Andy Warhol meets Paula Rego's Germaine Greer. Expansion has created much-needed space as well as The Portrait, the appealing rooftop bar restaurant. Exhibitions include the annual BP portrait award (Jun–Sep).

St Martin's Place, Covent Garden ☎ 7306 0055
⊖ Charing Cross; Leicester Square ◑ *10am–6pm daily (from 12pm Sun).*

Somerset House ꟷA14

Following restoration work, the 16th-century Somerset House now incorporates the Courtauld Gallery, the Gilbert Collection of gold and silver decorative arts, and the grand Hermitage Collection, straight from the heart of St Petersburg that includes some of the best Rembrandts, Van Dycks, and Picassos in the world.

The Courtauld is a relatively hidden enclave of Impressionist and Post-Impressionist works, where you'll find that Van Gogh self-portrait (with bandaged ear) and Manet's only medal-winning painting *Bar at the Folies-Bergère*. The collection is courtesy of philanthropist and textile magnate Samuel Courtauld, who snapped up works such as Cézanne's *The Card-Players*, Renoir's *La Loge*, and Gauguin's *Nevermore* in the 1930s. It also boasts Bellini's explicit *The Assassination of St Peter Martyr*, Cranach's sensual late Renaissance *Adam and Eve*, and critic and painter Roger Fry's early 20th-century British collection. ♿ Good bookshop; The Admiralty, an Oliver Peyton restaurant with outdoor courtyard.

Somerset House, Strand ☎ 7848 2526 ⊖ Temple; Covent Garden
◑ *10am–6pm daily (from 12pm Sun).*

Tate Britain & Tate Modern A15

The Tate is like an amoeba, ever-expanding and moving in new directions. As well as satellites in Cornwall and Liverpool, the Tate in London has been split between two buildings, allowing more of the collection to be shown. The Tate on Millbank is now called Tate Britain; it houses British art from the 16th century to the present day, including Turner, Gainsborough, Constable, Millais (with the famous *Ophelia*) and Hockney (including *Bigger Splash*). Tate Modern, housed in the former Bankside Power Station, opened its doors in May 2000 to a flood of media attention. And not without due cause: the new space shows an amazing array of international modern art from 1900 to the present day, including Picasso, Mondrian, Dalì, Bacon, Pollock, and Warhol. The building itself is worth attention: the former turbine hall forms the lobby, dwarfing visitors with its 30m high ceiling, and drawing them in to see Louise Bourgeois' three tower sculptures created specifically for the space; and the 82 rooms create an awe-inspiring 776sq m of exhibition space.

Both galleries have adopted a radical approach to arranging work; suites of rooms are thematic, allowing juxtapositions of styles and eras to reveal unexpected connections. ♿ 1| The 99m chimney will be converted into a viewing gallery for great vistas. 2| The Millennium Footbridge spans the river from St Paul's to the Tate Modern's gardens. 3| The roof-top restaurant stays open until 10pm Fri–Sat. ❗ 1| The Turner Prize will continue to show at the Millbank site. 2| Temporary exhibitions are held at both sites. Book ahead to avoid the queues (7420 0055).

Tate Britain, Millbank ☎ 7887 8000 ⊖ Pimlico ◑ 10am–5.50pm daily.
Tate Modern, Bankside ☎ 7887 8000 ⊖ Southwark
◑ *10am–6pm daily (to 10pm Fri–Sat).*

Wallace Collection *F6*

Considering the scale, grandeur, and location of this collection, it's surprising it's not always bustling. Hertford House is home to the largest collection of French 18th-century paintings, porcelain, and furniture outside Paris. It has an amazing array of armoury, and paintings by Poussin, Titian, Rubens, Hals, and Gainsborough. Gilt, marble, tails, and swags abound in the impeccably maintained rooms. The Wallace has joined the trend for refurbishing London's museums for the millennium; the makeover creates four extra galleries and an all-weather Sculpture Garden. You should always find what you're looking for here, whether it's Hals' *The Laughing Cavalier*; Murano glass; or a case full of tobacco graters.
Hertford House, Manchester Square, Noho ☎ 7935 0687 ⊖ Bond Street
◑ *10am–5pm daily (from 2pm Sun).*

major exhibition spaces

Barbican *D9*

The Barbican is a concrete paean to the arts; a mini-city with yellow lines leading through the maze to the main exhibition building. There's a charge for the main galleries, but other areas, such as the arabesque Curve Gallery, offer a free programme. With free foyer music in the evenings, a tropical garden, a cinema, theatre and concert hall, bars, cafés and restaurants, you can indulge all your senses at once.
Barbican Centre, 2 Silk Street, The City ☎ 7382 7105 ⊖ Barbican; Moorgate ◑ *7am–11pm daily.*

Camden Arts Centre *off map*

Camden is an innovative venue, with a strong programme of events to back up its international exhibitions. Artists-in-residence hold open studios, and the bookshop stocks artist's multiples. A regular fixture is the New Contemporaries exhibition (Aug–Sep).
Arkwright Road, Hampstead ☎ 7435 2643 ⊖ Finchley Road
◑ *11am–7pm Tue–Sun (to 5.30pm Fri–Sun).*

Hayward *D14*

The Hayward, part of the post-war riverside complex, is due to be revamped in the next few years, so don't be put off by its dour brutalist exterior. Instead, be guided by the flashing neon tower, and step into its vast white interior. Solo exhibitions of international artists such as Bruce Nauman and post-war group shows are complemented by the odd theme show.

South Bank Centre, South Bank ☎ 7261 0127 ⊖ Waterloo; Embankment
◑ ***10am–6pm daily.***

ICA *⌕A13*
The ICA (Institute of Contemporary Arts) is over 50 years old: half a century of championing contemporary art, dance, cinema, theatre, performance, and criticism. The ICA's exhibition programme is eclectic, and ranges from solo shows by the likes of the Chapman brothers and Lari Pittman, to group shows curated by guests such as artist Martin Maloney featuring art rarely seen outside alternative spaces.
The Mall, St James's ☎ 7590 4444 ⊖ Charing Cross; Piccadilly
◑ ***12–9.30pm daily.***

Royal Academy of Arts *⌕A13*
The Royal Academy doesn't exhibit its own collection in its neo-classical home, but chooses to utilise its galleries to present retrospectives of major artists – national and international – and the famous annual Summer Exhibition (Jun–Aug). Outside, the courtyard is often home to huge contemporary sculptures by the likes of Anthony Gormley and Richard Deacon RA.
Burlington House, Piccadilly ☎ 7300 8000
⊖ Piccadilly Circus; Green Park ◑ ***10am–6pm daily (to 8.30pm Fri).***

Royal College of Art *⌕E11*
The art college's ground floor is a prestigious exhibition venue next to the Albert Hall, and houses a broad spectrum of temporary shows throughout the year. Regular fixtures include the RCA curatorial students' show in April, and degree shows in June. There's also the notorious Absolut-sponsored anonymous postcard sale (usually Dec), where established names such as David Hockney and Tracey Emin submit unsigned works for sale for around £40 each. You find out the name of the artist's work that you bought at the end of the exhibition.
Kensington Gore, Kensington ☎ 7584 5020
⊖ High Street Kensington; South Kensington ◑ ***10am–6pm daily.***

Saatchi Gallery *⌕off map*
Manifested from the ex-ad-man Charles Saatchi's immense collection, the Saatchi Gallery, a vast white-washed warehouse space, shows a rotating selection of his holdings. His initial love of US 80s greats was replaced with a 90s young British art shopping spree, and recently he has bought from Germany and America again. Look out for Young National Artists exhibitions – there are generally three shows a year. Don't miss Richard Wilson's 20:50, a room disturbingly half-filled with sump oil, which is permanently installed in the gallery.

98a Boundary Road, South Hampstead ☎ 7624 8299
⊖ Swiss Cottage; St John's Wood ◑ *12–6pm Thu–Sun (closed August).*

Serpentine Gallery *E11*
This ex-tea pavilion on the edge of Kensington Gardens has reopened after major expansion. As well as running a stimulating programme of mainly solo shows, the gallery also commissions artists to work in the surrounding grounds. Artists and critics talk about the current exhibition on Sundays at 3pm.
Kensington Gardens, Kensington ☎ 7402 6075 ⊖ South Kensington; Lancaster Gate ◑ *10am–6pm daily.*

South London Gallery *off map*
This flagship gallery of South London opened in 1891, and is now flanked by Camberwell Art School. The poor transport links to the area are more than compensated by their exhibition programme, which mixes solo shows by artists such as Mark Quinn, Tracey Emin, and Julian Schnabel, with intriguing group shows.
65 Peckham Road, Peckham ☎ 7703 6120
⊖ Oval, then 🚌 36; or ⊖ Elephant & Castle then 🚌 12, 171
◑ *11am–6pm Tue–Fri (7pm Thur); 2–6pm Sat–Sun.*

Whitechapel *off map*
The Whitechapel Art Gallery is a striking exhibition venue, with a huge triple-height main gallery and a smaller, more intimate space upstairs. Their programme leans towards exhibiting work by international artists such as Guillermo Kuitca, Peter Doig, and Rosemarie Trockel. They often split the gallery and have smaller alternative shows upstairs.
80–82 Whitechapel High Street, Whitechapel ☎ 7522 7888 ⊖ Aldgate East ◑ *11am–5pm Tue–Sun (to 8pm Wed).*

galleries – alternative spaces

The umbrella term 'alternative space' encompasses everything from small rooms in condemned buildings, galleries in dedicated arts centres, to space above pubs and bookshops. Few receive grants, many are run by artists' groups or dedicated individuals, and new spaces seem to open weekly. Clerkenwell, Hoxton, and the fringes of the City are still popular artists' haunts, and are full of studio complexes and alternative galleries. The **Cubitt** is run by the artists who have studios in this disused laundry. They have a range of innovative group shows, as does **30 Underwood Street**, also in N1. Towards Liverpool Street, there is the strangely named road Tenter Ground: search around this seemingly derelict street for No. 1 and climb the rickety staircase that leads to the gallery, **One in the Other**, to view some intriguing installations.

The more substantial non-commercial spaces are further east. **The Showroom** is shaped like a slice of cake, and was responsible, along with the Chisenhale, for giving many of the British artists currently enjoying international fame and fortune their first solo shows. Further into Bow is **Matt's**, started by Robin Klassnik in the 70s and named after his dog (Matt E Mulsion). Klassnik continues to work with established and young artists in this vast industrial space.

Due South, near Tower Bridge, **Delfina** is a huge studio complex, set up four years ago by Spanish septuagenarian Delfina Entrecanales, who offers foreign and British artists free studio space and the option to show in the gallery. Most of the ground floor houses the Delfina restaurant which serves amazing (if expensive) lunches.

More and more galleries are opening near the river, especially round Vauxhall. **Milch** has relocated to the area from Charing Cross, and now sees itself as a 'culture shop' operating from the first floor of a disused elevator factory.

Chisenhale *off map*
64 Chisenhale Road, Bethnal Green ☎ 8981 4518 ⊖ Mile End; Bethnal Green ◑ *1–6pm Wed–Sun.*

Cubitt *off map*
2–4 Caledonia Street, King's Cross ☎ 7278 8226 ⊖ King's Cross ◑ *10.30am–6pm Fri–Sun.*

Delfina *D15*
50 Bermondsey Street, Bermondsey ☎ 7357 6600 ⊖ London Bridge ◑ *10am–5pm daily (from 2pm Sat–Sun).*

Matt's *off map*
42–44 Copperfield Road, Mile End ☎ 8983 1771 ⊖ Mile End ◑ *12am–6pm Wed–Sun during exhibitions.*

Milch *off map*
2–10 Tinworth Street, Vauxhall ☎ 7735 7334 ⊖ Vauxhall ◑ *12–6pm Thu–Sun.*

One in the Other *D10*
1 Tenter Ground, Shoreditch ☎ 7564 8282 ⊖ Liverpool Street ◑ *12–6pm Sat–Sun.*

The Showroom *off map*
44 Bonner Road, Bethnal Green ☎ 8983 4115 ⊖ Bethnal Green ◑ *1–6pm Wed–Sun.*

30 Underwood Street *A10*
30 Underwood Street, Hoxton ☎ 7336 0884 ⊖ Old Street ◑ *1–6pm Fri–Sun.*

photography & design galleries

1998 was the Arts Council's year of photography and the electronic image, boosting photography's standing as an artform. The same year, the V&A opened its **Canon Photography Gallery**, which shows a changing programme of photographs from its extensive archives. Other dedicated spaces abound: **Zelda Cheatle** deals in work by artist-photographers such as the late Helen Chadwick; the **Photographer's Gallery** in Covent Garden and further west the **Special Photographers' Gallery** are important venues for shows. The **Lux Gallery** has an innovative programme by contemporary artists working with photography, film, and digital imaging.

Design in London is the new black, and the capital now has international status as a design capital. For dedicated groupies, the **Design Museum** is the place to pay homage. Islington is design-heaven and home to the Crafts Council, which has a shop and large gallery with a changing exhibition programme.

The Lux Gallery *F4*
Lux Centre, 2–4 Hoxton Square, Hoxton ☎ 7684 2785 ⊖ Old Street
◑ *12–7pm Wed–Sun (to 6pm Sat–Sun).*

Photographer's Gallery *A14*
5 & 8 Great Newport Street, Covent Garden ☎ 7831 1772 ⊖ Leicester Square ◑ *11am–6pm daily (from 12pm Sun).*

Special Photographer's Gallery *A14*
21 Kensington Park Road, Leicester Square ☎ 7221 3489 ⊖ Leicester Square ◑ *10am–6pm Mon–Sat (from 11am Sat).*

V&A Canon Photography Gallery *A17*
V&A, Cromwell Road, South Kensington ☎ 7938 8500 ⊖ South Kensington ◑ *10am–5.45pm daily*

Zelda Cheatle *A13*
99 Mount Street, Mayfair ☎ 7408 4448 ⊖ Green Park; Bond Street
◑ *10am–6pm Tue–Fri; 11am–4pm Sat.*

commercial galleries

For a contemporary art junkie, the **White Cube** and its new sister gallery **White Cube^2** are where it's at. Jay Jopling deals in work produced by his super-artists: Damien Hirst, and others. Nicholas Logsdail also exhibits young artists at his **Lisson Gallery**, alongside the sculptors who made his name in the early 80s.

Cork Street used to be the art world mecca but now only a handful of interesting dealers rent space here. Look for **Entwhistle** for interesting new artists. Just north, Dering Street is awash with **Antony D'Offay Galleries**, mainly dealing in international stars.

The east has been home to Maureen Paley and her home-cum-gallery **Interim Art** for years. But there's also a flurry of alternative spaces in the area: **Andrew Mummery's** Great Sutton Street gallery and **The Eagle** (over a pub) are both located in Clerkenwell, while **Victoria Miro**, Chris Ofili's art dealer, recently opened a spacious gallery in North Shoreditch where she exhibits the best of the world's young artists.

Andrew Mummery *B9*
33 Great Sutton Street, Clerkenwell ☎ 7251 6265 ⊖ Farringdon

Antony D'Offay Galleries *F6*
Dering Street, Mayfair ☎ 7499 4100 ⊖ Bond Street

Eagle Gallery *C9*
159 Farringdon Road, Clerkenwell ☎ 7833 2674 ⊖ Farringdon

Entwhistle *A13*
For interesting new artists.
6 Cork Street, Mayfair ☎ 7734 6440 ⊖ Green Park

Interim Art *off map*
21 Herald Street, Bethnal Green ☎ 7729 4112 ⊖ Bethnal Green

Lisson Gallery *D5*
52–54 Bell Street, Marylebone ☎ 7724 2739 ⊖ Edgware Road

Victoria Miro *F3*
16 Wharf Road, Islington ☎ 7734 5082 ⊖ Angel

White Cube *D3*
44 Duke Street, Piccadilly ☎ 7930 5373 ⊖ Piccadilly Circus

White Cube^2 *F4*
48 Hoxton Square, Hoxton ☎ 7930 5373 ⊖ Old Street

kids' attractions

Coram's Fields *C8*
The park, pets' corner, and playground do not admit adults 'unless accompanied by a child'. Bring carrots to feed the goats, and a change of clothes for the 'beach'.
entrance: Guilford Street, Bloomsbury ☎ 7837 6138 ⊖ Russell Square
◑ *9am–dusk daily.*

London Zoo *C2*
The zoo is huge, so follow the free *What's On* guide, which gives details of feeding and bathing times. There's a revamped children's zoo and during the summer 'animals in action' is in the outside amphitheatre (12pm, 2pm, and 3.30pm daily in school holidays and at weekends).
Regent's Park ☎ 7722 3333 ⊖ Camden Town ◑ *Apr–Oct: 10am–5.30pm daily (Nov–Mar: 10am–4pm daily).*

Serpentine Lido ⚲D11

A splash in the water at the Serpentine is just the ticket on a hot day. For young kids there's a supervised play area with sandpits and slides. There's also the sandy-bottomed 'beach', where older kids can swim in deeper water.

Hyde Park, Knightsbridge ☎ 7706 3422 ⊖ Knightsbridge
◑ *Jul–Sep: 10am–6pm daily.*

Bethnal Green Museum of Childhood *⚲off map*

This branch of the Victoria & Albert Museum greets you with a huge collection of dolls' houses, model railways, puppets, board games, and more. Exhibits are mainly look-don't-touch.

Cambridge Heath Road, Bethnal Green ☎ 8980 2415 ⊖ Bethnal Green
◑ *10am–5.50pm Mon–Thu & Sat–Sun.*

London Aquarium ⚲F14

The two-storey, glass-sided shark tank is awe-inspiring and the luminescent jellyfish display surreal. The most popular interactive display is undisputably the tank of 'friendly' rays. Further on, the kids can tickle crabs.

County Hall, Westminster Bridge Road, South Bank ☎ 7967 8000
⊖ Waterloo, Westminster ◑ *10am–5pm daily.*

London Transport Museum ⚲A14

Kids can clamber on historic buses, trams, and trains to their hearts' content; play with touch-screen computers and videos; and have a go at 'driving' an underground train on the tube simulator. London Transport's wonderful posters, commissioned from many well known artists including Man Ray and David Hockney, are in a separate gallery.

Covent Garden Piazza, Covent Garden ☎ 7379 6344 ⊖ Covent Garden
◑ *10am–6pm daily (from 11am Fri).*

Pollock's Toy Museum ⚲D7

This old museum is more like a ramshackle home than an exhibition space. Discover an incredible array of old-fashioned toys, and marvel at the 4000-year-old Egyptian mouse and one of the world's oldest teddies. There are free toy theatre performances during school holidays.

1 Scala Street, North Soho ☎ 7636 3452 ⊖ Goodge Street
◑ *10am–5pm Mon–Sat.*

BBC Experience ⚲D5

Access to BBC equipment and archives will keep kids engrossed. They can present the weather, try sports commentating, and then edit their performances.

Broadcasting House, Portland Place, Marylebone ☎ 0870 6030304
⊖ Oxford Circus ◑ *10am–6pm daily (from 11am Mon).*

Holland Park Adventure Playpark *off map*
This is a huge space with super-sized castles and assault courses. Adults aren't allowed in but your kids are supervised so you can roam through the rest of the park. There's also a playground next door for kids aged 0 to 7.
entrance: Abbotsbury Road, Kensington ☎ 7603 6956
⊖ High Street Kensington ◑ ***10am–6pm daily.***

Sleepovers
Kids don't always want to spend 24 hours a day in the company of adults. They want to venture out, break free, hang out with people their own age. So several London museums and childcare services have set up pioneering sleepover schemes. The **Science Museum** runs monthly nights of fun that include playing in the Launch Pad and Fight Lab rooms; the **British Museum** has three to four themed nights a year, like the Egyptian night where kids bed down with mummies and weave bullrushes; and the **Golden Hinde**, the full-size replica of Francis Drake's ship, holds monthly Individual Living History nights where kids dress up in Elizabethan costume and act out roles on ship. Food is provided, but sleeping bags must be taken.

British Museum *C8*
Great Russell Street, Bloomsbury ☎ 7636 1555 ⊖ Tottenham Court Road

Golden Hinde *off map*
St Marie Overie Dock, Cathedral Street, Southwark
☎ 0870 0118700 ⊖ London Bridge

Science Museum *A17*
Exhibition Road, Science Museum ☎ 7938 8080 ⊖ South Kensington

Show Time
For free entertainment, go to Covent Garden Piazza, where there are often Punch & Judy shows, jugglers, and fire eaters. Cinemas that run special junior programmes are the **Barbican** and the **National Film Theatre**. There are several great children's theatres: London's only permanent puppet theatre is the acclaimed 110-seater **Little Angel Theatre**; but if you want to combine puppetry with a canal setting, go for the **Puppet Theatre Barge**. For new plays there is the purpose-built **Polka Children's Theatre** – also the largest venue with 300 seats. London's oldest children's theatre is the central **Unicorn Theatre for Children**. Recommended age groups and prices vary with productions.

Barbican Cinema *D9*
Barbican Centre, Silk Street ☎ 7382 7000

BFI IMAX *off map*
South Bank ☎ 7902 1234

Little Angel Theatre *D3*
14 Dagmar Passage, Cross Street, Islington ☎ 7226 1787

National Film Theatre *D14*
South Bank ☎ 7633 0274

Polka Children's Theatre *off map*
240 The Broadway, Wimbledon ☎ 8543 4888

Puppet Theatre Barge *off map*
Regent's Canal, Little Venice (Oct–May only) ☎ 7249 6876

Unicorn Theatre for Children *D3*
St Mark's Studios, Chillingworth Road, Islington ☎ 7700 0702

parks & gardens

Battersea Park *off map*
Play tennis, go boating, bowling or join in a game of softball in this park designed for the actively inclined. Kids can feed and stroke the animals at the children's zoo or go for a pony ride. The park is home to the serene Peace Pagoda and Henry Moore's statue, Three Standing Figures. Loads of activities.
Entrances: Albert Bridge Road; Queenstown Road ☎ 8871 7530
Sloane Square then 137, 319 Battersea Park ***8am–dusk daily.***

Chelsea Physic Garden *off map*
Set up over 300 years ago for the study of medicinal herbs and plants, the walled garden shelters glasshouses, ancient trees and an early rock garden. In this tiny space, there are, amazingly, around 5,000 species of plants and trees. An oasis of tranquillity.
Entrances: Royal Hospital Road; Swan Walk ☎ 7352 5646
Sloane Square then 11, 22, 211 ***Apr–Oct: 12–5pm Wed; 2–6pm Sun.***

Green Park *C13–E13*
A haven for cooped-up office workers. Find the bandstand (concerts Jun–Aug), hire a deckchair (Apr–Sep only), and immerse yourself in the English scene. Green Park remains green all year round thanks to water running just below the grassy surface. Half a million daffodils bloom in the spring.
Entrances: Piccadilly; Constitution Hill ☎ 7930 1793
Green Park; Hyde Park Corner ***dawn–dusk daily.***

Greenwich Park *off map*
In good weather you can admire wide swathes of London from here. Stroll around the 183 acres of parkland, wallow in royal history and see the Queen's House, Royal Naval College and the Old Royal Observatory.

From the comfort of a deckchair listen to music from the bandstand (Sundays); there are outdoor theatre performances in the summer. ☝ Great views; masses for kids to do in summer.
Entrances: Blackheath Gate; St Mary's Gate ☎ 8858 2608 Ⅲ Greenwich; Maze Hill ◑ *6am–dusk daily.*

Hampstead Heath & Parliament Hill *off map*
Hampstead Heath really feels like the countryside with its rolling woodland and meadows. The heath has many ponds, including three for swimming: Kenwood Ladies, Hampstead Mixed, and Highgate Men's. If you're after cultural options, there are lakeside concerts in summer, and an impressive collection of paintings at English Heritage's Kenwood House. ☝ Terrific views; easy to find a spot all to yourself.
Entrances: Hampstead Lane; East Heath Road; Highgate Road ☎ 8348 9908 ⊖ Hampstead Ⅲ Hampstead Heath ◑ *24 hours daily.*

Highgate Cemetery *off map*
Romantic resting place for Victorians eminent and otherwise. Karl Marx (east side) may be the most famous, but George Eliot (east side), Christina Rossetti and Michael Faraday (both west side) are also here among the striking statues and sarcophagi. ☝ The tour around the west side.
Entrance: Swain's Lane, Highgate ☎ 8340 1834 ⊖ Archway ◑ *Summer: 10am–5pm Mon–Fri, 11am–5pm Sat– Sun; Winter: 10am–4pm Mon–Fri, 11am–4pm Sat–Sun; cemetery is closed during funerals.*

Hyde Park *A11–C12*
Open to the public since 1637, Hyde Park's sheer size makes it popular for large gatherings and concerts (the Rolling Stones played here in 69). Speakers' Corner (northeast corner) has been a venue for public debates since 1872. ☝ Lots of uncrowded spots; boating on the Serpentine; swimming at the lido.
Entrances: Marble Arch; Bayswater Road; Park Lane; Knightsbridge; Hyde Park Corner ☎ 7298 2100 ⊖ Marble Arch; Queensway; Lancaster Gate; Knightsbridge; Hyde Park Corner ◑ *dawn–dusk daily.*

Kensington Gardens *off map*
Bang next door to Hyde Park, these gardens were originally part of Kensington Palace, where Diana, Princess of Wales lived. Since her death the number of visitors has gone up dramatically and there are plans for a Diana Memorial Walk. ☝ Exhibitions of modern art at the Serpentine Gallery; model boats on the Round Pond.
Entrances: Bayswater Road; High Street Kensington ☎ 7298 2117 ⊖ Lancaster Gate; Queensway; High Street Kensington ◑ *dawn–dusk daily.*

Kew Gardens *off map*

The Royal Botanic Gardens at Kew are a mecca for plant-lovers. The Palm House is a feat of Victorian engineering and the newest glasshouse, the Princess of Wales Conservatory, contains ten microclimates. Also check out the eccentric Great Pagoda, the Marianne North Gallery and the Plants+People exhibition. You can visit a desert, a rainforest, and a swamp all in one day.

Entrances: Kew Road; Kew Green ☎ 8940 1171 ⊖ Kew Gardens Kew Bridge ◑ *Summer: 9.30am–6pm daily; Winter: 9.30am–4pm daily; glasshouses & gallery close earlier.*

Regent's Park *maps 5–6 & 2*

Regent's Park was planned by the Crown architect, John Nash, in the early 1800s. The plan was never fully realized but the park is now surrounded by impressive classical-style villas. Main attractions are the zoo, three playgrounds, two boating lakes, open-air theatre (May–Sep) and bandstand concerts (May–Sep: Sat–Sun). Open-air theatre; Queen Mary's Rose Garden in the summer.

Entrances: Park Square Gardens; Prince Albert Road ☎ 7486 7905 ⊖ Regent's Park; Camden Town ◑ *dawn–dusk daily.*

Richmond Park *off map*

One of the wildest and largest of London's parks, and still home to herds of deer (red and fallow), which once provided venison for royalty. The Isabella Plantation is a mass of blooms in spring.

Entrances: Queen's Road; Roehampton Lane; Kingston Hill ☎ 8948 3209 ⊖ Richmond ◑ *dawn–dusk daily.*

St James's Park *F13*

London's first royal public park, created from a marshy field where lepers kept their pigs. Remodelled by Crown architect John Nash, it was a prototype for the later Victorian parks. The lake is the focal point and there are summer concerts on the bandstand. Views from Park Bridge; feeding the pelicans.

Entrances: Horse Guards' Road; The Mall; Birdcage Walk ☎ 7930 1793 ⊖ St James's Park ◑ *dawn–dusk daily.*

Wetland Centre *off map*

What used to be a West London derelict piece of land is now a remarkable wildlife habitat where birds of all kind flock from all over the world. Fantastic view over the main lake from the glass observatory.

Barnes ☎ 8409 4400 ⊖ Hammersmith, then the 'Duck Bus' Barnes ◑ *Summer: 9.30am–6pm daily (Winter: to 5pm)*

body and soul

Whether you fancy a whole day of luxury or just an hour's pampering, London has plenty of places to get in touch with your hedonistic self.

spas

The Porchester Spa *off map*

The Porchester has a delicious art deco feel. Lounge about in a wrap, or sweat it out in the Turkish baths, Russian steam rooms, or sauna. Non-members £18.70.

Porchester Road, Bayswater ☎ 7792 3980 ⊖ Queensway
◑ *women: 10am–10pm Tue, Thu & Fri; 10am–4pm Sun; men: 10am–10pm Mon, Wed & Sat (men only); mixed: 4–10pm Sun.*

The Sanctuary *A14*

Exclusively for women, this is the ultimate pamper. Don a white towelling robe and pad between sauna, steam room, meditation suite, swimming pool, and jacuzzi. Membership is £35 (evening: from 5pm Wed–Fri) or £58 (day).

12 Floral Street, Covent Garden ☎ 0870 0630300 ⊖ Covent Garden
◑ *10am–6pm Sun–Tue; 9.30am–6pm Wed–Fri; 10am–8pm Sat.*

Selfridges Spa & Health Oasis *F6*

What better place to rest after shopping? The hydrotherapy tub (huge bath with jets of warm water) is amazing (£25). Aromatherapy costs extra.

400 Oxford Street, Bond Street ☎ 7318 3389 ⊖ Bond Street ◑ *9.30am–7pm Mon–Fri (to 8pm Thu–Fri); 9.30am–7pm Sat; 12–6pm Sun.*

swim & float

Brockwell Park Lido *off map*

An old-fashioned lido with 30s multi-coloured bathing huts. Packed with families and trendies at weekends, but blissfully empty early morning (£2.50).

Dulwich Road, Brixton ☎ 7274 3088 ⊖ Brixton Ⅲ Herne Hill
◑ *May–Sep: 6.45am–10am & 12–7pm Mon–Fri; 8am–7pm Sat–Sun.*

Hampstead Heath *off map*

The men's pond is a gay cruising area, but the women's is secluded and friendly. One of the few chlorine-free places to bob about outdoors. Ring for a free diary of opening times.

North End Way, Golders Green ☎ 8348 9908 ⊖ Golders Green
◑ *times vary.*

South London Natural Health Centre *off map*

At the top of the building are two flotation cabins. Slip in for 1-hour (£40), and let Epsom salts suspend you in warm water. Surprisingly unclaustrophobic, it relaxes the muscles, and leaves you feeling serene.

7a Clapham Common South Side, Clapham
☎ 7720 4952 ⊖ Clapham Common ◑ *10am–10pm daily.*

fitness & dance

The Club *F14*

For the swankier gym-goer, The Club is the latest state-of-the-art health and fitness spa, located in County Hall, overlooking the Thames. Pamper days include use of the spa and the 75-station gym (£25).

County Hall, South Bank ☎ 7928 4900 ⊖ Waterloo; Westminster
◑ *24 hours daily.*

Danceworks *F6*

Waltz into this dance studio where day membership (£4) opens up a world of possibilities, from salsa to belly dancing (from £4–£6 per class).

16 Balderton Street, Mayfair ☎ 7629 6183 ⊖ Bond Street
◑ *8am–10pm Mon–Fri; 10am–6pm Sat–Sun.*

Oasis Sports Centre *E8*

The biggest gym in the West End. Compulsory induction session £7.90; unlimited gym use £5.20; step yoga, aqua, or tai-chi classes (1 hour) £4.75.

32 Endell Street, Covent Garden ☎ 7836 9722 ⊖ Covent Garden
◑ *6.30am–9.30pm Mon–Fri; 9.30–5.30pm Sat–Sun.*

Pineapple Studios *E8*

A funky dance studio with 150 different classes. It's popular with both pros and beginners – so stamp your feet to flamenco, tap or street jazz (£4– £6 per class). Day membership £1 before 4.30pm, £4 after.

7 Langley Street, Covent Garden ☎ 7836 4004
⊖ Covent Garden ◑ *7.30am–10pm Mon–Fri; 9am–8pm Sat.*

The Savoy *A14*

For a modest £20 you can spend a day at the Savoy's Fitness Gallery – including use of the gym, sauna, steam rooms, and one of only two roof-top swimming pools in London. Spend an extra £35 for an hour's personal training.

The Strand, Covent Garden ☎ 7836 4343 ⊖ Charing Cross; Leicester Square ◑ *6.30am–9pm Mon–Fri; 8am–8pm Sat–Sun.*

Triyoga *off map*

This innovative drop-in yoga centre is the talk-of-the-town. With the current popularity of yoga, it can't fail to succeed, with classes all day every day of varying style and levels. Prices range from £8 (for 1 hour classes) to £10 (for 2 hours). 16 alternative health treatments are also available.

6 Erskine Road, Swiss Cottage ☎ 7586 5939
⊖ Swiss Cottage; Chalk Farm ◑ *6.30am–9pm daily (from 7am Tue & Thu; to 8.30pm Fri; from 9am Sat–Sun).*

massage & alternative therapies

The Grove *off map*

A friendly alternative therapy centre, with spiral staircases and spacious rooms. Experience Indian head massage using the Ayurvedic method to soothe and invigorate (£25).

182–184 Kensington Church Street, Notting Hill ☎ 7221 2266
⊖ Notting Hill Gate ◑ *9am–7pm Mon; 9am– 8pm Tue–Fri; 9am–6pm Sat; 12–5pm Sun.*

Neal's Yard Therapy Rooms *E8*

Located in the hippiedom of Neal's Yard, these white-washed rooms have a cottage feel, and offer 30 therapies. For blissful relaxation there's reflexology, shiatsu or aromatherapy massage (£36–£50). Times vary, so book in advance.

2 Neal's Yard, Covent Garden ☎ 7379 7662 ⊖ Covent Garden
◑ *9am–9.30pm Mon–Fri; 1.30–5.30pm Sat.*

Walk-in BackRub *E8*

With no need to book in advance, and a typical wait of just 5 minutes (more on Sat afternoons), this promises a truly stress-free experience. Relax with a 10, 20 or 30 minute fully-clothed shiatsu massage (£8.95+).

14 Neal's Yard, Covent Garden ☎ 7836 9111 ⊖ Covent Garden
◑ *11.30am–7pm Mon–Sat (to 6pm Sat).*

beauty treatments

Aveda Concept Salon *E12*

Bathed in green light from a giant aquarium, this must be the most soothing of London's salons. There's a range of treatments using Aveda's luscious organic products, including the custom facial (£55).

Harvey Nichols, 109–125 Knightsbridge ☎ 7201 8610
⊖ Knightsbridge ◑ *9am–8pm Mon–Fri; 9am–7pm Sat; 12–6pm Sun.*

Cosmetics à La Carte *E12*

Staff can mix and match your choices from a vivid rainbow of cosmetics. A 90-minute lesson creates a new you for £100.

19b Motcombe Street, Knightsbridge ☎ 7235 0596 ⊖ Knightsbridge
◑ *10am–6pm Mon–Sat.*

Elizabeth Arden Red Door Hair & Beauty Spa *F6*

Among the facials on offer in this smart Mayfair spa are the skin-illuminating facial treatment (£55), guaranteed to give a healthy look; also CACI treatment (£55), a 'non-surgical face-lift', which uses electrical impulses to tone face muscles and smooth away wrinkles.

29 Davies Street, Mayfair ☎ 7629 4488 ⊖ Bond Street ◑ *10am–7pm Mon–Tue; 9am–8pm Wed–Thu; 9am–6pm Fri–Sat; 11am–5pm Sun.*

The Green Room *E8*

A whole host of treats (cheaper than most) can be had at the eight London branches of this treatment room. Enjoy massage (from £18.50), make-overs (from £18.50), and alternative therapies (including acupuncture and reflexology). Or try a 15-minute £10 fast fix.

The Body Shop, 23 Long Acre, Covent Garden
☎ 7379 9600 ⊖ Covent Garden ◑ *10am–7pm Mon–Sat (to 6pm Sat).*

Harrods Hair & Beauty Salon *F11*

Pass the neo-classical busts at the gateway to this salon, and you know you're heading into an arena of extravagance, with prices to match. A fantastic array of facials range from £52 to £85. For flawless beauty at any expense, hair and make-up duo, Andrew and Liz Collinge, will make you over for £425!

Knightsbridge ☎ 7893 8333 ⊖ Knightsbridge ◑ *10am–7pm daily.*

Joan Price's Face Place *C18*

A private one-hour make-up lesson (£40) will leave you looking dazzling, or do it yourself for free with a palate of 15 make-up brands.

4 Chelsea Manor Studios, Flood Street, Chelsea ☎ 7352 8113
⊖ Sloane Square ◑ *10am–5.30pm Tue–Sun.*

MOT & Ian Matthews *A13*

Pioneers of the male grooming industry, offering a wide range of specialist treatments exclusively for men, including oxygen treatments for the jet-lagged. Cut-throat shaving and barbering available.

28 Maddox Street, Soho ☎ 7287 3334/7499 4904 ⊖ Oxford Circus
◑ *8am–8pm Mon–Fri; 9am–6pm Sat.*

haircuts

Daniel Poole HumanResource Centre *B13*

Right in the heart of Soho and ferociously fashionable, it's the place to go for shocking pink colour (from £30) or green hair extensions (£5 each).

49 Old Compton Street, Soho ☎ 7287 0666 ⊖ Piccadilly Circus; Leicester Square ◑ ***11am–8pm Mon–Sat; 12–8pm Sun.***

John Frieda *B12*

This is where beauty editors and celebs, such as Catherine Deneuve and Diana Ross, get their locks chopped. Prices for a cut and blow dry range from £50 to £150 (for a senior stylist).

4 Aldford Street, Mayfair ☎ 7491 0840 ⊖ Bond Street; Marble Arch ◑ ***9am–6pm Mon–Sat.***

Vidal Sassoon, Men's Salon *B12*

A reliable, top-class chain for a good fashion cut. It's not cheap – £45–£70 for a tip-top stylist – but the price includes an out-of-this-world head massage.

56 Brook Street, Bond Street ☎ 7318 5222 ⊖ Bond St ◑ ***9am–6pm Tue–Sat.***

Worthington's *D7*

Centrally located, but also chic and informal. Here, customers read the daily newspapers and sip a complimentary glass of wine. A haircut that includes mini head massage and personalised hair care costs from £39.50 to £72.

7 Percy Street, North Soho ☎ 7631 1370 ⊖ Goodge Street ◑ ***8am–9pm Mon–Thu; 8am–8pm Fri; 9am–6pm Sat.***

piercings & tattoos

Into You *D9*

Tongue piercing, tiger tattoos, and gold-plated genitalia – internationally renowned artist Alex Binnie will pierce or ink you 'just about anywhere'. There's also a huge choice of body jewellery. Piercing from £25; tattooing £50 per hour. Book in advance.

144 St John Street, Clerkenwell ☎ 7253 5085 ⊖ Farringdon ◑ ***12–7pm Tue–Fri; 12–6pm Sat.***

alternative health

Farmacia *E8*

Brother and sister, Sanjay and Meenu Bhandari run this unique pharmacy combining conventional medicine with complementary therapies. All their medicines and products are organic and GM-free.

169 Drury Lane, Covent Garden ☎ 7831 0830 ⊖ Covent Garden ◑ ***9am–7pm Mon–Sat (to 6pm Sat).***

games & activities

Sometimes, only the pleasure of bouncing around on elasticated rope, floating high above the city or driving miniature cars round in circles is enough to raise the pulse. Check out some of these adrenalin-fuelled, endorphin-inducing activities.

ballooning

Wasn't it the New Seekers who sang 'Up and Away in my Beautiful Balloon'? Now sing it for yourself as you glide across the London skyline.

Adventure Balloons *off map*
Pick-up at Tower Hill Bridge & Vauxhall ☎ 01252–844222 ◑ *Apr–Sep: Tue–Thu.*

Virgin Balloon Flights *off map*
Departing from Alexandra Palace; Burgess Park; Blackheath ☎ 01952 200141 ◑ *Mar–Sep: daily; Oct–Feb: weekends.*

bungee-jumping

After leaving their permanent position at Battersea Bridge, UK Bungee Club is now a roaming tower, allowing adrenalin-junkies to jump all over London. Call for up-and-coming venues. Book at least a week in advance.

UK Bungee Club *throughout town*
☎ 07000 286433 ◑ *10am–5pm Sat–Sun.*

casinos

You don't have to be a black-tie-and-tux wearing millionaire to try your luck at roulette or blackjack. Many casinos offer free membership, but visit in person with your passport or driving licence, and be prepared for a 24-hour delay before you can take to the gambling tables.

The Golden Nugget *B13*
22–32 Shaftesbury Avenue, Piccadilly ☎ 7439 0099 ⊖ Piccadilly Circus ◑ *2pm–4am daily.*

Rendezvous *D12*
14 Old Park Lane, Mayfair ☎ 7514 9000 ⊖ Hyde Park Corner ◑ *12pm–4am daily.*

dance

From the foxtrot to the samba, the quickstep to the Cha-cha-cha, you'll find over 130 styles down at Pineapple Dance Studio. For steaming salsa, the Loughborough Hotel runs three club nights a week with classes beforehand. And for something a little different, try swinging the night away at Jitterbugs.

Jitterbugs *B13*
Notre Dame Hall, 6 Leicester Place, Leicester Square ☎ 7437 5571
⊖ Leicester Square ◑ ***7.45–midnight Wed (classes until 9.30pm).***

Loughborough Hotel *off map*
39 Loughborough Road, Brixton ☎ 7642 5806 ⊖ Brixton
◑ ***8pm–2am Thu–Sat (classes until 10pm).***

Pineapple Dance Studio *E8*
7 Langley Street, Covent Garden ☎ 7836 4004 ⊖ Covent Garden
◑ ***7.30am–10pm Mon–Fri; 9am–8pm Sat.***

go-kart racing

Nothing brings out the competitive spirit more than re-enacting the drama of Formula One racing from the confines of a nippy little kart. It's an activity best appreciated with a group of friends to expose the depths of interpersonal rivalry.

Daytona Raceway *off map*
Atlas Road, Willesden ☎ 8961 3616 ⊖ North Acton; Willesden Junction
◑ ***9am–10.30pm daily.***

Playscape Pro Racing *off map*
Streatham Park Raceway, Streatham High Road, Streatham ☎ 7801 0110
Streatham ◑ ***10am–10pm daily.***

helicopter tours

If you want a god's view of London but time is too pressing for a balloon ride, there are currently two companies offering helicopter tours of the capital: Cabair do a 30-minute trip, and Flightworks do a slightly more fulfilling 50-minute trip. Both take in most of London's sights. Helicopters can also be chartered for specifically requested journeys.

Cabair Helicopters *off map*
Elstree Aerodrome, Herts ☎ 8953 4411
⊖ Edgware (then 5-minute taxi ride) ◑ ***Sun.***

Flightworks *F7*
Wycombe Air Park, near Marlow, Bucks ☎ 01494 451111 ◑ ***daily.***

horse riding

Galloping around the city's parks is the perfect antidote to traipsing the crowded streets of central London. Hyde Park is the most central of rides, but the Wimbledon stables offer more interesting terrain.

Hyde Park Stables *off map*
63 Bathurst Mews, Bayswater ☎ 7723 2813 ⊖ Lancaster Gate
◑ *Tue–Sun (times vary).*

Wimbledon Village Stables *off map*
24 High Street, Wimbledon ☎ 8946 8579 ⊖ Wimbledon
◑ *Tue–Sun (times vary).*

ice skating

If the slippery pleasures of frozen water are your thing, here are a couple of places close to central London to keep your blades from rusting.

Broadgate Ice Rink *D10*
Broadgate Circle, Eldon Street, City ☎ 7505 4068 ⊖ Liverpool Street
◑ *Oct–Apr: 12–6pm Mon–Thu (10pm Fri); 11am–8.30pm Sat; 11am–7pm Sun.*

First Bowl *off map*
17 Queensway, Bayswater ☎ 7229 0172 ⊖ Bayswater
◑ *10am–10pm daily.*

karaoke

For a nation that trades on a character of reserve, karaoke has proved itself a strangely popular import to these shores. There are karaoke nights in pubs throughout the capital, but for a recommendation you could try the glammed-up karaoke night at the Retro Bar.

Retro Bar *A14*
2 George Court, Covent Garden ☎ 7321 2811 ⊖ Charing Cross ◑ *Wed.*

limousines

The stretched limo is, perhaps, the defining image of wealth and excess; behind the darkened windows hides an intangible world of easy leisure. But you too can taste a little of *la dolce vita* from £35 per hour.

A Limo Scene ☎ 0956 153116

Padrino Limousines ☎ 7254 4888

namco station

For kids who simply won't grow up, and who now want to eat their cake, drink their beer, and play their games, the Namco Station is the new solution. Bumper cars, special effect tenpin bowling, shooting games, an American pool hall, video games, and a bar. A veritable house of cheap kicks.

Namco Station *F14*
County Hall, Riverside Building, Westminster Bridge Road, Westminster ☎ 7967 1066 ⊖ Waterloo; Westminster ◑ *10am–midnight daily.*

reading the future

If you're keen to know your destiny, the area around Neal Street in Covent Garden is the place to head for. The Astrology Shop prepares a variety of horoscopes, including character profiles and compatibility charts. Mysteries offers an assortment of psychic readings.

Equinox at the Astrology Shop *E8*
78 Neal Street, Covent Garden ☎ 7497 1001 ⊖ Covent Garden
◑ *9am–7pm Mon–Sat (8pm Thu); 11am–7pm Sun.*

Mysteries, New Age Centre *E8*
9–11 Monmouth Street, Covent Garden ☎ 7240 3686 ⊖ Covent Garden
◑ *10am–6pm Mon–Sat.*

rollerblading & skateboarding

Rollerblading is one of the speediest ways of bombing around. Most of London's parks have good enough paths for skating, but one of the best areas is along the South Bank. The Playstation Ski Park has specially-designed space for skateboarding, rollerblading, and BMX racing, but they don't hire out equipment.

London Bicycle Tour Company *off map*
1A Gabriel's Wharf, 56 Upper Ground, South Bank ☎ 7928 6838
⊖ Waterloo ◑ *9am–6pm Mon–Sat; 10am–2pm Sun.*

Playstation Ski Park *off map*
Bay 65–66 Acklam Road, Notting Hill ☎ 8969 4669 ⊖ Ladbroke Grove
◑ *12–4pm & 5–9pm daily.*

Skate Attack *off map*
96 Highgate Road, Kentish Town ☎ 7485 0007 ⊖ Kentish Town
◑ *9am–6pm Mon–Sat; 10am–2pm Sun.*

snooker & pool

The green baize, the discreet lighting in smoke-filled halls, and the reassuring click of chalked cue meeting ball – the late-night pleasures of snooker. But if you're not entirely committed to the whole club atmosphere and just fancy playing the odd frame, pubs are good alternative places to play pool in.

The Elbow Room *D1*
103 Westbourne Grove, Notting Hill ☎ 7221 5211 ⊖ Notting Hill Gate
◑ *12–11pm daily (to 10.30pm Sun).*

King's Cross Snooker Club *off map*
225 Pentonville Road, King's Cross ☎ 7278 7079 ⊖ King's Cross
◑ *24 hours*

Players Snooker Club *off map*
63 Wandsworth High Street, Wandsworth ☎ 8874 1252 ⊖ Wandsworth Town ◑ *24 hours*

The Pool Room *B10*
104–108 Curtain Road, Hoxton ☎ 7739 9608 ⊖ Old Street
◑ *12–11pm daily.*

speak out

Since 1872, the law has recognised the right of free assembly in the Marble Arch corner of Hyde Park where orators speak and crowds gather to discuss, argue, and heckle. It is still a fun place to visit on Sundays, when subjects ranging from Esperanto to religion are aired by speakers who have only a milk crate for a stage.

Speakers' Corner *A12*
On the corner of Hyde Park near Marble Arch ⊖ Marble Arch ◑ *Sun.*

tenpin bowling

There are several bowling lanes throughout London, and for your nearest bowl it is best just to check in the Yellow Pages. Charges are either per game – ranging from £3.80 to around £5 (depending on the time) – or, if there is a group of you, by lane at £16 to £32 per hour for up to six players.

First Bowl *off map*
17 Queensway, Bayswater ☎ 7229 0172 ⊖ Bayswater
◑ *10am–midnight daily.*

Rowans Leisure Centre *off map*
10 Stroud Green Road, Finsbury Park ☎ 8800 1950 ⊖ Finsbury Park
◑ *10.30–1am Mon–Thu; 10.30–3.30am Fri–Sat; 10.30–1.30am Sun.*

hotels

London hotels are pretty pricey. The choice is good at the top end of the scale, but there are also plenty of cheaper sleeps clustered around the main railway stations and the backpacker stomping ground of Earl's Court. Price categories are for a double room.

under £100

Fielding *A14*

This 18th-century listed building in a pedestrianized Covent Garden side street offers exceptional value for such a fab location. Lacking in flashy amenities, it has a quaint feel. Bedrooms are simply furnished in pine and wicker with tidy shower rooms.

4 Broad Court, Bow Street, Covent Garden ☎ 7836 8305
F 7497 0064 W www.fieldinghotel.co.uk ⊖ Covent Garden 24 all
££ (singles: £76; doubles: £100)

La Gaffe *off map*

Under the long-standing artistic patronage of local Hampstead playwright, Bernardo Stella, La Gaffe hums with life. The bedrooms (quieter towards the back) are all attractively decorated in bright fabrics, and kitted out with crafty shower rooms.

107–111 Heath Street, Hampstead NW3 6SS ☎ 7435 8965 F 7794 7592
W www.lagaffe.co.uk ⊖ Hampstead 18 AE/DC/MC/V
££ (singles: £65; doubles: £90)

Generator *A8*

Futuristic twist on hostel accommodation, with hard-edge decoration and graphics, boldly designed for maximum impact. The friendly atmosphere encourages global travellers to meet and mingle. Good-value and fun.

Compton Place, Bloomsbury ☎ 7388 7666 F 7388 7644 W www.thegenerator.co.uk ⊖ Russell Square 217 MC/V £ (from £15/person)

Hotel 167 *off map*

An upbeat B&B run in a straightforward, hands-on style. Breakfast is served on marble tables beneath large abstract artworks in the elegantly proportioned reception lobby. All the bedrooms are ensuite with minifridges and in-house video. Book ahead for these affordable prices.

167 Old Brompton Road, South Kensington SW5 0AN ☎ 7373 3221
F 7373 3360 W www.hotel167.com ⊖ South Kensington 19
all ££ (singles: £72; doubles: £90)

Mabledon Court *off map*
A welcome budget oasis in the less than salubrious area of King's Cross. This reassuring little hotel is neat, very well-kept, and will meet basic needs. The bedrooms, all with ensuite facilities, are tiny yet practical. There's a bright sitting room and a small breakfast room.
10–11 Mabledon Place, King's Cross WC1H 9BA ☎ 7388 3866 F 7387 5686
w www.smoothhound.co.uk/hotels/mabledon.html
⊖ King's Cross; Russell Square 33 all ££ (singles: £68; doubles: £78)

Mad Hatter *14a*
This converted Victorian pub/hotel south of the river is an easy stride to Waterloo. The hats lining the walls are a reminder of the building's former existence as a hat factory, while the *Alice in Wonderland* theme is accentuated with paintings and pictures. Cozier-than-average bedrooms.
3–7 Stamford Street, Southwark SE1 9NY ☎ 7401 9222 F 7401 7111
w www.fullers.co.uk ⊖ Blackfriars 30 all
£ (singles & doubles: £60)

Morgan House *off map*
Classy budget B&B which operates more or less in tandem with Woodville House (no. 107), a few doors down. In both, you'll find original fireplaces, appealing breakfast rooms, and attractive patio gardens.
120 Ebury Street, Belgravia SW1W 9QQ ☎ 7730 2384 F 7730 8442
w www.morganhouse.co.uk ⊖ Victoria 11 MC/V £ (singles: £42; doubles: £62)

78 Albert Street *D2*
One of surprisingly few smart but relaxed B&Bs in central London, 78 Albert Street is housed in a stylish creeper-clad Georgian terrace. The bedrooms are light, clean, uncluttered, and user-friendly, with ensuite bathrooms. Breakfast is served in the airy open-plan kitchen.
78 Albert Street, Camden NW1 7NR ☎ 7387 6813 F 7387 1704
⊖ Camden Town 3 none ££ (singles: £40; doubles: £80)

Swiss House *off map*
A warm, cozy ambience pervades this country-cottage style Victorian house. Breakfast is served in rustic surroundings and room service operates from midday. Comfy bedrooms are traditional, some stunningly proportioned with tall windows. All have showers and cable TV. Opt for a quieter room at the back.
171 Old Brompton Road, South Kensington SW5 0AN ☎ 7373 2769
F 7373 4983 w www.swiss-hh.demon.co.uk ⊖ Gloucester Road 15
AE/DC/MC/V ££ (singles: £46; doubles: £80)

Windermere *off map*

A neat, bright, friendly option. Rooms are all shapes and sizes, hence there's a complex tariff. Communal areas consist of a small lounge and a relaxing restaurant which attracts increasing numbers of non-residents.
142–144 Warwick Way, Pimlico SW1V 4JE ☎ 7834 5163 F 7630 8831
w www.windermere-hotel.co.uk ⊖ Victoria 22
AE/JCB/MC/V ££ (singles: £80; doubles: £84)

YHA Oxford Street *E7*

Favoured by international backpackers, this busy hostel is just seconds away from London's most famous shopping street. Book well in advance.
14–18 Noel Street, Soho W1V 3PD ☎ 7734 1618 F 7734 1657
w www.yha.org.uk ⊖ Oxford Circus 75 MC/V £ (from £20.55 per person)

£100–£200

Academy *D7*

Shapely bay trees give way to floral sculptures as you enter these stylish Georgian terraced houses. Inside it's cool, urbane, restrained. Plain, light walls flatter bright contemporary fabrics and tasteful modern prints, but period features are still intact. A library-lounge opens onto lush patio gardens.
17–25 Gower Street, Bloomsbury WC1E 6HG ☎ 7631 4115 F 7636 3442
w www.etontownhouse.com ⊖ Goodge Street; Tottenham Court Road
49 all ££ (singles: £115; doubles: £145)

Basil Street Hotel *E12*

A stone's throw from Knightsbridge, this Edwardian retreat offers instant therapy. The relaxed country house has traditional bedrooms which are good value for such an exclusive location. Rare character and real charm.
Basil Street, Knightsbridge SW3 1AH ☎ 7581 3311 F 7581 3693
w www.thebasil.com ⊖ Knightsbridge 80 all
££–£££ (singles: £128 + vat; doubles: £190 + vat)

Beaufort *B17*

The Beaufort attracts discerning business folk and 'ladies who lunch'. Housekeeping is exemplary; the facilities endless. Each swish, individually designed lair offers luxuries such as brandy, Swiss chocs, video, and CD player.
33 Beaufort Gardens, Knightsbridge SW3 1PP ☎ 7584 5252 F 7589 2834
w www.thebeaufort.co.uk ⊖ Knightsbridge 28 all
£££ (singles: £170 + vat; doubles: £180 + vat)

Cannizaro House *off map*

Secluded landscaped gardens enhance the country-house feel of this elegant residence. Vast flower arrangements, chandeliers, frescoes, and

imposing *trompe l'oeil* fireplaces adorn public areas. The best bedrooms – with canopied four poster beds – are positively palatial.
West Side, Wimbledon Common SW19 4UE ☎ 8879 1464 F 8879 7338
w www.thistlehotels ⊖ Wimbledon 45 all
£££ (singles & doubles: £199)

Charlotte Street Hotel *D7*
With an old-meets-new design from Kit Kemp, this converted warehouse radiates privacy and simplicity. Bedrooms are individually designed, with a Bloomsbury set-inspired decor. Modern facilities complement boho luxury.
15 Charlotte Street, North Soho W1P 1HB ☎ 7806 2000 F 7806 2002
w www.charlottestreethotel.com ⊖ Goodge Street 52
all £££ (singles: £175 + vat; doubles:£195 + vat)

Claverley *B17*
Unfancy tariff for a small acclaimed B&B in a quiet, tree-lined cul-de-sac. Furnishings are elaborate – most rooms are romantic looking. Personal, warm, and well cared for. Enjoy complimentary tea in the reading room.
13–14 Beaufort Gardens, Knightsbridge SW3 1PS ☎ 7589 8541 F 7584 3410
w www.claverlyhotel.co.uk ⊖ Knightsbridge 29 all
££ (singles: £85; doubles: £140)

Dorset Square *C6*
A staggeringly beautiful Regency townhouse. Graceful English-style bedrooms are a treasure-trove of oils and glorious antiques. Each room is painted in bold colours and exudes character and charm.
39–40 Dorset Square, Marylebone NW1 6QN ☎ 7723 7874 F 7724 3328
w www.firmdale.com ⊖ Baker Street 38 AE/MC/V
££ (singles: £98 + vat; doubles: £140 + vat)

Durrants *E6*
Outside, Durrants is a picture of simple Georgian symmetry. Inside you'll discover softly lit oils, well-worn leather, and the polished clubbiness of a quintessentially English, family-run hotel.
22–30 George Street, Marylebone W1H 6BJ ☎ 7935 8131 F 7487 3510
⊖ Bond Street 92 AE/MC/V ££ (singles: £87.50; doubles: £135)

Five Sumner Place *C17*
This distinguished Victorian terraced house looks, and feels, like a quiet private home. Well-equipped bedrooms with trad furnishings make a smart, convenient, affordable base. Breakfast is served in a huge airy conservatory.
5 Sumner Place, South Kensington SW7 3EE ☎ 7584 7586 F 7823 9962
w www.sumnerplace.com ⊖ South Kensington 13 all
££ (singles: £88; doubles: £141)

Hazlitt's *F7*
An 18th-century hideaway in the heart of Soho, adored by media types. Rooms have clawfoot baths and antique hardwood furnishings – not modern gadgetry. Breakfast is served in your room.
6 Frith Street, Soho W1V 5TZ ☎ 7434 1775 F 7439 1524 W www.hazlittshotel.com ⊖ Piccadilly Circus; Leicester Square 23 all ££–£££ (singles: £140 + vat; doubles: £175 + vat)

Millers *off map*
The faintly bohemian feel and striking, antique-laden interiors are a supreme antidote to minimalism. The intimate, homely ambience lures an arty crowd who mingle in the elegant sitting room. A rare London find.
111a Westbourne Grove, Notting Hill W2 4UW ☎ 7243 1024 F 7243 1064 e millersuk@aol.com ⊖ Notting Hill Gate; Bayswater; Queensway 8 AE/JCB/MC/V ££–£££ (singles: £140 + vat; doubles: £160 + vat)

Mornington *off map*
Expect polished, courteous service in this Swedish-owned residence. The smart library-bar is a good place to browse the newspapers. Bedrooms have sparkling bathrooms and modern accoutrements.
12 Lancaster Gate, Bayswater W2 3LG ☎ 7262 7361 F 7706 1028 W www.mornington.se ⊖ Lancaster Gate 66 all ££ (singles: £110; doubles: £125)

Number Sixteen *C17*
A virtually unaltered, beautifully serene Victorian country-house-in-town. There are stylish, spacious bedrooms – many with balconies – and an inviting garden beyond the award-winning conservatory.
16 Sumner Place, South Kensington SW7 3EG ☎ 7589 5232 F 7584 8615 W www.numbersixteenhotel.co.uk ⊖ South Kensington 36 AE/DC/MC/V ££–£££ (singles: £95; doubles: £170)

Pelham *A17*
This luxury retreat is designed with terrific panache along fairly classical lines. It appeals to imaginative lovers of English tradition who dare to be a little different. The downstairs restaurant serves mouthwatering food.
15 Cromwell Place, South Kensington SW7 2LA ☎ 7589 8288 F 7584 8444 W www.firmdale.com ⊖ South Kensington 51 AE/MC/V ££–£££ (singles: £145 + vat; doubles: £175 + vat)

Pembridge Court *F1*
An upbeat Notting Hill townhouse, lavishly furnished, friendly, comfy, and popular with young trendsetters. Bedrooms are adorned with framed Victorian gloves, fans, and other whimsical ephemera.

34 Pembridge Gardens, Notting Hill W2 4DX ☎ 7229 9977 F 7727 4982
w www.pemct.co.uk ⊖ Notting Hill Gate 20
AE/DC/MC/V ££–£££ (singles: £120; doubles: £180)

Petersham *off map*

Wonderfully positioned, adjacent to 2000 acres of parkland. Bedrooms are traditionally styled; those with river views need to be pre-booked. An enviable setting for long romantic weekends, weddings, and parties.

Nightingale Lane, Richmond TW10 6UZ ☎ 8940 7471 F 8939 1098
w www.petershamhotel.co.uk ⊖ Richmond 60
AE/DC/MC/V ££–£££ (singles: £130; doubles: £165)

Portobello *C1*

This unusual pad offers Victorian adventure, with decor as eclectic as the wares of the nearby Portobello Market. Bedrooms range from spartan naval cabins to romantic dens draped with reams of gauzy fabrics. Celebs regularly troop through this bohemian dreamland.

22 Stanley Gardens, Notting Hill W11 2NG ☎ 7727 2777 F 7792 9641
w www.portobello-hotel.co.uk ⊖ Notting Hill Gate 24
AE/MC/V ££–£££ (singles: £140; doubles: £185)

The Rookery *C9*

Occupying six restored Georgian townhouses with period furnished bedrooms named after notable locals. Magnificent bathrooms have Victorian fittings, deep tubs, and polished copper pipework.

12 Peter's Lane, Cowcross Street, Clerkenwell EC1M 6DS ☎ 7336 0931
F 7336 0932 w www.rookeryhotel.com ⊖ Farringdon 33
all £££ (singles: £160 + vat; doubles: £195 + vat)

Sanderson *E7*

In fashionable Noho, this urban oasis is the new spiritual (Philippe Starck designed) home of Europe's rich and famous. A stay here focuses around the deluxe spa and gym. The loft-like rooms are romantic but modern.

50 Berners Street, North Soho W1P 3AD ☎ 7300 1400 F 7300 1401
⊖ Oxford Circus; Tottenham Court Road 150
all £££ (singles & doubles: £195 + vat)

Tophams Belgravia *B18*

This extremely well cared for hotel has been run by generations of Tophams (a family of artists). The very well connected Mrs T keeps the famous guests coming. Bedrooms are exceptionally inviting.

28 Ebury Street, Belgravia SW1W 0LU ☎ 7730 8147 F 7823 5966
w www.tophams.co.uk ⊖ Victoria 39 all ££ (singles: £115; doubles: £130)

Blakes *off map*

British designer Anouska Hempel's ultra-fashionable hotel is a magnet for the slick, beautiful, and glamorous. Totally unique, each room is a dramatic self-contained fantasy in daring, extravagant colour schemes. Eye-grabbing *objets* punctuate the spaces and every exotic detail is intrinsic to the design.
33 Roland Gardens, South Kensington SW7 3PF ☎ 7370 6701 F 7373 0442 e blakes@easynet.co.uk ⊖ South Kensington 51 all £££ (singles: £155 + vat; doubles: from £220 + vat)

Covent Garden *E7*

An understated exterior fronts a carefully themed dreamscape of individually designed rooms. Suitably theatreland, each bedroom resembles a stage set, with quirky furniture and unusual trademark mannequins.
10 Monmouth Street, Covent Garden WC2H 9HB ☎ 7806 1000 F 7806 1100 w www.firmdale.com ⊖ Covent Garden 58 AE/MC/V £££ (singles: £190 + vat; doubles: £220 + vat)

Dukes *C13*

An urbane and well hidden stopping-off point for top-level VIPs. Cozy, comfy, and full of attentive butlers, valets, and other bygone luxuries. Traditional luxurious rooms have period furnishings and fine paintings.
35 St James's Place, St James's SW1A 1NY ☎ 7491 4840 F 7493 1264 w www.dukeshotel.co.uk ⊖ Green Park 88 AE/DC/MC/V £££ (singles: £190 + vat; doubles: £210 + vat)

Great Eastern *D10*

Designed for corporate bigwigs, rooms are minimal but with all mod cons. If you haven't signed that big deal at lunch, you can clinch it on one of the three phone lines in your room or at one of four restaurants or three bars packed to the gills with city slickers. Definitely first class.
Liverpool Street Station, Hoxton & Shoreditch EC2M 7QN ☎ 7618 5000 F 7618 5001 w www.great-eastern-hotel.com ⊖ Liverpool Street 267 all £££ (singles: £195 + vat; doubles: £225 + vat)

Halcyon *off map*

The Halcyon's lavish style is there to satisfy its star-studded guest list. Bedrooms are romantically individual, overlooking gardens and lawn tennis courts, many with French windows and ivy covered balconies.
81 Holland Park, Holland Park W11 3RZ ☎ 7727 7288 F 7229 8516 w www.halcyon-hotel.co.uk ⊖ Holland Park 42 all £££ (singles: £205 + vat; doubles: £240 + vat)

Halkin ⁂F12

A fancy Belgravia address and an Italian theme (that even stretches to Armani-clad staff) sets the scene. Restaurants don't come any cooler than the Halkin's – the ultimate in minimalist chic, with food to match. Bedrooms are very designer too and everything is controlled by the touch of a button.

5 Halkin Street, Belgravia SW1X 7DJ ☎ 7333 1000 F 7333 1100 w www.halkin.co.uk ⊖ Hyde Park Corner 41 all ££££ (singles & doubles: £265 + vat)

Hempel *off map*

Lady Weinberg's (aka Anouska Hempel) second London hotel stands in a quiet Bayswater enclave. A Zen-like spirit infuses the peaceful and harmonious interior. Stone-floored bedrooms, with designs drawn directly on to the walls, have a stark, monochromatic simplicity.

31–35 Craven Hill Gardens, Bayswater W2 3EA ☎ 7298 9000 F 7402 4666 w www.hempelhotel.com ⊖ Paddington 61 all £££–££££ (singles: £245 + vat; doubles: £285 + vat)

Leonard *E6*

The elegant reception rooms of this Georgian townhouse – with billowing fabrics, lavish flowers, and stately antiques – raise expectations. Upstairs, the bedrooms and suites are just as classy, individual, and imaginative. It's little surprise this place attracts discerning glitterati and company directors.

15 Seymour Street, Marylebone W1H 5AA ☎ 7935 2010 F 7935 6700 w www.theleonard.com ⊖ Marble Arch 32 all ££ (singles: £180 + vat; doubles: £200 + vat)

Metropolitan *D12*

Not particularly cozy, but the Metropolitan's prime Mayfair location and it's ruthlessly contemporary approach, lure the young jet-setters. Design is *Zeitgeist* minimalist. The restaurant (Nobu) and intimidatingly hip Met Bar are good for star-spotting.

Old Park Lane, Mayfair W1Y 4LB ☎ 7447 1000 F 7447 1100 e sales@metropolitan.co.uk ⊖ Hyde Park Corner 155 all £££–££££ (singles: £230 + vat; doubles: £255 + vat)

Myhotel *D7*

Designed by feng shui expert William Spear, Myhotel is one of the new breed of designer hotels attracting music, fashion and TV execs. You are sent a questionnaire before your visit, so rooms are tailored to suit individual requirements. It's all affordable luxury and bang in the centre of town.

11–13 Bayley Street, Bedford Square, Bloomsbury WC1B 3HD ☎ 7667 6000 F 7667 6001 w www.myhotels.co.uk ⊖ Tottenham Court Road 76 P all £££ (singles: £170 + vat; doubles: £210 + vat)

No. 5 Maddox Street E7

If you don't want anyone to know you're in town, this is the place to stay. The 12 perfectly formed suites each have bathroom and bedroom, plus a generous living space and attached kitchen so guests can fend for themselves. The technology quota is high. Popular with media execs and fashion types.

5 Maddox Street, Piccadilly W1R 9LE ☎ 7647 0200 F 7647 0300 W www.living-rooms.co.uk ⊖ Oxford Street ◆ 12 ▤ ㉔ ✐ ▭ all £££ (singles & doubles: £215 + vat)

No. 3 Dorset Street C6

Set up by artist David Shapiro in a four-storey Georgian townhouse, this is a permanent gallery featuring the work of British artists. Each of the three suites takes up a floor, and there's a studio room in the basement.

3 Dorset Street, Marylebone W1H 4EH ☎ 7224 7172 F 7224 7182 W www.numbertwo.co.uk ⊖ Baker Street ◆ 3 ▤ ✐ ▭ ▭ all ££–£££ (singles: £128 + vat; doubles: £215 + vat)

One Aldwych B14

Housed in a listed Edwardian building. Luxurious, classic bedrooms are sleek and sumptuous, but chintz-free. There's also an 18m swimming pool (with piped underwater music) and a collection of modern art.

1 Aldwych, Covent Garden WC2B 4BZ ☎ 7300 1000 F 7300 1001 W www.onealdwych.co.uk ⊖ Covent Garden; Temple; Charing Cross ◆ 105 ▤ ㉔ ≋ ↔ ✐ ▢ P ♿ ▭ all ££££ (singles: £255 + vat; doubles: £275 + vat)

St Martin's A14

Ian Schrager's first London hotel offers the expected super-stylish and super-cool overnight sensation. Designed by Philippe Starck, the main theme is light – turn a dial and your room will turn anything from ruby-red to emerald green. The rooms are kitted out with web access and wide screen TVs. Hang out with the beautiful people in the Light Bar.

46 St Martin's Lane, Covent Garden WC2N 4HX ☎ 7300 5500 F 7300 5501 ⊖ Leicester Square ◆ 240 ▤ ㉔ ↔ ✐ ▢ P ♿ ▭ all £££ (singles & doubles: £235 + vat)

over £300

Berkeley E12

The Knightsbridge location and rooftop health spa attract the smart set. In good weather, the roof rolls back, opening the pool to the sun. Rave reviews shower its revolutionary, Thai-French restaurant, Vong.

Wilton Place, Knightsbridge SW1X 7RL ☎ 7235 6000 F 7235 4330 W www.savoygroup.co.uk ⊖ Hyde Park Corner ◆ 168 ▤ ㉔ ≋ ↔ ✐ ▢ P ▭ all ££££ (singles: £285 + vat; doubles: £345 + vat)

Claridge's F6

The grand old dame of Brook Street has succumbed to certain mod cons which slot in alongside art deco fixtures and fittings. It's so divine that Spencer Tracy allegedly said 'I don't want to go to heaven, I want to go to Claridge's'. Even the standard rooms are large enough to party in. The service is utterly attentive.

Brook Street, Mayfair W1A 2JQ ☎ 7629 8860 F 7499 2210 w www.savoygroup.co.uk ⊖ Bond Street 197 all ££££ (singles: £295+ vat; doubles: £345 + vat)

Lanesborough E12

Breathtaking, unashamed hedonism, no expenses spared. Cloaked in lavish period furnishings, the range of facilities is awesome. The conservatory is OTT – a fantasy of trickling fountains and exotic vegetation.

Hyde Park Corner, Knightsbridge SW1X 7TA ☎ 7259 5599 F 7259 5606 w www.lanesborough.com ⊖ Hyde Park Corner 95 all £££–££££ (singles: £240 + vat; doubles: £325 + vat)

The Connaught B12

The home from home for Britain's gentry between the wars, The Connaught still has the air of a stately home – exclusive, formal and trad. Staff outnumber guests by at least two to one. The restaurant is an English institution.

16 Carlos Place, Mayfair W1Y 6AL ☎ 7499 7070 F 7495 3262 w www.savoygroup.co.uk ⊖ Bond Street 90 all ££££–£££££ (singles: £290 + vat; doubles: £380 + vat)

The Savoy A14

A galaxy of stars have stayed here. Black cabs and limos glide past the entrance hall which is decked with marble reliefs. Behind lie a trio of celebrated restaurants where guests devour over 9500 sides of smoked salmon and 52,000 oysters a year. The palatial bedrooms – some overlooking the river – are finely restored art deco.

The Strand, Covent Garden WC2R 0EU ☎ 7836 4343 F 7240 6040 w www.savoygroup.co.uk ⊖ Charing Cross; Covent Garden 207 all ££££ (singles: £280 + vat; doubles: £330 + vat)

The Ritz C13

Piccadilly's centenarian pleasure-palace is still the ultimate London sleep. A visit is a reminder of just why The Ritz remains a synonym for the high-life. Bedrooms to die for are those with views over Green Park.

150 Piccadilly, St James's W1V 9DG ☎ 7493 8181 F 7493 2687 w www.theritzhotel.co.uk ⊖ Green Park 131 all ££££ (singles: £285 + vat; doubles: £325 + vat)

practical information

admission charges
Most sights of interest, including some churches and cathedrals, have an admission charge or ask for a voluntary contribution. Some sights offer free or reduced admission at certain periods. Ask about concessions for pensioners (over 60), students, and children.

banks
Banks usually offer a better exchange rate than bureaux de change. The main banks are HSBC, Lloyds TSB, National Westminster (NatWest), Barclays, Abbey National, and Halifax. Their opening hours are usually 9.30am–3.30pm Monday–Friday (but some don't close until 4.30pm). Saturday morning opening is also common. All banks are closed on public holidays. Most banks have cashpoint machines where you can obtain money by credit or debit card [→credit & debit cards]. To transfer money from abroad contact: Western Union ☎ 0800 833833.

bars
[→pubs & bars]

bureaux de change
Check commission and minimum charges before exchanging money and travellers' cheques [→travellers' cheques] as rates can vary dramatically. Beware of places advertising no commission as they may have very poor exchange rates. Sometimes, especially with large sums, it is possible to negotiate a little. Bureaux de change (generally open 8am–9pm) are in all airports and most major rail and central London underground stations.

The following are reliable places to change money:
American Express (AMEX) charges £2 commission on all cash transactions. Two conveniently located branches are:
102–104 Victoria Street SW1 ☎ 7828 7411 ◑ *9am–5.30pm Mon–Fri (from 9.30am Wed; to 4pm Sat).*
78 Brompton Road SW3 ☎ 7584 6182 ◑ *9/9.30am–5.30pm Mon–Fri (to 4pm Sat).*
Thomas Cook charges a £2 flat fee with commission-free buy back. Two conveniently located branches are:
1 Marble Arch W1 ☎ 7530 7150 ◑ *8am–8pm daily (10am–6pm Sun in winter).*
184 Kensington High Street W8 ☎ 7707 2300 ◑ *9am–5.30pm Mon–Sat.*

cafés
[→restaurants & cafés]

children
Transport: children travel free/more cheaply on most tube and bus services.
Activities: many London parks offer One O'Clock Clubs – free, enclosed areas for under-5's to play (they must be with an adult). In school holidays some stores and museums, including Harrods and Pollock's Toy Museum, lay on special kids' entertainment.
Eating out: unfortunately not all London restaurants welcome children with open arms so it's best to ring and ask. However, there are some child-friendly venues with special menus.
Child minders: for daytime and evening supervision Universal Aunts provides stand-in parents for children of all ages. They will take the kids out,

or collect/drop them at airports or stations: 19 The Chase sw4 ☎ 7738 8937
Should you require round-the-clock babysitting ring the **Childminders Information Line** for details of their 24-hour service ☎ 7487 5040.

conversion chart

Women's clothing

US	6	10	14	16
British	8	12	16	18
European	36	40	44	46

Men's clothing

US	36	40	44	46
British	36	40	44	46
European	46	50	54	56

Women's shoes

US	5	6	7	8
British	4	5	6	7
European	37	38	39	40

Men's shoes

US	7	8	9	10
British	6	7	8	9
European	40	42	43	44

courier services

National and international services:
DHL ☎ 0345 100300
Federal Express ☎ 0800 123800
UPS ☎ 0345 877877

credit & debit cards

Credit cards are widely accepted. Visa is the most popular, followed by MasterCard, Amex, Diners Club, and JCB. Cash advances can be obtained if you have your PIN number with an internationally recognized credit card at any cashpoint machine displaying the appropriate card sign. Fees vary according to the issuing bank, but range from 1.5% for a JCB advance to 3% for AMEX and 4% for Diners Club, MasterCard, and Visa. Often a cheaper way to obtain your money is to use a debit (cashpoint) card, although some banks charge for this service. Check with your bank which UK banks are part of the same network, so that you can withdraw money from your account at a minimal cost.
To report lost or stolen credit cards call:
AMEX ☎ 01273 696933 (personal cards)
Diners Club ☎ 0800 460800
JCB ☎ 7499 3000
MasterCard ☎ 0800 964767
Visa ☎ 0800 895082

currency

British currency is the pound sterling (£), divided into 100 pence. Euros are not accepted, but a few retailers will accept euro travellers' cheques (check with individual shops). There is no limit to the amount of cash that can be imported or exported.

customs

At airports, customs is divided into three routes: the blue lane is for anyone travelling from within the European Union (EU); the red and green lanes are for people travelling from outside the EU – red is for those with goods to declare, green for those with nothing to declare. Random checks may be made. All animals are subject to six months' quarantine before they can enter the UK unless they have the correct documentation from a vet. ☎ 0870 2411710 for details.

dental treatment

Free dental treatment is not available so keep all receipts for insurance claims. For practices within your area (many of which operate emergency

services) check the Yellow Pages directory or call:
Talking Pages ☎ 0800 600900
Patients will be seen in an emergency (but be prepared for a long wait) at:
Guy's Hospital Dental School
Guy's Tower, St Thomas Street SE1
☎ 7955 2186 ◑ *8.45am–3.15pm Mon–Fri; 9.30am–5pm Sat–Sun.*
King's College Hospital
Denmark Hill SE5 ☎ 7346 3894
◑ *6–11pm Mon–Sun; 9.15–9.45am Sat–Sun.*

disabled visitors

The majority of London sights have access for disabled visitors, but it is best to double-check first. A useful guide to buy is *Access in London* (£7.95), published by Quiller.
Artsline gives free information on disabled facilities at permanent and temporary cultural events and venues ☎ 7388 2227.
Holiday Care Service offers free information on accommodation ☎ 01293 774535.
Tripscope gives free information on transport for the elderly and disabled ☎ 8580 7021.

driving

You can drive in the UK with an overseas driving licence (which has been held for more than one year).

duty free

Duty-free goods are only available to non-EU nationals, with the usual limits of: 1 litre of spirits, 200 cigarettes, and £75 worth of souvenirs and gifts. The gift allowance is greater if you are entering from outside Europe – information is posted in every duty free store.

electricity

Electrical supply is 240 volts (V). Plugs are three-prong and adaptors are widely available in shops at airports and train stations.

email & internet

A number of internet cafés allow you to surf the net and send and receive emails for around £3 per 30 minutes. Most places also offer word processing and faxing facilities.

embassies & consulates

Australian High Commission
Australia House, Strand WC2
☎ 7379 4334
Canadian High Commission
38 Grosvenor Street W1 ☎ 7258 6600
Irish Embassy
17 Grosvenor Place SW1 ☎ 7235 2171
New Zealand High Commission
80 Haymarket SW1 ☎ 7930 8422
South African High Commission
Trafalgar Square WC2 ☎ 7451 7299
US Embassy
24 Grosvenor Square W1 ☎ 7499 9000

emergencies

Police, ambulance & fire services
☎ 999 (24 hours – strictly emergencies only)
For emergency 24-hour medical attention:
Charing Cross Hospital
Fulham Palace Road W6 ☎ 8846 1234
Guy's Hospital
St Thomas Street SE1 ☎ 7955 5000
London Royal Free
Pond Street NW3 ☎ 7794 0500
St Thomas's Hospital
Lambeth Palace Road SE1 ☎ 7928 9292
University College Hospital
Grafton Way WC1 ☎ 7387 9300

help & advice lines

Capital Helpline will tackle queries about anything, or put you in touch with someone who can help ☎ 7484 4000.
London Lesbian & Gay Switchboard offers 24-hour information ☎ 7837 7324.

hotels

Charges: budget hotels usually include breakfast, whereas upmarket hotels frequently exclude breakfast and VAT (currently 17.5%) from the room rate. Mandatory service charges and exorbitantly surcharged telephone calls may be extra. Few hotels have substantial numbers of single rooms and single occupancy of a double room results in little or no cost reduction. However, some hotels do offer reduced rates at weekends, off-peak periods and for regular corporate clients.
Tipping: it's common to tip 10–12.5% for extra services in flashier hotels.
Children: some hotels offer free stays for children under 12 sharing rooms with parents.
Check-out time: usually 11am or midday. Most hotels will store luggage.
Reservations: it's safer to make reservations in advance. Fax bookings are convenient and secure. Many hotels also have email addresses. The easiest way to book is to quote your credit card number, and many hotels insist on this. A booking, however made, is legally binding and if you make a last minute cancellation or don't show up, you might have to pay the cost of one night's hotel accommodation as a penalty.
At Home in London has a choice of over 70 private homes offering B&B accommodation in London ☎ 8748 1943.
Go Native specializes in short to medium-term stays in temporarily vacant homes of London professionals ☎ 7286 1088.
LTB Hotel Hotline gives information on hostels, camping, and self-catering ☎ 7604 2890.

immigration

Control on entry to the UK can be strict, particularly at Heathrow. Lanes are divided into EU nationals, who don't need visas, and other nationalities, who should check entry requirements well before leaving their country [→visas]. No vaccinations are needed.

insurance

Comprehensive medical insurance is highly recommended for non-EU members.

left luggage

Left luggage offices operate in all airport terminals and main railway stations. Most places charge £3 per item for 24 hours. Not all are open 24 hours, so check first.

lost property

Report all lost items to the police to validate insurance claims. A lost passport should also be reported to your embassy.

maps

The most comprehensive map is a *Collins London Street Atlas* or an *A–Z* (the Londoners' bible), both of which are available from bookshops and most newsagents.

measurement

As a rule, metric measures are used.

imperial: metric	metric: imperial
1 inch = 2.5 cm	1 mm = 0.04 inch
1 foot = 30 cm	1 cm = 0.4 inch
1 mile = 1.6 km	1 m = 3.3 ft
1 ounce = 28 g	1 km = 0.6 mile
1 pound = 454 g	1 g = 0.04 oz
1 pint = 0.6 l	1 kg = 2.2 pounds
1 gallon = 4.5 l	1 l = 0.2 gallons

medical matters

Hospital treatment: accident and emergency treatment is available free to all visitors at the discretion of the hospital [→emergencies]. For non-emergency treatment, however, visitors are liable to be charged. Anyone who is from within the European Economic Area (EEA), or from a country with which the UK has a reciprocal agreement, is normally eligible for free hospital treatment, if the need arises, during a visit to the UK. For more information, contact the Patient Services Manager or the Overseas Visitors Manager at your nearest hospital. Treatment is free to all visitors at major hospitals for clinics treating Sexually Transmitted Disease (STDs).

General Practitioners (GPs): emergency or immediately necessary treatment from a doctor is available free of charge to all, including overseas visitors. Whether the condition is deemed an emergency or requires immediate treatment is a clinical decision made by the GP concerned. It is also up to the GP to decide on what basis he accepts the patient for non-essential treatment. Check first; if one doctor doesn't accept you for NHS treatment, another may.

NHS (National Health Service) **Executive** offers general information about using the NHS system ☎ 7725 5300.

NHS Hotline gives free medical advice over the phone: ☎ 0845 4647

The Health Shop offers advice on illnesses and where to get treatment ☎ 0800 665544.

Great Chapel Street Medical Centre is a walk-in NHS surgery for anyone without a registered doctor. Opening times vary, so call first.
13 Great Chapel St W1 ☎ 7437 9360

Medicentres are private walk-in clinics charging a £40 consultation fee. There are branches at Waterloo, Euston, and Victoria Station (platform 15):
☎ 0870 6000870 ◑ *7am–9pm daily.*

Centre for Sexual Health
Jefferiss Wing, St Mary's Hospital, Paddington W2 ☎ 7886 1225

Holistic Health offers 14 complementary therapies: 64 Broadway Market E8
☎ 7275 8434 ◑ *9am–5pm Mon–Sat.*

medicine & chemists

Medicines can be purchased from chemists and large supermarkets, but many are only available with a doctor's prescription. If you are not eligible to receive free treatment in the UK you will be charged the full price (get a receipt for any insurance claims), otherwise you pay £5.90 per item. To ensure late-night opening in each area, chemists work on a rota – each should display information on which nearby chemists will be open late.

Bliss Chemist 5 Marble Arch W1
☎ 7723 6116 ◑ *9am–midnight daily.*

office & business services

Most five-star hotels operate 24-hour business centres – usually for residents only.

Rymans is a well-stocked stationer with many central London branches – they offer faxing and black & white photocopying:
57 Charing Cross Road WC2
☎ 7439 2058.

The Copy Stop is open 24 hours on weekdays for photocopying and printing (10am–4pm Sat):
112–114 Wardour Street W1 ☎ 7287 2341.

1st Translation offers translation services for every language: 24 Holborn Viaduct EC1 ☎ 7329 0032.

[→email & internet]

opticians

Eye Care Information Service offers advice on eye care, problems, and available treatments: ☎ 01673 857 847

Sight Care sells contact lenses and can make up glasses from an existing prescription in one hour. They carry out walk-in or pre-bookable eye tests for £10:
45 Oxford Street W1 ☎ 7434 2385

photography

Snappy Snaps can process films within an hour at many branches:
23 Garrick Street WC2 ☎ 7836 3040

Jessop's specializes in part-exchanging camera equipment. They also offer a range of excellent developing and processing services:
63 New Oxford Street WC1 ☎ 7240 6077

Camera Clinic Ltd will mend your camera equipment on the spot where possible:
162–168 Regent Street W1 ☎ 7734 6629

police

For local police stations look up Police in the telephone directory or call directory enquiries on ☎ **192**.
Only dial ☎ **999** in an emergency.

postal services

Post offices are usually open 9am–5.30pm on weekdays and 9am–12.30pm on Saturdays. The post office off Trafalgar Square (24–28 William IV Street WC2) is open until 8pm Mon–Sat, with the last collection at 7.45pm. Collection times elsewhere are posted on London's bright red postboxes.
To find your nearest post office, call:
Post Office Counters Helpline
☎ 0345 223344

Stamps can be bought from post offices and most newsagents, stationers, and supermarkets. Inland mail is 27p for first class, 19p for second class. Postage for a standard letter or postcard within the EU is 36p. Stamps for postcards cost 45p outside Europe. Other letters (and parcels) being sent outside the EU vary according to weight.

Poste Restante: to receive letters, mail should be addressed to Poste Restante, Post Office, 24–28 William IV Street, London WC2N 4DL.
Mail will be kept for up to 3 months and you need some form of ID to collect it.

pubs & bars

Opening times: generally 11am–11pm Mon–Sat; 12pm–10.30pm Sun. Most places allow 10–20 minutes drinking-up time. Last orders for cooked food tend to be 2pm for lunch or 8 or 9pm for an evening meal.

Late opening: for late-drinking bars try Soho, Islington, Hoxton, and Brixton.

Ordering: the usual system is to order and pay at the bar; food will be brought to where you are sitting.
Children: to drink alcohol you must be 18 or over. 14–17s can drink soft drinks, but under 14s are usually only allowed into pub gardens and family rooms. A few pubs have 'children's certificates', allowing children entry as long as they are accompanied by an adult.
Smoking: smoking is the norm, and only some pubs, such as the JD Wetherspoon chain, have no-smoking areas.

public holidays

Offices close, but many shops remain open on public holidays (known as bank holidays). The exception is Christmas Day when almost everything closes. Public transport runs less frequently on national holidays and not at all on 25th December:
Spring Bank Holiday – end May
Summer Bank Holiday – end August
Christmas Day – 25th December
Boxing Day – 26th December
New Year's Day – 1st January
Good Friday – March/April
Easter Monday – March/April
May Day Holiday – beginning of May

religion

For general enquiries about places and/or times of worship contact:
Baptist ☎ 7836 6843
Buddhist ☎ 7834 5858
Church of England ☎ 7898 1000
Evangelical ☎ 7207 2100
Jewish ☎ 7580 1663
Muslim ☎ 8840 4840
Quaker ☎ 7663 1000
Roman Catholic ☎ 7798 9097

restaurants & cafés

Bookings: to be sure of a table it's best to make a reservation.
Opening times: unlicensed cafés usually open 9am–5pm. Most restaurants take orders 12pm–2.30pm and 6.30–11pm.
Prices: menus are displayed at the window – prices include VAT. Minimum charges may operate at busy periods or after midnight.
A cover charge is sometimes added (for bread, etc); if so, it must be stated on the menu.
Tipping: some restaurants automatically add an optional service charge to the bill, so check this before tipping. Where service is not included, add 10–15%. When paying by credit card, fill in the total and the gratuity section on the slip.
Children: ring in advance to check whether restaurants welcome children.
Smoking: most restaurants and some cafés offer a choice of smoking or non-smoking seating. If you have a strong preference, mention this when booking.

safety

Take the usual safety precautions that you would in any big city. You shouldn't walk alone late at night; carry valuables with you; leave money or credit cards lying around; or let your belongings out of your sight. Avoid poorly lit, isolated areas. Beware of bag snatchers and pickpockets in central London restaurants, bars, markets, and on the underground. You may prefer to take a taxi rather than public transport late at night. Women can use a company that employs only women drivers: **Ladycabs** ☎ 7254 3501

shopping

Opening times: generally 9/10am–5/6pm Mon–Sat and often midday–6pm Sun. Some supermarkets open 24 hours on certain days, and

10am–4pm Sunday. Most areas have late night shopping one evening a week.
Payment: for individual purchases over £100, paying by credit card gives you extra protection. This is because the credit card company is equally liable for any claim you have against the trader (eg if the goods are faulty or if they are not what you ordered).
Export: non–EU members returning or exporting purchases within 3 months can get a VAT refund [→VAT]. Check with individual shops about the minimum amount which must be spent. Some department stores shipping your goods abroad can refund VAT at time of purchase.
Sales: mostly January and June.
Returns: keep receipts for refunds and exchange. If goods are faulty, you are entitled to your money back. If you change your mind about a purchase, most chains will exchange goods – but there is no legal obligation to do so.
Guarantees: manufacturers' guarantees give you additional rights, but often only if the retailer fills in the details of the purchase and you remember to send off the registration card. Electrical goods may come with the choice of an extended warranty. Watch out as these are often expensive and don't cover everything.
Deliveries: An internet-based service will deliver anything from ice-cream to videos in one hour within central London **w** www.urbanfetch.co.uk
Office of Fair Trading ☎ 0345 224499

smoking

Smoking is forbidden in most public buildings: all theatres, most cinemas, and everywhere on the public transport system. Many restaurants have no-smoking sections.

students

An International Student Identity Card (ISIC) entitles full-time students to some discounts on travel and museum admissions. An ISIC card costs £6, is valid for one year, and you can use it all around the world. Obtain one in London by taking two photos and proof of your full-time student status (a letter from your university/a valid student union card etc) to branches of Student Travel Association (STA) or Campus Travel.
ISIC Helpline ☎ 8666 9205
If you aren't a student but are under 26 you can apply for a Youth Card (IYTC). It will give you discounts on travel, some restaurants, and sights etc. It is valid for one year and available from any branch of STA Travel. You need proof of your date of birth and a passport photo.

telephoning

Phone sounds:
steady 'brrrrrrrr' = go ahead and dial
double 'brrr brrr' = number is ringing
repeated short 'beeps' = line is busy
continuous 'beep' = number is unobtainable
Telephone boxes: accept coins, credit cards and/or pre-paid phonecards. The minimum cost is usually 20p. Most phones have simple instructions, often in several languages. Pub phones may require you to press a button when the call is answered.
Phonecards: can be bought wherever phonecard signs are displayed. British Telecom (BT) phone cards can only be used in BT phones, but BT phones will accept some other cards – check when you buy.
Mobile phone hire:
Cellhire ☎ 7490 7799
Independent Phone Rentals
☎ 8878 6000

Local codes: all London numbers are eight digits; inner London numbers (used to have the code 0171) always start with a 7, outer London numbers with an 8 (used to have the code 0181). If you are dialling from outside London use the prefix 020.
International codes: dial ☎ 00 plus the country code; **USA and Canada** ☎ 1; **Australia** ☎ 61; **Ireland** ☎ 353; **New Zealand** ☎ 64; **South Africa** ☎ 27.
Operator ☎ 100 (for wake-up calls, credit card calls, help with telephone problems).
Directory enquiries ☎ 192 will give you any number in the directory. You need the name and address (free from payphones, 40p from private phones).
International operator ☎ 155 (for collect calls and help with international calls).
International directory enquiries ☎ 153
Talking Pages ☎ 0800 600900 will give you contact numbers for a particular service in a specified area.
Phone directories: The Phone Book, an alphabetical list of businesses and services, and Yellow Pages, lists by category, are available in post offices and libraries.
Private phone rates: standard local rate 8am–6pm weekdays is 4p/min; evening local rate 6pm–8am is approx 2p/min; weekend local rate midnight Fri–midnight Sun is 1p/min. National calls vary in price but are cheapest after 6pm and at the weekend.
Payphone rates: 9p/min for local calls and 14p/min for long distance/national calls.
Freephone numbers: numbers preceded by ☎ 0800 are free of charge.
Premium rates: all calls with the ☎ 0891 prefix are charged at premium rate of 50p/min at all times (£1 from payphones). There are many other prefixed numbers with similarly high charges.
International phone rates: these vary from country to country, but tend to be cheaper in the evening and better value still at weekends. Phone the international operator to check prices. Phonecards with a scratch-to-reveal pin number (there are several different brands) provide a cheaper way of making international phone calls via a freephone number. However, by far the cheapest option, for more than £20–£25 worth of international calls, is to use one of the independent phone companies which offer savings of 50–75%. Setting up an account usually takes about 15 minutes and money is taken from your credit card. You are given a PIN number and an account number and then you can make calls from any touchtone phone. Try the following companies for this service:
First Telecom ☎ 0800 3766666
Go Talk ☎ 0800 097 7777
Swift Call ☎ 0800 7690800

time

Clocks are set to Greenwich Mean Time (GMT) – they go back one hour in autumn (end of October) and forward by one hour in spring (end of March) at the start of British Summer Time. Dial ☎ 123 for the 24-hour speaking clock.

tipping

Tipping 10–12.5% in taxis, restaurants, hotels, and hairdressers is the norm. Make sure you fill in the total when signing credit card slips. Tipping is not customary in bars and pubs.

tourist information

The London Tourist Board (LTB) provides information and free transport maps of central London. Information centres are generally open from 8.30am–6pm daily at:

Heathrow Airport (underground station at terminals 1, 2 & 3)
Liverpool Street (underground station)
Victoria Station (railway forecourt)
Waterloo International (arrivals hall)
LTB ☎ 7932 2000
w www.londontown.com
General information:
w www.visitbritain.com
British Tourist Authority ☎ 8846 9000

travel agents

Two reliable agents for cheap flights are:
Trailfinders ☎ 7938 3366
STA Travel ☎ 7361 6262.

travellers' cheques

Travellers' cheques are the safest way to travel with money. The most widely accepted currencies are pounds sterling and US dollars. The best places to change travellers' cheques (you will need a passport) are bank-operated bureaux de change, American Express, or Thomas Cook [→bureaux de change]. American Express, Visa, and Thomas Cook are issuing travellers' cheques in euros.

VAT (Value Added Tax)

VAT is a sales tax added to all goods except for books and children's toys. Travellers from outside the EU are entitled to a VAT refund (just under 15% of the sales price) if they leave the UK within three months of the last day of the month in which the purchase was made. VAT on services and entertainments cannot be reclaimed. If you spend over £55–£100 (it varies) in a shop displaying the 'Tax Free for Tourists' sign, you are entitled to reclaim the VAT. The procedure can be complicated, so do ask. You need to get a form from the shop. It has to be certified by them so do this when making your purchase. Only one form should be completed per shop and you will need ID to prove you are from a non-EU country. Take your form(s) to the airport VAT/Customs desk at your last point of departure from Europe. The officer may ask to inspect the goods so it is advisable to keep them in your hand luggage – they should be unused and unopened. You will either receive the refund on the spot, in cash (often in your own currency), or it will be refunded to your credit card within two to three weeks.
For general enquiries phone:
Global Refund ☎ 0800 829373.

visas & entry requirements

Some visitors must obtain entry clearance before coming to the UK. For all EU visitors and many others, a valid passport is all that is required. Visitors from the US, Canada, Australia, New Zealand, and South Africa do not need visas for short tourist trips (less than six months); other nationalities should check with their nearest British Embassy or consulate well before leaving.

weather

Heatwaves reaching 90°F are possible in summer (Jun–Aug), as is snow in winter (Dec–Mar). Be prepared for all eventualities, including rain at any time of year. Keep abreast of the erratic British weather by checking forecasts in the newspapers or at the end of TV news broadcasts.
Weathercall ☎ 0891 500401 (premium rate) gives the latest forecast, or you can check the internet
w www.weather.com

arrivals

If you fly into London, you'll probably use one of the 'Big Three' international airports: Heathrow, Gatwick, or Stansted – London's newest. The capital is also served by two smaller airports: Luton and City Airport in Docklands.

✈ Stansted
[NE 34 miles/55 km]
✈ Luton
[N 32 miles/51.5 km]
✈ Heathrow
[W 15 miles/24 km]
✈ City
[E 6 miles/9.5 km]
✈ Gatwick
[S 24 miles/38.5 km]

Speedlink
Speedlink bus service links Heathrow and Gatwick airports, departing every 15–30 min. Journeys take 1 hr–1 hr 30 min; a single ticket costs £17. For bus services between airports call airport traveline: ☎ 0990 747777

heathrow [LHR]

The world's busiest international airport with four terminals handling over 90 passenger airlines; 170-plus destinations; over 57 million passengers, and around 420,000 flights annually. Terminal 4 is some distance from the other three, so check beforehand which one your airline uses. There's a free shuttle bus service for transfers between terminals.

☎ useful numbers
Enquiries: 0870 0000123
w www.baa.co.uk
Shopping info: 0800 844844
Business centre: 8759 2434
Car park info: 0345 405000
Lost property: 8745 7727/7750
Left luggage:
terminal 1; 8745 5301 (6am–11pm);
terminals 2 & 3; 8745 4599 (5.30am–10.30pm);
terminal 4; 8745 7460 (5.30am–11pm)
Forte Crest: 0870 4008595
Sheraton Skyline: 8759 2535

Terminal 1: domestic flights & British airlines to Europe, including Virgin Express
Terminal 2: non-British airlines to Europe & Virgin Atlantic arrivals from Miami & Johannesburg
Terminal 3: all long-haul flights (including Virgin Atlantic) except BA & SAS
Terminal 4: Concorde, Air Malta, BA Intercontinental, KLM & several non-European airlines

transport options: Heathrow–central London

⊖ underground
45–60 min to/from central London on the Piccadilly line.
5am–11.40pm Mon–Sat; 6am–11pm Sun. Every 1–4 min (every 10–15 min on Sun, early morning & late at night).
£3.50
Via: South Ealing, Hammersmith, Earl's Court, Knightsbridge, Leicester Square, King's Cross.

1| Generally reliable.
2| Cheapest option.
1| Gaps between services can be longer than scheduled.
2| Stations aren't user-friendly for those with luggage.
3| Trains are very crowded at peak times.
1| Terminal 4 has a separate stop on a one-way loop.
2| Avoid the queues and use ticket vending machines in the baggage reclaim areas.
3| To change from the Piccadilly to the District or Circle Lines, use Hammersmith or Barons Court – the lines share the same platform so it's easier if you have luggage.
4| Pick up underground (and bus) information and maps from the ticket office.
Information ☎ 7222 1234

Heathrow Express
15 min to/from Paddington from terminals 1, 2 & 3;
20 min to/from terminal 4.
5.10am–11.40pm daily, every 15 min.
£12
Serves Paddington Station only.
1| Quickest route.
2| You can check in your luggage at Paddington.
Buy tickets on the Heathrow Express, at any mainline station, Heathrow terminal, or some hotels or save £3 by booking online **w** www.heathrowexpress.co.uk
Information ☎ 0845 6001515

Airbus
1 hr 30 min to/from central London (depending on traffic)
6.30am–10.15pm daily, every 30 min.
£8
A1 route to Victoria station via: Earl's Court, Knightsbridge, Hyde Park Corner.
A2 route to King's Cross station via: Bayswater Road, Marble Arch, Baker Street, Russell Square, Euston.
Convenient if you have lots of luggage.
1| Journey times are unpredictable (particularly during peak traffic: 8–9.30am and 5–6.30pm)
2| More costly than the underground.
3| Stops at all terminals.
Tickets can be bought on the bus.
Airbus services:
☎ 7730 3466
Airport Traveline (bus & coach):
☎ 0990 747777

taxis & minicabs
45 min–1 hr to central London (depending on traffic and destination).
24 hours
from £38 for a taxi; from £25 for a minicab
1| Door-to-door service.
2| Convenient if you have lots of luggage.
The most expensive option.
1| Minicabs are usually cheaper than taxis.
2| Some upmarket hotels offer courtesy taxis.

☎ taxi numbers:
terminal 1: 8745 7487
terminal 2: 8745 5408
terminal 3: 8745 4655
terminal 4: 8745 7302
For a reliable minicab service, ask at an information desk.

Ticket prices represent a single adult fare, unless otherwise indicated. Journey times are approximate and subject to change.

gatwick [LGW]

The world's busiest single-runway airport, used by over 120 airlines serving more than 200 destinations. Its two terminals handle in excess of 28 million passengers and 230,000 flights each year. The two terminals are linked by a free monorail service, which runs every 3 min.

North Terminal: Air 2000, Air France, Britair, British Airways, Brymon Airways, Delta Airlines, Deutsche BA, Emirates, Finnair, GB Airways, Leisure International Maersk Air, Malev, Royal Nepal Airlines, TAT European
South Terminal: all other airlines, including Caledonian, Virgin Express & Virgin Atlantic

☎ useful numbers

Enquiries: 01293 535353
w www.baa.co.uk
Shopping info: 0800 844844
Car park info: 0345 405000
Lost property: 01293 503162
Left luggage:
north terminal 01293 502013;
south terminal 01293 502014
Copthorne: 01342 714971
Gatwick Hilton: 01293 518080
Le Meridien: 01293 567070

transport options: Gatwick–central London

Gatwick Express

30–35 min to/from Victoria.
daily, every 15 min; then hourly throughout the night.
£10.20
Serves Victoria Station only.
1| Fast, regular, and direct.
2| You can buy your ticket on the train.
Most expensive option after taxis.
Outbound British Airways and American Airlines passengers can check in at Victoria Station.
Information ☎ 0990 301530

Connex South Central

35–47 min to/from Victoria.
vary; 10 min–1 hr intervals; 24 hour service.
£8.20
Via: Clapham Junction & East Croydon. Some Connex services go to Charing Cross & Blackfriars.
Cheapest train service.
Departure instructions can be confusing.
1| Some services are much slower than others.
2| Check you're in the right section of the train for your destination as some stations have short platforms.
Information ☎ 0345 484950

Thameslink

1 hr to/from King's Cross (continues to St Albans, Luton, and Bedford).
5am–midnight daily, approx 4 trains per hour; then usually one an hour through the night.
£9.50
Via: London Bridge, Blackfriars, Farringdon, King's Cross, West Hampstead.
Information ☎ 0345 484950

Airbus

1 hr 20 min to/from Victoria
5.15am–9.50pm daily, approx every hour.
£8
Via: Wandsworth, Victoria, Hyde Park Corner, Marble Arch, Baker Street, Finchley Road.
Drivers can help with luggage.
1| Slowest option.
2| Journey times are variable, especially at rush hour.

Connects with nationwide services at Victoria Coach Station.
Information ☎ 0870 5808080

taxis & minicabs
1–2 hr to/from central London
24 hours
from £65 for a taxi; from £35 for a minicab
The most comfortable and convenient option.
Most expensive option.

☎ taxi numbers
Taxis North Terminal: 01293 507448
Taxis South Terminal: 01293 502808
Gatwick Airport Cars: 01293 562291
Gatwick Goldline Cars: 01293 568468

london stansted [LSN]

Britain's newest and sixth-largest passenger airport deals mostly with business and charter holiday traffic. It's also one of the most stylish (designed by Sir Norman Foster), and handles over 8 million passengers a year.

☎ useful numbers
Enquiries: 01279 680500
w www.baa.co.uk
Car park info: 0345 405000
Shopping info: 0800 844844
Left luggage: 01279 663213
Hilton National: 01279 680800

transport options: Stansted–central London

Stansted Skytrain
45 min to/from Liverpool Street station.
5am–midnight daily, every 30 min.
£12
Fast and convenient.
1| You need a separate ticket to use the underground.
2| Change at Tottenham Hale for connections to the Victoria line underground.
Information ☎ 0345 484950

Airbus
1 hr 45 min to/from Victoria Coach station.
24 hours daily, every 30 min
£8
Drivers will help with luggage.
Journey times are longer than the train and very variable, depending on traffic.
Connects with National Express services nationwide from Victoria Coach Station.
Information ☎ 0870 5808080

Stansted Airport Cars
(no black taxis at Stansted)
1 hr 30 min to/from central London (depending on traffic).
24 hours. £70
Most comfortable and convenient service.
Very expensive.
☎ 01279 662444

london city [LCY]

A small, privately owned business airport in Docklands, east of the City. Around 10 airlines serve 20 European and domestic destinations.

☎ useful numbers
Enquiries: 7646 0088
w www.londoncityairport.com
Business centre: 7646 0900

transport options: London City–central London

Docklands Light Railway (DLR)
1| 12 min between Bank and Canary Wharf station.

5.30am–12.30am Mon–Sat (from 6am Sat); 7.30am–11.30pm Sun, every 5–10 min Mon–Sat; 15 min Sun.
£1.80
Connect with the Airport Shuttlebus (blue), 20 min.
every 20 min.
£2
2| 18 min between Tower Hill and Prince Regent station.
every 5–10 min. £2.10
Connect with the 473 bus,5–10 min.
every 12 min. 70p

underground
30 min from Green Park via Waterloo on the Jubilee Line to Canning Town (regular shuttlebus from tube to airport).
6am–midnight daily, every 20 min.
£1.50
Cheaper than a taxi.

taxis & minicabs
50 min to/from central London (depending on traffic). 24 hours.
£25–£30
Painless and convenient.
Relatively expensive.
taxis 7646 0850
minicabs 7476 6633

london luton [LTN]

A smallish airport slightly closer to London than Stansted, dealing mostly with holiday charter traffic, but also scheduled flights, including Easyjet. Handles around four million passengers a year, and is expanding rapidly.

useful numbers
Enquiries: 01582 405100
w www.london-luton.com
Car park info: 01582 395456
Lost property: 01582 395219
Left luggage: 01582 405100
Luton Travelodge: 01582 575955

transport options: Luton–central London

train
30 min to/from King's Cross Station.
24 hours daily, every 15 min,
£9.50;
then shuttlebus (5-min trip) or taxi
The best option for getting to central London.
0345 484950

Greenline 757
1 hr 30 min to Victoria Coach Station.
4.30am–11pm daily; mostly every 30 min, but frequency varies.
£7.50
Long journey times.
Connects with National Express services nationwide from Victoria Coach Station. 0870 6087261

Cab Co
(no black taxis at Luton)
1 hr 30 min to/from central London (depending on traffic).
£45–£50
The most comfortable and convenient service.
Costly and slow in traffic.
01582 736666

in, out & about

Many visitors to London arrive from outside the capital, or venture out at some point.
For information on train services and ticket prices from all stations, contact the National Rail Enquiry service:
0345 484950 or try:
w www.thetrainline.com

rail ticket booking lines
Anglia Railways [A]
01473 693469
Connex South Central [CSC]

☎ 0870 6030405
Great North Eastern Railways [GNER]
☎ 0345 225225
Great Western Railways [GWR]
☎ 0345 000125
South Western Trains [SWT]
☎ 0845 6000650
Thames Trains [TT]
☎ 0345 300700
Virgin Trains [VT]
☎ 0345 222333
West Anglian Great Northern Railways [WAGNR]
☎ 0800 566566

main rail links
Charing Cross, serving the south coast.
Euston, serving Birmingham & the west.
Fenchurch Street, serving the east & Essex.
King's Cross, serving the northeast & Scotland.
Liverpool Street, serving East Anglia.
London Bridge, serving the southeast.
Marylebone, serving the Midlands.
Paddington, serving south Wales & the southwest.
St Pancras, serving the north.
Victoria, serving the south, Kent & Sussex coast.
Waterloo, serving the south & the Dorset coast.

coach information
National Express ☎ 0990 898989
Victoria Coach Station ☎ 7730 3466
Traveline (Green Line buses) ☎ 8668 7261

national airlines
Aer Lingus [AL] ☎ 0645 737747
British Airways [BA] & BA Express ☎ 0345 222111
British Midland [BM] ☎ 0345 554554
CityFlyer Express [CFE] ☎ 0345 222111
EasyJet ☎ 01582 702900
Go ☎ 0845 6054321
KLM UK ☎ 0990 074074

national air links
London has five airports all serving different parts of the UK.
Gatwick: BA & CFE fly to most major UK airports.
Heathrow: BM & BA fly to most major UK airports.
Stansted: KLM UK & BA Express fly to airports in Scotland & to Manchester & Newcastle; Go flies to Edinburgh.
Luton: EasyJet flies to all main airports in Scotland.
London City: KLM UK flies to Manchester & Edinburgh.

entry points & destinations

Bath
GWR to/from Paddington, 1 hr 30 min £29; 3 hr 20 min £18.50
Birmingham
VT to/from Euston, 1 hr 30 min £21.40; 2 hr 30 min £13
Brighton
CSC to/from Victoria, 49 min £13.70; 1 hr 30 min £10
Cambridge
WAGNR to/from King's Cross, 49 min; or Liverpool Street, 1 hr 30 min £13.40 1 hr 30 min £10
Canterbury
CSC to/from Victoria, 1 hr 30 min £14.70; 1 hr 50 min £11
Dover
CSC to/from Charing Cross/Victoria, 1 hr 45 min £17.50; 2 hr 30 min £14
Edinburgh
GNER to/from Kings Cross, 4 hr £68; 9 hr £30

Exeter
GW to/from Paddington, 2 hr 30 min £39; 4 hr £26

Fishguard
GW to/from Paddington, 5 hr £44; no direct coach service

Folkestone
CSC to/from Charing Cross, 1 hr 30 min £17.50;
2 hr 15 min £13

Glasgow
GNER to/from King's Cross or VT to/from Euston, 5 hr 30 min £69;
8 hr £29

Harwich
Anglia to/from Liverpool Street, 1 hr 15 min £16.40;
no direct coach service

Holyhead
VT to/from Euston, 5 hr £50.50; 8 hr £30

Liverpool
VT to/from Euston, 2 hr 45 min £40; 4 hr 30 min £22

Manchester
VT to/from Euston, 2 hr 30 min £40; 4 hr 30 min £22

Newcastle-upon-Tyne
GNER to/from King's Cross, 3 hr £66; 6 hr £27

Newhaven
CSC to/from Victoria, 1 hr 30 min £14.60; 2 hr 15 min £11

Oxford
TT to/from Paddington, 1 hr 30 min £12.40; 1 hr 40 min £9

Portsmouth
SWT to/from Waterloo, 1 hr 30 min £18.50; 2 hr 5 min £14.50

Plymouth J
GWR to/from Paddington, 3 hr £44; 4 hr 40 min £41

Ramsgate
CSC to/from Charing Cross/ Victoria, c.2 hr £17.50;
2 hr 40 min £13

Southampton
SWT to/from Waterloo, 1 hr 15 min £19.40; 2 hr 15 min £10

Stratford-upon-Avon
TT to/from Paddington, 2 hr 20 min £17.50; 2 hr 30 min £14.50

Swansea
GW to/from Paddington, 3 hr £39; 4 hr £24

Windsor
SWT to/from Waterloo, 50 min £5.80;
(Green Line) 1 hr 15 min £7.30

York
GNER to/from King's Cross, 1 hr 50 min £52; 4 hr 20 min £27

train tips

1| Ticket prices given are based on an adult cheap-day return or 'supersaver' fares.

2| You can save up to 50% by booking an APEX ticket at least 7 days in advance or a Super APEX at least 14 days in advance.

coach tips

1| Ticket prices given are based on an adult, off-peak, weekday return. Friday and Saturday travel is more expensive; advance fares and same day travel, cheaper.

2| National Express coaches all leave from Victoria Coach Station. Other coach operators may charge less, but this might be because the journey is less direct.

Eurostar

A high-speed train service linking London (Waterloo Station) with Paris (3 hr) or Brussels (2 hr 40 min). Check in at least 20 min before departure. Booking ahead is recommended especially at weekends, during the summer, and for cheaper tickets.

⏱ 5.15am–8pm daily: to Paris every hour; to Brussels every 2 hr.
£ from £69 (Leisure APEX booked 14 days in advance) ☎ 0990 186186

Please note ticketing and price structures for trains and coaches are very complex, and subject to frequent change.

general information

£ travelcards
The cheapest way for most visitors to get around London is to buy a one-day Travelcard (valid after 9.30am on weekdays and all day at weekends). This is available from underground ticket offices, machines, and some newsagents, and enables you to use the underground, buses, and suburban trains as much as you like. You save money on fares, and time queueing for tickets. Greater London is divided, for transport purposes, into six concentric fare zones. Travelcards are priced according to how many zones they cover. For travel within central London, you'll only need a zones 1 & 2 card (daily £3.90; weekend £5.80), but if you're based some way out of the centre, you'll probably need a three-or-more-zones Travelcard. Weekend Travelcards are the best value, costing approx 25% less than two one-day cards.
Weekly or monthly Travelcards are available, too. These allow travel before 9.30am, and are a sensible option if you are in town for five days or more. To get one, you need a photocard (free from any station when you supply a passport photo).
❶ Neither daily nor weekend Travelcards are valid on night-buses or the Airbus.
❶ A daily Travelcard valid before 9.30am is also available and is called a London Transport card: for zones 1 & 2 it costs £5. Travelcards for children aged 5–15 are also available; a one-day (all zones) card costs £2; a Weekend (all zones) Travelcard costs £3. Family Travelcards (valid for any group of 1–2 adults and 1–4 children travelling together) offer even cheaper rates.

maps & leaflets
Free maps and information are available at underground stations, especially those with a Travel Information Centre: Euston, Hammersmith, Heathrow, King's Cross, Liverpool Street, Oxford Circus, Piccadilly Circus, St James's Park, and Victoria. These outlets also tickets to some major attractions.

♿ disabled travellers
London Transport publishes *Access to the Underground* – a guide to each station for passengers with limited mobility. ☎ 8580 7021

kids
Children up to 15 (with proof of age) get reduced-price tickets (about 50% of adults') on the underground and on buses. Child bus fares are not valid after 10pm. Kids aged 14 or 15 must pay an adult fare if they do not have a photocard. To get one, proof of age is required. Accompanied children under five travel free.

excess fares & penalties
If you don't have a valid ticket, or travel beyond a destination covered by your ticket or Travelcard, you may be liable to a penalty. You can get a ticket extension (valid for two hours for a single journey) from self-service machines, or ask the ticket office, driver, or conductor what the extra fare is before you travel. If caught with an invalid ticket on the underground or

trains, you're liable to an on-the-spot £10 penalty: on the buses it's £5. You may also be prosecuted – inspectors are not lenient.

☎ useful numbers
London travel information ☎ 7222 1234
Travelcheck updates ☎ 7222 1200

the tube

London's underground or 'tube' system is one of the most extensive – and expensive – in the world. Most of the time things run fairly smoothly, but you'll find varying rates of reliability on different lines.
The Circle Line can be slow and erratic and the Northern Line is dubbed the 'Misery Line'. But apart from walking or taking a taxi, the underground is still the best way to get around town.

Tube map [→back cover]
Highly schematic, this map bears little relationship to actual distances between stations. Sometimes it's quicker and easier to walk than go underground, but check distances on a street map before you hit the road.

using the underground

• Buy tickets from a ticket office or a machine.
• To pass through an automatic barrier, put your ticket through the slot at the front. Don't forget to collect it again (unless it's a single and you're at the end of your journey).
• On each platform there's at least one underground map. Use the map to select which line(s) you have to take (each line is colour-coded); follow directions to the relevant line; decide which platform you need by checking the list of stations displayed on each. On some routes, more than one line operates, and certain lines split and go to more than one destination. Check where lines interchange (indicated by a circle or a double circle).
• Most stations have electronic signs above platforms saying when the next train is due and its final destination. Each train has its destination marked on the front.
• Announcements are often made regarding delays or changes in train destinations – but they can be hard to hear or understand.
• Avoid travelling at peak times (8–9.30am & 5–6.30pm Mon–Fri) if possible.

underground essentials

Around 5.30am–midnight (from 7am Sun) daily; approx every 2–10 min.
If you're not using a Travelcard, buy single tickets (return tickets cost twice the single fare and are same-day only) from station offices or self-service machines, which usually give change. Tickets are priced according to the number of zones covered: A single ticket in zone 1 costs £1.50; zones 1 & 2 costs £1.80; zones 1–6 costs £3.50.
Carnet: books of 10 single tickets (for travel within zone 1 only) cost £11 from underground ticket offices, transport information centres, ticket machines, and newsagents displaying the LT sign. Each ticket is valid for one year for any journey within zone 1 only, and must be validated as you start your journey.
1| Frequent services on most inner city routes.
2| Easy connections to other routes and public transport.
3| Fairly user-friendly.

👎 **1|** Crowded, especially at peak times.
2| Certain lines are renowned for delays.
3| Some stations may be unsafe at night.
4| Services stop around midnight.
5| Operating problems and security alerts can cause delays.

do

1| Make sure your ticket is valid for your entire journey.
2| Keep your ticket throughout your journey; fines are imposed on passengers without a valid ticket.
3| Stand on the right of escalators (or walk up or down on the left).
4| Mind the gap! At some stations, the carriages don't meet the platform edge.
5| Press the button to open the doors on newer trains.

don't

Smoke anywhere on the system.

London travel information ☎ 7222 1234
Lost property ☎ 7486 2496

suburban trains

Suburban trains depart from all the mainline train stations, plus several others. These services are used mainly by commuters, so services are especially busy and frequent during rush hours, and fares are cheaper after 9.30am. A few local railways cross London and occasionally interchange with the underground:

1| Silverlink Metro: linking Richmond to North Woolwich via several stations including Camden Road and Highbury & Islington; every 15–30 min, prone to delays on Sundays.
2| Thameslink: connecting King's Cross, Farringdon, London Bridge, and Elephant & Castle (every 15–30 min).

These trains are useful if you're staying on the outskirts of London (particularly in parts of south London where there's no underground network), or if you're taking a day trip. Buy tickets from departure station offices or machines. ☎ 7222 1234

docklands light railway [dlr]

This overground railway is one of the best ways to get around the Docklands. Though fully automated, there are 'captains' to keep an eye on things and on-board guides give a running commentary. Trains run from Bank and Tower Gateway stations to Beckton, and Island Gardens – where you can walk through a tunnel to Greenwich. Travelcards are valid on the DLR. Sail & Rail tickets offer unlimited travel on DLR plus a single riverboat trip (either direction) between Westminster and Greenwich. ☎ 7222 1234

buses

The mention of London's buses instantly conjures up an image of old-style red double-deckers. There are still plenty of these iconic Routemasters about, but since privatization, modern versions and single-deckers – more able to weave their way through the traffic – have appeared. Overall, buses can be a relaxing, inexpensive, and enjoyable way of seeing London – if you're not in a hurry.

bus map

Thirty-six bus maps cover the huge Greater London region in detail, but the All London Bus Guide, which includes day and night services, should be adequate. Get this free at any tourist information centre.

using the buses

• Many bus stops display timetables. Where there are lots of routes serving an area, bus stops are letter-coded and mini maps help you work out which bus stop you need. Some stops display alphabetical lists of destinations, with the relevant bus numbers.
• Buses should stop automatically at points marked with the red-on-white LT symbol; at 'request' stops (white-on-red), they only halt if signalled – put your hand out when your bus approaches. If they're full, they may not stop at all.
• Make sure you're going in the right direction; if in doubt, ask the driver or conductor as you get on.
• Most new buses are one-person operated (OPOs), so have your Travelcard, bus pass, or some change ready. Routemaster buses (with rear access) have a conductor to collect fares.
• For request stops, ring the bell as the bus approaches. On Routemasters, do not get on or off between stops.
• Certain bus services (prefixed with an N) run nightly; their fares are structured differently and most depart from Trafalgar Square.
• Stationlink services, with ample luggage space, run hourly services from mainline stations: SL1 buses go clockwise from Paddington (via Marylebone, Euston, St Pancras, King's Cross, Liverpool Street, Fenchurch Street, London Bridge, Waterloo, Victoria); SL2 buses go anti-clockwise.

bus essentials

Day buses: 5–12.30am, but frequency and regularity vary greatly with traffic. Timetables and electronic displays should be used only as a rough guide.
Night buses: around midnight–6am, approx every hour.
Stationlink: SL1 8.15am–7.15pm: SL2 8.40am–6.40pm. 70p–£1
Any journey taking in zone 1 is £1; any zone, excluding zone 1, is 70p. A one-day three-zone bus pass costs £2.40. Weekly bus passes cost £7.50–£11.50; night bus fares are £1–£1.50 in central London.

1| It's a scenic way to get around.
2| Buses go where tubes and trains don't.
3| Cheaper than most other types of transport.
4| Conductors/drivers can give help (but won't necessarily!)
5| Skeleton services run through the night.

1| Complicated route system.
2| Can be crowded and slow in rush hour.
3| Erratic service.

1| Like one-day Travelcards, bus passes aren't valid on night buses or the Airbus.
2| Buy passes at tube stations, tourist information centres, or newsagents displaying the LT sign.
3| Buy your single bus ticket from the driver or conductor.
4| A few bus routes link major London landmarks and are a cheap, easy way to see the sights.

do
1| Have change ready for your fare.
2| Store your luggage in the compartment near the exit doors.
3| Keep your ticket for inspection until the end of your journey.

don't
Smoke on buses.

London travel information:
☎ 7222 1234
Lost property: ☎ 7486 2496

taxis

These days London's famous taxis or 'black cabs' come in all colours, sometimes splashed with advertising. There are several different types too, but newer models are accessible to wheelchair users. Minicab drivers are the cabbies' arch rivals; minicabs can only be summoned by phone or by going to their offices.

taxi test

Before London 'cabbies' get their licence, they have to pass a rigorous exam called The Knowledge. This requires them to know London inside out – including all the main places of interest.

using taxis & minicabs

• Licensed taxis are available for hire when the yellow sign on the roof is illuminated.
• You can hail a taxi in the street, or go to a rank (eg at a mainline station), or order a taxi by phone [see below].
• By law, cabbies are supposed to take the quickest route to your destination (this may not necessarily be the shortest in heavy traffic), and are not permitted to refuse any fare within a six-mile radius of central London. But they do not have to take you if you are drunk, abusive, or otherwise 'undesirable'.
• Some minicab companies have better reputations than others; most operate within local areas, so ask locally for a reliable company or check in *Yellow Pages*. Avoid solitary street touts (who are illegal operators) like the plague.
• Women travelling alone may prefer to use **Lady Cabs**, who only uses female drivers [see below].

limobikes

One of the quickest ways to zoom around the city is to hop on a Virgin Limobike. Helmets and waterproofs provided; prices compare with taxis. Book in advance. ☎ 7499 6233

trishaws

For short hops, a fun way to beat the traffic is to pick up a trishaw from Bugbugs in the City and the West End. ☎ 7675 6577

taxi & minicab essentials

Ⓞ Cabs operate on a 24-hour basis.
£ Taxis are metered; the meter starts ticking at £1.40 – after that, charges escalate in a convoluted way. Expect to pay £3–£5 for shortish central London hops, and up to £25 for any significant journey out of the centre. Supplements are charged for each additional passenger, piece of luggage over 60cm long, and in the evening, at weekends, or on public holidays.
£ Minicab fares should be agreed upon in advance, and are generally cheaper than black cabs.
👍 **1|** Taxi drivers are among the safest and most skilful drivers in town.
2| If you're in a group (maximum five) it can be cheaper, as well as more convenient, to travel by taxi instead of public transport.
3| Competition keeps minicab fares to popular destinations, like airports, fairly similar and reasonable.
👎 **1|** Taxis mysteriously vanish when it rains and are sometimes hard to come by, eg in the West End after the theatre, and even on main streets in the early hours.
2| Minicabs are not licensed by the police, nor are they always insured. Driving standards can be low and

minicab drivers don't know London as well as cab drivers so they may not always take the most direct route.

❶ A 10% tip is expected by both taxi and minicab drivers.

do

1| Check the minicab price before setting off.

2| Have suitable notes handy for your fare.

don't

Get in unlicensed minicabs on the street.

☎ taxi numbers

Computer Cabs (they charge an extra £1.20 call-out fee): 7286 0286

Radio Taxis: 7272 0272

Lost property: 7833 0996

☎ minicab numbers:

Greater London Cars: 8883 5000

Lady Cabs: 7254 3501

Meadway Cars: 8458 5555

driving

The best advice for driving in London is 'don't'. If you're determined to bring a car into central London, plan carefully. Parking is the main hurdle. There are plenty of car and some motorbike rental companies, or you could consider hiring a bicycle to beat the meters, car park fees – and the traffic.

street maps

Geographer's A–Z or Collins's London Street Atlas are invaluable for anyone needing to know London in detail. Available from most newsagents and bookstores.

rules of the road

1| Remember to drive on the left in Britain.

2| Give priority to traffic approaching from the right at roundabouts.

3| Do not pass on the inside (left) lane.

4| Seatbelts are compulsory at all times (including rear-seat passengers).

5| Drink-drive laws are strict.

6| Speed limits in urban areas are 30mph unless otherwise indicated.

at the wheel

Car hire in the UK can be expensive (the best deals are arranged from abroad): expect to pay around £80–£200 per week for a small car (most of which are not automatic). You'll need a valid driving licence of at least one year's standing and some additional ID (eg a passport). Most large firms insist on a minimum age of 21. The well-known international rental companies all have offices in central London and at the airports.

☎ car hire numbers

AIM Rent-a-car: 8742 8955

Avis: 0870 6060100

Europcar: 0870 6075000

Hertz: 8679 1799

Holiday Autos: 0990 300400

National Car Hire: 0990 365365

Transhire: 7978 1922

petrol

Most hire cars take unleaded petrol (colour-coded green on petrol pumps). There aren't many places to fill up in the heart of London; the main routes through town, or large supermarkets such as Tesco and Sainsbury which have petrol stations (and offer some of the lowest fuel prices) are a better bet. Most petrol stations are self-service.

clamping & towing

One thing London motorists dread is having their cars clamped. A large notice is slapped across your windscreen informing you which payment centre you need to visit to unclamp your car; fines are up to £80. Even worse, if you can't find your vehicle at all, it may have been towed to a central car pound. Arranging for retrieval will cost £105 upwards: ☎ 7747 4747.

using meters & car parks

• You'll need to collect lots of change to park in the street; alternatively, head for a National Car Park (NCP).

• Meters close to the centre cost as much as £3 per hour (on Sat pm and Sun, parking is usually free). Two hours is often the maximum stay allowed without refilling the meter (which officially you're not supposed to do).

• In the evening and on Sundays, street parking on single yellow lines is allowed, and using places marked 'cardholders only' or 'residents' may be allowed, but always check always check the parking notices on lampposts first.

• Never park on double yellow lines or red lines (no stopping allowed at all).

• Parking offences incur hefty fines, but you get a 50% reduction if you pay up within 7–14 days.

alternatively...

• If you've taken the car and had one too many, **One for the Road** will sort you out. A driver arrives on a scooter (which folds up and goes in the boot of your car) and chauffeurs you home. Slightly more expensive than a taxi. ☎ 7924 4141

easy riding

Only intrepid visitors would venture onto the mean streets of London on a motorcycle, but if you are such a person and you know your way around, there are a number of companies who rent bikes from 50cc scooters to the latest sports rockets. Helmets and insurance are usually included in the hire price. You then have the speediest way of getting through the city. Parking is free in the many bays scattered around the centre.

☎ motorbike hire numbers

Scootabout, King's Cross WC1: 7833 4607

Metropolis Motorcycles, Vauxhall SE11: 7793 9313

on your bike

Cycling is a good way to cut costs, though traffic fumes can be terrible and it can also be dangerous. In quiet districts and some parks, it's a pleasant option, and in rush hours, bikes are often the fastest things on the road. The London Cycle Network is in the process of setting up over 1000 miles of dedicated cycle routes throughout the capital. For more information (and a central London cycle route map) contact the London Cycling Campaign: ☎ 7928 7220.

bicycle hire

Hiring a bicycle costs from £2–£5 per hour, £5–£10 per day or £30 per week (you're expected to leave a hefty deposit). Outside rush hour, bikes can be taken for free on overland sections of the underground and on Silverlink Metro and Thameslink, but not on the DLR. Make sure you get a good, secure padlock and a helmet. Cycling without lights at night is illegal.

☎ bicycle hire numbers

Bikepark, Covent Garden WC2: ☎ 7430 0083

Dial-a-Bike, Victoria SW1: ☎ 7828 4040 (delivery to major central London hotels)

London Bicycle Tour Co, Gabriel's Wharf SE1: ☎ 7928 6838

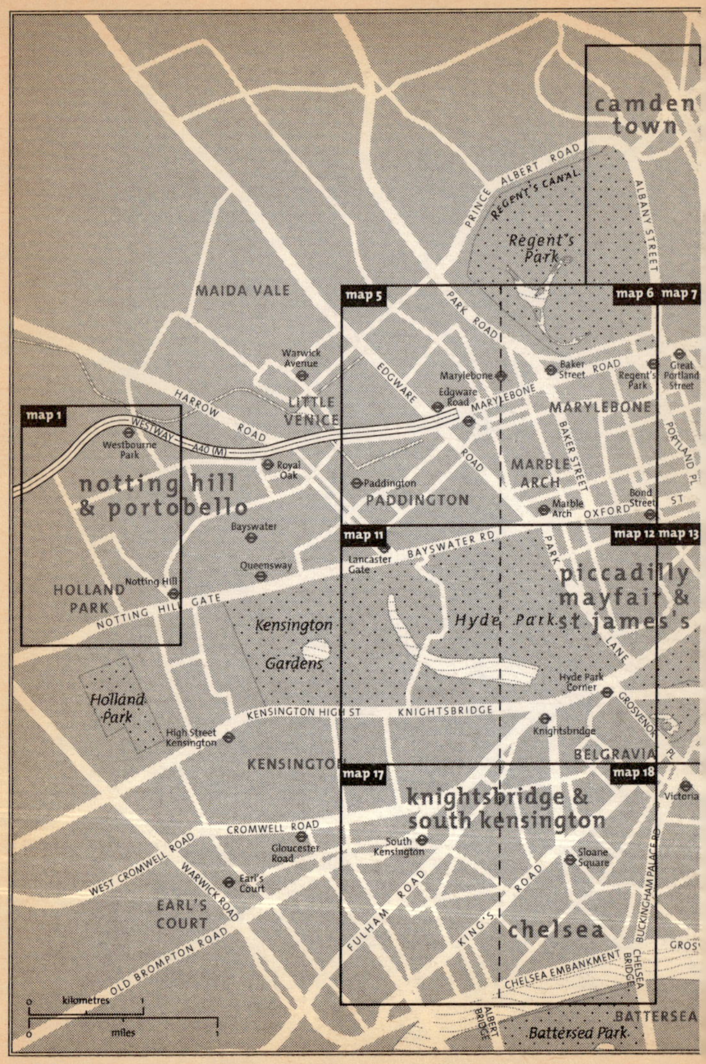

camden town
PRINCE ALBERT ROAD
REGENT'S CANAL
Regent's Park
ALBANY STREET
MAIDA VALE
map 5
map 6
map 7
PARK ROAD
Warwick Avenue
EDGWARE
Marylebone
Baker Street
ROAD
Great Portland Street
Regent's Park
HARROW
ROAD
LITTLE VENICE
Edgware Road
MARYLEBONE
MARYLEBONE
map 1
WESTWAY
A40 (M)
Westbourne Park
Royal Oak
ROAD
BAKER STREET
PORTLAND PL
notting hill & portobello
Paddington
PADDINGTON
MARBLE ARCH
Marble Arch
OXFORD
Bond Street
ST
Bayswater
map 11
Lancaster Gate
BAYSWATER RD
map 12
map 13
PARK
piccadilly mayfair & st james's
Queensway
HOLLAND PARK
Notting Hill
NOTTING HILL GATE
Kensington
Hyde Park
LANE
Gardens
Hyde Park Corner
GROSVENOR PL
Holland Park
KENSINGTON HIGH ST
KNIGHTSBRIDGE
Knightsbridge
High Street Kensington
BELGRAVIA
KENSINGTON
map 17
map 18
Victoria
knightsbridge & south kensington
CROMWELL ROAD
WEST CROMWELL ROAD
Gloucester Road
South Kensington
Sloane Square
WARWICK ROAD
Earl's Court
ROAD
EARL'S COURT
FULHAM ROAD
KING'S
chelsea
BUCKINGHAM PALACE RD
OLD BROMPTON ROAD
CHELSEA EMBANKMENT
CHELSEA BRIDGE
GROS
kilometres
0
1
miles
0
1
ALBERT BRIDGE
BATTERSEA
Battersea Park

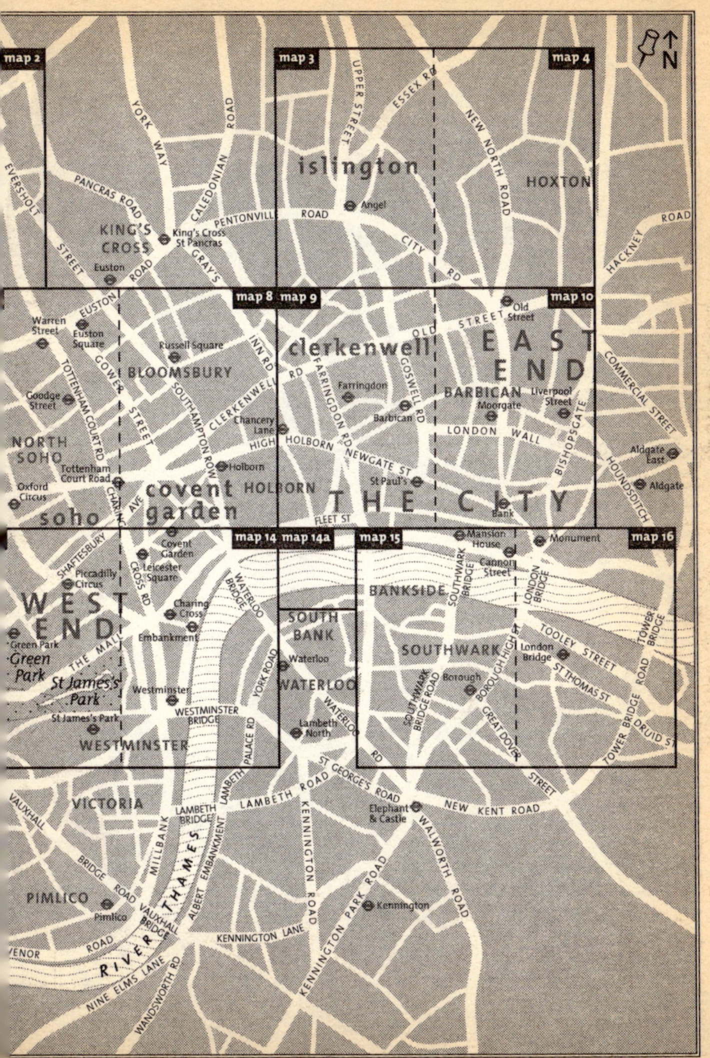

map 2
map 3
map 4
N
EVERSHOLT
YORK WAY
CALEDONIAN ROAD
UPPER STREET
ESSEX RD
NEW NORTH ROAD
islington
HOXTON
PANCRAS ROAD
PENTONVILLE
ROAD
Angel
HACKNEY
ROAD
KING'S CROSS
King's Cross St Pancras
CITY
RD
STREET
Euston
ROAD
GRAY'S
map 8
map 9
map 10
EUSTON
Warren Street
Euston Square
Old Street
OLD STREET
clerkenwell
EAST END
INN RD
Russell Square
COWER STREET
BLOOMSBURY
RD
FARRINGDON RD
GOSWELL RD
COMMERCIAL STREET
TOTTENHAM COURT RD
Goodge Street
SOUTHAMPTON ROW
Farringdon
BARBICAN
Liverpool Street
Moorgate
Barbican
CLERKENWELL
Chancery Lane
LONDON WALL
BISHOPSGATE
NORTH SOHO
HIGH
HOLBORN
NEWGATE ST
Aldgate East
HOUNDSDITCH
Tottenham Court Road
Holborn
Oxford Circus
CHARING
AVE
covent garden
HOLBORN
St Paul's
THE CITY
Aldgate
soho
FLEET ST
Bank
map 14
map 14a
map 15
map 16
Mansion House
Monument
SHAFTESBURY
Covent Garden
Piccadilly Circus
Leicester Square
CROSS RD
WATERLOO BRIDGE
SOUTHWARK BRIDGE
Cannon Street
LONDON BRIDGE
BANKSIDE
WEST END
Charing Cross
SOUTH BANK
TOWER BRIDGE
Embankment
TOOLEY STREET
Green Park
Green Park
THE MALL
SOUTHWARK
London Bridge
Waterloo
St James's Park
YORK ROAD
WATERLOO
BOROUGH HIGH ST
ST THOMAS ST
Westminster
SOUTHWARK BRIDGE ROAD
Borough
TOWER BRIDGE ROAD
WESTMINSTER BRIDGE
WATERLOO
GREAT DOVER
DRUID ST
St James's Park
Lambeth North
WESTMINSTER
PALACE RD
RD
STREET
LAMBETH
ST GEORGE'S ROAD
VICTORIA
LAMBETH BRIDGE
LAMBETH ROAD
Elephant & Castle
NEW KENT ROAD
VAUXHALL
BRIDGE
ROAD
MILLBANK
RIVER THAMES
ALBERT EMBANKMENT
KENNINGTON ROAD
WALWORTH ROAD
KENNINGTON PARK ROAD
PIMLICO
Pimlico
VAUXHALL BRIDGE
Kennington
KENNINGTON LANE
ROAD
VENOR
NINE ELMS LANE
WANDSWORTH RD
KENNINGTON

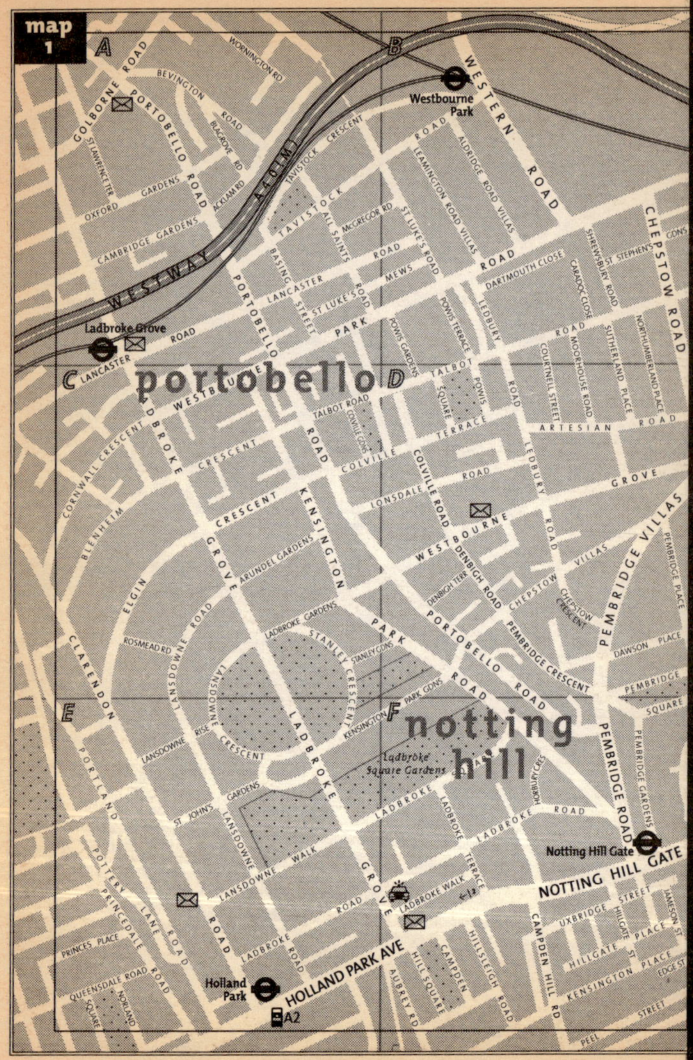

map 1
A
B
C
D
E
F
portobello
notting hill
Westbourne Park
Ladbroke Grove
Notting Hill Gate
Holland Park
WESTWAY
A40(M)
GOLBORNE ROAD
PORTOBELLO ROAD
WESTERN ROAD
LADBROKE GROVE
KENSINGTON PARK ROAD
WESTBOURNE GROVE
PEMBRIDGE VILLAS
PEMBRIDGE ROAD
NOTTING HILL GATE
HOLLAND PARK AVE
CHEPSTOW ROAD
LANCASTER ROAD
ELGIN CRESCENT
CLARENDON ROAD
LANSDOWNE ROAD
Ladbroke Square Gardens
A2

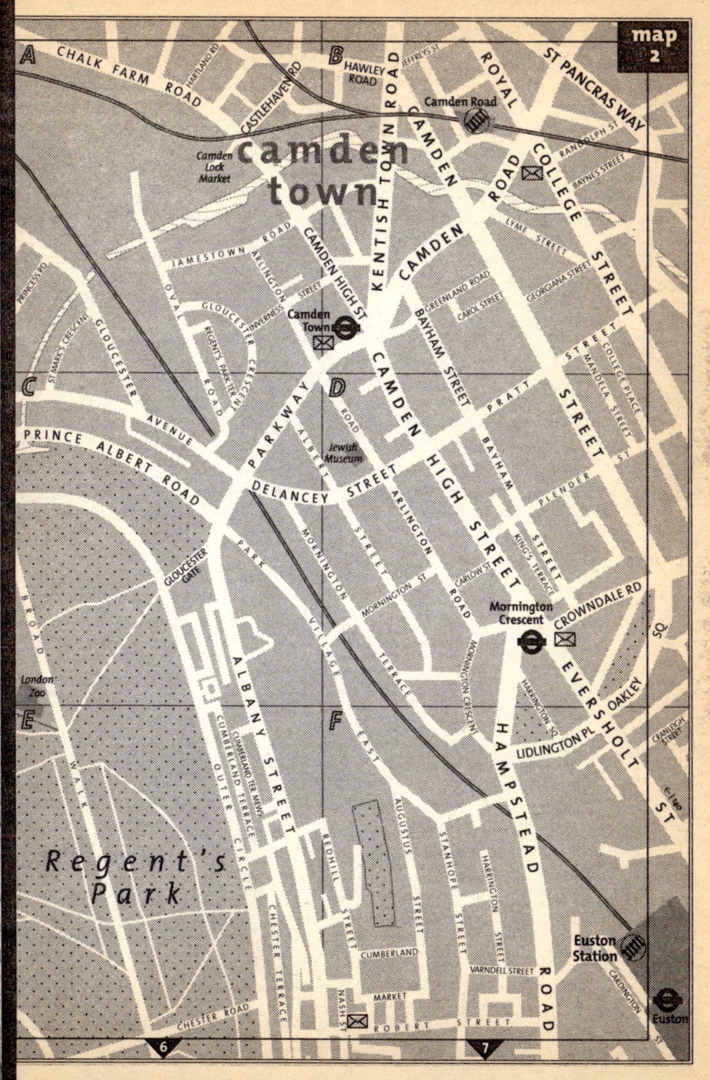
camden town
Camden Lock Market
Camden Road
Camden Town
Jewish Museum
Mornington Crescent
Euston Station
Euston
London Zoo
Regent's Park
Gloucester Gate
CHALK FARM ROAD
HARTLAND RD
CASTLEHAVEN RD
HAWLEY ROAD
JEFFREYS ST
KENTISH TOWN ROAD
ROYAL COLLEGE STREET
ST PANCRAS WAY
RANDOLPH ST
BAYNES STREET
CAMDEN ROAD
LYME STREET
JAMESTOWN ROAD
ARLINGTON ROAD
CAMDEN HIGH ST
CAMDEN HIGH STREET
INVERNESS STREET
GLOUCESTER CRESCENT
OVAL ROAD
REGENT'S PARK TER
PRINCESS RD
ST MARK'S CRESCENT
GLOUCESTER AVENUE
PRINCE ALBERT ROAD
PARKWAY
ALBERT STREET
DELANCEY STREET
GREENLAND ROAD
CAROL STREET
GEORGIANA STREET
BAYHAM STREET
PRATT STREET
COLLEGE PLACE
MANDELA STREET
PLENDER ST
KING'S TERRACE
ARLINGTON ROAD
MORNINGTON STREET
MORNINGTON ST
MORNINGTON CRESCENT
CARLOW ST
CROWNDALE RD
PARK VILLAGE EAST
MORNINGTON TERRACE
HARRINGTON SQ
EVERSHOLT ST
OAKLEY SQ
LIDLINGTON PL
CRANLEIGH STREET
HAMPSTEAD ROAD
BROAD WALK
ALBANY STREET
CUMBERLAND TER MEWS
CUMBERLAND TERRACE
OUTER CIRCLE
CHESTER TERRACE
CHESTER ROAD
REDHILL STREET
AUGUSTUS STREET
STANHOPE STREET
HARRINGTON STREET
CUMBERLAND MARKET
VARNDELL STREET
NASH ST
ROBERT STREET
CARDINGTON ST
6
7

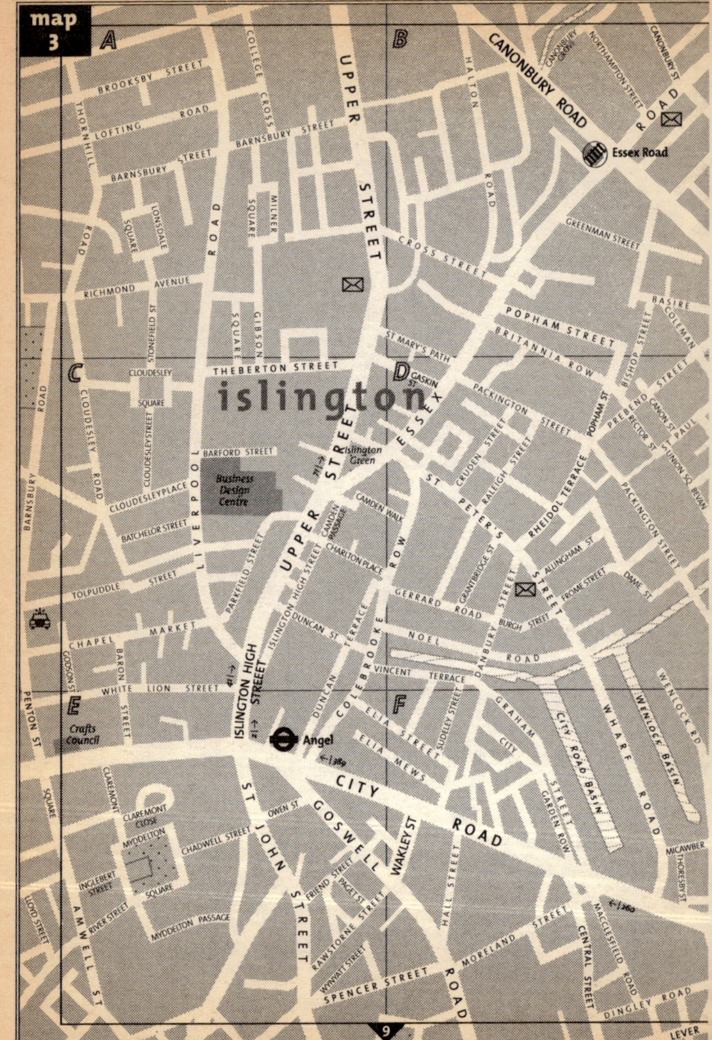

map 3
islington
Upper Street
Essex Road
Angel
Business Design Centre
Crafts Council
Islington Green
City Road
Canonbury Road
Liverpool Road
Islington High Street
St John Street
Goswell Road
Pentonville Road
Essex Road
St Peter's Street
Colebrooke Row
Noel Road
Wharf Road
Wenlock Basin
City Road Basin
Spencer Street
Amwell St
Myddelton Square
Barnsbury Street
Cloudesley Square
Theberton Street
Cross Street
Popham Street
Packington Street
Rheidol Terrace
Gerrard Road
Duncan Terrace
Chapel Market
White Lion Street
Chadwell Street
Moreland Street
Central Street
Dingley Road

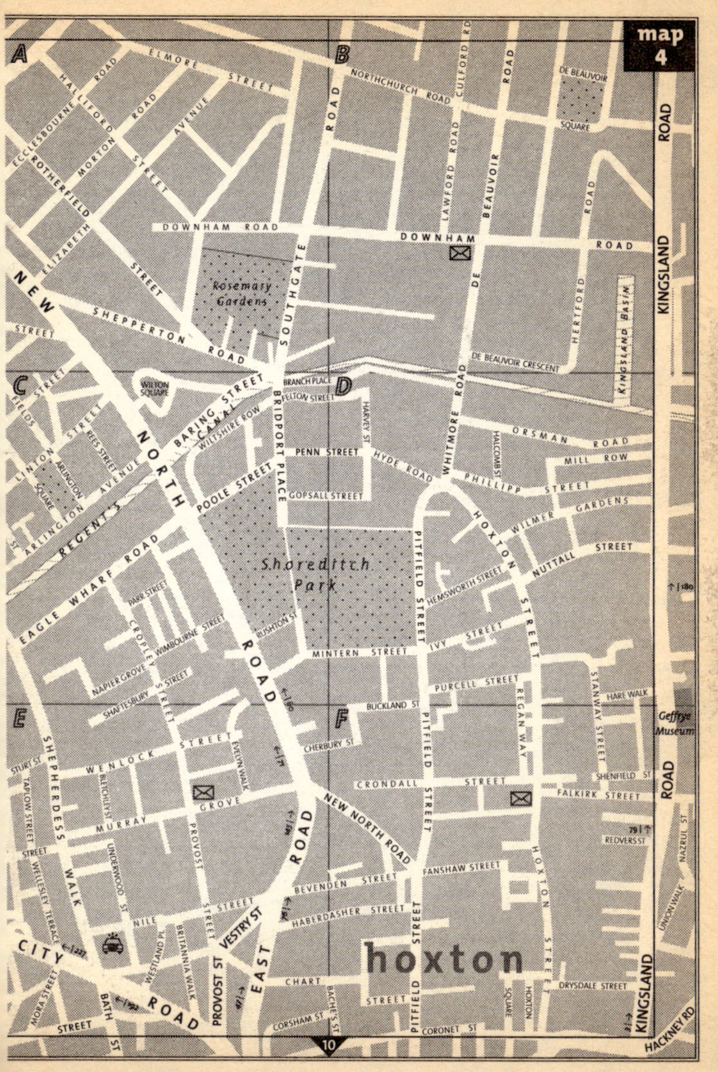
map 4
hoxton
Shoreditch Park
Rosemary Gardens
Geffrye Museum
Regent's Canal
New North Road
East Road
City Road
Kingsland Road
Hoxton Street
Pitfield Street
Southgate Road
Downham Road
De Beauvoir Road
De Beauvoir Square
Whitmore Road
Kingsland Basin
Hackney Rd
10

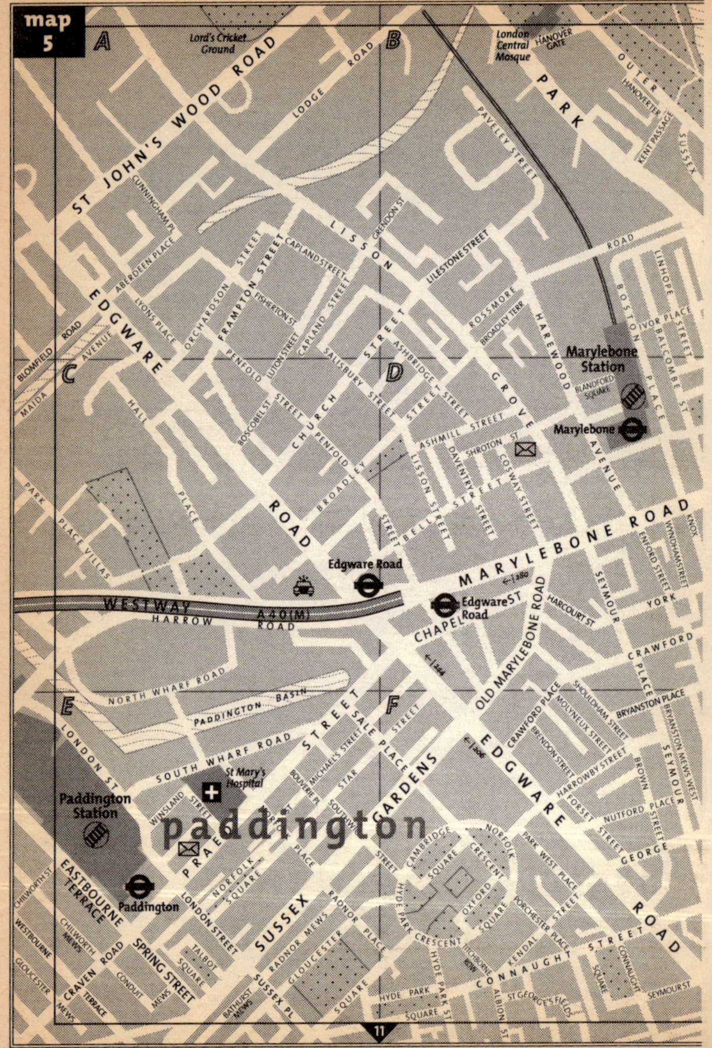
map
5
Lord's Cricket Ground
London Central Mosque
Marylebone Station
Marylebone
Edgware Road
Paddington Station
Paddington
St Mary's Hospital
paddington
WESTWAY
A40(M)
ST JOHN'S WOOD ROAD
EDGWARE ROAD
MARYLEBONE ROAD
PRAED STREET
SUSSEX GARDENS
11

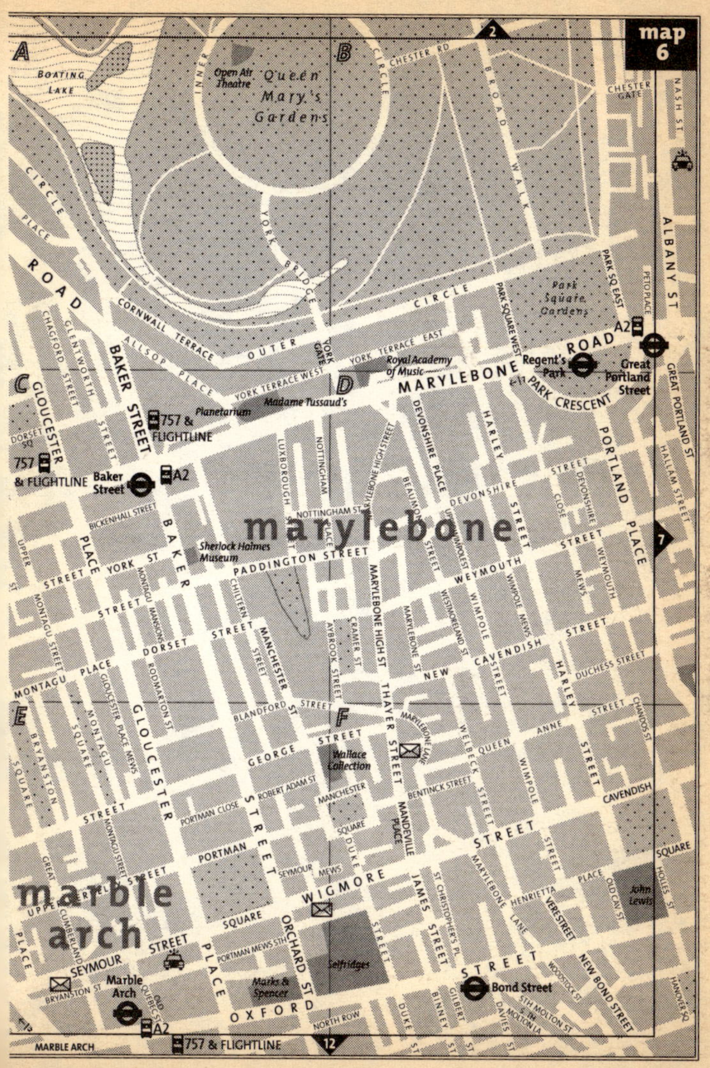
map 6
2
7
12
A
B
C
D
E
F
BOATING LAKE
Open Air Theatre
Queen Mary's Gardens
INNER CIRCLE
CHESTER RD
BROAD WALK
CHESTER GATE
NASH ST
ALBANY ST
CIRCLE PLACE
ROAD
YORK BRIDGE
CORNWALL TERRACE
ALLSOP PLACE
OUTER CIRCLE
YORK GATE
YORK TERRACE EAST
YORK TERRACE WEST
Park Square Gardens
PARK SQUARE WEST
PARK SQ EAST
PETO PLACE
A2
Royal Academy of Music
MARYLEBONE ROAD
Regent's Park
Great Portland Street
PARK CRESCENT
GREAT PORTLAND ST
GLOUCESTER
CHAGFORD STREET
GLENTWORTH STREET
BAKER STREET
757 & FLIGHTLINE
Planetarium
Madame Tussaud's
DORSET SQ
Baker Street
STREET
LUXBOROUGH
NOTTINGHAM
MARYLEBONE HIGH STREET
DEVONSHIRE PLACE
BEAUMONT
HARLEY
PORTLAND
HALLAM STREET
DEVONSHIRE STREET
DEVONSHIRE CLOSE
BICKENHALL STREET
NOTTINGHAM ST
marylebone
UPPER WIMPOLE
PLACE
Sherlock Holmes Museum
PADDINGTON STREET
UPPER MONTAGU STREET
YORK ST
MONTAGU MANSIONS
BAKER
CHILTERN
WEYMOUTH STREET
WEYMOUTH MEWS
UPPER WIMPOLE
WESTMORELAND ST
WIMPOLE STREET
WIMPOLE MEWS
DORSET STREET
MANCHESTER STREET
AYBROOK STREET
CRAMER ST
MARYLEBONE HIGH ST
MARYLEBONE ST
NEW CAVENDISH STREET
DUCHESS STREET
MONTAGU PLACE
GLOUCESTER PLACE MEWS
RODMARTON ST
BLANDFORD STREET
THAYER STREET
MARYLEBONE LANE
CHANDOS ST
BRYANSTON SQUARE
MONTAGU SQUARE
GEORGE STREET
Wallace Collection
QUEEN ANNE STREET
ROBERT ADAM ST
MANCHESTER SQUARE
BENTINCK STREET
WELBECK STREET
CAVENDISH SQUARE
PORTMAN CLOSE
MANDEVILLE PLACE
MONTAGU STREET
PORTMAN SQUARE
SEYMOUR MEWS
DUKE STREET
WIGMORE STREET
JAMES STREET
HENRIETTA PLACE
VERE STREET
OLD CAV ST
HOLLES ST
John Lewis
marble arch
GREAT CUMBERLAND PLACE
UPPER BERKELEY STREET
ORCHARD ST
PORTMAN MEWS STH
ST CHRISTOPHER'S PL.
Selfridges
SEYMOUR STREET
Marks & Spencer
Bond Street
NEW BOND STREET
WOODSTOCK ST
HANOVER SQ
BRYANSTON ST
Marble Arch
QUEBEC ST
OXFORD STREET
NORTH ROW
BINNEY ST
GILBERT ST
DAVIES ST
STH MOLTON ST
S. MOLTON LA
MARBLE ARCH

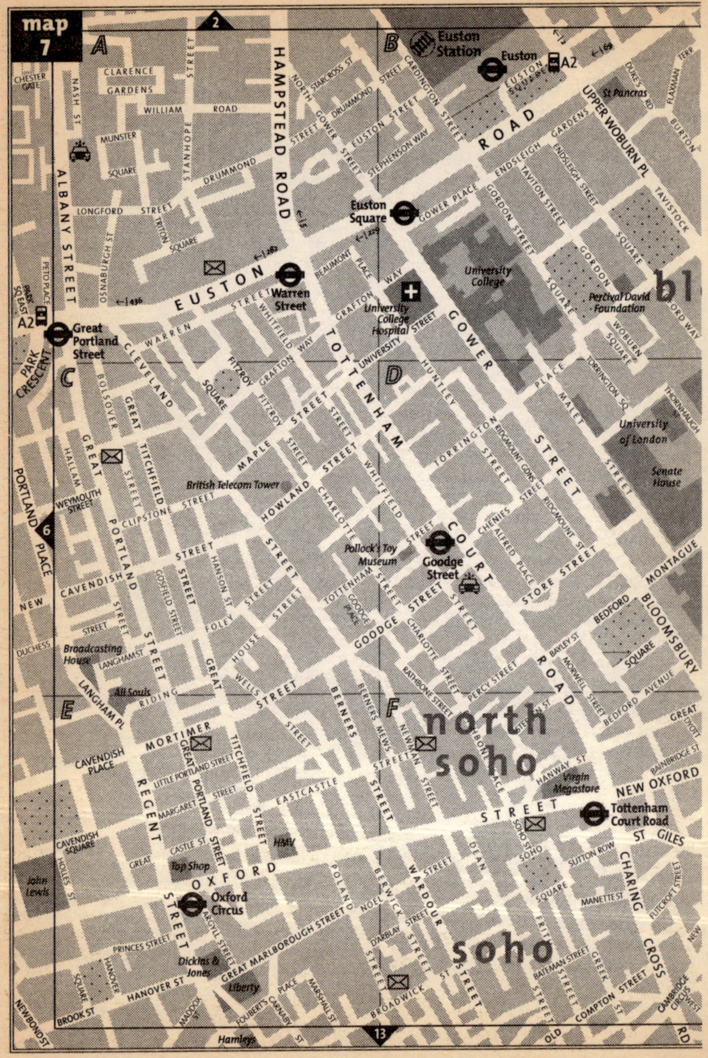
map 7
north soho
soho
Euston Station
Euston
Euston Square
Warren Street
Great Portland Street
Goodge Street
Tottenham Court Road
Oxford Circus
University College
University College Hospital
Percival David Foundation
University of London
Senate House
British Telecom Tower
Pollock's Toy Museum
Broadcasting House
All Souls
Virgin Megastore
HMV
Top Shop
John Lewis
Dickins & Jones
Liberty
Hamleys
St Pancras
Euston Road
Hampstead Road
Tottenham Court Road
Gower Street
Oxford Street
New Oxford Street
Charing Cross Road
Regent Street
Great Portland Street
Albany Street
Wardour Street
Berners Street
Charlotte Street
Bloomsbury

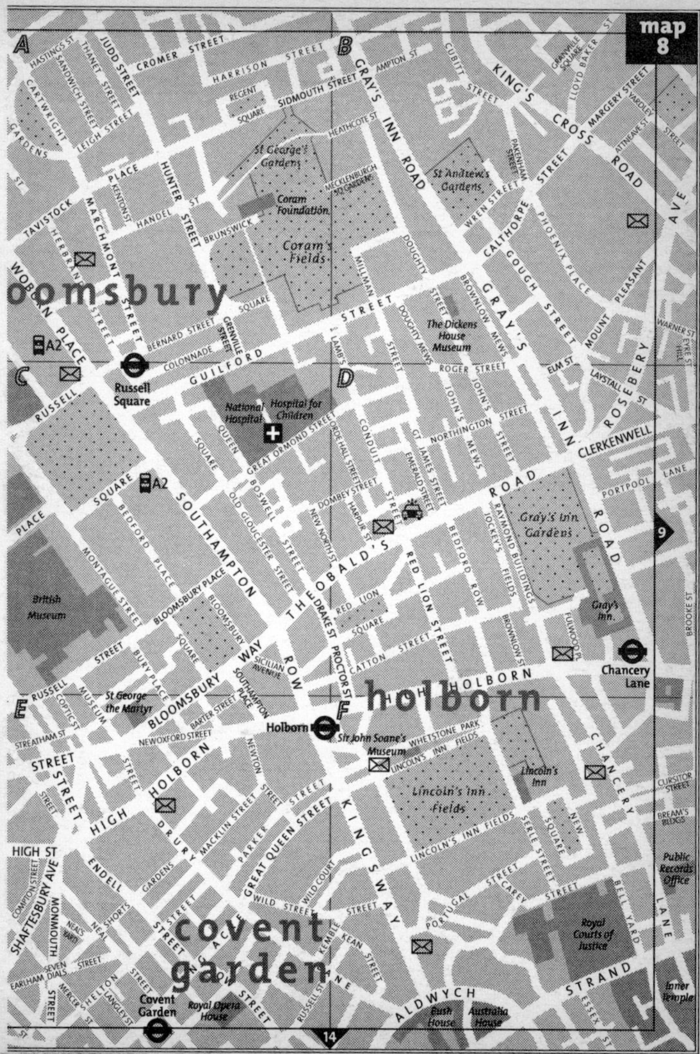

map 8
A
B
C
D
E
F
9
14
Bloomsbury
holborn
covent garden
Hastings St
Thanet St
Judd Street
Cromer Street
Harrison Street
Sandwich Street
Cartwright Gardens
Leigh Street
Regent Square
Sidmouth Street
Ampton St
Gray's Inn Road
Cubitt Street
Granville Square
Lloyd Baker St
King's Cross Road
Margery Street
Vardley St
Heathcote St
St George's Gardens
Mecklenburgh Sq Garden
Hunter Street
Place
Kenton St
Tavistock Place
Marchmont Street
Handel St
Brunswick Square
Coram Foundation
Coram's Fields
St Andrew's Gardens
Pakenham Street
Wren Street
Calthorpe Street
Phoenix Place
Atneave St
Herbrand Street
Woburn Place
Millman Street
Doughty Street
Gough Street
Pleasant
Mount Pleasant
Ave
Bernard Street
Grenville Street
Guilford Street
Lamb's Conduit Street
Doughty Mews
Brownlow Mews
The Dickens House Museum
Warner St
Eyre St Hill
Colonnade
Russell Square
Roger Street
John's Mews
Elm St
Laystall St
Rosebery
A2
National Hospital
Hospital for Children
Queen Square
Great Ormond Street
Orde Hall Street
Conduit Street
Gt James Street
Emerald Street
Northington Street
John Street
Clerkenwell Road
Portpool Lane
Boswell Street
Old Gloucester Street
Dombey Street
Harpur St
New North St
Theobald's Road
Raymond Buildings
Jockey's Fields
Gray's Inn Gardens
Gray's Inn
Southampton Row
Bedford Place
Montague Street
Bloomsbury Place
Bloomsbury Square
Red Lion Street
Red Lion Square
Bedford Row
Brownlow St
Fulwood Pl
Brooke St
British Museum
Drake St
Proctor St
Catton Street
Sicilian Avenue
Bury Place
Russell Street
Chancery Lane
Coptic St
Museum Street
St George the Martyr
Bloomsbury Way
Barter Street
Southampton Place
High Holborn
Holborn
Sir John Soane's Museum
Whetstone Park
Lincoln's Inn Fields
Lincoln's Inn
Streatham St
New Oxford Street
Newton Street
Cursitor Street
Bream's Bldgs
Drury Lane
Macklin Street
Parker Street
Great Queen Street
Kingsway
Serle Street
New Square
Public Records Office
High St
Shaftesbury Ave
Compton Street
Monmouth Street
Endell Street
Gardens
Wild Court
Wild Street
Portugal Street
Carey Street
Bell Yard
Royal Courts of Justice
Neal's Yard
Neal St
Shorts Gardens
Long Acre
Kemble Street
Kean Street
Seven Dials
Earlham Street
Shelton St
Mercer St
Langley St
Covent Garden
Royal Opera House
Bow Street
Russell St
Aldwych
Bush House
Australia House
Strand
Essex St
Inner Temple

map 9
clerkenwell
A
B
C
D
E
F
b
3
8
15
AMWELL ST
WILMINGTON SQUARE
YARDLEY
ATTNEAVE ST
KING'S CROSS RD
ROSEBERY AVENUE
MYDDELTON
ST
EXMOUTH MARKET
SKINNER STREET
Spa Fields
NORTHAMPTON ROAD
CORPORATION ROW
WOODBRIDGE
MEREDITH ST
ST JOHN STREET
NORTHAMPTON SQUARE
WYCLIF ST
SEBASTIAN ST
GOSWELL RD
PERCIVAL STREET
LEVER STREET
CENTRAL STREET
IRONMONGER ROW
NORMAN ST
SEWARD STREET
PEAR TREE STREET
MITCHELL ST
CYRUS STREET
GOSWELL ROAD
COMPTON STREET
BASTWICK STREET
GEE STREET
GARRETT ST
DALLINGTON ST
NORTHBURGH ST
BERRY STREET
GREAT SUTTON STREET
OLD STREET
BALTIC STREET
GOLDEN LANE
MOUNT PLEASANT
AVE
FARRINGDON ROAD
BOWLING GREEN LANE
SANS WALK
CLERKENWELL CLOSE
AYLESBURY STREET
CRAWFORD PASSAGE
WARNER STREET
EYRE ST HILL
RAY ST
FARRINGDON LA
CLERKENWELL GREEN
BACK HILL
HERBAL HILL
ROSEBERY
CLERKENWELL ROAD
BRITTON STREET
ST JOHN'S LANE
ST JOHN STREET
TURNMILL STREET
ALBION PL
BENJAMIN ST
FANN STREET
SAFFRON STREET
HATTON
LEATHER LANE
PORTPOOL LANE
CROSS ST
KIRBY STREET
SAFFRON HILL
FARRINGDON ROAD
CHARTERHOUSE SQUARE
Barbican
ALDERSGATE ST
BEECH
Barbican Centre
Farringdon
COWCROSS ST
CHARTERHOUSE STREET
LONG LANE
BALDWINS GDNS
GREVILLE STREET
GARDEN
BROOKE ST
GRAY'S INN RD
Gray's Inn
Chancery Lane
CLOTH FAIR
MIDDLE ST
Smithfield Market
WEST SMITHFIELD
Museum of London
HOLBORN
HOLBORN CIRCUS
HOLBORN VIADUCT
WEST SMITHFIELD
HOSIER LANE
SNOW HILL
COCK LANE
GILTSPUR ST
St Bartholomew's Hospital
MONTAGUE STREET
LONDON
LITTLE BRITAIN
FURNIVAL STREET
FETTER LANE
NEW FETTER LANE
ST ANDREW ST
SHOE LANE
FARRINGDON STREET
KING EDWARD ST
ALDERSGATE ST
NOBLE STREET
OAT LANE
CURSITOR ST
BARTLETT CT
National Postal Museum
ANGEL ST
GRESHAM
NEWGATE STREET
CHANCERY
BREAM'S BUILDINGS
LT NEW ST
Old Bailey (Central Criminal Court)
WARWICK LANE
ST MARTIN'S LE GRAND
FOSTER LANE
GUTTER LANE
Public Records Office
Dr Johnson's House
ST BRIDE STREET
City Thameslink
OLD BAILEY
St Paul's
BELL YD
Royal Courts of Justice
FLEET STREET
STRAND
LUDGATE CIRCUS
LUDGATE HILL
ST PAUL'S CHURCHYARD
NEW CHANGE
St Paul's Cathedral
WATLING
CANNON
BREAD
PILGRIM STREET
CARTER LANE
CREED ST
BLACKFRIARS LA
Apothecaries Hall
NEW BRIDGE ST
BOUVERIE STREET
WHITEFRIARS STREET
SALISBURY CT
TEMPLE LA
KING'S BENCH WALK
Temple Church
Inner Temple

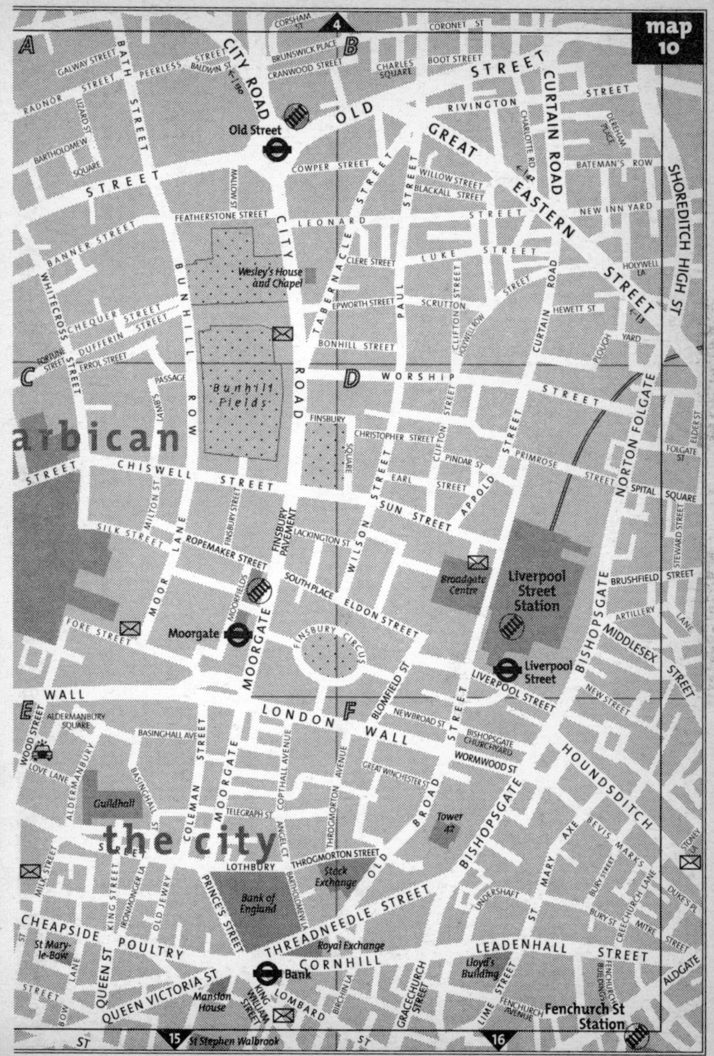

map 10
Old Street
Wesley's House and Chapel
Bunhill Fields
Barbican
Moorgate
Broadgate Centre
Liverpool Street Station
Liverpool Street
Guildhall
the city
Tower 42
Stock Exchange
Bank of England
Royal Exchange
Bank
Lloyd's Building
Mansion House
St Mary-le-Bow
Fenchurch St Station
St Stephen Walbrook

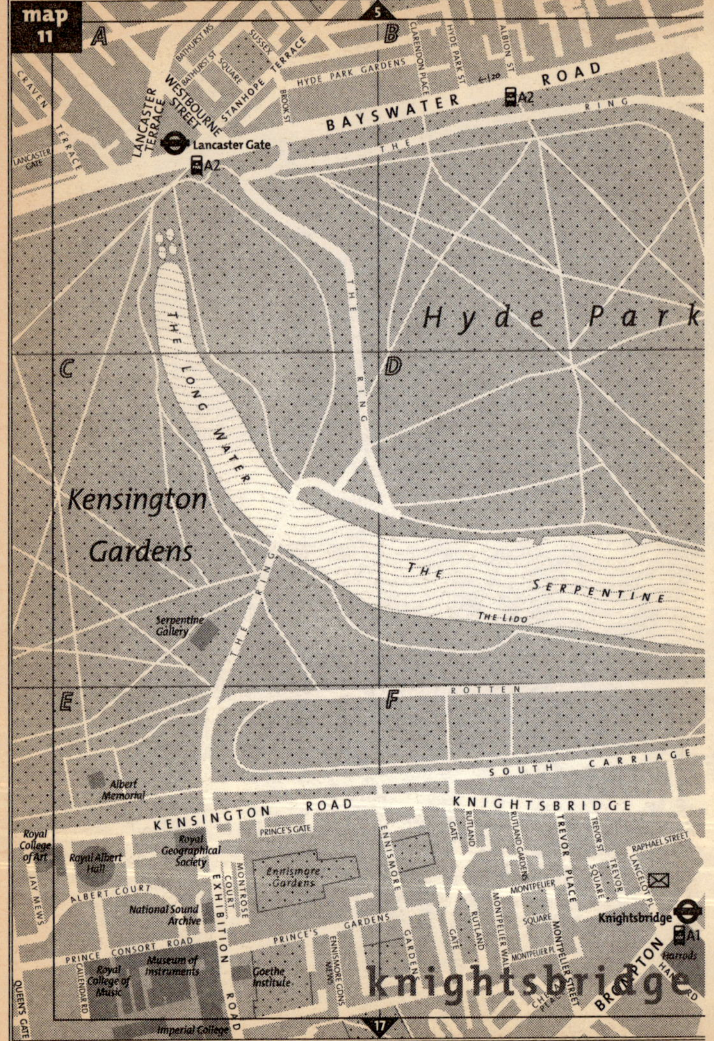

map
11
5
17
A
B
C
D
E
F
Hyde Park
Kensington
Gardens
THE LONG WATER
THE SERPENTINE
THE LIDO
THE RING
BAYSWATER ROAD
KENSINGTON ROAD
KNIGHTSBRIDGE
SOUTH CARRIAGE
ROTTEN
Lancaster Gate
A2
A1
Serpentine Gallery
Albert Memorial
Royal College of Art
Royal Albert Hall
Royal Geographical Society
National Sound Archive
Museum of Instruments
Royal College of Music
Imperial College
Goethe Institute
Ennismore Gardens
Knightsbridge
Harrods
knightsbridge
CRAVEN TERRACE
LANCASTER GATE
LANCASTER TERRACE
WESTBOURNE STREET
BATHURST MS
BATHURST ST
SUSSEX SQUARE
STANHOPE TERRACE
HYDE PARK GARDENS
BROOK ST
CLARENDON PLACE
HYDE PARK ST
ALBION ST
PRINCE'S GATE
ENNISMORE
RUTLAND GATE
RUTLAND GARDENS
TREVOR PLACE
TREVOR ST
TREVOR SQUARE
RAPHAEL STREET
LANCELOT PL
MONTPELIER SQUARE
MONTPELIER WALK
MONTPELIER PL
MONTPELIER STREET
BROMPTON
ALBERT COURT
JAY MEWS
MONTROSE COURT
EXHIBITION ROAD
PRINCE'S GARDENS
PRINCE CONSORT ROAD
CALLENDAR RD
QUEEN'S GATE
ENNISMORE GDNS MEWS

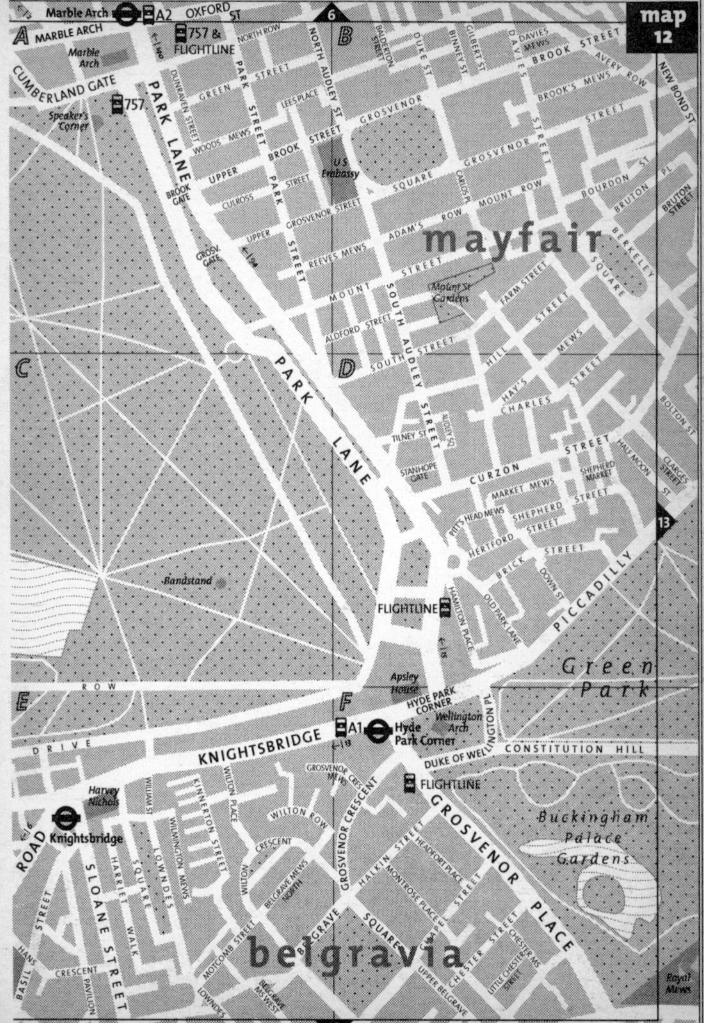
map 12
Marble Arch
A2
OXFORD ST
757 & FLIGHTLINE
757
MARBLE ARCH
CUMBERLAND GATE
Speaker's Corner
PARK LANE
NORTH ROW
NORTH AUDLEY ST
BALDERTON STREET
DUKE ST
BINNEY ST
GILBERT ST
DAVIES MEWS
DAVIES STREET
BROOK STREET
AVERY ROW
BROOK'S MEWS
NEW BOND ST
GREEN STREET
PARK STREET
DUNRAVEN STREET
LEES PLACE
GROSVENOR STREET
WOODS MEWS
UPPER BROOK STREET
US Embassy
GROSVENOR SQUARE
CARLOS PL
MOUNT ROW
BOURDON ST
BRUTON PL
BRUTON STREET
BROOK GATE
CULROSS STREET
UPPER GROSVENOR STREET
ADAM'S ROW
mayfair
BERKELEY SQUARE
GROSV. GATE
REEVES MEWS
MOUNT STREET
Mount St Gardens
FARM STREET
SOUTH AUDLEY STREET
ALDFORD STREET
HILL STREET
HAY'S MEWS
SOUTH STREET
CHARLES STREET
BOLTON ST
TILNEY ST
AUDLEY SQ
STANHOPE GATE
CURZON STREET
HALF MOON ST
SHEPHERD MARKET
CLARGES STREET
MARKET MEWS
SHEPHERD STREET
PITTS HEAD MEWS
HERTFORD STREET
BRICK STREET
DOWN ST
PICCADILLY
OLD PARK LANE
HAMILTON PLACE
FLIGHTLINE
Bandstand
Green Park
Apsley House
HYDE PARK CORNER
ROW
Wellington Arch
WELLINGTON PL
A1
Hyde Park Corner
KNIGHTSBRIDGE
DRIVE
CONSTITUTION HILL
DUKE OF WELLINGTON
GROSVENOR MEWS
GROSVENOR CRESCENT
FLIGHTLINE
GROSVENOR PLACE
Harvey Nichols
Knightsbridge
WILLIAM ST
KINNERTON STREET
WILTON PLACE
WILTON ROW
WILTON CRESCENT
LOWNDES SQUARE
WILMINGTON MEWS
HARRIET WALK
SLOANE STREET
HALKIN STREET
HEADFORT PLACE
MONTROSE PLACE
Buckingham Palace Gardens
ROAD
BELGRAVE MEWS NORTH
BELGRAVE SQUARE
CHAPEL STREET
CHESTER STREET
CHESTER MS
LITTLE CHESTER STREET
belgravia
MOTCOMB STREET
HANS CRESCENT
BASIL ST
PAVILION RD
LOWNDES ST
BELGRAVE MS WEST
UPPER BELGRAVE ST
Royal Mews
A
B
C
D
E
F
6
13
18

map 13
piccadilly
st james's
soho
westmin
Green Park
St James's Park
Buckingham Palace Gardens
Buckingham Palace
Queen's Gallery
Royal Mews
Liberty
Hamleys
Royal Academy of Arts
Fortnum & Mason
St James
Tower Records
Piccadilly Circus
Trocadero Centre
National Gallery
New Zealand House
Canadian Embassy
Institute of Contemporary Arts
Queen's Chapel
Marlborough House
St James's Palace
Lancaster House
Duck Island
Foreign & Commonwealth Office
Cabinet War Rooms
Guards Museum
New Scotland Yard
Dean's Yard
Green Park
St James's Park
REGENT STREET
SHAFTESBURY AVENUE
CHARING CROSS ROAD
HAYMARKET
PALL MALL
PALL MALL EAST
COCKSPUR ST
THE MALL
CONSTITUTION HILL
BIRDCAGE WALK
BUCKINGHAM GATE
VICTORIA STREET
PICCADILLY
NEW BOND ST
OLD BOND STREET
JERMYN STREET
ST JAMES'S STREET
WATERLOO PLACE
CARLTON HOUSE TERRACE
HORSE GUARDS ROAD
QUEEN'S GARDENS
SPUR ROAD
STABLE YARD ROAD
MARLBOROUGH ROAD
TOTHILL STREET
PETTY FRANCE
CAXTON STREET
PALACE STREET
BROADWAY

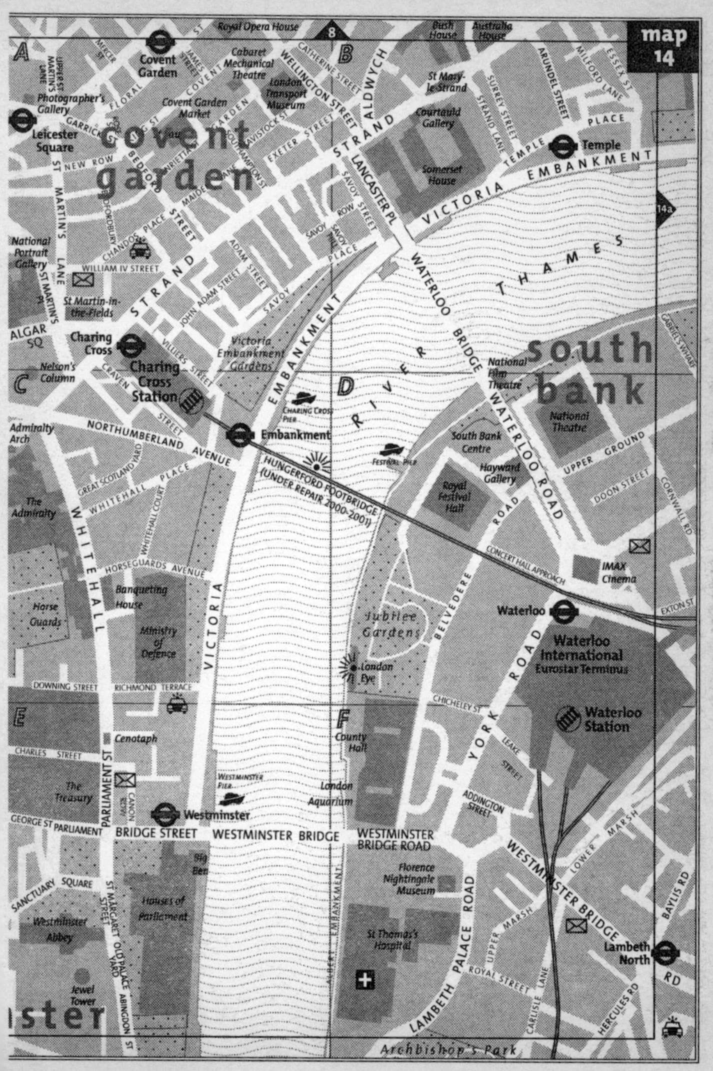

map 14
covent garden
south bank
River Thames
Royal Opera House
Covent Garden
Leicester Square
Photographer's Gallery
Cabaret Mechanical Theatre
London Transport Museum
Covent Garden Market
Bush House
Australia House
St Mary-le-Strand
Courtauld Gallery
Somerset House
Temple
National Portrait Gallery
St Martin-in-the-Fields
Charing Cross
Charing Cross Station
Nelson's Column
Admiralty Arch
Victoria Embankment Gardens
Embankment
Charing Cross Pier
Festival Pier
Hungerford Footbridge (under repair 2000-2001)
National Film Theatre
National Theatre
South Bank Centre
Hayward Gallery
Royal Festival Hall
IMAX Cinema
The Admiralty
Banqueting House
Horse Guards
Ministry of Defence
Jubilee Gardens
London Eye
Waterloo
Waterloo International Eurostar Terminus
Waterloo Station
Cenotaph
County Hall
London Aquarium
The Treasury
Westminster Pier
Westminster
Big Ben
Florence Nightingale Museum
Houses of Parliament
Westminster Abbey
St Thomas's Hospital
Jewel Tower
Lambeth North
Archbishop's Park
Strand
Aldwych
Wellington Street
Catherine Street
Arundel Street
Milford Lane
Essex St
Surrey Street
Strand Lane
Temple Place
Victoria Embankment
Lancaster Pl
Savoy Street
Savoy Row
Savoy Hill
Savoy Place
Waterloo Bridge
Waterloo Road
Upper Ground
Doon Street
Cornwall Rd
Gabriel's Wharf
Concert Hall Approach
Exton St
Belvedere Road
York Road
Chicheley St
Leake Street
Addington Street
Lower Marsh
Westminster Bridge Road
Baylis Rd
Upper Marsh
Royal Street
Carlisle Lane
Hercules Rd
Lambeth Palace Road
Albert Embankment
Westminster Bridge
Bridge Street
Parliament St
Parliament Square
George St
Canon Row
Charles Street
Downing Street
Richmond Terrace
Horseguards Avenue
Whitehall
Whitehall Place
Whitehall Court
Great Scotland Yard
Northumberland Avenue
Craven Street
Villiers Street
John Adam Street
Adam Street
William IV Street
Chandos Place
Bedford Street
Maiden Lane
Henrietta St
Southampton St
Exeter Street
Tavistock St
Floral St
Garrick St
New Row
St Martin's Lane
Upper St Martin's Lane
Mercer St
James Street
Bedfordbury
Trafalgar Sq
Sanctuary
St Margaret Street
Old Palace Yard
Abingdon St

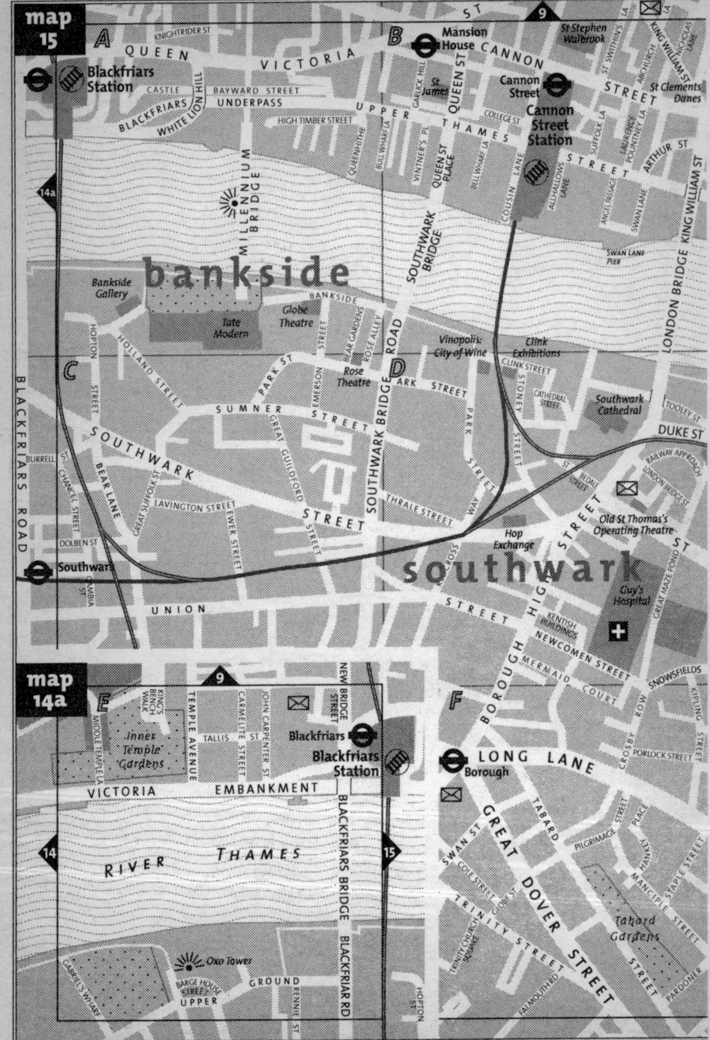

map 15
A
B
C
D
E
F
9
14a
14
15
QUEEN VICTORIA
KNIGHTRIDER ST
Blackfriars Station
CASTLE
BAYWARD STREET
BLACKFRIARS UNDERPASS
WHITE LION HILL
UPPER THAMES STREET
HIGH TIMBER STREET
Mansion House
CANNON STREET
St James
QUEEN ST
GARLICK HILL
Cannon Street
Cannon Street Station
COLLEGE ST
St Stephen Walbrook
ST SWITHIN'S LA
ABCHURCH
KING WILLIAM ST
NICHOLAS LANE
St Clements Danes
QUEENHITHE
BULL WHARF LA
VINTNER'S PL
QUEEN ST PLACE
BELL WHARF LA
COUSIN LANE
ALLHALLOWS LANE
SUFFOLK LA
LAURENCE POUNTNEY LA
ARTHUR ST
ANGEL PASSAGE
SWAN LANE
SWAN LANE PIER
MILLENNIUM BRIDGE
SOUTHWARK BRIDGE
LONDON BRIDGE
bankside
Bankside Gallery
Tate Modern
Globe Theatre
BANKSIDE
HOPTON STREET
HOLLAND STREET
PARK ST
BEAR GARDENS
ROSE ALLEY
Rose Theatre
Vinopolis: City of Wine
Clink Exhibitions
CLINK STREET
STONEY STREET
CATHEDRAL STREET
Southwark Cathedral
TOOLEY ST
DUKE ST
SUMNER STREET
EMERSON STREET
GREAT GUILDFORD STREET
SOUTHWARK BRIDGE ROAD
PARK STREET
SOUTHWARK STREET
BLACKFRIARS ROAD
BURRELL ST
CHANCEL STREET
BEAR LANE
GREAT SUFFOLK ST
LAVINGTON STREET
EWER STREET
THRALE STREET
WAY
RAILWAY APPROACH
LONDON BRIDGE ST
BEDALE STREET
ST
Old St Thomas's Operating Theatre
Hop Exchange
DOLBEN ST
Southwark
CAMBIA ST
southwark
CROSS
UNION STREET
HIGH STREET
KENTISH BUILDINGS
NEWCOMEN STREET
MERMAID COURT
Guy's Hospital
GREAT MAZE POND
ST
SNOWSFIELDS
ROW
KIPLING STREET
CROSBY
PORLOCK STREET
BOROUGH
map 14a
KING'S BENCH WALK
TEMPLE AVENUE
CARMELITE STREET
JOHN CARPENTER ST
NEW BRIDGE STREET
Inner Temple Gardens
MIDDLE TEMPLE LA
TALLIS ST
Blackfriars
Blackfriars Station
LONG LANE
Borough
VICTORIA EMBANKMENT
BLACKFRIARS BRIDGE
TABARD
GREAT DOVER STREET
SWAN ST
PILGRIMAGE STREET
PLACE
HANKEY
STAPLE STREET
MANCIPLE STREET
RIVER THAMES
COLE STREET
GLOBE ST
TRINITY STREET
TRINITY CHURCH SQUARE
Tabard Gardens
STREET
PARDONER
Oxo Tower
GABRIEL'S WHARF
BARGE HOUSE STREET
UPPER GROUND
RENNIE ST
BLACKFRIAR RD
HOPTON ST
FALMOUTH RD

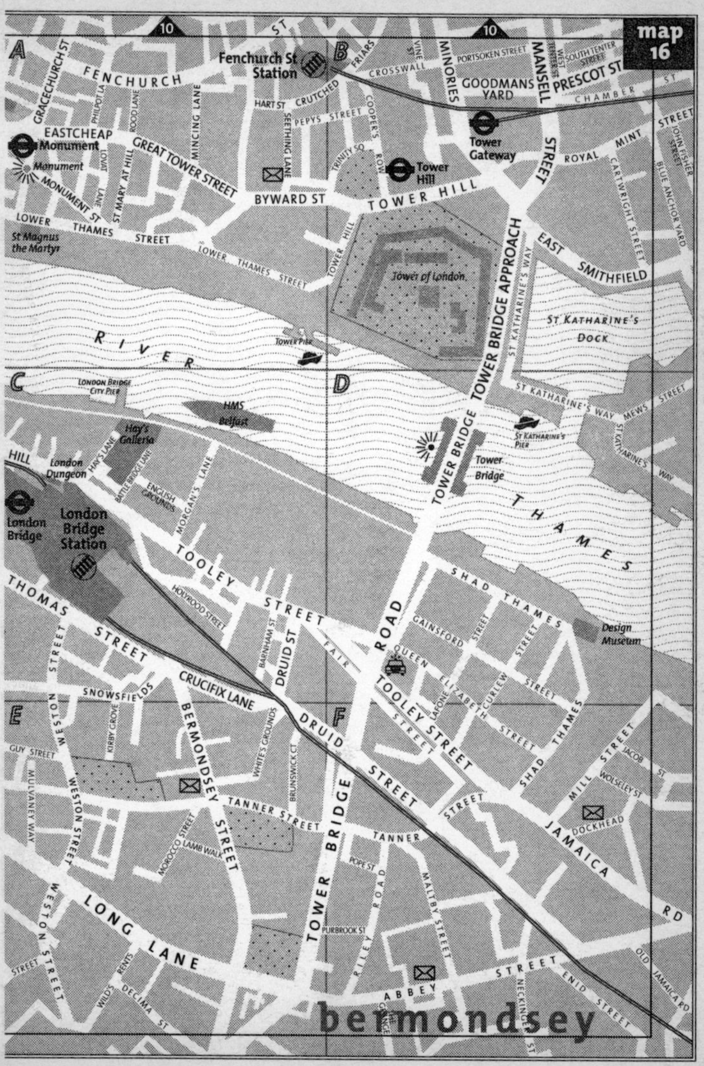
map
16
Fenchurch St Station
Monument
Tower Gateway
Tower Hill
Tower of London
St Katharine's Dock
Tower Pier
London Bridge City Pier
HMS Belfast
Hay's Galleria
London Dungeon
London Bridge
London Bridge Station
Tower Bridge
St Katharine's Pier
Design Museum
St Magnus the Martyr
River Thames
bermondsey

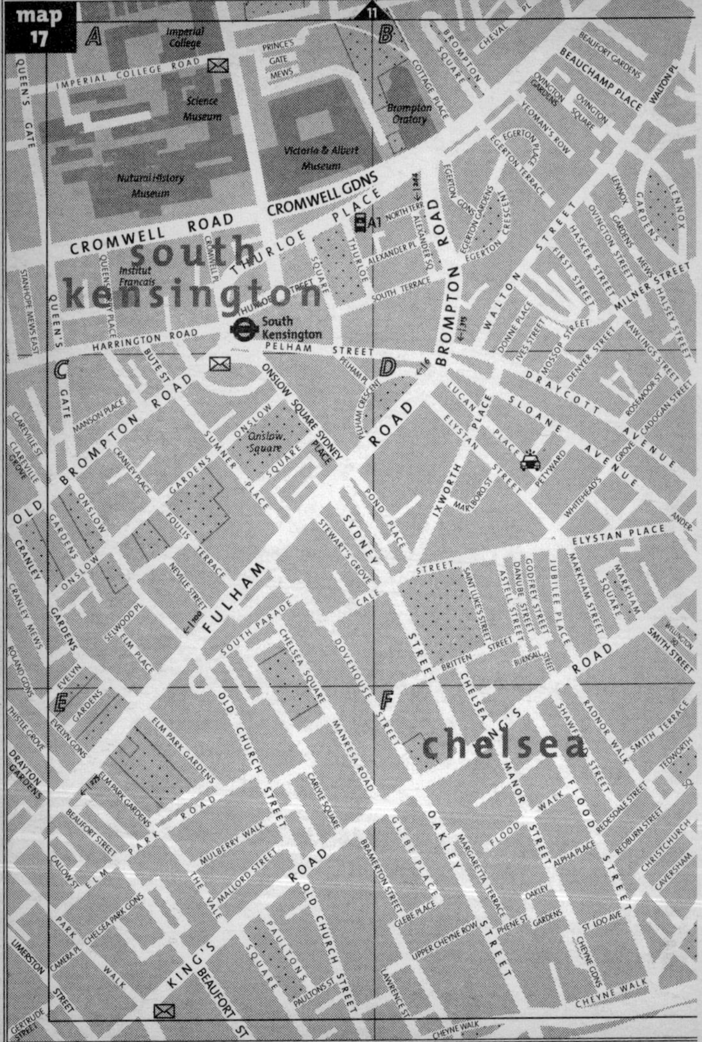

map 17
south kensington
chelsea
Imperial College
Science Museum
Natural History Museum
Victoria & Albert Museum
Brompton Oratory
Institut Francais
South Kensington
Onslow Square
CROMWELL ROAD
CROMWELL GDNS
BROMPTON ROAD
FULHAM ROAD
KING'S ROAD
OLD BROMPTON ROAD
SLOANE AVENUE
DRAYCOTT AVENUE
PELHAM STREET
HARRINGTON ROAD
THURLOE PLACE
IMPERIAL COLLEGE ROAD
QUEEN'S GATE
ELYSTAN PLACE
OAKLEY STREET
OLD CHURCH STREET
CHEYNE WALK

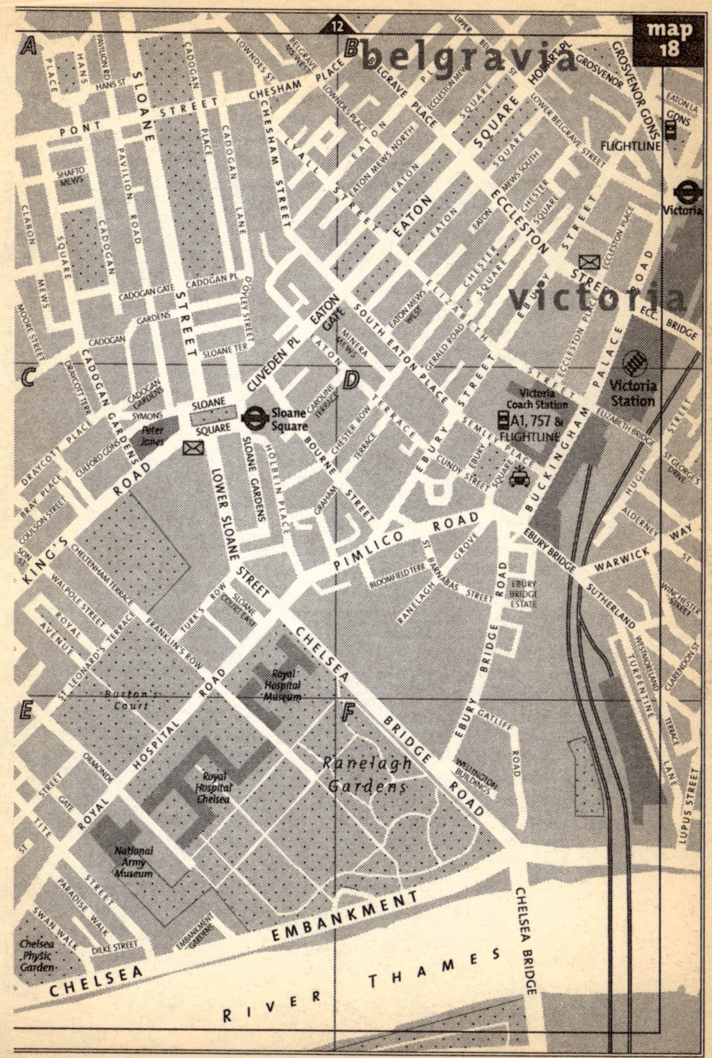
map
18
belgravia
victoria
Victoria
Victoria Station
Victoria Coach Station
A1, 757 & FLIGHTLINE
FLIGHTLINE
Sloane Square
Peter Jones
Royal Hospital Museum
Royal Hospital Chelsea
National Army Museum
Ranelagh Gardens
Burton's Court
Chelsea Physic Garden
RIVER THAMES
CHELSEA EMBANKMENT
CHELSEA BRIDGE
CHELSEA BRIDGE ROAD
ROYAL HOSPITAL ROAD
KING'S ROAD
SLOANE STREET
LOWER SLOANE STREET
PIMLICO ROAD
BUCKINGHAM PALACE ROAD
EBURY STREET
EBURY BRIDGE ROAD
ECCLESTON STREET
EATON SQUARE
BELGRAVE PLACE
CHESHAM PLACE
CHESHAM STREET
PONT STREET
WARWICK WAY
SUTHERLAND

notes

acknowledgements

Conceived, edited & designed by
Virgin Publishing Ltd
London w6 9HA

Editorial assistance: Tim Brown, Jessica Hughes
Index: Hilary Bird
Cartographic editor: Dominic Beddow
Cartographer: Simonetta Giori
Draughtsman Ltd, London 020 8960 1602 | Email: mail@magneticnorth.net

Printed by Omnia Books Ltd, Scotland

Based on information from the Virgin Guide to London written and researched by:
Transport: Lindsay Hunt, Naomi Peck | **Soho:** Oliver Bennett, Charlotte Packer | **Covent Garden:** Ros Belford, Michael Ellis, Ian Wisniewski | **Piccadilly, Mayfair & St James's:** Paul Myers, Charlotte Packer, Ian Wisniewski | **Knightsbridge & South Kensington:** Jonathan Aris,Paul Myers, Charlotte Packer | **Chelsea:** Paul Myers, Charlotte Packer, Ian Wisniewski | **Notting Hill & Portobello:** Ros Belford | **Clerkenwell:** Oliver Bennett, Kara O'Reilly | **Islington:** Oliver Bennett, Kara O'Reilly **Camden:** Siobhan Dolan | **Hampstead:** Naomi Coleman | **Greenwich:** Julia Kaminski, Emma Warren | **Sights & Museums:** Mary Lu Bakker, Michael Ellis, Ella Milroy, Naomi Peck, Ferdie McDonald | **Parks & Gardens:** Fiona Wild | **Galleries:** Charlotte Mullins | **Children:** Josie Barnard | **Sport:** Michael Ellis | **Game for a Laugh:** Michael Ellis | **Body & Soul:** Leise Spenser | **Shopping:** Miranda Eadie, Charlotte Packer, Melanie Rickey, Sean Swallow, Simon Yates | **Restaurants & Cafés:** Ros Belford, Oliver Bennett, Matthew Byam Shaw, David Gould, Ella Milroy, Danielle Peck, Naomi Peck, Mark Tindall, Fiona Wild, Ian Wisniewski | **Pubs & Bars:** Emma Warren Media: Liese Spenser | **Cinema:** Michael Ellis, Paul Myers | **Theatre:** Richard Lintern | **Poetry:** Michael Ellis | **Dance:** Gill Clarke | **Opera & Classical Music:** Charles Searson **Popular Music:** Ian Gittins | **Comedy:** Ivor Dembina **Clubs:** Emma Warren | **Events:** Claire Fogg, Clare Tomlinson | **Hotels:** Lindsay Hunt | **Practical information:** Ella Milroy.

Acknowledgements and credits:
London Underground Map was produced by permission of London Regional Transport (Reg user number 00/3362)

Great care has been taken with this guide to be as accurate and up-to-date as possible, but details such as addresses, telephone numbers, opening hours, prices and travel information are liable to change. The publishers cannot accept responsiblility for any consequences arising from the use of this book. We would be delighted to receive any corrections and suggestions for inclusion in the next edition.

Please write to or email:
Virgin Publishing Ltd
Thames Wharf Studios
Rainville Road
London w6 9ha
Fax: 020 7386 3360
Email: travel@virgin-pub.co.uk

key to symbols

- telephone number
- recorded information line
- F fax
- e email
- w worldwide web
- hot tips
- opening times
- wheelchair access
- hotel
- price
- frequency/times
- map reference
- ☆ recommended (featured in listings section)
- must see
- capacity
- dress code
- good points
- bad points
- underground
- bus/coach
- shuttle bus
- taxi
- trains
- airport
- ferry port/river boat pier
- number of beds
- breakfast included
- air conditioning
- 24-hour room service
- fitness facilities
- business facilities
- outdoor area/garden
- restaurant/café
- bar/pub
- parking
- credit cards
  AE = American Express
  DC = Diners Club
  MC = Mastercard
  V = Visa
  all = AE/DC/MC/V
  are accepted
- £ cheap restaurant (main courses under £6)
- ££ moderately priced restaurant (main courses between £6–£12)
- £££ expensive restaurant (main courses over £12)

key to map symbols

- sight/museum/gallery/land-mark/notable building/shop
- park/garden/square
- train station
- underground station
- bus terminal
- river bus
- viewpoint
- street number
- police station
- post office
- hospital casualty unit
- grid reference
- tourist information
- one-way street
- hotel